A
Research Primer
for the
Social and Behavioral Sciences

A
RESEARCH PRIMER
for the
SOCIAL AND BEHAVIORAL SCIENCES

Miriam Schapiro Grosof
Yeshiva University
   and
Pace University
New York, New York

Hyman Sardy
Brooklyn College
Brooklyn, New York

1985

ACADEMIC PRESS, INC.
(Harcourt Brace Jovanovich, Publishers)
Orlando   San Diego   New York   London
Toronto   Montreal   Sydney   Tokyo

ACADEMIC PRESS, INC.
Orlando, Florida 32887

United Kingdom Edition published by
ACADEMIC PRESS INC. (LONDON) LTD.
24–28 Oval Road, London NW1 7DX

Library of Congress Cataloging in Publication Data

Grosof, Miriam.
    A research primer for the social and behavioral sciences.

    Bibliography: p.
    Includes index
    1. Social sciences--Research. 2. Social Sciences--
Methodology. I. Sardy, Hyman. II. Title.
H62.G7658   1985   300' .72   84-16763
ISBN 0-12-304180-5 (alk. paper)

PRINTED IN THE UNITED STATES OF AMERICA

85 86 87 88   9 8 7 6 5 4 3 2 1

Contents

16. Endgame

Preface

This book is directed to novice investigators in the broad category "social and behavioral sciences" who are already knowledgeable in their respective disciplines and whose research problems primarily concern human subjects, yield quantitative or quantifiable evidence, and involve statistical or related procedures for the analysis of that evidence. Most researchers, unless they have had years of experience, possess substantial technical skills but may need help in coordinating them or in filling in uneven preparation. Moreover, they may want to use as yet unfamiliar methodologies from related areas. Research requires a shift in attitudes and expectations from the patterns of earlier training; we outline the research process as a whole and emphasize the importance of organizing information and planning sequences of tasks. We discuss the selection of methodologies, not the details of their use. We cover such fundamental matters as how to choose a research topic and evaluate its suitability. Our approach is practical rather than sentimental or inspirational, because we believe that the best incentive to continue in a productive career is the successful completion of a commendable first project.

This book had its genesis in our experiences, working with doctoral students and other beginning researchers, over a period of several years, variously as instructor in statistics and research courses, principal dissertation advisor, committee member, informal and formal consultant, and friend. We believe the research task to be amenable to rational analysis. The needs for assistance in the decision-making aspect of research, and for an overview of how the many component pieces fit together in the entire process, seemed to us to be urgent for many individuals. We have tried to meet these needs in a way which combines common sense and sophisticated erudition.

Acknowledgments

In this ambitious endeavor we have relied upon the contributions of many others. (Any errors and shortcomings are of course our own.) Richard A. Stein and Gerald Marotznik generously permitted us to use their data set. Elisa Adams edited the final draft of the manuscript with elegance, wit, and skill. Kathleen O'Donnell-Maguire typed and retyped with extraordinary diligence and meticulous accuracy.

Many colleagues, students, and friends provided special expertise, comments on early drafts, general advice, and the opportunity for helpful discussion; among these are: Stuart Blum, Linda Schapiro Collins, Thomas J. Conroy, Juliana A. Corn, Gene S. Fisch, Benjamin N. Grosof, Laurel T. Hatvary, Rochelle Hendlin, Leon F. Landovitz, Marc Levine, Gerald Marotznik, Vivian McRaven, Donald Michelli, Kathleen A. Pistone, Bernard Pollack, Sandra M. Pulver, Lucille Raines, "Reviewer #4", Julian Roberts, David Rogers, Theresa F. Rogers, Terry Salinger, Susan J. Sardy, John J. Simon, Judith M. Walter, and Solomon Weinstock.

Also, for support and encouragement before and during the writing, we thank: Benjamin N. and David H. Grosof, Ernest Kafka, Donald J. Newman, Lillian Milgram Schapiro, Meyer Schapiro, and Shulamith Simon.

Last and most, we acknowledge with deep gratitude the participation of Gene S. Fisch and Susan J. Sardy, for their loving good humor, for their effort in helping us get the project under way, for reminding us continually of its value, for constantly challenging us to refine our ideas and their presentation, and for "being there" with reinforcers.

Introduction

"We face insurmountable opportunities"

Pogo (Walt Kelly)

This book is entitled *A Research Primer for the Social and Behavioral Sciences*. Traditionally, a primer is intended for beginners; it is gentle and friendly in tone; it offers an introduction to some domain of knowledge in a simple and direct way, and provides some suggestions for learning more about it, usually through further, more intensive reading. This primer is perhaps somewhat unusual in that it is addressed to individuals who have already acquired at least a fair degree of knowledge or expertise in one of the social or behavioral sciences. They may, nonetheless, need guidance in undertaking that most difficult of tasks, independent original research.

The goal of this book is threefold: to provide you with

- an introductory but comprehensive overview of the research process,
- a description of the difficulties you will probably encounter and the skills you will have to master in order to overcome them, and
- a discussion of differing and possibly conflicting points of view concerning certain aspects of your task.

We delineate the different facets of research, and offer guidelines for formulating and managing the interdependent procedures needed to attack your research problem. We make no attempt to duplicate the many excellent works on specific topics: manuals of design, textbooks on statistics, expositions of philosophy or methodology in the various social sciences, and handbooks of style, etc. We see this book as a primer of research concepts, not of techniques, and not directed to any one discipline. It deals with questions that arise in applied or cross-fields and that require researchers to integrate or decide among the methodologies and viewpoints of several different disciplines. It is not a book of "know-how." It is certainly not encyclopedic and does not pretend to be.

The book is for you if you are undertaking a first research project in your own or a related field in the social or behavioral sciences, be it a doctoral dissertation or a substantial master's thesis, senior honors, or major area paper.

1

Among the social and behavioral sciences we include social psychology, sociology, certain aspects of individual psychology (e.g., clinical, human learning, child and adolescent development), political science, anthropology, economics, history; also all the applied social relations (multidisciplinary or interdisciplinary) fields[1] such as education, ethnic, area and women's studies; the health sciences such as delivery of medical care, epidemiology, kinesics, and public health; human ecology, social work, and theory of management. We also include certain work in linguistics and analysis of style and period in the arts. We assume your research question is primarily concerned with human behavior, and exploits the application of statistical or related quantitative methods in the analysis of evidence.

We make certain assumptions about you, the reader, in addition to those mentioned above concerning fields of interest.

- You are sufficiently knowledgeable about the discipline within which the problem lies (e.g., education, sociology, public health) so as to be aware of related problems, fundamental definitions, pertinent theories. (You may, however, be unfamiliar with strategies of data collection and analysis more typical of work in other disciplines but quite adaptable to problems in your own.)
- Your are able to obtain access to such needed facilities as calculating devices, a library, etc.
- You are informed about statistics to the extent of an intensive 1-year course,[2] and reasonably unperturbed at the prospect of learning and using additional techniques.
- You are oriented towards research as a problem-solving enterprise, whether the desired outcome is primarily theoretical or practical.
- You are energetic, persistent, and willing to assign a high priority to the research project for its duration: in other words, strongly motivated.

Many people find the prospect of undertaking their own research overwhelming. Why is this so?

- New researchers are neither selected nor trained for this set of tasks. Their earlier training, which may have concentrated on another field, emphasized different skills, those that are relevant to course work. In addition, it may have been very uneven or have taken place long ago. Throughout the college and earlier graduate years, retention and the ability to summarize and synthesize the work of others were emphasized. The shift from being consumer to producer of research is the shift from asking "What is known?" to "What do I want (or need) to know?" Formulating a coherent proposal for a research project and laying out the methodology can be formidable: It requires keeping several balls in the air at the same time.

- Beginning researchers frequently do not know which skills they need, nor how to acquire them. They are often uncertain about what is expected of them. Their most important—and perhaps most difficult—task is learning to take responsibility for their own work, to develop and use their own critical ability rather than depending on the traditional "grading" by an authority. Doing this involves willingness to undertake a risk.

  To address these concerns, this primer outlines the research process as a whole, from the initial selection of a problem area, through problem formulation, identification of variables, development of design, decisions about sampling and instrumentation, exploitation of the computer, choice of statistical analysis, and finally presentation of findings.[3] It describes the steps involved under each of these headings, with particular attention to the interdependence of decisions and warnings of common pitfalls. It indicates what skills the researcher will need, and which can be best obtained in the form of a consultant's services. Although each chapter deals with its topic in some detail, the book's main purpose is to convey the importance of intelligent choice among alternatives.

  We emphasize the importance of organizing information for research purposes.

  We stress the decision-making that goes into research, not how to use specific techniques but when to use them. We make a consistent effort to employ terminology that will be compatible with usage in all, or at least several, disciplines.

- Research requires asking as well as answering questions. It requires a skeptical rather than an accepting attitude towards intellectual authority.

  This primer emphasizes the need to accomplish a major shift in attitudes about knowledge. It consistently describes the research process as a set of plausible procedures together with a set of questions to be answered, and emphasizes that the investigator's choices among these alternatives determine and characterize the particular piece of research.

- This book is practical in its approach. It emphasizes realistic estimates of time, money, and other resources, and careful planning of procedures so as to make the most effective use of whatever is available. Almost everyone operates under constraints of time and money. Research is an open-ended enterprise: unlike the set curricula for the training of lawyers and physicians, it offers no guarantee of completion at the end of a fixed time.

- This book acknowledges the inevitable difficulties instead of implying that their occurrence is somehow the beginner's fault. Here are some facts of life we recognize and take into account: finding sources, checking references, revising endlessly, setting up calculations, and summarizing statistical results are frustrating tasks; rewriting can be tedious; finding the appropriate way to state what seems already obvious may be very difficult, especially if one finds writing burdensome; the problem may be elusive and difficult; unexpected snags may develop; the researcher, having lost some initial enthusiasm, may become impatient; subjects may be uncooperative, supervisors who give permission may change their minds (or their assignments); books may mysteriously disappear from the library that has the only copy within 200 miles, etc., etc. A heavy investment must be made in a search for what often turns out not to be there.

Researchers cannot depend on external approval as a source of motivation. Neither is there usually available an ongoing collaboration from which they can obtain the social support to which they may be accustomed. Friends and family may not understand their work or even why it is worth doing. Researchers must set their own standards and proceed in a frequently lonely enterprise.

Finally, beginning researchers are likely to be intimidated by examples of "great research." While there is much to be said for ambition and elevated goals, it is painful to have to accept the greater wisdom of striving to do a workmanlike job on a well-defined and contained problem whose solution is valuable and interesting.

We address these concerns directly. We make every effort to assist you to develop a sense of proportion—and a sense of humor—about the enterprise in which you are entangled. We do not minimize the uncertainty or the gratuitous character of some of the snags that may impede your progress. This is likely to relieve some of your "it's just me" feelings of inadequacy. We believe that straightforwardness about certain problems is helpful even when no direct solutions can be offered.

For convenience, we frequently refer to the beginning researcher as *the student*, using this in both the specific sense of graduate (or undergraduate) student and the more general one of learner. We hope any necessary distinction will be self-explanatory. *We* almost always means the authors; very occasionally it means "the profession." *He* should be understood as *he or she* unless the antecedent is clearly male. *You* means you, the reader.

The best way to use this book is to read the table of contents and the preface, skim the first few paragraphs of each chapter, then return to read more carefully the chapters that seem most relevant to your interests and state of progress. Some of the "philosophical" material seems very simple and the "statistical" very difficult, but it is important not to confuse technical and profound.

Despite the informal style, some parts need to be studied very closely. (If you are an aural learner, try reading difficult bits out loud.) You will probably find it helpful to reread certain chapters and to consult the list of references.

The chapter on writing up your results serves as a general guide. Superb models (as well as an assortment of horrible examples) are undoubtedly available in the literature of your own field. In this book, we cite many studies, some quite popular; not all are good ones but all serve an exemplary purpose.

At the end of most chapters, in addition to the usual notes, a briefly annotated list of additional reading is given. These include general (elementary) reference texts, specialized technical manuals, and special reference texts, or specialized chapters thereof. We have tried to indicate their potential for direct usefulness. We are not including research reports and material prepared for professional colleagues with the same or related academic research specialty. All authors mentioned in the text, notes, or reading lists appear with full citation in the bibliography.

Appendix: Decision Trees

We will make frequent use of decision trees.

A decision tree is a graphic representation of decision procedure. To be practicable, it must consist of a finite number of steps (but not too many, one hopes). Each step presents a finite number of alternatives, exactly one of which must be selected. The alternatives at any step or branch point should (1) be mutually exclusive and (2) exhaust the universe of possible alternatives at that step, that is, every possible alternative should appear. Put in terms perhaps more familiar, a decision tree is a flow chart for decision-making. A simple example will illustrate the conventions (see Figure 0.1).

Start at the left of Figure 0.1 and read across. (Other trees may start at the top and work down to take advantage of available space.) Note that at each branch point, exactly one alternative applies; there is no "missing case" and no overlap of cases. For example, in our Figure 0.1, "The Bedtime Snack," you start at the initial question, "Are you thirsty or hungry?" Your answer can only be *yes* or *no*. If your answer is *no*, proceed to the branch or arrow which terminates with the command, "Brush teeth now." If your answer is *yes*, you can ask the next question, "Are you hungry?" Follow the branch corresponding to the selected alternative until you reach the next branch point and repeat the decision procedure. In a more general setting, a branch may connect (loop or bridge) to another branch or even to another parallel tree. Referring again to Figure 0.1, suppose you had come out of "The Bedtime Snack" by satisfying your thirst with a root beer; a branch could be

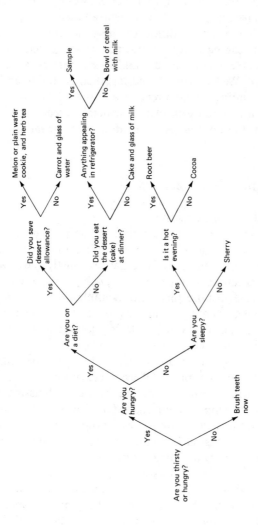

FIGURE 0.1 Decision tree: The bedtime snack.

constructed so that you could again consider the first question, "Are you thirsty or hungry?" The answer *no* would bring you to the command, "Brush teeth now."

Some main branches are longer than others in that to arrive at the final alternative (plum) you need to traverse more branch-points: that is, you need to make a longer sequence of decision-steps. It is very important not to skip or bypass any branch-points, and not to leap from one branch to another unless they are connected by a loop or bridge. It is also possible that in such trees the same plum will appear at the end of more than one sequence of branches—this simply means that the same outcome can be achieved using different sets of initial assumptions. (It is further possible that two individuals can construct quite distinct trees leading to the same final decision set; this need not concern you if you are mainly a consumer of plums.)

A great many so-called real life problems entail for their solution decision sequences, which can be represented graphically in the form of a tree. Among these are:

medical diagnosis;
taxonomic (classification) systems for gemstones, flowering plants, animals;
trouble-shooting a mechanical device or electrical circuit (e.g., auto or TV repair);
purchasing decisions;
"prioritizing" tasks; time planning;
choosing a menu, a costume, a travel itinerary; and
identifying the criminal by elimination in the classical detective story.

In Chapters 5 and 6 you will find trees used to exhibit a classification of research types. In Chapter 11 you will find a tree for each of several pertinent questions about the data, to help you choose an appropriate type of data analysis.

Associated with decision trees is a large technical vocabulary, which we see no need to introduce, and a substantial literature on analysis and applications. A good reference, especially if you anticipate constructing such trees, is Anderson et al. (1978, pp. 90–93) or Hillier and Lieberman (1974, pp. 610–613). This book will not demand that you construct any trees but only "climb" or "descend" them. We hope our metaphoric description will be clear without explicit definitions.

Notes

[1]These are characterized by Meyer Schapiro (private communication) as *Zwissenschaften*.

[2]Our emphasis is on interpretation of statistical analysis, and selection of appropriate procedures. We follow the spirit of the remark (attributed to Montaigne) "Everything the child learns in school he forgets, but the education remains."

[3]Sommer (1963) classifies researchers as the creative "idea-person," the scientific middleman or operationalizer (methodologist), and the technologist. He observes that all of these are essential for success (pp. 32–34). We would add to this list: the interpreter, the exploiter, and the politician. A more serious discussion of the different but interrelated roles of the researcher can be found in Hyman (1964).

1

Preliminaries

Introduction

The human species exhibits persistent curiosity. In every society of which records survive, some individuals have been preoccupied with exploration, the acquisition of information, and the speculative ordering or systematization of this information into explanations of the phenomena of everyday life. The outcome of this process is knowledge. Every answered question suggests more questions and more speculation, so later exploration often appears far removed from the starting point.[1] For example, the casual observation that one can often "read" someone's "message" before he opens his mouth to speak, or that the "message" directly contradicts the spoken words, leads eventually to the work of Birdwhistell (1952), Goffman (1959), and investigators of cultural differences in stance and gesture.

Questions, or their answers, reflecting some common theme of substance or style are grouped together into disciplines that possess characteristic strategies of investigation and a common vocabulary. New fields of inquiry may develop from time to time in response to the need to attack novel problems or out of dissatisfaction with already-existing points of view. Examples abound: Political economy, which was concerned initially with the wealth of nations, gave rise to economics as the analysis of systems. Economics specialized into many fields, including econometrics, economic geography, and management science. Anthropology, primarily an outgrowth of European explorations in Africa, the Americas, and Oceania, divided into physical and cultural; it now overlaps archaeology, ethnology, and sociology (which was defined as a separate discipline in 1857 by Comte, a philosopher interested in laws governing the social order). Medicine has among its many subfields public health and epidemiology. There is every reason to expect that this proliferation of methodologies and repeated differentiation of labels will continue.

Our first task is to look at how one goes about acquiring knowledge, or finding belief. Throughout any discussion of knowledge, it is helpful to distinguish between:

9

Statements that are *true*: those in which you have a high degree of belief; and

Statements that are *valid*: those that have been obtained by a procedure, agreed upon in advance, whose usefulness has been acknowledged.

In this primer we avoid the question of truth. Our concern is with validity. Our goal is to offer guidance in procedure and strategy. The profound and very important philosophical issues underlying all research must be pursued elsewhere.[2]

Methods of Acquiring Knowledge

Some of the many ways of acquiring knowledge have been classified[3] into hierarchies that reflect a progression from the less to the more "scientific."

1. A person with authority may tell us; he may represent a powerful or awesome institution (the priesthood, the government, the university, or the business community) or he may be reputed to possess the qualification of great knowledge in his own right. In any case, this knowledge is accepted because of its source. Compare the effect of a scholarly comment made by a well-regarded senior professor and that of the same comment made by a very young graduate student!

2. Not too far removed from this is knowledge that has "always been so": its continued acceptance strengthens the claim of tradition as a basis for knowledge. We may tend to accept as true whatever we regard as "self-evident", or we may be inclined to reject as invalid everything we have not directly observed. It is quite possible that our personal experiences are themselves contradictory, leading us uncritically to accept conflicting statements.[4]

3. Starting with what we already know (from whatever source) we may arrive at further knowledge using agreed upon rules of logic. Statements so obtained must be labeled "valid" providing we regard the rules of logic as leading us inevitably to a conclusion; we do not demand further evidence or a further appeal to authority or intuition (our sense of the self-evident). This process is called *deduction* or *deductive inference*. The familiar joke about the tourist on a tight itinerary who reasons, "If this is Tuesday, it must be Belgium," provides a frivolous but apt illustration. More serious, and far more elaborate, examples can be seen in synthetic Euclidean (plane or solid) geometry when properly axiomatized,[5] the laws of Mendelian inheritance and their predictive consequences, and the complex econometric models developed systematically from relatively simple assumptions.

4. On the other hand, using a widely accepted but poorly understood sequence of repeated observation, abstraction, and generalization, we may

arrive at further knowledge that represents an extension or unification of what we knew at the outset. For example, the young child somehow decides on the basis of his familiarity with his pet cat that the leopard in the zoo is a big pussycat. This procedure, called *induction* or *inductive inference*, is evidently nondeductive: logic alone will not permit you to choose between competing generalizations. Experience, taste, and anticipated usefulness are all factors.[6] In many cases the inductive step is a fortuitous identification of a plausible relationship between apparently disparate phenomena. A famous example involved the districts with high incidence of cholera and the location of (polluted) wells in London.[7]

Most classification systems or taxonomies are developed through application of the inductive process.[8] The establishment of classifications is an essential fundamental step in the organization of knowledge because until objects can be assigned to appropriate classes, it is impossible to establish relationships between membership in one class and membership in another. Examples of so-called taxonomic research are readily seen in the work of Mendeleev on the classification of chemical elements or Linnaeus on botanical classification. With induction, the emphasis is on a search for invariants across experience. There is no prescription or procedure that will identify or validate plausibility.

Statistical inference is often regarded as a special case of induction.

5. In most hierarchies of ways of acquiring knowledge, the position of greatest sophistication is occupied by the scientific method.

The Scientific Method

"The scientific method may initially be described as a cyclic process through which human beings learn from experience. As evidence accumulates, theories in better and better agreement with the actual functioning of nature can be formulated."[9] *Research* is the process, procedure, or strategy by which the scientific method is applied.[10]

Research begins with curiosity. It involves an active effort to find new facts and to order them into meaningful patterns. It entails a point of view on the nature of knowledge and a set of agreed-upon conventions as to what constitutes science. A large body of literature sets forth various positions on both of these issues. The essentials for a science include *systematic observation* of *identifiable, specified events* and a coherent *theoretical framework* within which to *evaluate these observations*. This framework is susceptible to *modification* as a result of the observations. Any necessary *assumptions* must be *stated explicitly* and the *procedures* for making and evaluating observations are *specified in advance* so as to be *reproducible* by other qualified individuals. Usually, the goal of the scientific endeavor is the formulation of *predictions*:

statements of what is likely to be observed under comparable or slightly modified conditions. Beyond this, each discipline has a philosophy of its own and a tradition (not to say a mystique) of investigation. (You have an obligation to make yourself familiar with the agreements in force in your own field, and the controversies you may need to understand while doing your own work.)

Thus research involves asking questions and seeking answers in a context so contrived as to permit you (1) to identify the relationships among selected factors, while the (possible) effects of other factors are suppressed either by construction or by happenstance, and (2) to describe the relationships in such a form that, ideally, some inference can be made about comparable constellations of events.

IDENTIFYING A PROBLEM AS RESEARCHABLE

Finding a suitable problem can take a long time, and so can deciding whether it is researchable. The first consideration is that the problem can be clearly stated so that any reader can understand specifically what it is that you want to know, what you are assuming at the outset, and what you expect to find out.

Formulation in vague terms, such as, Are people who have lots of social contacts and belong to many (informal) social groups, likely to be better informed about matters of everyday importance? is unacceptable, because in almost every important respect it will be difficult or impossible to make decisions about evidence and validity. Many beginners find it difficult to move from the problem-area, in this case the relationship between gregariousness or sociability and possession of information, to a more precise formulation as a problem-question. Asking yourself repeatedly, What can I realistically find out? may help you. Before you proceed you must be comfortable with your answers to the following: Is there a clearly identified, well-stated problem-question here, or is there just a general problem-area of interest and concern? Can I refine the question so it will be easier to work on or so its answer will be sharper? You can expect to have to specify suitable definitions (see Chapter 4), an arena (see Chapters 5, 6, and 8), procedures for measuring (see Chapter 7), and criteria for evaluating your findings (see Chapters 4 and 10–15).

The question posed above can be restated as follows: when gregariousness and integration (group membership) are defined operationally in an appropriate way for their respective university departments, and the difference between high and low group density environments is taken into account: (1) Are more gregarious graduate students more likely to be integrated? and (2) Are more gregarious, more integrated graduate students more likely to indicate that they are informed about departmental financial aid?[11]

Here are some specific criteria that will help you decide whether a problem is researchable:

1. You must be able to identify and list the variables or factors which may affect the outcome of the study, and to specify those you plan to study.
2. You must be able to specify what assumptions (whose validity will not be tested in your study) you will be making.
3. You must be able to describe, at least tentatively, the possible outcomes.
4. You must be able to state one or more conjectures, about one or more specific expected (anticipated) outcomes.
5. In particular, you must, if you wish to use the techniques of inferential statistics, be able to formulate for each conjecture a so-called bifurcated hypothesis: a pair of mutually exclusive statements that together exhaust all possibilities; one of these must be compatible with your conjecture.
6. You must be able to identify the kinds of evidence that would support or refute the conjecture.
7. You must be able to specify the kinds of observations which would yield such evidence. (Our discussion of feasibility will be found in Chapter 2.)
8. You must be able, on the basis of plausible arguments, to trace relationships between facts (pieces of evidence or summaries of evidence previously collected), and between facts and explanations, so that the consumer of your research will be convinced that there is indeed some connection between the evidence you have obtained from your observations and the conclusions you propose to draw from it.
9. You must also be able to identify alternative explanations and, using the facts you expect to bring forward, eliminate them or reduce the likelihood that they apply.

A well-explored and cleverly exploited theoretical frame of reference makes it easier to recast a vague question into researchable form, so that a study sticks together in this sense.

THE ROLE OF THEORY

Fundamental to the scientific method is the notion of theory: A statement or set of statements that integrate and summarize, in as general a way as possible, what is already known and can be used to predict what the researcher may expect to observe in the future. Statements like, "The theory accounts for (or explains) the evidence" or "The theory is not supported by the observations" describe ways in which new findings are regarded as compatible with already existing knowledge.

The goal of theory-construction is the development of a causal chain: where genius, or an inexplicable conceptual leap, is required, it is most likely to take place at this stage. Developing new theory usually involves the process of induction. The crucial role of observation and classification as a basis for theory-development is frequently deprecated.[12] No researcher need be apologetic about any study that provides raw material for later conjectures.

The effort to justify a particular theory—or to refute it—and the use of theory for predictive purposes serve to guide a scientific investigation and distinguish it from a mere fishing expedition, a casual casting about for interesting phenomena. (Many studies do indeed involve what appears to be the simple accumulation of factual data, e.g., NASA expeditions or the collection of specimens of animals or artifacts, but in most cases the desire to extend or modify already-existing theory underlies this research.)

On the basis of relevant theory the researcher formulates one or more hypotheses or conjectures[13]—plausible guesses or hunches. It is at this step that general knowledge, sophistication, and ability to use both deductive and inductive processes come into play. In general, if several competing candidate theories are compatible with the observations, it may be difficult to decide which is to be preferred.[14] The researcher tries to pursue the logical implications of what is already known and to combine them with insights drawn from experience with the field, so as to formulate predictions. The next step is the establishment of a criterion for evaluating any observational evidence (data) to be collected: What evidence will permit the retention of the theory? What evidence will require modification or even abandonment of the theory? More specifically, What evidence will force rejection of the conjecture that has been deduced from the underlying theory? Ideally this can be decided in advance of the observational phase of the study.

In all fairness, we must point out that exploratory and clinical research, whose main goal is to obtain data for later classification and the development of new theory, often proceed without clearly stated hypotheses of the kind described. Also in the "real world" many (if not most) studies proceed without explicitly stated hypotheses. Dalton's essay (1964) describing the development of concepts and methods used in his study *Men Who Manage* (1959) offers a thoughtful justification for a much broader and looser approach to problems; Dalton feels that hypotheses stated as such tend to "bind both one's conscience and vanity,"[15] and indicates that in practice he cannot formulate hypotheses until he is already familiar with the situation under study. Like many others, Dalton regards the conventional model of research as oversimplified or useful, at best, to evaluate the finished product rather than as a blueprint for carrying out the process. He does acknowledge, however, that his research was guided by hunches, some of which were dropped and replaced as his knowledge increased.

Despite the hazards of overcommitment to preconceptions embodied in the conjectures, first research projects need clearly stated testable hypotheses and should not be "let's take a look" types.

The relationship of theory and evidence is such that evidence cannot *prove* a theory to be correct, that is, establish its validity, but evidence can *disprove* a theory, that is, refute it and so force a modification in its formulation. Evidence can also make theory more plausible or believable. (We discuss this point at greater length in Chapter 4.) For instance, if theory predicts that children of working mothers will exhibit more antisocial behavior than the children of full-time homemakers—everything else being equal—then observations to the contrary will establish that the theory as stated is in error, but observations compatible with the prediction will simply lend support to the theory.[16] No amount of case-by-case evidence will prove a universal statement, whereas any one counterexample will destroy its (universal) validity.

There are obvious hazards in accepting the principle that when a test of the inference "if A then B," yields evidence B is in fact true, we can have increased confidence in the truth of A. From a logical point of view, affirming the consequent is an evident fallacy.[17] On the other hand, "few students in the elementary logic course have been told that affirming the consequent. . . is very nearly the life blood of science."[18] Extensive and thoughtful discussions of this point can be found in Sidman (1960, pp. 127–137) and in Stinchcombe (1968, Chapter 2 passim); see also Chapter 4 (section on the Logic of Hypothesis Testing).

Despite the wide acceptance of the conventional formulation of the role of evidence in testing theory, it is all too often the case that once a powerful theory has become well-established, that is, once it has withstood numerous empirical tests, it is increasingly difficult to overturn. Researchers tend to set aside or simply to ignore evidence that contradicts it. To put this another way, the mindset of the community of researchers virtually excludes alternative theories. The history of science provides several examples of this.

CAUSALITY

One of the most complex, elusive, and difficult notions with which any researcher struggles is that of causality. Philosophers and scientists of all kinds have been preoccupied with the need to present a suitable definition and a set of criteria by which causal relationships can be recognized.[19] "In scientific theory there is really no need for the concept of causation. It is an esthetic dimension added for esthetic reasons. . . . The statement of scientific laws does not include or require causality; it simply requires statements of invariant association in given orders."[20] A counsel of despair? It is generally easier to formulate criteria for *determination* (a necessary connection between variables of which causation is only one among many types); the determining conditions for an effect E are those which make the occurrence of E probable. It is only rarely that a question can be so formulated that its answer is of the form "C is necessary *and* sufficient for E." More generally, the researcher seeks to establish (1) evidence of concomitant variation of C and E (the form of the variation as predicted by the hypotheses of the study); (2) evidence that E did not occur before C; (3) evidence ruling out other factors than C as alternative determining conditions of E in the situation under study; (4) evidence of the effects of contributory and contingent conditions that make E more probable. Thus, the outcome may be stated as "the frequency of occurrence of C is positively correlated with the frequency of occurrence of E" or "when A is present, the frequency of occurrence of C is significantly more positively correlated with the frequency of occurrence of E than when A is not present," "In the social sciences. . . the connections between antecedents and consequents will be probabilistic. This is not to deny that social scientists can better approximate inevitable causal connections by studying the contingency conditions that codetermine when a particular putative cause affects an outcome. We merely deny that they will ever be totally successful in this attempt."[21]

Underlying all scientific endeavour is the assumption that nothing "just happens," but that everything happens for a reason. Notwithstanding the absence of certainty and the reliance on probabilistic (i.e., statistical) inference, researchers really want to establish cause-and-effect sequences. The hazards of confusing even very strong correlations with the existence of a causal relationship are illustrated in many studies; for example, the numerous attempts to relate income and years of schooling. Causal inference is an essential aspect of all research and the ultimate goal of all science. You may want to seek out and read discussions of causality written with particular reference to the problems of your own field. We will return to this topic in Chapter 12.

CONTROLLED OBSERVATIONS

The notion of controlled observation distinguishes the scientific method from other ways of acquiring knowledge. In the classical formulation of science, the researcher identifies the variables of interest, controls—or some would say selects—the values of all except a specified few, then observes the associated values of the latter. In effect, he constructs the events to be observed. A more general point of view is that the observer is controlled:[22] the observer carefully specifies what observations will be made, within what conceptual framework and under what conditions. We prefer to refer to this as systematic observation in controlled circumstances. After all, the astronomer and the meteorologist cannot construct events! (We will have more to say about this in Chapters 4 and 5.)

The social and behavioral sciences have frequently been the subject of criticism from those in the "hard" sciences, on the grounds that they do not lend themselves to the "true" scientific (by which is meant, experimental) method. It is true that the manipulation of variables, as done by the physicist, is generally not possible; moreover, the presence of the observer may effect a substantial alteration in the events under observation. (However, this is true in any experimental situation.) The work of anthropologists like Margaret Mead[23] and Oscar Lewis, as well as much research in education, exemplifies the last difficulty. Social scientists often invoke the "intervention"[24] or "participation" argument to justify other, gratuitous, violations of careful research procedure. We believe that social and behavioral science research has been pauperized rather than enriched by an overzealous adherence to a physical-sciences experimental model, and that some of the controversy over selection versus control of variables is a great waste of time, the result of misunderstanding or excessive self-consciousness. Equally wasteful is the (often) self-imposed demand for specific causal models or functional relationships which are neither necessary nor sufficient for good social science research.[25]

STATISTICAL ANALYSIS

The most effective exploitation of observations as a basis for retaining or rejecting hypotheses, that is, for supporting a theory or forcing its modification, may entail the development of suitable measurement schemes and a more or less complex statistical analysis. (Many sound and valuable studies make no quantitative analysis of findings, but we have indicated earlier that we are not concerned with them in this book.) The statistical component of research permits exploration of patterns and relationships, provides a summary of certain aspects of the observations, and yields a basis for the decision that the criterion for acceptance or rejection of the hypotheses has been met. Inferential methods need not be in question: descriptive statistical procedures (data reduction) may be sufficient for the purpose of the study, or may be all that is possible. Other forms of summary and analysis of data than the conventional inferential statistical procedures may yield far richer results. This is commonly the case in exploratory studies such as Bott's (1955) investigation of possible determinants of conjugal roles, and in such community studies as Poll's (1962). Findings and conclusions are presented in an informal discursive fashion reflecting the researcher's experience and judgment. The choice of a statistical strategy and the designation of the events to be observed are interdependent. A satisfactory analysis reflects a coherent and plausible taxonomy that permits the ordering of data. On the principle, "garbage in, garbage out," it is most unwise to expect to be able to extract conclusions of substance from data that are inadequate because of poor planning, carelessness in collection, or inept design.

OVERVIEW OF THE SCIENTIFIC METHOD

The scientific method, as embodied in research, comprises the following components:

- Assumptions: knowledge not susceptible to challenge in the particular study;
- Theory: framework for the study;
- Evidence previously obtained;
- Conjectures: stated in the language of theory;
- Predictions (hypotheses): obtained deductively from the conjectures, stated in the language of observations;
- Criteria for possible rejection or acceptance of the hypotheses;
- Observations: made systematically under controlled circumstances;
- Analysis of the observations; and
- Modification of the theory or increased confidence in it.

Needless to say, working through this apparently clean, rational process may involve many human fallibilities and disagreements; moreover, the motivations of the researchers may be quite other than the thirst for knowledge. Nonetheless, this is the model to which most scientists aspire.

Classification of Research

Research, like most other complex activities, lends itself to classification, with many different bases for the establishment of categories. The distinction between research with human subjects—specifically, research in human behavior—and research with subjects other than human, is obvious. Equally obvious is the distinction between research in which the principal focus is on subjects as isolated individuals and research which concerns itself with social systems, interactions, behavior in groups, etc. One can classify research according to the number of factors or variables, according to the kinds of measurements possible, according to the size of the study population, according to whether the events under study are replicable, according to the methodologies used for making and analyzing observations, and so forth.

FORMULATIVE AND VERIFICATIONAL RESEARCH

A research project can be classified as formulative or verificational according to its purpose(s). *Formulative* research has as its goal the formulation of problems for more precise investigation, the development of hypotheses, the gaining of insights, and increasing familiarity with all aspects of the problem area including practical priorities. So-called exploratory research is frequently formulative; studies employing discriminant analysis to establish classes or factor analysis to identify underlying variables may also fall into this category. Studies whose goal is formulative admit great flexibility.[26] Multivariate exploratory research is too demanding as a first project except in very unusual circumstances; we recommend the choice of some alternative. *Verificational* research, as its label suggests, is directed toward obtaining evidence to support or refute hypotheses that have already been formulated, that is, to test the conjectures or predictions which have been deduced from the theory. (In Chapter 4 we discuss issues involved in stating and testing hypotheses.)

Research whose goal or outcome is the establishment of a taxonomy is often regarded—incorrectly—as prescientific rather than scientific. However, it provides a basis for both types of research: until and unless the identification and classification of phenomena can be carried out, no investigation of relationships between categories can proceed. Thus, for example, Hilson (1980) reports first a classification of women mathematicians into trait-types, and then an investigation of family and other variables which may be characterizing for this typology.

BASIC, APPLIED, AND ACTION RESEARCH

Research can also be classified as basic, applied, or action according to its purpose. It is important for you to identify your own project correctly. The differences are reflected in your criteria for the outcomes, the context of your interpretations, and your methodology, as well as your target audience for the findings.

The goals of *pure* or *basic* research are (1) to provide support or refutation for theory, (2) to establish evidence on which new theory can be developed, and (3) to contribute to general knowledge. Basic research studies should be framed so as to permit the greatest possible generalizability of the results. This must not be confused with research that involves issues so hypothetically formulated that they are "not about anything": presumably if a question needs answering, that necessity can be made apparent to a reasonably well-informed and unbiased reader.

As the circumstances to which they might apply become more particular, or as the constraints under which observations are to be made become more confining, the conclusions which may be drawn are more limited. Certain studies are designed specifically to determine whether theory adequately predicts outcome in a designated set of circumstances or whether modifications peculiar to the situation must be introduced. Such research can be properly called *applied*. The distinction between pure and applied research is not absolute: the various possibilities fall along a continuum which ranges from completely pure to applied.[27] Applied research, even at its most extreme, has generality as one of its important goals. There is very little entirely pure research in the behavioral and social sciences.

Even further removed from basic research is so-called *action* research. It often involves the analysis of the outcome of a very particular, perhaps nonreplicable, sequence of events, such as the evaluation of the effects of social intervention or of differing conditions, sometimes called *treatments*[28] in a "natural" setting. The researcher is primarily concerned with providing information on which an immediate decision can be based, or developing or applying decision criteria. In a proposed sequence of activities, the choice of each one may be predicated on the outcome of the one(s) preceding; hence research findings may be of great importance and possess considerable time value. For instance, in order to proceed with an investigation of the relative effectiveness of specified instructional schemes an educational experimenter may need to determine that a large proportion of 7-year-olds already possess certain cognitive or motor skills. Or, a survey researcher may wish to ascertain the issues that most concern voters in a particular area, in order to advise a political candidate. This research may be very restricted in its generalizability. Since such events may not be known in advance, the design and methodology must be flexible; nonetheless, these studies can meet the criteria for safeguarding internal validity (see Chapter 5). The pressure to obtain useful findings may lead to careless mistakes; if you undertake an action study you should be on your guard. Action research may be regarded as a special subcategory of the case-study approach.

To illustrate the differences between basic, applied, and action research we offer the following:

Example 1: Learning

Basic: carefully matched, naive subjects, controlled environment, explicit behavioral criteria, "machine" teacher.

Applied: quasi-experimental design[29] to test effectiveness of different methods of teaching reading.

Action: case study of implementation of new curriculum for reading instruction, intact groups.

Example 2: Pain-Causing Behavior

Basic: Milgram's (1974) studies of effect of persuasion on willingness of subjects to inflict pain on their fellow subjects.

Applied: identification of personality variables in individuals convicted of crimes of violence.

Action: evaluation of programs of rehabilitative therapy for child-abusers.

(Note: There are those who prefer to classify research according to the type of statistical analysis. This is rarely a useful point of view, because such a classification is not exhaustive nor is it unambiguous. As new techniques are developed the categories will shift, and one study may employ several statistical techniques.

Classifying your proposed study is most easily done after you have planned its design and data-collection procedures. In reading reports of earlier studies, you should attempt to identify them as falling under one or another of the headings mentioned above. Further discussion of classification will be found in Chapters 5 and 6.)

Your first task is to choose and appropriately state a researchable problem-question. In Chapter 2, we present some of the factors, theoretical and practical, that you should consider in making your selection.

Notes

[1]"If we cannot see things clearly, we will at least see clearly where the obscurities are" (Sigmund Freud).

[2]A good introduction to such problems is still Cohen and Nagel (1934). More detailed and specific is Nagel (1961).

[3]For example, Cohen and Nagel (1934) (pp. 193–196).

[4]"It ain't so much the things we don't know that get us in trouble. It's the things we know that ain't so" (Artemus Ward). "It is the customary fate of new truths to begin as heresies and to end as superstitions" (T. H. Huxley).

[5]Indeed, in many other parts of modern mathematics including formal logic itself.

[6]"The inductive attitude aims at adapting our beliefs to our experience as efficiently as possible" (Polya, 1954, Vol. 1, p. 7). "For every complex problem there is a simple solution. And it is always wrong" (H. L. Mencken).

[7]See Mechanic (1968). Medawar (1979) also offers several examples in biological research, as does Sidman (1960) in experimental psychology, Hammond (1964) in sociology, and Cannon (1945) in physiology.

[8]There are, however, a number of statistical procedures that identify groupings in data and allow the assessment of the strengths of the groupings. A number of these are exhibited and compared in Mezzich and Solomon (1980) and in Gordon (1981).

[9]Kemeny and Snell (1972, p. 3). See also Kuhn (1970) for an analysis of how new theory is generated. "If politics is the art of the possible, then surely research is the art of the soluble" (Arthur Koestler, quoted New York *Times*, June 28, 1983, p. C4).

[10]The term *research* is also widely used to refer to the outcome of the process, the body of information and theory so obtained. We make an effort to avoid the latter usage.

[11]This is based on the very interesting paper by Erbe (1962). The answers, by the way, are *yes* and *yes*, but the methodology and analysis are well worth reading. We refer again to this study in Chapter 4.

[12]See Rist (1979); Medawar (1979); and Hyman (1964). It is easy to overlook the importance of "purely descriptive" research as a component in theory building, and to place excessive emphasis on experimental or quasi-experimental testing of theory already formulated.

[13]In this book, we will with fair consistency use *hypothesis* to mean a predictive statement that is tested statistically, and *conjecture* in a more general way to mean a predictive statement, formulated in terms of theoretical constructs, which will be supported or refuted by the evidence. Thus, hypotheses are conjectures of a particular kind, cast into a particular form, and decisions

are made about them in a particular way. "The possibility of constructing hypotheses rests on the assumption that there is some order in nature. This is not the same as the assumption that all parts of nature are ordered" (Wilson, 1952, p. 26). Even in purely exploratory studies, the choice of what to observe and what to record embodies a conjecture as to what may be important. This conjecture is testable in the sense that analysis of observations either will reveal a pattern of difference of association, or will not.

[14]Systematic attacks on this problem are to be found in such works as Ackerman (1966).

[15]Dalton (1964) in Hammond, (1964, p. 54).

[16]Nye and Hoffman (1963).

[17]Cohen and Nagel (1934, p. 98).

[18]Sidman (1960, p. 127).

[19]In addition to those specifically quoted, we are drawing on points of view expressed by Plutchik (1974) (especially Chapter 8, pp. 174–175) "Concepts of Causality in Experimentation" which includes an analysis of J. S. Mill's methods; Rosenberg (1960, pp. 7–20 passim); Selltiz et al. (1976); Simon (1957); Stinchcombe (1968); Nagel (1961, various locations); Rapaport (1953, pp. 57ff.). For a brief summary of the history of the concept of causation see Cook and Campbell (1979, pp. 13–20). See also Blalock (1961), Hirschi and Selvin (1973), and Asher (1983) in connection with causality in nonexperimental studies.

[20]Greer (1969, pp. 120–121).

[21]Cook and Campbell (1979, p. 15).

[22]For an elaboration of this viewpoint, see Hyman (1964, Chapter 4).

[23]Mead's work has become the subject of renewed controversy in recent years. See, in particular, New York *Times* Jan. 31, 1983, Feb. 1, 1983, and Feb. 17, 1983 (Letters).

[24]Not to be confused with issues raised by so-called *action research*, whose goal is the identification and measurement of the effects of intervention (see p. 20).

[25]See Achen (1982, pp. 1–16) for a persuasive exposition of this viewpoint.

[26]See Selltiz, et al. (1976, Chapter 4, part I, pp. 91ff.); also Blalock (1970, Chapter 3).

[27]Lazarsfeld distinguishes between "autonomous" and "field-induced" research, while Cronbach and Suppes refer to these as "discipline-oriented" and "decision-oriented."

[28]The use of the term *treatment* to mean, most generally, different values of some discrete independent variable, can be disconcerting. It is, however, widespread, so no effort should be made to visualize a medical or other therapeutic procedure.

[29]For elucidation of this term, see Campbell and Stanley (1963).

Additional Reading

For further reading in the scientific method in general, on the role of theory as opposed to empirical evidence, and on theory construction:

Nagel (1961): first rate, touches all the bases, well repays hard work; covers a wide range of "sciences."

Cohen and Nagel (1934): simple analysis of the scientific method.

Stinchcombe (1968): sensible and straightforward, very helpful in clarifying quite difficult issues.

Merton (1968): reflects vast experience and a developed viewpoint, sophisticated.

Blalock (1969) (and Chapter 5 in Blalock and Blalock (1968)): technical but very clear.

Braithwaite (1960): more philosophical than practical.

Lazarsfeld and Rosenberg (1955): many technical issues.

Skyrms (1966): inductive logic.

Denzin (1978): role of theory in practice of research.

The references on causality are listed in Note 19 of this chapter.

Beveridge (1959); Medawar (1979); Sidman (1960), and Cannon (1945, 1965) offer interesting accounts of the role of intuition and "luck."

Tukey and Wilk (1965) suggest the importance of "data snooping" and preliminary statistical analysis in suggesting problems or reformulations.

Hyman (1964): an interesting and thoughtful account of the interplay of different aspects of research; examples are thoroughly described to illustrate his main points.

2

Choosing the Research Problem and Stating the Problem-Question

The Importance of a Well-Chosen Problem

The selection and formulation of the problem are the most important steps in any research project. This chapter addresses a variety of issues related to problem-selection.

The aphorism "well begun is half done" nicely describes the crucial role of the problem statement. It is virtually impossible to plan design and to estimate costs in the absence of a clear specification of what is to be investigated. If a research problem resists systematic attack, it may well be that the right question has not been asked. It is, of course, unfortunately the case that an investigation, no matter how well conceived and formulated, may yield unacceptable results or develop unforeseen complications; nonetheless, research of the highest quality has a well-stated question as its foundation. Problem-formulation is a (perhaps *the*) truly creative aspect of research;[1] meticulous care directed toward the effort we will describe in this chapter will be repaid many times over.

Sources of Problems

Problems calling for investigation can be found in several different ways. A good question for research is most likely to emerge from a theory that is in some way unsatisfactory, that is, a theory inadequate for prediction or explanation of observed phenomena. In the course of becoming knowledgeable in your own field, you will very often speculate concerning some event or set of relationships by asking yourself, "What if . . .?" or "Why not . . .?" or even "So what?" or "But . . . ." To some such questions you may seek answers by conversing and reading; as you pursue the answers, you find yourself narrowing the interrogation by repeatedly asking, "What do I want to know?" As this focusing process continues, it may be possible to find a suitable answer on the basis of existing theory. A particular theory makes sense because its logical consequences include predictions or sufficient explanations for the phenomena under consideration. (See Chapter 1.)

You may encounter interesting problems while taking courses. In lectures and in the literature of your field, issues are raised that may attract your attention and continue to pique your curiosity; it is wise to make a note of them. Further reading and conversation with more experienced researchers (colleagues or faculty) may reveal open questions worth following up. Published research reports frequently indicate the direction for further investigation. Disappointing findings or inappropriate procedures in previous studies can inspire a renewed attack on an unresolved question. Professional society meetings, at which explorers on the frontier give accounts of their latest expeditions, often yield a rich supply of research ideas, and you will have the advantage of learning who is working in different areas.

A thorough understanding of the fundamental theories in those parts of your field you find most interesting, and a broad acquaintance with recent research, will make it much easier for you to identify potentially fruitful questions.[2] (It is a sad fact that the beginner frequently lacks the depth of scholarship from which "mature" investigators generate an apparently endless supply of problems.)

For example, based on their earlier studies of factors associated with delinquency and their familiarity with the somatotyping of Sheldon (1940, 1942) and his efforts to associate these body types with personality types, Glueck and Glueck (1956) conjectured that delinquent boys might display a characteristic distribution of somatotypes; moreover, they hoped that strong associations might be useful for prediction and, hence, preventive efforts.

Ideally, then, a research question arises from a consideration of theory and its implications. In every domain of the social and behavioral sciences there are competing theories whose existence suggests contradictions or makes prediction difficult. This equivocal state of affairs can be usefully mined for a research problem. It is, however, useful to keep in mind that "When . . . competent observers advocate strongly divergent points of view, it seems likely on *a priori* grounds that both have observed something valid about the natural situation, and that both represent a part of the truth. The stronger the controversy, the more likely this is."[3] Accordingly, the researcher should adopt a multidimensional or longitudinal approach and avoid the temptation to conduct a so-called crucial (i.e., definitive) experiment in the hope of identifying a causal chain.

A study which tries to resolve a controversy is Birnbaum's (1975) investigation of self-esteem in gifted women, aged approximately 35–45. Earlier studies indicated that in their mid-20s, family-oriented women had higher self-esteem than career-committed women. Traditional theorists asserted that in midlife, career-oriented women continue to experience conflicts over career versus family roles; in contrast, other theorists suggested that the traditional role loses its power as a continuing basis for self-esteem. Birnbaum found that in midlife both married and single professional women displayed higher self-esteem than homemakers.

The events of the day may suggest problems. Your professional experience—for example, as a teacher, a clinician, or practitioner in some area related to your future research—can if properly exploited supply interesting problems. It is necessary to ask yourself: What would be helpful for me to know, of a general nature, so I can be more professionally effective? What am I taking for granted that needs to be verified or set temporarily aside? What might happen if . . .? Playing with possibilities can be very rewarding.

Often a good question arises in response to a pressing and immediate need: in some sense, something doesn't work, or doesn't work well enough.

Rapid social or economic changes in a population or in regulatory mandates can be expected to have manifold effects on community institutions. For example, the aging of the population, a result of increased longevity and decreased birthrate, is reflected in shifts in voting patterns for school-related budgets. Similarly, the study of Veroff et al. (1981) on mental health help-seeking patterns, described later in this chapter, is a systematic attempt to assess the impact of broad social changes. It is, however, frequently not clear just what such effects will be, nor how institutions can best respond so as to provide optimal service per taxpayer dollar. Research is required to evaluate the effects and account for them in a systematic way, and also to predict which response strategies will be most promising.

Here are some examples: Caplovitz's (1967) study of the consumer behavior of an urban poor population evolved from an attempt on the part of three settlement houses to develop an effective consumer-education program in a neighborhood undergoing rapid rebuilding and renewal. (His later [1979] study of the perceived effects of inflation can also be seen as a response to a social need.) Deutsch's (1971) investigation of the impact of Head Start on later school performance represented an effort to resolve conflicting and highly politicized assertions as to cost-effectiveness of this controversial program. Government policies concerning birth control give rise to a variety of studies[4] as to relative effectiveness of public information and persuasion campaigns.

This urgency to obtain an answer on which some action will be based can lead to the formulation of a sound research question.

Many research problems are suggested by supervisors. The dissertation advisor or project director who says, in effect, "I'm working on this and I'd like you to look into a related problem." is giving you a lead (if not an order!). The list of seminar topics should be taken seriously. Your fellow students often have problems to give away, particularly if their own advisors are actively engaged in several projects. If worse comes to worst, *ask*.

If it is necessary, for reasons of expediency, to ask an authority for a research problem, or to accept one suggested by an authority, you should be aware of the hazards in this procedure. It does not demonstrate your ability to generate research questions. You may find yourself committed to an inquiry that does not genuinely engage your interest, so the entire project can become an exercise in frustration and boredom. Be certain that you can sustain the effort to carry it to a conclusion. Try to use the suggested problem as a basis for your own formulation, not as a fully stated question; be sure to explore the pertinent theoretical material yourself.

Finally, you must not overlook the possibility of a happy accident, the serendipitous experience in which you almost literally "fall over" a problem.[5] Do not bet that this will happen to you, but if it does, be prepared to take advantage of your good fortune.

How then do you recognize a well-stated research question? How do you pose such a question? There is no single prescription that will meet the requirements of every area of knowledge open to scientific investigation, but there are some conditions to be met by questions amenable to systematic inquiry. They include these:

1. The element of genuine curiosity should be present as motivation for the researcher.
2. A comprehensive theoretical basis for the question should be developed.
3. The answer(s) to the question should represent an original contribution to knowledge. (This obviously does not apply to exact replications of earlier studies.)
4. The study as formulated must be systematically replicable.
5. The practical aspects of study procedure must be evaluated.
6. The usefulness of expected findings should be weighed against costs.
7. The political and ethical realities should be recognized and weighed.
8. The common errors in problem formulation must be avoided. (These will be discussed at length in this and later chapters.)

When you have examined the proposed problem-question in the light of each of these items, you can then make appropriate decisions concerning method and design, and can develop a tentative research plan.

In the rest of this chapter, we consider the list above in detail.

The Role of Curiosity

Curiosity is a fundamental motivating force in the process of scientific inquiry, in that the entire process hinges on the desire to know more about something. Its presence is essential in order that you can sustain the effort needed to pursue an investigation over a substantial period of time. Curiosity fuels your desire to reconcile discrepancies and repair omissions. Thus it is wise that you ask yourself, at the outset, questions such as the following:

1. Does this problem engage my attention and beg for solution? Is it appealing?
2. Do I have a profound interest in how it will turn out, or is my attitude just "so what?"
3. Are my curiosity about this problem and its ramifications, and the expressed interest of others, sufficient to motivate me for a sustained period? It may be a long haul.
4. Will I derive satisfaction from working on it? Will finding a solution give me a real boost, professionally or personally? Will anyone else be interested in my findings or conclusions?

No matter how your curiosity may have been aroused initially, it should be supported by the placement of the problem-question into the sort of systematic scheme called theory.

A Theoretical Basis for the Study

No matter how a research idea has come to mind, your best strategy is to relate the problem to a body of theory that suggests either an answer to or a refinement of the question. It is important that you turn early to an examination of relevant theories: First, because theory may point the direction in which an answer may be found—or, if not, the direction in which a sharpened or slightly shifted version of the question may lie—and second, because the theoretical frame of reference lends value and importance to the answer. The recognition and exposition of a suitable theoretical base, or matrix, for the problem permits the researcher

1. to collect data with a clearly identified purpose;
2. to tie together masses of evidence in a systematic way;
3. to develop an answer to the research question which can
   a. advance knowledge in the field rather than remain isolated;
   b. be of value in the attack on other, specific, problems; and
   c. generate other research ideas and investigations.

As a beginning researcher, you must assign your highest priority to broadening and deepening your knowledge of your own field so as to place a possible problem in suitable theoretical context and to decide whether it may be researchable. You need to have access to recent dissertations, and it is also very desirable for you to be reasonably well informed about current research preoccupations in neighboring fields.

Make an effort to formulate a problem-question, and to identify its place in a theoretical framework in such a way that whether the outcome of the study involves "positive" or "negative" results, they will be interesting and useful. While this goal is not always feasible, the "fail-safe" strategy is worth keeping in mind. For example, the findings of a study whose purpose is to verify the applicability of a model, such as Piaget's for cognitive development, or Kohlberg's for moral development, to a social subgroup possessing distinctive characteristics, will be valuable whether or not they support the conjecture; in the latter case, new questions and, thus, new lines of inquiry will be generated.

Even studies that involve primarily a catalogue or taxonomic outcome can be firmly anchored to a theory, perhaps one whose applicability is limited because of the absence of base–line data or identifying information about possible cases.[6]

We now look at some fairly well-known studies from the point of view of the research questions and their theoretical contexts. (Later in this book we will refer to several of them for other illustrative purposes.)

1. Zborowski, M. (1952). "Cultural Components in Responses to Pain." A study of differing reactions to pain in a hospital setting, by Jewish, Irish, Italian, and "Old American" patients. Theoretical framework: illness behavior is a culturally and socially learned response in primitive societies and in American life. Proposed explanation of differences was in terms of maternal protectiveness attitudes. Earlier studies focused on social–class status of the patients. Later studies attempted to test hypotheses that differences are attributable to income level, to extent of religious involvement, and to other variables. (See brief review, in Mechanic [1968, pp. 117–123].) This is a fail-safe study: *any* finding would have been of interest, even that of "no difference."

2. Rosenthal, R., and Jacobson, L. (1968). *Pygmalion in the Classroom: Teacher Expectations and Pupils' Intellectual Development.* A study designed to identify effects of manipulated teacher expectancies on student achievement. Theoretical framework: the notion of the self-fulfilling prophecy: differing expectancies induce differing responses to student behavior and differing "investment" in the students. This study has been extensively criticized for methodological weaknesses (see Thorndike, 1968), but has generated many related studies (see Brophy and Good, 1970).

3. Broverman, I. K., Broverman, D. M., Clarkson, F. E., Rosenkrantz, P. S., and Vogel, S. F. (1970). "Sex-Role Stereotypes and Clinical Judgments of Mental Health." A study of responses of clinicians asked to describe

a healthy, mature, competent (1) adult, (2) man, (3) woman. In previous studies mental health and social desirability were strongly related; and so also were stereotyped sex-role characteristics and social desirability. Authors hypothesized that the definition of mental health would be closer to stereotypic male characteristics than to female. Findings supported the conjecture.

4. Rosetta, Pa.: A longitudinal (panel) study of diet, stress, and incidence of heart disease designed to identify certain factors related to heart attack. The population was selected because its diet was high in cholesterol and various other "undesirable" components as exhibited in other studies. Findings were a surprise; for instance, diet appeared to be an unimportant factor for the older generation, and younger married women (with children) employed at clerical jobs had a high incidence of heart disease (cf. Stout et al., 1964, Bruhn & Wolf, 1979). Related longitudinal studies focusing on other factors such as stress are Dawber et al. (1963), Haynes and Steinlieb (1980), and Haynes et al. (1978a, b, 1980).

5. Coopersmith, Stanley. (1967). *The Antecedents of Self-Esteem*. A series of studies of preadolescents designed to identify the conditions that lead an individual to value himself as worthy. The research was intended to clarify methodological and conceptual issues raised in earlier studies, which are strongly related to various formulations of personality structure. The researcher expected the role of the parents, rather than sociological variables, to be crucial; the data suggested that the ability of the parents to interpret social demands to the child and to identify his behavior as successfully goal directed was of great importance. The series can be interpreted as providing construct validation for the Coopersmith Self-Esteem Inventory.

6. Thornton, A., and Freedman, D. (1979). "Changes in the Sex Role Attitudes of Women, 1962–1977: Evidence from a Panel Study." Documentation for the hypothesized existence of a major shift in sex role attitudes, and identification of the variables associated with such changes. The authors concluded that additional education, work for pay, and exposure to divorce were factors associated with a shift between 1962 and 1977 toward more egalitarian attitudes, but they do not account for the magnitude of the shift, nor was every group in the survey population equally affected. The analysis in this study is subtle and the discussion is excellent; as is frequently the case, the hypotheses are stated after rather than before the analysis.

7. Innes, J. M. (1978). "Selective Exposure as a Function of Dogmatism and Incentive." A study designed to clarify previous findings that individuals tend to seek out material expressing viewpoints or opinions

consistent with their own, by incorporating two additional variables: dogmatism (rigidity), and an "incentive", namely the prospect of a later opportunity to express their opinions. Two hypotheses were tested, using a sample of Australian undergraduate engineering students: high-dogmatics will be less likely to read belief-incongruent material than low dogmatics (supported, but not strongly), and those offered the "incentive" are more likely to read belief-incongruent material than those not offered it (not supported). (The author expressed surprise at the latter finding, but we suggest that the construct "incentive" may require a different operationalization than the one used here.)

8. Bell, A. P., Weinberg, M. S., and Hammersmith, S. K. (1981). *Sexual Preference: Its Development in Men and Women*. An analysis of the effects of a large number of developmental, familial, and other social variables on adult sexual preference. Findings were obtained from about 1500 extensive interviews, nearly 1000 with homosexuals. The authors indicate their purpose to be a test of the many (conflicting) theories concerning family and peer-relationship factors in the development of homosexuality and evidently hoped to settle part (or all) of the controversy definitively. They concluded, based on elaborate path analysis, that no theory currently "on the market" can be supported, but that certain patterns in adolescence (e.g., social nonconformity) are associated with later homosexual preference. They speculated that a biological basis for homosexuality is plausible. Here again, all findings were potentially of interest.

9. Coutts, L. M., and Schneider, F. W. (1980). "An Investigation of the Arousal Model of Interpersonal Intimacy." A study to test a model of behavioral changes (arousal levels) associated with increases or decreases in immediacy (intimacy), depending on previous state of arousal. The experimental design involved an accomplice, observers to record smiles, postural adjustments, etc., and some equipment for physiological variables (e.g., heart rate); self-reports were also collected. Two hypotheses were formulated: only one was supported but the discussion suggests that the model is nonetheless compatible with the findings. Implications for understanding nonverbal behavior are discussed rather superficially as the main concern of the authors appears to be theoretical.

10. Caplow, T., Baker, H. M., Chadwick, B. A., et al. (1982). *Middletown Families*. A study designed to test the assertion that family structure, family relationships, and the role of the family in the larger community have changed dramatically since 1929 and 1937. Base-line data from the two earlier Middletown surveys were used for comparison. The researchers concluded that the changes are far fewer and less dramatic than most speculative writers have predicted. (The Middletown III investigation

[1982] also addressed other issues, and these findings will appear separately. See, for example, McNamara and Bahr [1980].)

11. Farley, J. E., and Hansel, M. (1981). "The Ecological Context of Urban Crime: A Further Exploration." A study designed to test a specifically stated hypothesis as to the relationship between suburbanization and inner-city crime rates; the authors concluded that with the introduction of a suitable control variable, the relationship can be exhibited. The most interesting aspect of this report is the meticulous comparison of explanations based on competing theories; it can be taken as a model. The data were obtained from census material (population) and police records (criminal statistics).

12. Jacobson, C. G. (1978). "The Effects of Campaign Spending in Congressional Elections." This study was intended to increase understanding of the effect of spending on election outcomes in view of enacted and proposed legislation concerned with campaign finance reforms. Principal conjecture was that increased spending by challengers has some impact—that is, it buys voter recognition—but spending by incumbents has very little impact. Data supported this conjecture; the analysis (multiple regression) is very detailed and clearly set forth, and discussion is extensive. Implications for campaign finance policy also can be drawn from the projections obtained from the regression equations.

13. Veroff, J., Kulka, R. A., and Donvan, E. (1981). *Mental Health in America: Patterns of Help-Seeking from 1957 to 1976.* The study is a replication of a 1957 survey on what sorts of help Americans seek for (self) perceived mental health problems: family difficulties, periods of unhappiness, etc. The rationale was based on identification of social changes which in turn affect expectations for psychological health, and access to traditional sources of support. (Informal social help-seeking strategies are not analyzed for their own interest, but the data analysis suggests the importance of this domain of behavior for further study.) The authors' fundamental conjecture was that patterns have changed, and their selection of variables embodies specific conjectures as to significant factors: this is a common procedure in a large survey. They concluded that, for instance, income was not related to seeking professional help in 1976, as it was in 1957; women made much greater use of social support structures than men did; and individuals "in crisis" expected to use professional services and were able to do so. This is a very rich set of findings, quite conservatively interpreted; a good discussion of background, instrumentation, and data analysis is included. This study required substantial funding, 5 years, and more than 20 staff members.

Originality

It is usually necessary to justify the problem you plan to work on as in some way "original." Originality in the sense of "my, what a clever idea" is satisfying, but far from essential. For the beginner, innovation is more important than invention.

To satisfy yourself, and your supervisors, that your problem as posed is in fact an open problem will require a literature search and, if necessary, consultation with those actively working in the same or related fields. You must, of course, verify that someone else has not already satisfactorily settled the precise question you plan to pursue. It is, however, usually possible for you to shift or reformulate the problem-question so that you can attack it anew. Replication is an important part of scientific research; however, most institutions will not accept an exact replication of an existing study as the basis for a doctoral dissertation. If yours is the exception, originality is not a virtue.

Originality is an elusive quality and is often clearly identified only in retrospect. Two observations on the subject are worth repeating. "Everything of importance has been said before by somebody who did not discover it."[7] "Nearly all great discoveries have had anticipations which the historian digs up afterward."[8]

Amenability to Replication

We noted in Chapter 1 that the research question must be amenable to attack within the constraints imposed by the scientific method; this means that the procedures used must be replicable. For research in the social and behavioral sciences this may mean simply that the procedures for making observations are specified in sufficient detail, so that another investigator interested in the same events would be able to follow these same procedures. More generally, *replicability*[9] means that the populations under observation (or comparable populations) will permit re-examination under the same conditions. Sometimes the nature of the problem precludes precise replication; the classical examples are provided by studies of suicide, riots, behavior in wartime, communities in rapid change, and so forth. (In any case, the data gathered must be stored and available for scrutiny by others.)

Your answers to the following questions may help you to evaluate your proposed study:

1. What is already known about the situation or problem area with which this particular study is concerned?
2. What do you expect, on the basis of existing theory and any earlier studies, to observe?

3. How will an answer to this problem-question relate to what is already known? Will new or better evidence to support, refute, or extend some theory result from this study?
4. Is the problem-question formulated in such a way that anyone with reasonable experience in the problem area can decide what is to be found out, and why the answer is being sought?

Finally,

5. Is there a procedure or method of investigation which will lead to an answer?

Determining the do-ability of a problem—that is, deciding whether a research question is workable—is extremely difficult for the novice investigator; indeed, seasoned researchers undertaking a study in an unfamiliar area may be equally hard put to judge whether it is feasible within the practical constraints under which they must operate. Substantial experience with comparable research problems, a strong intuition based on scholarship, and a "feel" for the problem area, are the best guides. In their absence, you must rely on the advice of your mentors (dissertation committee members, project directors, or other supervisors), who will, we hope, possess these assets as well as a real interest in helping you achieve a successful result.

Practical Aspects of Problem Formulation

There is no universal criterion of practicality that can be applied to every proposed research project. There are, however, certain factors that you should consider in deciding whether a given research problem is workable:

1. Time
2. Costs
3. Availability of other resources
4. Availability of information
5. Usefulness of the findings
6. Approval and interest on the part of supervisors (e.g. the committee)
7. Background capabilities and limitations of the researcher

Examining each of these in some detail will enable you better to determine what weight to assign each in your evaluation.

TIME

Most researchers operate under some time constraints. It must be possible to fit the proposed project into these constraints. Answers to the following questions will help you better understand the time dimension of your proposed research:

1. What are your time constraints? Do you have a deadline for degree completion, a grant expiration date, a publication deadline, a job promised but contingent on the completion of research, or a planned relocation?
2. Does the problem have built-in time parameters, such as progress in a specified school year, growth in a specified population group, or a planned event that is the study situation?
3. Can the problem be investigated in a time interval compatible with your answer to Item 1 above? If you have 2 years available, a longitudinal study which requires you to take data over a 2-year period is unsuitable, because no time will be available for analysis and writing-up of results. A survey instrument may take many months to develop and validate, and so forth.
4. What delays can you realistically anticipate? You must allow time for such things as return of questionnaires, replies to inquiries by mail, delivery of equipment, and training of subjects.
5. Can you retain support from others during the time required to carry through the research? Will your committee or editor or grant project manager be responsive to the demands on their time?

It should be evident that time must be budgeted, like any other resource. Identifying and formulating your problem-question may take much longer than you anticipated. It is all too common to overestimate the time needed for data collection and analysis, and seriously underestimate that required for literature review and other so-called preliminaries. Writing up and interpreting findings can also be unexpectedly time consuming. Experience with many projects suggests that very often the researcher expects to complete the study in an unrealistically short period. In later chapters we will briefly examine the Program Evaluation and Review Technique (PERT), which can be very helpful in planning an optimal schedule for the project.

COSTS

A research project involves both out-of-pocket expenditures and in-kind services. Carelessness or oversight in listing costs can jeopardize the success of an otherwise valuable and well-conceptualized study. It is important for you to work out a tentative budget; it will help you to decide if the problem you intend to pursue is feasible. Wishfulness is entirely out of place here. Try to be hardheaded about probable expenses. You will find it useful to keep the following categories in mind:

1. Personnel: full and part-timers such as typists, consultants, technicians, interviewers, coders, etc. (Don't forget the cost of any benefits.)

2. Travel expenses: to subjects, conferences, etc.; living expenses for field studies.
3. Equipment: computers, measuring instruments, etc.
4. Supplies: tests, questionnaires, stamps and stationery for mailings, etc.
5. Contractuals: rent, telephone, utilities, etc.
6. Construction, e.g. special rooms, storage facilities, etc.
7. Other: publication fees, reproduction (photocopy) services, abstracts and reference materials, computer time, etc.

These categories are typical of the cost estimation breakdown required by the federal government in awarding grants or contracts. Close adherence to these categories will make it easier for you to carry out the application procedure, if, as is so often the case, it is necessary for you to seek financial support for your study. Familiarity with "grantsmanship" is frequently a fundamental requirement on the researcher. The list will also be helpful if you must budget on the basis of personal and/or family resources. Doctoral students in particular may be disagreeably surprised by the cost of what appears to be a simple research project. If insufficient funds are available, you may be unable to pursue your project. It is wise to recognize this state of affairs at the outset.

AVAILABILITY OF OTHER RESOURCES

Even if you find yourself in the enviable position of having enough money to conduct your research, you may be unable to buy the needed equipment or tools at any price. Very often they have to be invented, or at least modified from existing prototypes. For example, specialized counting and timing machinery, sensitive cameras and sound recorders, controlled environments, etc., may simply be unavailable as stock items. Instruments, whether mechanical devices or questionnaires, may have to be developed and checked for reliability. Sometimes it is impossible to obtain staff with essential skills, and the cost or time required for training is out of the question. Not the least of the resources whose availability must concern you is a suitable study population of adequate size (see also Chapter 8). If it appears unlikely that you will be able to obtain subjects of the needed number and distribution, you must reassess your study as formulated. Certain types of subjects (such as individuals with specific genetic defects: for example, hemophilia) may not be available, or may be obtainable only at great cost for transportation. In educational or health research, it may be necessary to get permission from hundreds of parents of young children. Suitable quantities of drugs or nutritional supplements may be impossible to get. Finally, political and/or ethical factors (e.g., invasion of privacy, revelation of unpopular truths) may make individuals or community organizations reluctant to participate.[10]

The interrelationships between the cost of a project, the time needed, and the special resource requirements, can be complex, and may arouse some hesitation among those approached to underwrite the project. For example, a foundation may be willing to sponsor a given research study only if the subjects do not object to the special treatment they may be given, while a university may be willing to allow students to be used as subjects only if the "control" group also receives the beneficial "treatment", after the observation period. Studies of long-term effects on student achievement of such factors as high pupil turnover, as in urban renewal districts, may require access to information from many school districts, as well as record keeping in a form incompatible with that in general use in these districts; such studies will probably fail to receive funding or encouragement.

AVAILABILITY OF INFORMATION

Under this heading consider such aspects of a research problem as the following: Certain kinds of base-line data about the situation you plan to investigate may be necessary for comparison purposes (e.g., in cohort analyses). If base-line data are unavailable or unreplicable, your project may be entirely impossible to carry out; if you have to obtain them before beginning the "treatment" phase of your study, the additional time and cost may be prohibitive. Earlier results pertinent to your problem may be in the folklore of your field but may be unpublished, or so located that they are inaccessible to you. An all-too-common example is provided by instruments that have been used in other studies but for which adequate reliability analyses have never been reported (or carried out). Papers may have been written in a language which you do not read, and for which translators are hard to find. Likewise, other researchers whose work is crucial to yours may be unreachable during the period that you will need information and advice. These matters must be taken into account in the planning stage.

In the foregoing, we have emphasized that before committing yourself to a particular research problem you should consider the costs and availability of resources needed to answer the question you have posed. There are, in general, several ways to approach a given question; comparison of alternatives may suggest formulations which lead to cheaper, easier, more readily feasible procedures. Seek those that feel workable. Avoid those that, in the opinion of your mentors, pose technical difficulties of a formidable kind. Do not embark on a project that more experienced researchers regard as dubious unless you are willing to risk wasted time and money, and great frustration and disappointment.

USEFULNESS OF THE FINDINGS

In choosing a research problem you should ask yourself: If I find an answer to the problem-question, will anyone care? More specifically, will the answer be useful in any of the following senses: (1) immediate: Will it provide knowledge that can assist someone in making a decision? What effect will there be on some behavior (mine or that of others)? (2) long-term: Will it generate more questions, and so contribute to the development of more theory and to the overall growth of my field? Will it help refute an inappropriate assumption? (3) personal: Will my having answered this question enhance my professional reputation and help me to establish a career in this field? Will it allow me to satisfy the requirements for a suitable degree or other credential? Failure to consider these issues represents a serious oversight. Your responses may suggest a revision, or replacement, of your problem question.

A proper statement of a research question includes an indication that an answer will appreciably advance knowledge in the field. In many cases— although this need not always be true—an answer will have immediate practical application. For example, public-health studies can serve as the basis for regulatory legislation or vaccination campaigns; the findings of studies in nutrition affect school lunch program planning. The problem statement should delimit expected breadth of findings in terms of population, areas of coverage, and other parameters, and describe limitations such as lack of access to information or weakness of the only available instruments. Make an effort to conceptualize applications and to address the expected conclusions to those who might need the information embodied in the outcome of the study. It is important also to suggest directions in which your work can be extended or generalized and to mention open questions to which your expected findings are relevant. A research project that duplicates work done by others without extending the subject beyond its present limits will not, in general, be regarded as useful. In certain instances, however, such a study can be interesting if new tools or novel methodologies are applied.

POLITICS OF PROBLEM SELECTION

Except in unusual circumstances, the members of a research committee or editorial board must recognize the possible findings as worthwhile if they are to continue to support and guide the project. If the outcome appears sufficiently glamorous, some of the committee may seek coauthorship in subsequent publications. Coauthorship with a researcher of established reputation has advantages that you should not quickly dismiss. Your supervisor, a more experienced researcher, may assist you in a creative way with suggestions concerning methodology or interpretation; moreover, senior project staff or committee members have probably already published on related problems and can therefore make it easier for you to publish. We cannot overstate the value of findings that will promote not only your own future work but the careers of your research committee as well. Remember: sound research on the part of a student or subordinate is worth money or repute to the supervisor.

If you pick your research problem judiciously, taking into account the questions that are exciting current attention in your field, various segments of your report will lend themselves to publication as articles, and the entire document may be published as a book or monograph. Ideally, you will be able to exploit the research area for books, articles, talks, etc. and can thus establish yourself as an expert. Think of the potential for milking the project for such by-products in making your choice of a research question. As you analyze the possible answers for the selected problem question, you should not be put off by the new questions that they generate. A strong research effort usually provides a firm basis for further research, and the pursuit of these new questions will help "bond" you to the problem area.

Probably no single decision in your professional career will have more significance in determining your direction in future investigations, than your selection of a first research problem.

POLITICAL PROBLEMS PECULIAR TO DOCTORAL STUDENTS: THE COMMITTEE

The initial choice of a dissertation committee always involves the careful weighing of alternatives, and an awareness of what may be very delicate relationships among the faculty members in your department. To the extent that the choice is yours—and most frequently, a student has a limited role in the choice, or, at best, a limited population from which to make a choice—you will seek individuals whom you like, respect, and admire, who possess relevant knowledge, and who express a commitment to the success of your project, both theoretically and as an ongoing effort. This last is essential for your principal advisor. You will probably have to balance specialized expertise against general interest as criteria for inclusion.[11] No matter how carefully selected, each member inevitably has more or less strongly expressed preferences and individual goals which may not be entirely compatible with yours. It helps to keep in mind that dissertation committee members or research sponsors may have idiosyncrasies, usually not directed against you personally, but reflecting their own histories and temperaments.

It is important that you become familiar with the power alignments within this group and aware of possible conflicts, whether intellectual or personal, between committee members. (A rereading of Machiavelli may help you understand departmental politics.) In order to avoid the painful and destructive experience of getting caught in the cross-fire of intracommittee disputes, as well as for other reasons we will mention later, (see sections below on Trouble and Common Errors) you will do well to adopt early the policy of meeting with your committee members (and, when possible, your entire committee) at regular intervals. You may also find it helpful to use a tape recorder at such conferences, if it is agreeable to all present, so your attention will not be distracted by the need to take notes. This will enable you to remain aware of everyone's reactions, to keep everyone equally informed about your progress, to involve everyone in rethinking questions and evaluating procedures where necessary, and in general, to make the success of your research a matter of direct concern to them all.

You must accept the guidance and (perhaps very insistent) direction of the committee but at the same time be prepared to receive relatively little support should the project fail to yield acceptable results. Even very experienced mentors may be at a loss to suggest ways to save or repair the study. Sometimes they lack sufficient energy or commitment to try very hard on your behalf, and sometimes the problem is truly unworkable in ways that could not have been foreseen.

Perhaps the only unresolvable problem a doctoral student has to face in dealing with a committee is that of the unresponsive advisor. Such a person, for whatever reason, is inaccessible or delays beyond acceptable limits. If you sense that this is your situation, seriously consider a change of advisor (no simple matter), even if it entails a change of topic, for you will make no progress otherwise.

CAPABILITIES AND LIMITATIONS OF THE RESEARCHER

You need self-awareness in order to make an intelligent choice of research project. Each scientist undertakes research, in part, in order to experience the honor and status which reward such activity. However, if you tackle a question designed to meet overly grandiose expectations, you will probably not be able to answer it. Realistic goal expectations, based on your abilities and limitations, will lead you to examine feasible projects and avoid common pitfalls. Your research can be interesting and manageable even if it is not earth shattering.

It is essential that you acknowledge the existence of your own biases, so that you can avoid questions in which they might contaminate the outcome.[12] You must also make an accurate assessment of your skills and aptitudes in order to avoid a topic that is beyond accomplishment. You may very well have to master new skills: for example, you will undoubtedly acquire a fair amount of statistical and computer know-how during the course of your research. It makes no sense, however, to choose a topic which involves you deeply in an area in which you are particularly weak, or which you find distasteful. For instance, the need to learn two or three new foreign languages to a level of fluency, should suggest that the problem be reconsidered. Likewise, if you have no training whatsoever in the techniques needed for historical research, such as authentication of documents, and no access to archives, you should not plan to pursue a question which requires these. Commitment and motivation must be, and remain, extraordinarily high if you are to carry such a project to completion. You should plan to utilize mainly those skills with which you are comfortable, and to develop new ones only to extend or strengthen these. You should not have to learn or relearn an inordinate amount of new basic material.[13]

You also need a clear perception of your best working style. For example, if coordinating and directing efforts of a team of assistants, or interviewing large numbers of strangers, represents a great strain for you, then a project requiring these activities frequently over the period of a year should be avoided. On the other hand, if you find it difficult to work without access to colleagues with whom you can discuss matters, an isolated field study may be an unsuitable choice. In the long run, such personal, social, and intellectual issues must be resolved if you are to be able to work effectively toward your goal, and to earn the recognition you want.

Stating the Problem-Question: Avoiding Common Errors in Formulation

Early in the research report or proposal it is desirable to present an explicit statement of the problem you will investigate. Ideally, this will include one or more questions which constitute the problem. It need not include a formal list of hypotheses; it must, however, provide a specific and accurate synopsis of the goal of the study. Thus it may be in the form of an exploratory question, or it may embody a testable conjecture. Many of the difficulties that arise in formulating conclusions can be avoided if the problem-question is clearly stated at the outset. The problem statement should be located so as to be highly visible. It should identify and describe the domain of investigation (comparatively narrow in scope, but avoiding triviality), the major independent and dependent variables, the target population, the relationships or phenomena you are investigating, and the anticipated outcome.[14] It is difficult to state any problem cleanly and economically until you have identified variables and formulated hypotheses, so you can expect to make several revisions. For a thoughtful discussion of the discrepancy between the process of developing ideas and their formal exposition, see Merton (1968)[15] and Hammond (1964).[16]

The statement should not reflect researcher bias, nor should it attempt to justify itself. No research is truly value-free but assertions with a moralistic flavor have no proper place in the problem statement.

After reading the statement of the problem, the consumer of your research should understand clearly what problem-question you seek to answer. If you can't state it clearly you probably don't understand it yet, yourself. Complex, profound ideas do not demand complicated, tortuous, sesquipedalian language: on the contrary, aim for simplicity. The title, in addition to meeting the requirements of your university, your employer, or your professional journal, should be specific and informative, so that future researchers can recognize the problem area without mind-reading.

What follows is a sample, hardly exhaustive, of defects in the formulation of the research problem question.

A poorly identified goal is the most likely cause of an inadequate research proposal. Ambiguously stated objectives can hamper a project by confounding priorities and confusing the central with the peripheral. A poor literature review can lead to duplication of the work of others or a misjudgment of the value of an investigation. Lack of the firm conviction that the research is worth doing may lead you to overlook fruitful possibilities in variable selection, methods, and alternative conjectures. Sometimes a question is chosen merely because data are available which can be exploited beyond the goals for which they were originally collected. Undertaking too vast a project invites disaster, as does accepting in its entirety and without modification a problem suggested by someone else.

Lacking a sound theoretical base, the researcher will almost certainly fail to make clear and explicit the assumptions underlying the project or to justify the potential interest of the findings. The study of events unique to a particular situation—ad hoc research—may be of little or no use as a basis for the generalization and (theoretical or practical) application of results. Failure to recognize rival hypotheses can lead to weak conclusions.

Among other related sources of difficulty may be the following: failure properly to enumerate cases and to eliminate overlapping cases; failure to make clear what relationships between variables are under study; failure to distinguish between relationships and possible causality; failure to specify the population to which conclusions may apply; failure to specify the unit of analysis (individual, classroom, community, hospital, etc.); failure to specify what sort of evidence will be sufficient to draw the desired conclusion; failure to distinguish between necessary and sufficient evidence; and failure to operationalize definitions. All of these reflect a pervasive vagueness, perhaps confusion of a description of the problem-area with a sharp formulation of the problem-question.

It is obvious that failure to think through cost, time, and resource availability can severely damage any project. Failure to obtain support from a research committee, granting organization, or other component of the institutional hierarchy, may render a good research question totally unworkable. Putting off preliminary consideration of research until coursework or other training is completed is a mistake, in that you lose the opportunity to direct your learning appropriately.

Perhaps the most common and the most serious error made by the novice researcher is the failure to develop a research plan; that is, to consider design issues at the outset, well before data collection has begun.

A Research Plan

A good research plan follows the pattern of the scientific method but expands and rearranges the components set out in Chapter 1 (p. 18) into a detailed list which is fairly well-standardized:

1. Describing the background of the problem.
2. Identifying the problem area.
3. Establishing a rationale (theoretical base).
4. Stating the problem question(s) to be answered by the study.
5. Indicating the importance of the study.
6. Stating the major hypothesis(es).
7. Stating the assumptions (conceptual or substantive) underlying the question.
8. Describing the constraints on the study (delimitations).
9. Defining needed unusual terms.
10. Presenting the limitations of the study.
11. Formulating design of procedures, for sampling, data-collection, and analysis; this includes operationalizing definitions and hypotheses.
12. Enlisting the support of your committee or comparable supervisory group.

You must explore each of these aspects before you arrive at a decision concerning the quality of the problem. The process frequently, perhaps necessarily, involves much retracing of arguments and reworking of ideas. This initial investment has a large long-term payoff.

In the next several chapters, we will elaborate on the items in the list.

DESIGN: PRELIMINARIES

In what follows, *design* is used in the most general sense to mean *plan*. Many related decisions must be made about research type and procedure for isolating effects (see Chapters 5, 6, and 8), procedure for measurement and data collection (see Chapter 7), and analysis (see Chapters 10–15). These decisions take into account the nature of the problem, the purpose(s) of the study, and the alternatives for its investigation; in particular, you need to evaluate available evidence, available instrumentation, and available population. Although the research question will usually suggest an appropriate design, other factors will come into play: previous related research, cost, your supervisor's policy on "the way we do it here," etc. It is important not to confuse the decisions concerning methodology with those concerning procedures for analysis of data. The latter are dictated by the kinds of data you obtain and also by the goals you hope to achieve in your study. The major functional categories of methodology are based on problem characteristics.

For each of the alternative research types described in Chapter 6, there is a conventional set of procedures, each with its associated strengths and weaknesses. Do not be intimidated by the many formal design models set forth in the standard research handbooks. Many of these were developed originally for agricultural experimentation and so are inapplicable to most social science research.

TROUBLE: THE BEST LAID PLANS . . .

Despite your best efforts and the most meticulous attention devoted to the anticipation and resolution of every possible difficulty, your project may prove, once under way, to be unworkable. Research is messy, fraught with unplanned contingencies.[17] The procedure may develop unforeseen difficulties. Sometimes these have theoretical resolutions: a slight shift in the problem formulation, with a corresponding shift in focus to so-called secondary phenomena, or a further refinement in the procedure to eliminate excessively rich and confusing observations, may well permit you to continue within the overall framwork of the original problem. A most entertaining account of such modifications in practice is that of Davis (1964), on the history of the Great Books Survey. The ideal, an experimental longitudinal study, was impossible, but longitudinal effects of participation in the Great Books groups were an important issue. High subject mortality, in the form of dropouts from the groups, made it difficult to distinguish effects from retention factors. The practical solution was to oversample those participants who were returning for a second or later year.

Some authors seem to us to shrug off this sort of trouble with the remark that the researcher should simply pursue a new line suggested by the difficulty itself; this option is not open to those who must conform to an accepted proposal or who must keep all modifications within specified limits. It is hard to accept the idea that the entire enterprise is fundamentally unsystematic or fortuitous in character, but chance *is* an important factor in success.[18]

Perseverance is a desirable trait, up to a point. Knowing when to give up is an aspect of your personality as well as of your developing professional judgment. Finding a new problem or making a major modification is indeed a disheartening task, and you may experience a period of great discouragement. We can offer only the reassurance that the process of problem formulation is usually easier on subsequent trials.

A far more serious, even disastrous, state of affairs arises when a study yields unacceptable results. The point of view[19] that there is no such thing as "negative" results, is cold comfort for most doctoral students and those meeting publication requirements. The unpleasant truth is that you are largely helpless in such a situation, and it would be deceitful for us to claim otherwise. The role of your committee, with whom you should have been holding regular meetings, will be crucial. Seek experienced and compassionate guidance.

If you feel that you must reassess your personal and professional goals, remember that research is a high-risk endeavor in that there is no guarantee in advance that any particular problem will yield a satisfactory solution. You can only do your best.

Appendix: Difficulties Nobody Mentions Because They Figure You Shouldn't Have To Be Told (Maybe You Don't!)

- Conflicts arise when mutually incompatible demands are made on the individual. So-called reality conflicts (e.g., you must put in so many hours in the library but your family makes demands which must be met) may be unresolvable except on an ad hoc basis. Don't expect any extra consideration from your mentors because you have extra obligations; the most you can expect is an acknowledgment that you have a reason for failing to perform, not an excuse for the failure. If you schedule your own time, you may be particularly vulnerable to demands which distract you from your research efforts. If you find that your own work is always taking second place, perhaps you need to reassess your goals or devise new alternatives for meeting them. Be honest about what you are asking of others, such as children, spouse, parents, friends: What's in it for them? You do have to decide how much you can expect other people to concede to your needs. We do not advocate a policy of total self-centeredness no matter how worthy your goal, but it is surely true that if you are afraid to make demands of your own it is very unlikely they will be met.
- Your family of origin, mate, children, extended family and/or friends may disapprove of what you are doing. Those on whom you depend the most may resent your preoccupation, and the heavy diversion of your time and energy, especially during stages of literature review, data

collection, and report writing. Sometimes this is expressed as advice that you abandon an activity that is so fatiguing, sometimes as double messaging with ostensible support plus escalating demands, and sometimes as a steady barrage of negative comments. You may find it an effective strategy to devote some effort to convincing these significant others that their assistance, including moral support, is crucial in making it possible for you to reach your goal and that the discomfort is finite. Don't let short term discouragement convince you that their feelings aren't as mixed as yours: if these people care about you, your success will bring joy to them also.

- Women, minorities, older students, and members of certain other categories may experience special problems in achieving acceptance or recognition by supervisors and/or colleagues (see, e.g., Sidner, 1982). The consequences include difficulty in being taken seriously, absence of suitable mentors, failure to obtain financial support for the research, and diminished access to the "old boy network" as a result of exclusion from the informal social life of the group. All this is grossly unfair: our only suggestion is that you make the effort to seek out members of your own group who have already achieved some success, and to identify individuals who are positively disposed to you and in a position to give you encouragement.

We think it is a pity and a scandal that at present such individuals must so often meet higher standards in performance and in personal qualities,[20] so that they are forced to choose between fighting the system and achieving within it. We deeply admire those who succeed both in accomplishing scientific work of good quality and in maintaining their personal equilibrium.

- Time and money management are crucial, particularly for the person who returns to school or to work after a lapse of several years during which he or she takes on (variously) responsibility for self-support, children, older parents, or whatever. The effective utilization of resources—time, money, personnel—is the key to effective functioning. There are many books on management of time and money.[21] Their advice boils down to:

  - Stay healthy. Do not neglect your physical well-being.
  - If you can afford to buy help, do so.
  - If not, you may have to compromise your standards for level of consumption, your overall style of living, your household, your child care, your role as helpmate, and your community participation.
  - Learn to accept assistance when and where it is offered.
  - Budget time for relaxation and, if possible, a little money for fun. Reward yourself when you accomplish a task.

- Many activities may have to be deferred or omitted for the duration. If everything else is too important to give up, you can't do research.
- Plan everything. Combine tasks. Efficiency and economy can be learned.
- Expect to be tired a lot.

In general, self-pity is destructive. You must be strongly goal directed (and able to tolerate a fairly high level of frustration) to be successful in research.[22]

Notes

[1]You may find helpful: Resta and Baker (1967); Polya (1945, 1954); and Anderson (1966, pp. 133–136).

[2]We strongly urge your reading Merton (1968, pp. 157ff.) on the interrelation of theory and empirical evidence.

[3]Campbell and Stanley, (1963, p. 3).

[4]See Chapter 5 in Bennett and Lumsdaine (1975) for a review of a number of such studies and a discussion of methodology.

[5]Both Sidman (1960) and Medawar (1979) have accounts of such experiences.

[6]An example is provided by the cluster analysis of ten ethnic populations using 58 genetic variables, described in Mezzich and Solomon (1980).

[7]A. N. Whitehead (1967).

[8]E. G. Boring, quoted in Merton, (1968, pp. 12–13). Merton has further relevant comments on the general topic of the originality of discoveries. The (unattributable) remark "Your conjectures are trivial, false, already in the literature, or all the above" also comes to mind.

[9]For an interesting discussion of replication, and of the role of pilot studies, see Sidman (1960); see also Chapter 5.

[10]See Denzin (1978, Chapter 13).

[11]See Sternberg (1981, pp. 86–91, 138–154).

[12]Another point of view is expressed by Fowlkes (1980, pp. x–xi). She feels it is better and more scientific for the researcher to *announce* his or her biases, so that the reader's assessment of findings and conclusions can take them into account. This issue is extremely pertinent to the recent (1983) and ongoing controversy over the work of Margaret Mead.

[13]The foregoing is written on the assumption that your course work or previous experience has prepared you adequately with the skills and knowledge that are central to work in your field. Sometimes unexpected gaps show up and must be filled in, and almost everyone is unevenly prepared in some respects.

[14]Many handbooks of research—for example, Kerlinger (1973, Chapters 2, 3)—offer criteria for evaluating a problem statement. Since none of these is a recipe but rather a checklist, consult one appropriate to your own field, but use it as an adjunct to your own self-critical judgment.

[15]This book also contains a provocative essay on "middle level" theory.

[16]This is a collection of essays by sociologists describing the development of both conjectures and methodologies for a number of well known studies. The introduction is particularly interesting and valuable. It is extremely readable throughout.

[17]See Denzin (1978, Chapter 13).

[18]Beveridge (1950) is very reassuring on this point. "What is a weed? A plant whose virtues have not yet been discovered" (R. W. Emerson).

[19]Sidman (1960, pp. 8–9) states rather strongly his conviction that any results properly obtained are a contribution to knowledge, and Barber (1976, pp. 32ff.) agrees. Smart (1964) notes that negative results should be incorporated into the prior probabilities in a Bayesian analysis. Medawar (1979, Chapter 11) has some instructive examples of exploiting negative results. The doctoral student may discover that his committee feels otherwise, and has quite different criteria for acceptability of a study. Editorial boards are usually unwilling to accept reports of negative findings: see Smart's (1964) survey of published articles. See also pp. 393ff.

[20]Entirely apropos is the following: "Equality is not when a female Einstein gets promoted to assistant professor; equality is when a female schlemiel moves ahead as fast as a male schlemiel" (Ewald B. Nyquist, quoted N.Y. *Times*, October 8, 1975).

[21]Bliss (1976); Winston (1978—directed primarily to women); Scott (1980); Lakein (1973).

[22]One of the few books that addresses personal problems of doctoral students is Sternberg (1981). A serious study of responses to the stresses of graduate work is Mechanic (1978). The article "Colleges Called Major Culprits in Thesis Delay" (New York *Times*, March 8, 1983, p. C1) may also be of interest.

Additional Reading

For further reading on how to find a problem and formulate it, we recommend:

Polya (1945, 1954): problem solving in the best tradition.

Beveridge (1950): strong emphasis on conjecture, imagination, intuition, fortuitous aspects of discovery; "the art of investigation."

Hammond (1964): ancedotal; description of genesis of several well-known studies and modifications along the way.

Bell and Encel (1978): more ancedotal material on social research projects.

Riecken and Boruch (1974): practical, useful.

Resta and Baker (1967): for graduate students.

Stinchcombe (1968): philosophical and sensible.

Merton (1968): may be very helpful, assumes a broad background.

Sidman (1960); Plutchik (1974): both of these are written by experimentalists, but are useful and interesting for all researchers.

Selltiz et al. (1976): Chapter 2 has a good discussion of finding, formulating and evaluating a problem.

Nuts and Bolts

Simon (1969, 1978): very practical, *very* basic; deals with many of the topics of this chapter.

Allen (1960); Smith (1963): both of these discuss criteria for funding of research proposals.

3

The Background of the Problem: Review of the Literature

Introduction

You cannot begin your work until you know what has already been done. In your final write-up you must, at the very least, report on and discuss published material which supports your conjectures and is confirmed by your findings. Thus, as soon as you have identified your problem area you should begin to review the pertinent literature.

A review of the literature is an ongoing enterprise. It takes place in several phases as you develop a clearer, better-focused understanding of your problem. Each modification of the problem will suggest further reading of relevant sources.

The community of scholars regards as *known* that which is available in published form or has, at least, been presented at a meeting and abstracted.[1] The review process enables you to hook your study onto the chain of scientific knowledge; in isolation, your work might not be of interest to other researchers, or its importance might be overlooked. Presenting the problem background thus serves the following purposes:

- Proper placement of your study in the context of current theory. The consumer of your research should be able to identify its theoretical base and the implications of this theory which you have pursued in formulating your testable propositions.
- Appropriate connection of your study to prior studies. The consumer of your research will see clearly in what ways it extends, contradicts, or complements already-existing knowledge, fills in gaps (e.g., in methods, populations, analysis) identified by other researchers, and opens new lines of investigation. The place of your study in its overall disciplinary setting will be clear,[2] as will its connection to work in related fields.

Locating Reference Materials: Bibliographic

Your main payoff for the many hours you have invested in undergraduate and graduate study in your own and related fields is your familiarity with reference materials and other resources, and your ability to recognize pivotal theories, their most prominent expositors, and the most significant evidence in their support. No shortcut or evasive strategy can substitute for scholarship of this sort. You will need to make effective and efficient use of libraries and other repositories of published material in order to develop the problem background.

At present "libraries" range from the awe-inspiring fully computerized state-of-the-art examples to the nineteenth-century survivals with only minimal cross-indexing. Somewhere in between is the typical card-catalogue model. Whether traditional or modern, the one(s) to which you have access must be exploited as effectively as possible. Following are some useful procedures.

The first step in locating appropriate reference materials is to make a list of all the topic or author headings under which such materials might plausibly be classified in a library card-file or other information-retrieval-system catalogue. In any case you will need to mind-read the cataloguer. You may want to carry out a free-association exercise on the subject of your problem area. Be sure to jot down what you regard as key words as you do your preliminary reading, because each of them will provide possible additional leads to related studies. As you refine the formulation of your problem, you should survey the literature associated with each of the major variables (in suitable context), even if the research was done under the umbrella of a discipline different from your own. Reading outside your field can be instructive; the points of view and formulations may allow you a novel insight into your own problem. Differing usages of important terminology or variations in methodology may be disconcerting, but the enrichment of your understanding will outweigh them. In fact, an effort to find related studies in nearby disciplines is an essential part of any background search. This is particularly valuable for formulative studies, and is crucial if you are working at the edge of your field or in an area usually regarded as applied. Examples include analysis of conflict (Coser, 1956), management science, women's studies (Kanter, 1977), and investigations of stress and burnout (e.g., Cherniss, 1980).

You must become familiar with the card catalogue at the university library or other research institution at which you plan to work. It may be arranged differently from the one(s) with which you are already familiar. Consult both author and subject headings. Do not overlook dissertations or in-house research reports which may be catalogued separately. Always ask about special departmental collections in areas related to yours. Also inquire about interlibrary loan services and reciprocal privileges at other libraries.

If you use such computerized systems as DATRIX or ERIC, you must understand the use of the Keyword-in-Context locators. For instance, to obtain a list of studies on curriculum modifications in mathematics instruction in community colleges, use the headings MATHEMATICS and CURRICULUM and COMMUNITY COLLEGE, but if you want information about mathematics instruction postsecondary without specific setting, you use the heading MATHEMATICS/INSTRUCTION/POST-SECONDARY and sort through the print-out list yourself. Both overspecification and excessive generality will restrict you, the former because you will lose titles that are tangential but relevant to your problem, the latter because you will be inundated by the irrelevant at great expense. Familiarize yourself with the instructions for using each of these systems; there is often a special reference librarian assigned to help users. Many computerized systems involve a delay of several days for each request; allow for this in planning your time.

You may expect a trial-and-error learning experience in using catalogues: this can be very frustrating and time-consuming. Articles published in medical and legal journals present special classification and retrieval problems: we strongly advise establishing a good relationship with the library staff.

In many of the disciplines included among the social and behavioral sciences, materials are available to help the researcher locate books, articles, dissertations, reviews, etc. A few examples:

- Indexes of research and abstracts of current or recent publications are available in many fields. (We have compiled a list; see the Appendix to this chapter.)
- Every professional journal publishes a yearly index, by author, subject, and title.
- Dissertation abstracts are computerized in the retrieval system DATRIX. Reprints are available, for a fee, from Dissertation Abstracts, c/o Xerox, Inc., Ann Arbor, Michigan.
- Educational Resources Information Center has established the computerized system ERIC. Most articles, etc., dealing with issues related to education are catalogued. There are also ERIC catalogues for other subjects such as reading, psychological dysfunction, etc.
- Index of learned journals will give you an idea of what journals exist, and clues as to the whereabouts of obscure or discontinued journals. Always check the library's list of journal titles.
- *Science Citation Index*, "An International, Interdisciplinary Index to the Literature of Science, Medicine, Agriculture, Technology, and the Behavioral and Social Sciences," is a computerized cross-referencing of several hundred journals and all articles and books cited.
- Certain disciplines, such as anthropology and management science, present difficulties for the researcher, because articles in these subjects appear in a great variety of journals, many published in other countries.

- American Documentation Institute (ADI), is maintained by the Library of Congress. Material relevant to a published work but too detailed or bulky for inclusion in the original article, such as data,[3] details of analysis, tables, etc., can be deposited with the ADI through the journal editor. A small charge covers cost of microfilm or photo copies.

Your mentors, fellow students, and former instructors can be most helpful. Do not be shy about asking what resources there are in your own and related fields. University library staff members should be thoroughly familiar with the entire range of resource materials, and if not should be able to refer you to specialists elsewhere.

The standard references for theory and well-established observational results, and for recent dissertations and articles, will be less elusive than middle-aged or cross-field books and research reports. Sometimes just plain luck makes the difference: cultivate a detective's alertness to coincidence. Always have a note pad and pen with you; change for the photocopy machine is a good idea, too.

Reviewing and Abstracting

When you have assembled a list of references, you will have to read them. How do you evaluate the research of others, so as to decide whether their procedures, arguments, or conclusions will be useful to you? Needless to say, the more experience you have working in your field, the better the perspective you will have on a given piece of research. We cannot offer a prescription for identifying relevance. There are, however, checklists that will help you spot weaknesses in research reports; an example is given at the end of this section.

Whatever you read should be abstracted and reviewed, even though you do not plan to refer to it in your report, and whether or not you have a complete copy in your possession. *Abstracting* means identifying the principal theoretical and/or observational issues treated by the researcher, summarizing the major conclusions, and listing the most important implications. *Reviewing* means briefly stating the strengths and weaknesses of the study, and also indicating the headings under which it should be classified. Make notes on each source while you read, or soon after; you may wish to expand or cross-reference them later.

For two or three key articles, you should not only check but read all citations and references to be certain they exist, are described correctly, and are relevant to the study. This procedure, while time-consuming, will provide good training for you and will increase both your familiarity with your field and your sophistication in dealing with its literature.

In any event, there is no excuse for failing to read, in its entirety, any report of previous research fundamental to your study. This applies equally to construct validation of an instrument you plan to use, to the analysis of the effect of the same treatment(s) applied to different populations, and to a discussion of the theoretical issues.

CHECKLIST FOR EVALUATING THE REPORT OF A STUDY[4]

1. Problem area or basic problem situation: clearly identified? clearly described? sufficiently delimited? significance exhibited? importance indicated?
2. Problem statement: question concisely and unambiguously stated? formulation value free? selection of variables justified? dependent versus independent variables identified? important terms defined? assumptions explicitly stated? limitations stated?
3. Problem background: clearly presented? relationship to previous findings clear? underlying theory thoroughly expounded? rationale logically developed? literature review complete and to the point? bibliography sufficient?
4. Hypotheses: clear? precise? all variables accounted for? statistical hypotheses appropriate for problem statement? operationalized?
5. Design and methodology: clearly described? completely specified for replicability? appropriately chosen for problem? free of specific weaknesses? In particular: instruments appropriate? correctly applied? validity and reliability established? population suitable? sample size appropriate? subjects selected properly? pilot study conducted, if needed? procedures appropriate? correctly carried out? data analysis appropriate? correctly carried out?
6. Presentation of findings; orderly, clear, well-displayed and complete? weaknesses identified? analysis consistent with facts? relationship to previous findings indicated?
7. Discussion of implications and conclusions: justified by data? generalizations suitably restricted? useful new questions raised? possible applications indicated? thoughtful recommendations for further study? reference to appropriate theoretical modifications? clear distinction between speculation, theory, and evidence in support of theory?
8. Style: title precise, concise, and informative? well-written? interesting? logically organized? scientific attitude implicit?

In view of the importance of inadequate previous research in generating new studies,[5] we urge you to carry out this sort of evaluation even when you are certain its subject is far from first-rate, so that you can identify clearly where the major exploitable weaknesses lie. Both qualitative and quantitative results, even if incomplete, may be important.

Locating Reference Materials: Other Researchers

Important up-to-date information about your problem area and related problems will emerge in conversation or correspondence with other researchers. You will be able to identify such individuals from lists of speakers at section or national meetings of the professional societies of your discipline, from the index of authors of papers in recent issues of your professional journals, and from notices of colloquium guests at your own or nearby universities. A truly conscientious committee member or other advisor will make it his/her business to refer you to potentially helpful sources, and will try to arrange an introduction. Most investigators are willing to send reprints or preprints of their research reports. In addition, they are usually willing to respond to a letter or telephone call, but you may have to travel to another city for an interview: remember to budget the cost.

If you undertake to communicate directly with other researchers:

- Be specific in asking questions. Avoid vague sweeps of the form, "How is X related to Y?" A fishing expedition is no fun for the fish. Prepare in advance for any interview, in person or by telephone, with a list of topics to be covered. Take notes or ask permission to use a recording device. Ask only for reprints that promise some value for your work.
- Be reasonably specific in describing your own problem area. However, don't give away your whole proposal until you develop confidence in the trustworthiness of your informant. Even very senior faculty members have been known to steal ideas and techniques; younger investigators may try to exploit your work for their own professional advancement.
- Be meticulously prompt in responding to requests for information, and courteous in calling only at convenient times, but do not take as an affront a failure to receive reciprocal treatment.
- Keep a record (names, dates, times) of all phone calls to your sources. Keep a copy of your half of correspondence and make appropriate note cards for letters received.
- Without fail, acknowledge the assistance you have received. References in the report follow a form such as "Private communication with (name, date)." Consult the appropriate style manual or check other reports. (Acknowledge informal assistance such as reading of preliminary drafts, "sounding board" conversations, and so forth, in an introductory or closing paragraph in the completed report. In this matter, it is wise to err on the side of generosity.)
- Send a note of thanks after an extended interview or on receipt of material written or assembled specially for you.
- Avoid celebrity hunting, but seek out individuals who are prepared to share knowledge and opinions that may be directly helpful to you.

Format: Notes and Bibliography

It is unfortunate that no single format for notes and bibliographic references is universally accepted. Thus the first and overriding rule is: As early as possible in your literature review obtain the style manual or instructions to contributors from your university registrar, journal editors, or whomever will be deciding whether the form of your report is acceptable. If you obtain these format criteria in advance you may avoid extensive time- and money-wasting retyping and the tension of last minute revisions. You should find guidance on the following:

How to abbreviate journal titles.
How to identify journal issues (volume–number versus dates).
How to list anthologies, collections, reprints.
How to cite newspaper articles.
How to cite conversations and correspondence and other unpublished material.
How to group bibliographic items: by type, by author, other.
How to code several items by the same author for compact reference.
How to list repeated references to the same source.
Whether to use endnotes or footnotes.
How to number notes: sequentially from first to last, sequentially for each chapter, or sequentially on each page.

The foregoing list is by no means exhaustive.

Name and date references are preferable to numbering schemes such as the one specified by the American Mathematical Society, because they avoid repeated renumbering of listed items. Endnotes, although they have the drawback of requiring an extra bookmark or index finger, simplify typing and allow the reader to locate earlier references more easily.

Turabian (1969) discusses almost every contingency. If you have no other guidelines, we suggest that you use hers. Another widely followed set of standards can be found in the American Psychological Association's *Publication Manual*. (Both of these give instructions for margins, labeling of graphs, presentation of tables, etc.). *The MLA Style Manual* (1977) is also used by many disciplines.[6] Whichever style you use, be consistent.

Recording and Storing Bibliographical Material

Some modification of your techniques for taking notes may make the literature review easier to carry out and, eventually, easier to write up. (Note taking is rapidly becoming a lost art for those who depend heavily on photocopying.) We will describe one system for recording and storing bibliographic material that many researchers have found effective.

A full citation of each book, article, dissertation, review, or whatever, should be written on its own 3 × 5 or 4 × 6 index card. Follow the format that you expect to use in the bibliography of your report. For ease of reference, you can code by author and year. Indicate at the bottom or on the back of the card where to find this piece of material (e.g., university library or personal collection). These cards should be kept together, arranged alphabetically by author, chronologically, topically, or in any other fashion; they can easily be rearranged as necessary.[7] Mark the cards for works you have already consulted to distinguish them from those whose promising-looking citations you have culled from other sources. Do not take notes on your bibliographic cards: you will have to file the cards alphabetically for your reference list, and chronologically or by topic for the notes—nothing can be in two places at once!

When you read, summarize and abstract; be sure to indicate the source on each page of your notes. It is essential to record page references for all quotes and paraphrases. This will facilitate obtaining the necessary copyright releases if you anticipate publication of your report. Mark all photocopies with the source. Even if you expect not to use the reference, make out the appropriate citation card and mark it distinctively.

It is wise to separate notes on different topics. Certain references are so rich in material that you may need to cross-index your notes. Write headers or topic labels in colored ink; in general, exploit color coding which can be a useful device for many purposes. Avoid taking notes on both sides of the paper. Make it as easy as you can for yourself to find or rearrange information. You may be surprised to see how much bibliographic material accumulates. As you proceed, try to develop a system that facilitates retrieval without becoming too unwieldy. A proper filing system for reprints and photocopies is a must.

When to Stop

It is hard to decide when to stop seeking further background material. Your informed judgment is ultimately your only guide, although you will do well to seek advice from mentors. You must be satisfied that you have surveyed all pertinent aspects of your problem as it has evolved, all significant studies on related problems, and the important theories that touch on your problem area. As a beginner embarking in a new research area, you will find it desirable to buttress your case more strongly than if you were already experienced in the field: you need the reassurance that comes from relying on the authority of others' work. At some point you will become aware that the marginal increments in your knowledge from additional references are diminishing. You will become aware, also, that reading other people's research reports has its pros and cons: you are learning about the many facets of your problem but may be distracted by small distinctions which should play no part in the formulation of your study. It is time to move on to the next stage of your project.

We cannot repeat too often that the entire process is a helical one. Do not be surprised or disconcerted if you have to return several times to seek further sources concerning the same general issues. Later, when your study is complete, you may wish to reread some of your earlier sources for comparison, or to check on related references that did not seem promising at first. You will find as you go along that your sophistication and ability to evaluate the importance of what you read has increased, and that you can focus more quickly on the essential details.

Whether you are working on a dissertation, preparing a project report, or planning to submit your results to a learned journal, you must keep abreast of the literature until you complete your research report, for at least two reasons. First, reference to very recent related findings will greatly enrich your discussion, so that you establish yourself firmly as one of the group actively involved in your problem area. Second, and less happily, publication of the same or a similar study while you are at work on your project will require an immediate reaction. In such a case, consult your mentors as quickly as possible, making every effort to avoid panic. You may be able to introduce a shift or modification which will make your work a contribution rather than a repetition. It is rare in the social or behavioral sciences that two projects pursue exactly the same problem, but even a small degree of overlap may be unacceptable. You may be able to convince your supervisors that a replication is urgently needed because of some weakness or contradiction. More promising is the possibility of leapfrogging the completed study by using its citations and, in effect, carrying out a follow-up. An example of this strategy is provided by two papers in the field of sports medicine. Michelli et al.'s (1981) investigation of the relationship between factors in exercise training and cholesterol level reduction was anticipated by Bonchard et al. (1980). Michelli and his associates then shifted their question to a study of *how much* training (i.e., what percentage of maximum capacity) is required to achieve specified reductions in cholesterol levels.

These salvage strategies may be unworkable if your own project is well under way. The situation ranks among the major crises for researchers, along with total absence of interpretable results and accidental destruction of data.

Common Errors

Several pitfalls await you in the course of your efforts to develop the background of your problem. Some of the most common errors are by no means restricted to beginning researchers.

An improper allocation of time or insufficient reflection leads to a hurried review. The outcome(s) may be superficiality, omission of pertinent areas, inadequate followup of important references, or overreliance on secondary sources. The other extreme, excessive sweep or failure to limit topic search, also reveals that the process of focusing on the problem area is incomplete. Be sure to make clear whether a source is empirical, speculative, or itself a review of earlier research in the problem area. Do not accept reported data without some skepticism; even the best reputations may rest on incomplete, "selected," or inaccurate data, so if what you read does not jibe with other sources, you must protect yourself by pointing out the discrepancies. You also do your readers a service! In your evaluation of sources, do not overemphasize findings at the expense of a critical examination of techniques or an analysis of underlying theory. Finally, errors or omissions in citation are frustrating and distracting. Meticulous accuracy at every stage and repeated checking are essential.

Outcome of the Background Search

In the course of your review of the literature you will become familiar with

closely related problems,
alternative definitions of concepts,
populations used in previous studies,
design of previous studies,
observational evidence obtained in related situations,
data analysis strategies used for related evidence,
faults and pitfalls in others' procedures, instruments, inferences, etc., and
recommendations of others for further research.

As a result of a timely and thorough review, you will be able to

identify the strategic variables and classify them according to the role they play in the formulation of your problem-question;
describe clearly the relationships for which you will attempt to obtain evidence, and the meanings of these relationships;
attach your problem firmly to current theory, and make it part of a chain of evidence-plus-inference;
avoid duplicate arguments or formulations; and
avoid repeating the errors of previous researchers.

It is your task to present your review of the literature in such a fashion that your reader will be able to follow your train of thought as you justify your problem formulation, your choice of variables, your conjectures, and your elimination of other possible factors or explanations. A short section on presentation of the problem background will be found in Chapter 16.

You should now be able to proceed to the precise statement of your research hypotheses.

Appendix: Research Indexes

Abstracts for Social Workers
Abstracts in Anthropology
Abstracts on Criminology and Penology
Accountants' Index Supplement
American History and Life
British Education Index
Business Periodicals Index
Canadian Education Index
Child Development Abstracts and
   Bibliography
College Student Personnel Abstracts
Contemporary Sociology
Criminology Index
Criminal Justice Abstracts
Current Index to Journals In Education
Current Sociology
Deafness Speech and Hearing Abstracts
Dissertations Abstracts
Education Index
Educational Administration Abstracts
Education Finance
Exceptional Child Education Resources
Historical Abstracts

Index Medicus
Index of Economics Articles
Index to Current Urban Documents
Index to Legal Periodicals
Information Science Abstracts
International Political Science Abstracts
Journal of Economic Literature
Journal of Human Services Abstracts
Language and Language Behavior Abstracts
Language Teaching and Linguistics Abstracts
Library Literature
Personnel Management Abstracts
Peace Research Abstracts
Population Index
Poverty and Human Resources Abstracts
Research in Education
Research Relating to Children
Sage Urban Studies Abstracts
Social Science Citations Index
Sociological Abstracts
Sociology of Education Abstracts
State Education Index
Woman Studies Abstracts

Notes

[1]Needless to say, there may exist other valid data or convincing theoretical explanations that have never been exposed and challenged (refereed). Such material enjoys an inferior status and provides weaker support for later studies. On the other hand, exposés such as those of Broad and Wade (1983) and articles like Bradley (1981a,b) raise serious questions as to the validity and reliability of the refereeing process. Perhaps Voltaire was right: "The multitude of books is making us ignorant."

[2]Stinchcombe (1982) is a witty and thoughtful discussion of the various purposes served by tying your research to one of the classics.

[3]A brief but comprehensive list of sources of survey data, suitable for secondary analyses, can be found in Glenn (1977, pp. 24ff.).

[4]For more detail and further discussion, see Isaac with Michael (1971).

⁵Light and Pillemer (1984) have made an effort to develop a strategy for combining findings from different studies, but we do not regard their procedure, which involves pooling data obtained under dissimilar conditions, as feasible. More useful is Glenn's (1977) discussion of comparability of results in cohort analyses (pp. 27ff.): his observations have great generality in all kinds of survey studies. Also pertinent here is Jacob (1984).

⁶Weidenborner and Caruso (1982) contains a list of citation formats by discipline.

⁷If you have ready access to a computer, use of a text-editor can make storing, correcting, and rearranging your bibliographic material and notes an easy rather than (as usual) a burdensome, time-consuming task. Such a device can also be helpful if you need to keep track of large quantities of documentary or archival material.

Additional Reading

Useful resources that may help direct your research are:

Buros (1965, 1972, 1978): for instruments.
Glock (1967): superb bibliographies in several areas of survey research.
Berelson and Steiner (1967): out-of-date, but still useful, list of papers.
Miller (1970): lists many resources.
Katzer et al. (1978): evaluating research.
Rose (1983): extended discussion, with examples, of how to analyze, evaluate, and interpret a report.
Weidenborner and Caruso (1982): bibliographic and note forms in various fields, lists of dictionaries, indexes, etc.
Handy and Kurtz (1964): a critical index of research in behavioral science, now somewhat obsolete.
Light and Pillemer (1984): attempts to set forth guidelines for evaluating conflicting findings. Worth reading critically. Excellent bibliography.
Peters and Ceci (1980): an iconoclastic small study of the review and referee system.
Stinchcombe (1982): a provocative essay on the varied uses of the classics in one's field.

The literature of your own field is your best resource.

4

Definitions and Major Research Hypotheses

Introduction: The Relationship between
Theory-Building and Hypothesis-Testing

The tasks of science include the building of theory and the systematic gathering and evaluating of evidence to support or refute such theory (see Chapter 1). In order to participate in this process, you must identify a problem area that presents interesting and useful open questions, formulate a problem statement that embodies the question you expect to answer, determine whether the problem as posed is researchable, and find out what is already known (or conjectured) that is pertinent to this and related problems. You must place your problem-question and its anticipated answer in the context both of some theory—either already-existing theory or your own—and of already-available findings. These steps in the research process have been described in Chapters 2 and 3.

If your study is exploratory, its goal may include the formulation of hypotheses. Thus much of what we say below concerning hypothesis testing will not apply to it. On the other hand, our discussion of definitions, operationalizing, and the different roles of variables is quite pertinent.

A substantive or research hypothesis is a statement of what you expect to observe, the conditions of such observations, and the way other events affect the outcome. The statement is first posed as a conjecture in the language of the theory, that is, the *construct language*. It must then be operationalized, that is, translated into the data language. The data language uses the vocabulary of measurements, records of observations and manipulations, and outcomes of other procedures including computations (see pp. 66 and 73ff.). The record of your observations constitutes the evidence to justify or refute your expectation. This part of the research process is called hypothesis testing. (Even if hypotheses are not to be tested formally, it is a good idea to state them, at least tentatively, for your own guidance. This will help eliminate much of the confusion that arises when a mass of evidence has to be sorted out, evaluated, and interpreted. It also makes a bit easier the not unusual task of shifting the direction of a study already underway.)

Thus, your next step is the formulation of your major research hypotheses. Decide first what variables are appropriate for incorporation into your hypotheses. (The theory to which you relate your question, and previous pertinent studies, will suggest these.) The *arena*, that is, your particular setting and population, may virtually force additional variables on your attention. These variables must be clearly defined and operationalized. Then restate your anticipated answer in operational form so that a decision can be made as to whether the answer has actually been obtained. This means, criteria for making the decision must be set forth. This book deals with those areas of research for which data are quantitative or quantifiable. We often assume, in addition, that it is possible and appropriate to restate the substantive hypotheses in statistically testable form and to invoke the conventional machinery of significance testing.

Role of Definitions in Hypothesis Formulation

Typically, an hypothesis embodies a statement that a certain variable occurs in a specified distribution, or that two or more variables are associated in a particular way. Before you can formulate your hypotheses, you must select your variables. Specifically, you must identify the constructs that are to be operationalized as variables, and provide clear, precise, and unambiguous definitions so that there is no doubt, either in your mind or that of the consumer of your research, what you are talking about.

As a novice investigator, you will probably not need to develop new definitions or identify new concepts. If your study is an application or extension of the theory of earlier researchers, you must use their definitions of key constructs because that theory deals with relationships among constructs as *they have defined them.*

It is pointless to introduce a definition proposed by one researcher and expect to exploit the procedure and conclusions of another, unless there is fundamental agreement on the meaning of the constructs they employ. The use of different definitions may limit the possibility both of comparing different situations and of making generalizations. An example is the many conflicting or overlapping definitions of anxiety in current use.

The development of a definition is easier to prescribe than to carry out. The identification of a concept is itself a theoretical procedure, not an arbitrary and irrational assignment of a label as is often supposed. "Definitions are not the beginning of theory but a part of it."[1] The advance of a science thus implies progressive refinements of the concepts. Unfortunately, "concepts do not automatically generate operational definitions, and theories do not fall into place once all the data are in. Rather, theoretical formulations arise from strange sources . . . and many times [they] bear only a distant relationship to data."[2]

Homans[3] distinguishes between *nonoperating definitions* and *operating definitions*. Examples of the former are "role" and "culture." These are clusters of variables, but are not themselves variables because they are not operationalizable and so cannot be incorporated into testable propositions.

It is useful to bear in mind that "constructs . . . are nonobservables; . . . variables, when operationally defined, are observables." More exactly, "a *concept* expresses an abstraction formed by generalization from particulars . . . a *construct* is a concept . . . deliberately and consciously invented or adopted for a specific scientific purpose . . . a *variable* is a construct that takes on different values: a symbol to which numbers or values are assigned."[4] "A *variable* is something that varies."[5]

"The making of pedagogically or heuristically useful definitions is an *art* rather than a *science* . . . the choice of a good definition is more often guided by intuitive feelings about the needs of a particular situation rather than by application of well-defined principles."[6] In general, any first attempt at a definition is an application of common sense and everyday life experience. As information is gathered and evaluated, however, the need for new concepts becomes evident, and new terminology is introduced into the language of science. New concepts make already-developed concepts either more precise or more general, or they may replace a bundle of related concepts by a single word or phrase. The last types are frequently called *intervening variables*, a "term invented to account for internal and directly unobservable psychological processes that in turn account for behavior,"[7] for example, anxiety. The term *hypothetical construct* is used to imply the existence of an underlying reality.[8] (See also p. 68.) *Type concept* (typology) means a concept constructed out of a combination of the values of several variables;[9] frequently, such concepts are identified by a factor analysis or similar procedure. Among the familiar examples are (1) disease as a symptom package; (2) Warner's (1949) social class index; (3) classification of folklore or other material according to presence of designated motifs. See Mezzich and Solomon (1980) for other taxonomic examples.

A hazard in the use of a hypothetical construct is reification, the assumption (explicit or implicit) that the construct refers to something material, and the subsequent reference to that "something" as if it were actually observable (e.g., anomie, self-esteem, utility, the superego). Reification should not be difficult to recognize if you make an effort to inspect your variables carefully.

A definition can be established by example or by stipulation. Both these procedures require an agreement that terminology be used in a particular way. Usually, the conventions of the discipline have to be taken into account. A constitutive definition involves ultimately the replacement of one construct, or several, by another; an operational definition, on the other hand, specifies the activities needed to measure the construct or to manipulate it. The old joke "intelligence is what an intelligence test tests" reflects this distinction. Kerlinger (1973) asserts that if all the constructs in a theory are defined operationally, the theory is "thin", and that extreme operationism is narrowing, restrictive, and scientifically unsound: "No operational definition can ever express all of a variable."[10] The opposite position is taken by Rapaport (1953), namely, that definition is the process of making a word usable: in the absence of a common experience for the user and the reader, the word is not usable. Plutchik (1974) points out that the crucial objection to an operational definition is that when the operation changes, so does the concept. It is important, in any case, that you be able to give the specific operational definitions of all the constructs you intend to use, that is, to formulate the definitions in the data-language (see following section).

Although it is extremely difficult to specify how one identifies or formulates a concept, it is relatively easy to set forth criteria for a successful definition. It must be clear, unambiguous, and precise in its statement, and include neither too many nor too few aspects of the original intuitively identified construct. If the variable is multidimensional, it is necessary to be able to specify the dimensions; unidimensional variables are easier to work with in a first research project but may not serve your purpose. For instance, the analysis of leader behavior has led to the two dimensions, Consideration (relating) and Initiating Structure (directing) (see Hemphill and Coons, 1957). If a type concept (typology) is in question, the variables that make it up should be *in fact* connected. Finally, in order to yield a useful variable, the construct must be operationalized or, at least, operationalizable (see section below on Operationalizing Definitions and Hypotheses). The work of Coopersmith (1967) can thus be seen as an effort to achieve a workable operational definition of self-esteem through the development of a measuring device.

Among the most common pitfalls, aside from the obvious ones such as insufficient precision, excessive narrowness, and ambiguity, is an impatience with the definition process, which results in an arbitrary, thus less fruitful, formulation. A construct with no specifiable operational form should be suspect.

Using a construct whose definition is unacceptable or unfamiliar to other researchers in the same problem-area is an almost certain guarantee that your conclusions will come under challenge. Disagreements in interpreting findings frequently arise from disagreement or lack of clarity in operationalizing the constructs.

Finally, the effort to resolve discrepancies between differing formulations of a concept from disparate sources may result in combining incompatible theories.

Selection of Variables and
Identification of Their Role in the Hypothesis

Your conjecture or guess of an answer to your research problem-question will reflect your overall familiarity with the problem area and related research, as you have identified it in your review of the literature. A powerful conjecture is based on intuition (knowing what you don't know you know), and scholarship (prior knowledge). It has two aspects: the selection of variables and the statement of a relationship between the variables.

A potentially fruitful study may fail to progress, or may have a disappointing outcome, unless appropriate variables are chosen. Thus, identifying the variables that you will measure and deciding, tentatively, which ones "do the work" are crucial steps in the process of reducing your problem-question to testable hypotheses.

In effect, your choice of variables justified by the background of the problem is itself a conjecture as to plausible relationships. One of the best ways to obtain a preliminary list of variables is to "brainstorm," to free associate on the problem. Ask yourself: What might be important in this situation, either as an outcome or as a possible determining factor? Do not eliminate whatever comes to mind until your list is as complete as you can make it. Do not concern yourself at this stage with questions of design, measurement, or analysis, but keep in mind that suitable definitions must be available for each variable. Now go back over your list and look at each item in turn.

Most writers on research[11] offer schemes for the classification of variables. Underlying any scheme is the notion that two variables may be related in one of three ways: (1) *symmetrical*: neither influences the other; (2) *asymmetrical*: one influences the other but not vice versa; (3) *reciprocal*: both influence one another. (We are not defining "influence"!). Note that although causality or determination is a central concern of most research, and the ultimate goal of all science, the terminology that follows carefully avoids the word *cause* and exploits the vocabulary of mathematics. Here are some of the categories in general use:

- Independent variables are the predictive antecedents, dependent variables the consequents. Ideally, the values of independent variables are experimentally manipulated or selected, while the dependent variables are observed for concomitant variation. In practice, large numbers of variables are often measured without an a priori designation of which ones are which; the identification of dependent variables is made after preliminary analysis; for example, a canonical correlation analysis. Designation of a variable as independent reflects a presumption of causation or determination, while the label "dependent" reflects a presumed effect. Your decision as to which variables fall into which category is a direct translation of your conjecture. Bunches of variables can be collectively identified as dependent or independent. Many statistical procedures require identification of variables as independent or dependent, even though you are not asserting the existence of any causal relationships (see Chapters 11–14).

- It may be useful to distinguish between active (manipulated) and attribute (measured but not manipulated, "organismic") variables, according to their role in your study. What may be an active variable in one context may be an attribute in another. In any particular study, the demographic (sorting) or background variables may be regarded as attributes.
- Each variable can be classified according to its level of measurement: discrete versus continuous, and nominal or categorical (including dichotomies), ordinal, ordinal-metric, interval, or ratio. Both study design and data analysis will depend to a greater or lesser extent on the measurement levels of the variables involved. (Extended discussion of this aspect can be found throughout Chapters 7, 11–14.)
- Directly observable variables may be contrasted with hypothetical construct variables. The latter are inferred from observations of behavior, and their measures are obtained by manipulating behavioral measures. Thus they are in effect operationally defined. Among the many hypothetical construct variables are intelligence, anxiety, social class, and leadership.
- A variable may be classified as antecedent or intervening according to its location in a proposed causal chain:

Antecedent variable	→	Independent variable	→	Intervening variable	→	Dependent variable

If a variable is indeed an intervening variable, controlling it should cause the statistical relationship between independent and dependent to diminish or vanish; this will not be the case if it is an antecedent variable. Thus these categories can be distinguished on both logical and statistical grounds. Since the tracing of causal sequences can be of great importance in the analysis of social phenomena, the identification of a variable as antecedent or intervening can be a useful adjunct to what Rosenberg (1968) calls "informed and imaginative speculation."

- Variables may be classified according to the kind of misleading ("spurious") interpretations of the data they suggest. This can be particularly important in large survey or experimental studies with many attribute variables. An extraneous variable appears to be related to the dependent variable, but is in fact associated with a third variable which is the true independent (causal) variable. A component variable typically reflects one aspect of a hypothetical construct, or of a typology. For instance, education and income are components of social class, so changes in social class may in fact be changes in either component or in both; therefore, it will be difficult to describe the relationship between social class and some other variable, such as political party membership. A suppressor variable is one that intercedes to cancel out, reduce, or conceal a "true" relationship: in the extreme case, the researcher may conclude from the absence or weakness of an hypothesized relationship that the underlying theory is defective. (A suppressor variable may also suggest that a relationship does exist, in an analysis designed to show there is none.) A distorter variable is one that converts a positive relationship into a negative one, or vice versa. These last classifications can ordinarily be made only after some kind of data analysis. They are of importance primarily, but not exclusively, in analysis of quasi-experimental or nonexperimental studies.[12]

- If a variable "causes an effect" and is in turn "altered by that effect," it is called a canonical variable. Evidently, tracing the paths of canonical relations can be crucial to an understanding of interactions.

When you see the list of variables you have generated, you may feel overwhelmed by their number and variety. You must reduce the list to manageable size by judicious formulation of your hypotheses and by careful design of your study. We address these issues in the rest of this chapter and the four which follow.

Pitfalls in variable selection include:

- Ambiguity, excessive generality, or overrefinement of constructs.
- Omission of potentially useful variables or inclusion of irrelevant ones.
- Confusion of a general nonoperating definition of concept such as "social status," or "sex role," or "job involvement" with measurable variables such as income, years of education, and occupation, or preference for specified activities or presence of specified behaviors or expressed perceptions.
- Failure to operationalize, of which the foregoing is a special case. Until a variable is operationalized, no translation of the hypothesized relationships into the data-language is possible.

It should be evident that implicit in your identification of the role of the variables you have listed is a tentative formulation of their relationships. We now look at the steps involved in stating your research hypotheses.

The Hypothesis: What Is It?

The purpose of hypotheses is to direct inquiry; observations must support or refute some assertion if they are to be scientifically useful.[13] Properly formulated hypotheses guide investigation, motivate design, and suggest interpretations of the findings. Beveridge (1950), Medawar (1979) and Sidman (1960) emphasize the need for flexibility and adaptability on the part of the researcher, the value of data snooping, and the importance of serendipity and the fortuitous juxtaposition of events: they would allow, as in formulative and some taxonomic studies, the generation of hypotheses after inspection of the data, as a goal rather than a guide. We agree that explanation and pattern recognition are enterprises of great value, challenging the imagination of the researcher and providing new insights for further analysis. The use of techniques such as those developed and explicated by Tukey (1977) and Ehrenberg (1982) complement or supplement, but do not replace, conventional hypothesis testing. Most authors of research manuals in the social and behavioral sciences stress the value of precise hypotheses, explicitly and formally stated in advance of data collection and certainly in advance of any inspection of the data.[14] They appear to agree that "If an explanation cannot be formulated in the form of a testable hypothesis, then it can be considered to be a metaphysical explanation and thus not amenable to scientific investigation."[15]

In practice, most researchers find that hypotheses need to be modified as procedures for sampling, measuring, and analysis are tried out and debugged. Both experimental and nonexperimental (e.g., survey) studies often proceed without specifically stated hypotheses (let alone a proposed causal order!). This state of affairs is very common now that efficient and powerful data processing is available, so that the investigator can indulge the impulse to explore all possible relationships. The hypotheses are in effect evolved afterwards (see comments of Dalton, 1964, cited earlier); to put this another way, results are announced with "trial hypotheses" accepted or rejected on an ad hoc basis. Such a procedure represents a sharp departure from conventional hypothesis testing, and may also entail great difficulties in writing up findings.

Some hypotheses can be stated precisely only after analysis of the findings; the outcomes of a discriminant analysis, ex post facto ANOVA (analysis of variance) or cross-tabulation, cluster analysis, or canonical correlation procedures provide examples. (The notion of a test of such an hypothesis, which is really a conclusion based on inspection of the data, is quite different from the test of an hypothesis stated a priori.) Certain expected results, such as normality of populations or homogeneity of variance, may not need to be stated as hypotheses. Methodological decisions are generally not regarded as subproblems, so hypotheses should not appear for them; their effectiveness should be "tested" in a pilot study.

The conservative view—specification of null and alternative hypotheses *before* data-inspection—is the more appropriate if conventional significance testing is to be carried out. Any study, no matter how elaborate, in which hypotheses are generated *after* data inspection should be regarded as formulative and a good subject for replication.

Stating the Expected Relationships

As a general rule, a research hypothesis is a statement about the distribution of one (or more) variable(s), or about the relationship between two or more variables (or sets of variables). The relationship may involve an association, weak or strong, which may be causal or deterministic, or may reflect a clustering or trend. (The functional descriptions of the associations may be mathematically precise, or they may be quite general; for example, direct or inverse.) The hypotheses may involve differences between values of one or several variables, in two or more groups. The conjecture may entail the establishment of a typology (a classification system), so the hypothesis will state that certain values or combinations of values of one or several variables do not occur.

In addition, the statement of the hypotheses must imply a test of these relationships. Thus it is essential that the variable(s) be measurable, and that a decision procedure be available. The hypotheses (conjectures) embody the anticipated answer to the research question. All constructs appearing in the hypotheses must be operationalized, that is, given empirical referents and rendered measurable, and the relationships must be specific in terms of operations and predictions. Without an appropriate conjecture, a study has no direction. Without testable hypotheses, a (verificational) study cannot be put into motion.

Properly framed hypotheses reflect a thoughtful analysis of your problem in the light of some body of theory; they are not merely a juxtaposition or conjunction of variables. A problem involving many variables may require a large number of hypotheses. In each you must clearly identify which effects are to be isolated, as well as the domain, magnitude, and direction of effects. You must also specify whether certain variables are to be suppressed or controlled. Anticipated interaction effects, such as those teased out in an analysis of variance or a multiple chi-square, may be described in a variety of ways: consult the literature of your field for the conventions in use. Diagrams may be useful to illustrate causal sequences.

A useful preliminary step may be the formulation of "orienting statements"[16] or "guiding metaphors",[17] in contrast to real propositions: for example, the individual's level of moral maturity as an adolescent reflects the demands of the culture for adult behavior. Such rather general assertions, while they are not useful in prediction or explanation, are nonetheless important because they suggest more precise formulations. Real propositions are stated in a form that allows a decision based on evidence.

There are no universally applicable prescriptions for stating hypotheses, because of the great variety of problems in the social and behavioral sciences. On the one hand, too great generality or vagueness, frequently arising from weaknesses in the definitions, may render the hypotheses untestable, hence of no scientific use. On the other hand, too much specificity makes them trivial or uninteresting. Making the necessary compromise requires experience and the critical analysis of other related studies. Well-stated, a set of hypotheses allows the reader to recapture the original problem; it must answer the research question as asked. Every assertion you hope to support, and only those assertions, should be translated into testable form.

A common error is the incorporation of value judgments: even if the question does not involve "ought/should" phrases, it may reflect a bias in the choice of constructs or criteria. Research cannot answer moral or ethical questions.

Deciding whether a set of hypotheses will actually permit the desired inference in response to the research question is a difficult matter. Read your hypotheses out loud to a cooperative colleague, who should then be able to reconstruct the question. If he or she is not able to do this, or appears to miss the point, or omits some essential aspect, you should carefully revise what you have written until there is no doubt that your hypotheses "fit" your problem and your conjecture.[18]

In our experience, beginning researchers often have trouble achieving this goal. You can help yourself learn how to formulate operationalized research hypotheses and recast them—where appropriate—as statistically testable. Find a published report of a study on a topic that interests you and carry out an intensive analysis. Look up the citations, restate the problem, outline its background, and reframe the hypotheses in various forms. Whether the research is of good or poor quality, this sort of conscientious dissection will give you invaluable insight into the decision process of the investigator, and an understanding of how variables, populations, and instruments were selected. Critical assessment of the appropriateness of the overall methodology and of the data analysis, and the presentation of conclusions will increase your awareness of alternatives. (For example, despite its defects, the Rosenthal and Jacobson [1968] study has stimulated a great deal of new research in the area of teacher expectancies.) Two or three such exercises will vastly enhance your power to identify suitable problems and generate new ones on the basis of existing results, and will increase your self-confidence in undertaking your own study.

Operationalizing Definitions and Hypotheses

We have referred in the preceding sections to the importance of operationalizing both the definitions and the hypotheses. *Operationalizing* means "talking about (1) one's observations, (2) the manipulational and computational procedures involved in making them, (3) the logical and mathematical steps which intervene between earlier and later statements, and (4) nothing else."[19] This point of view has advantages and disadvantages.[20] In order to develop a design for your study, you must specify how you will measure and/or manipulate each construct which appears in your hypotheses, that is, provide a translation from the theory or construct-language to the data-language. This is accomplished in part by describing the instruments and procedures used to obtain measurements for your variables, and in part by describing the criteria you will use to decide whether your observations lead to the expected answer(s) to your problem-question.

The crucial step in operationalizing a definition is selecting an observable *indicant* for each variable. Many, if not most, attributes of interest in social and behavioral science research are not directly observable, hence you cannot measure the variables until you specify these indicants. For instance, an indicant of hostility is the number of times a child strikes other children; an indicant of creativity is the number of different uses an individual suggests for a common object. Operationalizing the conjectures means formulating them in terms of the measurements of indicants.[21] (See Chapter 7, section on measurement.)

Moving back and forth between the theoretical and the empirical (observational) is intrinsic to the scientific method: operationalizing is constructing the bridge between them, which allows a theoretical inference based on empirical evidence. Problems of replication in the social sciences often reflect vagueness or inconsistencies in the operational forms of the crucial concepts. If you are in doubt as to how to operationalize a construct, you will find it helpful to read reports of other studies that make use of this construct or ones closely related. When hypotheses do not feel right, it may be that the operationalized form is a poor fit to the construct form. For example, Singleton and Smith (1978) hypothesized that grade inflation does not decrease grade reliability if the available scale allows for sufficient discrimination. They tested their hypothesis by an analysis of a systematic sample of grades and grade-point averages at a large state university over the period 1965–1975. (In 1970 a plus–minus system was introduced.) The study rests on the operationalizing of "reliability" as the average intercorrelation of all pairs of the students' first 20 course grades. The operationalizing of reliability as intercorrelation leads in the extreme case to the absurd conclusion that if all students get all *A*'s (so the intercorrelation is perfect) then the grades are more "reliable"—no one will believe this! The authors assert their hypothesis is supported by the evidence. It is obvious, however, that so many alternative explanations and additional variables need to be taken into account that the conclusions become most questionable.

Validity, specifically, *referent validity*, (also called *epistemic correlation*) is really the "goodness-of-fit" between the operationalized and construct forms of a definition (see Chapter 7, section on validity). Obtaining a good fit is not easy. It is difficult even to decide whether the fit is good, and we know of no systematic procedures to guarantee achieving this goal.

Erbe's (1962) study, already mentioned in Chapter 1, is an instructive example of the entire procedure. Use of the terms *gregariousness* and (*social*) *integration* overlapped in earlier investigations of information flow. No previous studies had treated these two variables simultaneously; alternative theories can be advanced about their differential effects on the possession of information. The extreme cases are the "gadabout" (gregarious but nonintegrated) and the cliquish person (integrated but not gregarious). Previous analyses of social networks also suggested the possible importance of contextual effects, namely, high or low density of group interaction (defined below), in the reference population. Erbe conjectured:

1. Integration with a peer group is conducive to the possession of information, even on a highly salient subject, compared to nonintegration.
2. High gregariousness, the maintenance of extensive acquaintanceships with other individuals in the referent population, is also associated with the possession of information, but this effect seems to be caused mostly by the fact that high gregarious persons are also more likely to be group members.
3. High density of group interaction in the population of reference is, in and of itself, conducive to the possession of information, especially among non-integrated students, although the integrated students within such a population are more likely to be informed than the non-integrated.[22]

The variables were *integration, gregariousness, cohesiveness* (density of group interaction), and *informedness*. They must be operationalized before the study can proceed.

This step requires the selection of an "*arena*" (see Introduction in Chapter 5). The study population consisted of a national two-stage stratified cluster sample (see Chapter 8, section on cluster sampling) of graduate students at universities offering a Ph.D. in the traditional arts and sciences. Twenty-five universities were selected and in each a sample was drawn at random from the total enrollment; quotas for the schools and students were set so that every current Ph.D. student was equally likely to be drawn. Total sample size was 3000. The size (number of students) of each subject's department was determined. The subjects were also classified according to certain other variables we will not discuss here.

Gregariousness was defined by the subject's indication of how many students in his department he knew well enough to chat with casually: the distribution of responses was quartiled for each department size and the subject was classified according to quartile. ("High gregarious" meant first quartile, etc.)

Integration was defined by the subject's response (yes/no) to the question whether he maintained informal contact with some group(s) of students that met outside the classroom. ("Integrated" means the answer is yes.)

Cohesiveness was defined by the responses (yes/no) to the question whether fellow students in the same department tended to form such groups. (If a majority of subjects said yes, their department was classified as "high cohesive"; if not, "low cohesive.")

Finally, for the purpose of this study, "information" concerned availability of financial support and the factors of importance in its allocation. Subjects were asked ten questions about these and were classified "uninformed" on each subtopic if they admitted to having no idea of the answer. The investigator presents a fairly long justification of the operational decisions, especially the last.

This study as reported did not make use of a conventional hypothesis-testing format in that no null hypotheses were stated and no level of significance assigned (see next section). Using percentage tabulations, interpreted as contingent probabilities, Erbe exhibited findings in support of the following operationalized hypotheses:

1. The higher the gregariousness, the more likely subjects were to be integrated (monotone relation).
2. The higher the gregariousness, the more likely subjects were to be informed, on 8 of the 10 items (monotone relation).
3. Integration was associated with a greater likelihood of informedness than was nonintegration, on 9 of the 10 items.
4. The variable of integration had a greater effect on the probability of being informed than the variable of gregariousness.
5. The integration effect on informedness did not disappear when cohesiveness was held constant.

Erbe concluded that his data support the three conjectures stated earlier. (p. 74).

The Logic of Hypothesis Testing

A conjecture is in general not testable until it is operationalized (translated into data-language). This operational form we call a *research hypothesis*. In the sorts of studies with which we are concerned, what is actually tested is a *statistical hypothesis*: a statement (prediction) about a population parameter, or parameters. Such a statement should be a logical consequence of the research hypothesis(es) and must refer to populations actually available for sampling purposes. The test involves the outcome of a statistical analysis applied to data obtained from these populations. Conventional hypothesis testing reflects the following logic:

Call H the hypothesis (conjecture) you believe or hope to be true. Write the implication[23] $H \Rightarrow E_H$ where E_H is a prediction, based on theory and previous findings, about the evidence (data): for example, the values of some computed statistic. It would be agreeable to prove "H is true" by asserting "if H is true than E_H occurs" and showing that E_H does occur; unfortunately, the logical argument

$$H \Rightarrow E_H$$
$$E_H$$
$$\therefore H$$

is fallacious. To be sure, H becomes more credible, but there is no way to be certain that E_H had no antecedents other than H. In effect, this means no amount of evidence can prove the truth of H.

On the other hand, the argument

$$H \Rightarrow E_H$$
$$not\text{-}E_H$$
$$\therefore not\text{-}H$$

is logically valid: the assertion "if H is true then E_H occurs" together with the demonstration that E_H does not occur, allows the conclusion "H is not true." This means an hypothesis can be *disproved* by the exhibition of evidence: either you can *reject* an hypothesis on the basis of your evidence or you can *fail to reject it*.

In view of the foregoing, we now replace the original conjecture (hypothesis) H by a new one. In the simplest case, write "H_0" the logical negation not-H of the H you are actually interested in, and $H_0 \Rightarrow E_{H_0}$ is a prediction about evidence, typically the value of a test statistic, deduced from H_0. Next, the evidence E is collected; it is necessary to decide, has not-E_{H_0} been exhibited? More exactly, is E compatible with the prediction E_{H_0} or not? The decision is based on the probability that the evidence E is described by the distribution embodied in the statement E_{H_0}: if this probability is below a preassigned value α (see below), the decision is "not-E_{H_0}." Following the format

$$H_0 \Rightarrow E_{H_0}$$
$$not\text{-}E_{H_0}$$
$$\therefore not\text{-}H_0$$

we conclude H_0 is false, we reject H_0, and hence must fall back on H, the logical negation of H_0. Of course, if E *is* compatible with E_{H_0} we fail to reject. Note that "failure to reject" is not the same as "accept." No hypothesis is ever directly shown to be true but survives only by probabilistic elimination of alternatives.[24]

The Null Hypothesis

The statement "H_0 is true" (i.e., "H is false") referred to above is generally called *the null hypothesis*. The strategy of rejecting the null hypothesis was introduced by R. A. Fisher, who used this term to mean the the negation of the research hypothesis "H is true." (Frequently *null* is used to specify a population parameter of zero, that is, no effect, no difference, zero correlation, etc.) Significance testing, which results in a decision about the validity of the null hypothesis, generally requires that "H is false" be stated in such a way that this decision can be based upon a statistical analysis of the sample data; hence, the null hypothesis implies a prediction (here E_{H_0} about the outcome of the statistical analysis. E_{H_0} is the statistical form of the null hypothesis. The decision rule is: eliminate (reject) the null hypothesis if the values of the test statistic computed from sample data would be very unlikely if the null hypothesis were true, otherwise suspend judgment. To put it more informally: if the consequence of "H is false" is unlikely, then "H is true" is more credible.

In addition to the assertion "if H_0 is true then E_{H_0} is observable" a number of other assumptions, often untested or untestable, must be made in order that the chosen statistical procedure can be applied (for instance: that an appropriate probability sample has been obtained, that the populations are normally distributed, that the samples are independent or correlated, that variances are equal, and, more fundamentally, that measurements are valid and of a suitable level).

The null hypothesis is formulated in the data language: it predicts distributions, relationships, or differences involving measurements. These relationships or differences are reflected in the computed values of one or more test statistics (difference of means, value of correlation, etc.). Ideally there is a single ("exact") alternative hypothesis that describes the same distribution, relationship, or difference as the null hypothesis. Rejection of the null *may* imply acceptance of the alternative, so the alternative is a more-or-less incomplete negation of the null.

"Every experiment may be said to exist only in order to give the facts a chance of disproving the null hypothesis."[25] (One can also say the null hypothesis exists only in order to be rejected.)

In practice, several alternative hypotheses are identified as likely and one specified hypothesis plays the role of H_0 and is shown to be false, so that the others achieve increased credibility. "Knowledge, when viewed from this perspective, is problematic. What are considered to be scientific truths are simply those statements which we consider to have a low probability of being proven incorrect in the future."[26]

The decision whether the null and, more especially, the alternative, should be exact or inexact, directional or nondirectional (see section on One-Tailed versus Two-Tailed Tests, below), reflects your experience and judgment as a researcher, rather than statistical considerations. Familiarity with the phenomena under study, based either on theory or prior empirical findings, necessarily suggests the null and alternative(s) just as it does the conjectures toward which your entire research project is directed. Choice of a suitable statistic is determined by what distribution, comparison or relationship you wish to exhibit, what sort of data you have, and other considerations. (This topic is discussed in some detail in Chapters 10–15.)

Level of Significance, Region of Rejection, and Type I or α-Error

As we have indicated above, the null hypothesis is rejected if the difference between the value of the test statistic computed from the data, and the value of the parameter predicted from the (assumed) null hypothesis, is too great to be attributable to chance fluctuations (sampling error). "Too great a difference" is specified in terms of a probability, called the level of significance, the *Type I error*, or the *α-error*.

For example, using .05 as the level of significance means that a value of the test statistic which would occur with a probability of .05 or less if the null hypothesis were true is to be regarded as sufficient evidence for rejecting the null hypothesis.[27]

The decision procedure involves either direct calculation of the probability of the test statistic, or comparison of the computed value of the test statistic with the tabled value(s) of the test statistic occurring with probability not exceeding the specified α. The latter strategy, finding so-called critical value(s), defines a critical region (region of rejection) for the statistic: if the test statistic falls into the region of rejection, the null hypothesis is rejected. In any case, the sampling distribution of the test statistic must be known.

Henkel (1976) points out that in addition the observed value of the test statistic must be likely if the alternative hypothesis is assumed true. This is easy to decide when the null and alternative hypotheses are logical opposites, otherwise, not so.

The chosen probability α can be interpreted as the probability of falsely rejecting a true (null) hypothesis. Thus the so-called α-error represents the risk of drawing this kind of erroneous conclusion. Most frequently, the α is chosen to reflect conventional practice in the discipline within which the study is conducted, but there are many specific criteria that reflect the design or the purpose of the study.[28]

> The risk level which would be unacceptable as the basis for a firm decision or for any action which was dangerous or expensive may be entirely adequate for suggesting the continuation of an experiment. In fact, it is probably true that the first evidence leading to important scientific discoveries is often very slender and could be accepted as proof only at very great risk. Therefore, it is unwise to set α too low in the preliminary stages of an investigation. Later on, however, when it is a question of asserting that something has been proved, more rigorous criteria are usually necessary.[29]

The application of the study is thus evidently an important determinant of your choice of α, as is the possible cost of an error.

To summarize: testing a statistical hypothesis involves a number of steps:

1. specifying the null and (if possible) the alternative hypotheses;
2. choosing the appropriate statistic;
3. deciding what will constitute a sufficiently unlikely value for the statistic to permit the decision that the null hypothesis is false, that is, choosing a Type I or α-error;
4. calculating the statistic for data obtained from a suitably chosen sample; and
5. deciding whether or not to reject the null hypothesis.[30]

Type II or β-Error

The false rejection of a true hypothesis is not the only error to be avoided. It is also important not to miss real effects, that is, erroneously to fail to reject a false null hypothesis. (This means one mistakenly rejects the alternative hypothesis.) This risk is called the Type II or β-error. In general, the α-error and β-error are antagonistic in that minimizing the probability of a Type I error increases the probability of making a Type II error. It is difficult to figure the relationship between α and β because, statistically, not-E_{H_0} is not necessarily the equivalent of E_H.[31] Calculation of β is possible only if the alternative hypothesis is exact, which is rare in the social and behavioral sciences; in any case, the technicalities are beyond the scope of this book. Related to β is the *power* of a statistical test, defined as $1 - \beta$, the probability of (correctly) rejecting a false null hypothesis. Power increases to some degree with sample size n; tables of the value of $1 - \beta$ (power of the statistic for a given sample size) are available for commonly used statistics.[32]

Your order of choice is thus: test statistic; α; power (table), hence β; and n (table). Once α is fixed, β and n must be balanced in view of cost and possible applications of the study outcomes (see the section on Determining Sample Size in Chapter 8). Ultimately, the purpose for which you are carrying out your investigation will determine whether α should be minimized at the expense of β, or vice versa. In general, exploratory studies call for a small β (lest a finding of possible importance get away), while those one hopes will be definitive in permitting a choice between competing hypotheses for clear-cut effects suggest a small α.

One-Tailed versus Two-Tailed Tests
(Directional versus Nondirectional Effects)

In stating your null and alternative hypotheses, you must decide whether the effect(s) you expect to exhibit is (are) directional or nondirectional. For example, suppose you hope to show that first-born high-school students tend to have higher (measured) verbal skills than those lower in the birth order. It will not be appropriate for you to adopt as the null "there is no difference," because the rejection of this null will leave you in midair; rather, a null of the form "$M_F \leq M_L$" (mean verbal-skill-measure of first-borns does not exceed mean of later-borns) and an alternative of "$M_F > M_L$" (mean verbal-skill-measure of first-borns exceeds mean of later-borns) would be better for your purposes. Here, your conjecture is embodied directly in your hypotheses. Your data must give you a value of the test statistic, which is unlikely if the assumption $M_F \leq M_L$ is true: this is a so-called one-tailed test.[33] On the other hand, an "exact" null hypothesis, in particular one that specifies a zero value for some parameter, calls for a two-tailed test; another way to say this is that the rejection region is symmetrical.

There is no general rule specifying whether the statistical test should be one- or two-tailed. You must refer to your conjecture. If your conjectures, and hence your research and statistical hypotheses are asymmetrical, then the null hypothesis should be directional and the test one-tailed.[34]

To illustrate the foregoing, we have formulated null hypotheses for several of the studies described in Chapter 2 (pp. 30–33). Many articles do not contain explicitly stated nulls, either because of space limitations or for some other reasons. (As we have indicated, in practice, much large-scale survey research proceeds without clearly formulated hypotheses, let alone nulls.)

We can reconstruct null hypotheses from Erbe's (1962) report of his study, already cited. A nondirectional null hypothesis might be "there is no significant difference in the proportions of those who possess information, among integrated and nonintegrated individuals." A directional null hypothesis, corresponding to operationalized hypothesis #3 (p. 75) might be "the proportion of those who possess information is lower or is not significantly different among integrated individuals than among nonintegrated individuals."

Thornton and Freedman (1979) report their findings and conclusions based on a multiple classification (dummy regression) analysis. They do not specify any criteria for accepting or rejecting a conjecture; it appears that they repeatedly test their data against implied nulls of the form, for example, "there is no difference in sex-role attitudes between 1962 and 1977 among those who received further education" or "there is no difference in the amount of change in respondents' attitudes between 1962 and 1977 associated with the number of respondents' children".

Null hypotheses in a study such as Jacobson's (1978) may be of the form "there is no significant linear relation between the probability that respondents know the candidate and expenditures by the candidate" or "there is no significant difference in the slopes of the bivariate regression lines for the above two variables for incumbents and challengers."

It is difficult to formulate null hypotheses for a study which employs a path analysis, like that of Bell et al. (1981). For example, in considering variables reflecting females' relationships with their fathers, the authors found homosexual women described their parents less favorably (cold, weak, rejecting, etc.) than did heterosexual women, but the path analysis did not show these variables to have a significant association with the daughters' adult sexual preference. Thus, the null "tested" is an hypothesis of "no significant total effect."

In their test of the Gibbs–Erickson model relating suburbanization and central-city crime rates, Farley and Hansel (1981) conjecture that this relationship is not a spurious one, arising from the effect of population size. Their null hypothesis is, in effect, that partial correlations (controlled for population size) between crime rates and suburbanization indexes, will vanish. Since the partials are only diminished somewhat, they "rejected" the null. (No alpha error is specified.)

Veroff et al. (1981) use a log-linear analysis to test multivariate contingency tables for significant differences and relationships among the numbers of responses in specified categories. One model implicitly tested is the "no difference" or "no relationship" assumption. Another procedure involves a comparison of models with the assertion that a proposed model B gives a better fit to the data than existing model A; when the "improvement" is not statistically significant, the competing model B is eliminated (see Veroff et al., 1981, Appendix G).

When Significance Tests Are Not Appropriate or Useful

Significance testing—following the procedures set forth by Fisher—is so much taken for granted as a part of the research process in the sciences with which we are concerned that it is easy to overlook the many serious questions that have been raised about its suitability.

Significance tests rest on probability theory which is a formal mathematical model. The assumptions of this model must be satisfied in order that the appropriate sampling distribution can be used as a basis for inference:

> [The] test of significance provides the probability. . . that a particular unique event (the particular sample result), or a more extreme event, would occur in a hypothetical situation which has three components—the null hypothesis is true, the study can be thought of as one of a very large sequence of identical studies, and the various assumptions underlying the test are met by the data, or have been shown empirically or theoretically to be unimportant for the valid interpretation of the results.[35]

These assumptions are more or less stringent but always involve random sampling from the population to which inferences are to be made. Consequently, case studies, studies with volunteer subjects, exploratory studies whose purpose is to suggest factors or conjectures for later more systematic research, and many quasi-experimental designs (see Chapter 5) may not lend themselves to classical significance testing. Likewise, there are difficulties associates with use of probability samples other than simple random sampling, inadequately defined populations, unavailability of power estimates for the inexact hypotheses in much social science research, and overreliance on an arbitrary level of significance, in addition to problems that arise from misuse of techniques or faulty design.

A number of objections have been raised, based upon the nature of the null hypothesis, the logic of rejecting the null if the probability of a test statistic is low, the disregard for the cumulative nature of science ("prior knowledge"), and the intended application of the decision: prediction versus action.[36] In many research contexts, the passage from the probability associated with the value of a test statistic to the (subjective) probability of the truth of a conjectural statement is a dubious inferential step. It may be more appropriate simply to cite the probability of the observed event without attempting to assign a truth value to the theory which predicts this event.

You should regard classical significance testing as one among several techniques for the evaluation of data, not the only one. It should not become a straitjacket for creativity and exploration. However, some explicit criterion for evaluating evidence must be set forth (Davis, 1968), as the alternative is for the researcher simply to select the data that suits his purpose.

A Final Word

There are many things whose *existence* we cannot prove but whose *effects* we can point to: "between what one observes and what one concludes there is a long and tortuous chain of reasoning, inference, and evaluation."[37]

A set of hypotheses, properly formulated and appropriately tested, should permit conclusions which will partly or wholly answer the original research question. Conjectures are in general stated in the construct language, research hypotheses are in general operationalized, that is, written in the data language, and statistical hypotheses comprise predictions in mathematical form about the probabilities associated with sets of data. It may be difficult to decide whether these successive translations do indeed allow the chain to be constructed, and also, whether the chain will bear much weight. We do not know of any systematic way to make this decision; knowledgeable fellow reseachers and not-yet-convinced colleagues can make useful criticism.

Last but not least, do not confuse significance and importance.[38] The former is mathematical; the latter is subjective, based on experience and judgment. Small differences in large samples can be highly significant but not important; large differences in small samples can be very important but not significant. The two criteria are independent and, while every researcher hopes to achieve both in his/her results, importance is by far the more valuable.

Notes

[1]Plutchik (1974 [2nd ed.], p. 39). The section pp. 39–41 is extremely clear and succinct. See also Stinchcombe (1968, pp. 38–40) for an elaboration of the role of causal hypotheses in concept formulation.

[2]Denzin (1978, p. 315).

[3]Homans (1967, pp. 10–21). Nonoperating definitions seem to be what Lastrucci (1967) calls "concepts" while operating definitions correspond to "constructs."

[4]Kerlinger (1973, pp. 28–29, 40). See also discussion at the beginning of our Chapter 7.

[5]Kerlinger (1973, p. 29).

[6]Rapaport (1953, p. 19). This author writes from a strict operationist viewpoint.

[7]Kerlinger (1973, p. 40).

[8]See MacCorquedale and Meehl (1948). Kerlinger (1973) calls these "intervening variables."

[9]Stinchcombe (1968, p. 41). We warmly recommend this reference.

[10]Kerlinger (1973, p. 32, see also pp. 30–34). This reference contains many examples of operational definitions.

[11]A fairly concise, if conventional, presentation can be found in Kerlinger (1973, Chapter 3). Much more thoughtful and thought provoking is Rosenberg (1968), not restricted in its usefulness to survey studies. Our discussion is based on both of these, in terminology and in point of view.

[12]Terminology follows Campbell and Stanley (1963). For further discussion, see Rosenberg (1968, pp. 94–98) or Bell et al. (1981).

[13]A frequent reason given for failure to fund grant proposals is poor hypotheses. See Allen (1960) and Smith (1963).

[14]See Morrison and Henkel (1970), and the interchange reprinted in Steger (1971, pp. 199–310; see also Zeisel (1970).

[15]Kerlinger (1973, p. 25). This author follows Popper (1959, 1962) who insists on testable hypotheses. The importance of testable theory has been an important issue in the recently renewed discussion of the status of psychoanalysis as a science (*New York Times*, Jan. 15, 1985, p. C1, and Jan. 22, 1985, p. C1). Another, differing, point of view is expressed by Babbie (1973, pp. 227–231), who emphasizes the back-and-forth aspect of hypothesis formulation.

[16]Homans (1967, pp. 14–18).

[17]Greer (1969, p. 138ff.).

[18]An interesting aspect of this, the level at which a theory is supported or refuted, and alternative explanations, is discussed in Stinchcombe (1968, pp. 47–53); see also Merton (1968).

[19]Skinner (1945).

[20]Consult Rapaport (1953) for the former, and Plutchik (1974 [2nd ed.], pp. 48–55) for a thoughtful analysis of the latter.

[21]An extended and thoughtful discussion of the relationship between conceptualization and measurement can be found in Blalock (1982). Our terminology follows Kerlinger (1973, pp. 432–433); see also Carmines and Zeller (1979) who use the term *indicator* for indicant.

[22]Erbe (1972, pp. 515–516).

[23]"$\Rightarrow$" means "implies"; "$\therefore$" means "therefore"; "not-H" is a proposition that is true if and only if the proposition "H" is false.

[24]Spielman (1974) argues strongly that the logic described here is incomplete, and that what might be called quasi-Bayesian analysis of possible outcomes is necessary before a decision can be made. Iverson (1984) summarizes the Bayesian viewpoint very simply; see especially pp. 72–77.

[25]Fisher (1966, p. 16). In contrast, note the remark of T. H. Huxley, "The great tragedy of science—the slaying of a beautiful hypothesis by an ugly fact."

[26]Henkel (1976, p. 35); see also Braithwaite (1960, Chapter 7) and Stinchcombe (1968, pp. 17–22, 24–25). "A reasonable probability is the only certainty" (Edgar Watson Howe).

[27]An anonymous cynic has remarked: this means that if a journal prints the reports of 20 studies, each with $\alpha = .05$, then the conclusions in one study are likely to be in error, but the reader does not know which one.

[28]Labovitz (1970) lists 11 criteria.

[29]Wilson (1952, p. 172).

[30]Our discussion closely follows the pattern established by Fisher. We strongly recommend further reading in the philosophy of significance testing and the use of null hypotheses, for example, Wilson (1952, pp. 170–174, 293–298) for discussion of logical problems of stating and testing hypotheses (philosophy of probability) and good references. For other views see Morrison and Henkel (1970) and the last two sections of this chapter. You will also find Meehl's (1954) discussion of inference based on clinical studies both provocative and informative, and Binder (1963) or Grant (1962) instructive concerning the role of the theoretical model.

[31]See Hays (1973) and Whittemore (1981).

[32]See Cohen (1969). Smith (1985) has an entertaining discussion of the hazards of data snooping (pp. 372–379) and offers guidelines for choosing null, alternative, α and β (pp. 358–363).

[33]See Steger (1971) for an extensive interchange on this issue.

[34]The F and the chi-square sampling distributions are used in most situations in a one-tailed test, even though the alternative hypothesis is nondirectional. This is an unfortunate source of confusion. For one- versus two-tailed procedures, see any standard text (e.g., Hays, 1973).

[35]Henkel (1976, p. 78).

[36]Extended discussion of these issues, and both the Neyman–Pearson–Wald and Bayesian approaches, can be found in Morrison and Henkel, (1970); see also Hays (1973, pp. 382ff.), Wilson (1952, pp. 170ff.), and Steger (1971, pp. 229–309). Luce and Raiffa (1957) have a short section on the relation between statistical inference and decision theory. McNemar (1960) is an agreeably opinionated summary of the shortcomings of conventional statistical tests.

[37]Rapaport (1953, p. 22).

[38]Bolles (1962) compares statistical hypotheses and scientific hypotheses and observes that when the statistician has rejected the null his job is done, whereas the scientist's is just begun. Achen (1982, pp. 44–51) refers to "substantive" (as opposed to "statistical") significance. Bakan (1967) raises serious questions as to the appropriateness and usefulness of significance tests in psychological research. See, also, Morrison and Henkel (1970, Chapters 20–22, 25–28).

Additional Reading

For further reading on operationalizing, see:

Rapaport (1953): first several chapters are extremely readable and useful; an operationalist.
Plutchik (1974): a balanced presentation.
Underwood (1957): Chapter 3.
Greer (1969, Part III): thoughtful and controversial.
Coleman (1964, Chapters 1–4).

On formulating definitions, and their importance;

Blalock and Blalock (1968)
Selltiz et al. (1976)

Hypothesis Formulation and Testing

Fisher (1973): the standard model for hypothesis testing.
Stinchcombe (1968): the logic of hypothesis testing simply explicated; also a clear introduction to the use of path diagrams.

Savage (1954) ⎫
Iverson (1984) ⎬ Bayesian viewpoint.

Footnotes 30 and 36 this chapter contain extensive references to the significance testing controversy.

Steger (1971): well-chosen readings on the foregoing.
Morrison and Henkel (1970): excellent bibliography; informative and thought-provoking readings.
Skyrms (1966): very simple.

α- and β-Error

Bradley (1968): clear.
Festinger and Katz (1953, Chapter 12).
Cohen (1969): emphasis on decisions concerning β and sample size.

Most elementary texts, especially Levine (1981), Hays (1973), and Freedman et al. (1978), will clarify this for you without excessive technical detail.

5

Evaluating Method and Design

Introduction

Do-able research begins with problem formulation and requires a sequence of inter-related decisions. This chapter addresses general issues which must be considered in choosing a method and design for answering your problem-question. It offers a classification scheme for research based on the nature of the evidence to be collected and the possibilities for controlling extraneous variance; it summarizes the criteria for evaluating research design. (It is not our purpose to set forth in detail the techniques that may be needed.)

Method means "an orderly procedure or process; . . . hence, a set form of procedure adopted in investigation," whereas *methodology* is defined as "the science of method or arrangements." Some authors refer to methodology as "the logic of procedure" but regard methods as techniques specific to a discipline. We agree with this usage. Confusion enters when *methodologies* is used to mean technicalities of procedure (as in Blalock and Blalock, 1968). *Design* means the arrangement of the conditions of observation.

Until a problem is properly stated, neither method nor design can be determined. On the other hand, the difficulties you encounter in making decisions about method or design can suggest refinements you might need to make in problem formulation. The way you operationalize your constructs makes certain methods feasible and renders others out of the question; the method then lends itself to certain designs.[1] Your hypotheses as operationalized reflect the available measurement schemes and may in fact force a design. This circular aspect of planning research can be frustrating, but in the long run the additional reflection it forces on the researcher pays off many-fold. Barber (1976) observes that the choice of methodology (e.g., the experimental paradigm) reflects a definition of what is "knowable" and also "worth knowing." Ultimately, your selection of an appropriate method is an act of judgment.[2]

All theory is formulated in general and tested in particular. To set this process in motion, you must chose a unit of analysis, a setting, suitable variables, instrumentation and procedures. An effective design will permit you to measure the variables you want to study or to identify relationships among these variables, unconfounded by the unwanted and irrelevant effects of impertinent variables. It will also permit you to analyze your observations so as to make inferences possible. Design selection thus specifically involves resolving such issues as control and randomization. Ideally, a design would permit you to compare everything of interest to everything else, and would control or suppress everything not of interest; in practice, all designs represent accommodations to feasibility. Not surprisingly, certain designs are strongly associated with certain statistical procedures (for instance: factorial designs and analysis of variance, repeated measures and the Friedman test, matched pairs and the correlated t-test, cross tabulations and the chi-square), but it is a mistake to base decisions about design primarily on availability or ease of statistical analysis.[3] It goes without saying that the planning of design and all aspects of measurement—data-collection procedures and record keeping— should be done, so far as possible, in advance of actual data-collection.[4] Data analysis has, to be sure, an exploratory aspect[5] but cannot reconstruct uncollected or improperly collected data. The key to successful research, as opposed to a sort of empirical browsing, is thinking through in a systematic way what you want to find out and what will constitute an answer to your questions.

Classification of Research

An appropriate classification of research can help you choose a method and design suitable for your problem-question. In Chapter 1 we presented briefly two conventional theory-based classifications:

- From the standpoint of the role of hypotheses, research can be formulative or verificational.
- From the standpoint of its distance from the "real world", research can be basic, applied, or action.

These two classification schemes take into account the goals of the study, but in different ways, so the resulting categories lie along different axes, so to speak.

Another taxonomy is based on data-collection techniques: observations, interviews, and questionnaires; and yet another is based on the degree of intervention of the researcher, classified under such headings as automated data-collection, participant observation, objective versus subjective instruments, and reactive versus nonreactive procedures. It is also possible to classify studies according to the data-analysis techniques employed.[6] Each of the foregoing schemes can be useful, but none is very helpful to you in your task: the selection of an appropriate method and design.

Over the years much effort has been devoted to development of a classification scheme based on methodology. The most familiar typology uses three categories: historical, descriptive, and experimental. Unfortunately, these categories need to be clearly specified so that a particular study may be readily classified. As it stands, the classification scheme is insufficiently informative. A modification[7] of this system, reflecting the work of J. S. Mill, classifies a study under one of two headings, according to whether or not the conditions under which the observed events take place can be controlled:

1. Experimental (control possible)
    a. Factorial (agreement and differences)
    b. Functional (concomitant variation)
2. Historical (control not possible)
    a. Retrospective (post facto)
    b. Progressive (developmental)

We prefer a classification that uses the conventional terminology and incorporates both the nature of the evidence and the possibility of control.

We describe *research* not as the study of events but rather as the collection and analysis of evidence from which inferences are made as to the events and their characteristics. We can then classify research according to the nature of the evidence and the kind of inferences, by asking a sequence of questions.

Figure 5.1 sets forth the questions and illustrates this classification scheme. Within the major categories (capital letters), subtypes can be identified by asking further questions (such as, Is time a variable?).

The existence of multiple taxonomies almost guarantees overlap of labels; thus a study can be basic, experimental, verificational, and observational, or applied, descriptive, formulative, and interview-based. Our purpose in assigning labels is to help you consider a variety of possible strategies for answering your problem-question, rather than to construct a perfect set of pigeonholes.

In the next section, the terminology used in Figure 5.1 is amplified. The classification scheme is further refined in Chapter 6.

If you have already formulated your problem and selected a tentative procedure for solving it, you should be able to locate your proposed research type in Figure 5.1. However, if you are still in the process of developing a strategy for solving a not-yet-formulated problem, you must proceed somewhat differently in your decision-making, as follows.

After you have identified the theories and previous research that will provide the framework for your study, you still need to select an *arena*. This decision is an essential step in operationalizing your theory, a transformation of

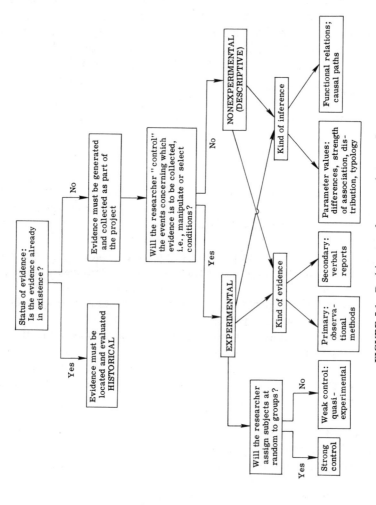

FIGURE 5.1 Decision tree for research types: I.

language we have discussed in the last chapter and will address further in Chapters 6–8. You will select a setting and a population (the arena) because in your judgment they offer a way to test or explore your conjectures. Sometimes the nature of the problem forces a choice of arena because of its specificity or an urgent need to address a particular set of issues. The arena may be a laboratory or a field setting; the latter includes a vast array of possibilities as disparate as the PTA in a new suburb, a university department or class, a large corporation with several locations and levels of employees, a therapy group, a summer camp, a health district, an urban school system, a union, a consortium of nations, or an isolated village.

You may need to evaluate different arenas for their feasibility and their potential for allowing you to isolate the phenomena (effects) you want to study. In particular, you should consider the following (by no means an exhaustive list):

1. Can I identify a research population suitable for the purpose of this study?
2. Is the research population appropriate, in quality and quantity, for the unit of analysis? Can I acquire sufficient data on the research population to answer the research question?
3. Do the constraints jeopardize my obtaining a generalizable answer?
4. Is appropriate instrumentation available for the variables in this arena?
5. Are procedures or methods sufficiently tested or do I need to carry out a pilot study?
6. Are there practical difficulties in the use of this arena, or these procedures?

When you are satisfied with the selection of your arena, you can go on to consider the next questions:

7. Is control possible?
8. Is control desirable?

Control

It is appropriate to ask what "control" means. While precise definitions are hard to find, there is some general understanding that it refers to the manipulation or selection of conditions, often referred to as *treatments*,[8] carried out by (or at the direction of) the investigator.[9] The term *control* is usually specialized to cover two different aspects of a study: the manipulation or selection of the values of the independent variable(s), and the selection of subjects and/or their assignment to comparison groups in which the independent variables have different values. The term *control* is also used to refer to statistical techniques, such as covariance and partial correlation, and deterministic procedures, such as partial differentiation, which permit isolation of effects and therefore substitute for the control of conditions or subject groups. A *control group* is a comparison or base-line group, often one to which no treatment is applied.

Your answers to the questions 7 and 8 above reflect your overall goal. If your research is formulative, or if you are interested the range of variation as it occurs in nature, then control may be of less importance: the more effects the better. Increasing control may diminish validity (see next section) in social and certain behavioral science research, because manipulation, especially in field settings, may change the relationships you wish to describe, or because the laboratory setting may be so artificial that generalization to natural settings is impossible.[10] Moreover, ethical issues arising from the manipulation of conditions for human subjects may make such an approach distasteful.

In contrast, if your research is verificational, the greater your degree of control over conditions the stronger the probability (in the Keynesian sense of degree of belief) that a functional or causal statement can be supported by the data. You may, at best, be able to draw very strong conclusions about a relatively restricted state of affairs. It is only when you are clear about what you want to achieve that you can assess the desirability of control.

In practice, control of conditions may be impossible for any one of the following reasons:

- The evidence you need to study is already in existence.
- The events you want to study (e.g., responses to a catastrophe) are beyond your power as an investigator to alter. (It may still be possible to have comparison groups of subjects, however.)
- The number of individuals in your target population may be limited, so comparison groups cannot be formed systematically.
- Too many variables, whose possible effects cannot be overlooked, may be present in the population. It may be wise to consider a different arena, or a shift in the problem-question.

Among the many thoughtful discussions of the feasibility and/or importance of achieving control, few compare with Chapter 13, "Methodological Problems of the Social Sciences," in Nagel's *Structure of Science* (1961). Nagel reviews the problems that arise from the use of the classical experimental physical science model for social science research. In place of the search for explanations incorporating a small number of factors, controlling other variables, leading to precise predictive laws, he proposes controlled inquiry as a broader methodological strategy. Basically, this requires a relaxation of the predictive criterion, a multivariate formulation, and a search for patterns of relationship, as well as taking into account what we now call feedback, (awareness of history) as a variable. Nagel makes a strong case for behaviorism as a frame of reference, and points out that the value-free ideal need not preclude the researcher's evaluation of the relations found to exist between variables. He observes that the usual reasons given for the "intrinsic impossibility of obtaining objective (i.e.. value free and unbiased) conclusions for the social sciences"[11] are far from definitive or even convincing, but in fact serve to direct attention to important practical difficulties.

Internal and External Validity

Your plan for isolating the effects you wish to study and identifying outcomes must provide a basis for logical inference. The notions of internal and external validity give rise to a useful set of criteria for evaluating a plan for research of any type.[12] Most simply put, *internal validity* means that conclusions about the treatments can be drawn, within the specific study situation; *external validity* means that the conclusions can be generalized, to other populations, settings, conditions, treatments, or measurement devices.[13]

Many strict experimental studies have high internal validity. Reliance on volunteer subjects, as in the Kinsey studies (1948, 1953), tends to diminish both internal and external validity, because unexamined variables associated with volunteering may have substantial effects, and because the volunteer population may be unrepresentative. The absence of internal validity renders the findings useless except insofar as the researcher has gained some insight into the problem; study conclusions cannot be incorporated into an inferential chain. In contrast, external validity may have relatively low priority, as in some action research where the interest lies in identifying the effects of treatments in the particular situation. A familiar example of a class of studies with low external validity is that of clinical reports of psychotherapeutic success: it is not at all clear that the results can be generalized to other therapists, other patients, and other slightly differing diagnoses. Internal and external validity may conflict, but they do not present a problem like that of balancing α - and β-errors when choosing a statistical test. Their relative importance varies according to the type of research being conducted.[14] Thus, the purposes of the study as well as considerations of feasibility must be taken into account in deciding which has a higher priority. The design may be modifiable to increase one or both kinds of validity.

Campbell and Stanley[15] have enumerated a total of 12 sources of unwanted effects: 8 which must be controlled in the design in order to protect internal validity, and 4 which may jeopardize external validity. The former are:

1. History effects reflect the subject's experience of events inside or outside the study situation during its course.
2. Maturation effects arise from changes consequent on the passage of time, like aging, fatigue, etc.
3. Test effects occur when the subjects' responses to a later test or procedure are modified by what they learned in an earlier test or procedure.
4. Instrumentation effects reflect changes in measuring instruments or in the observers or scorers.
5. Statistical regression occurs when units of study are selected on the basis of their extreme differentiation on one variable. The averages of the several groups will cluster more around the central location of the overall distribution on a later measure, unless earlier and later measures are perfectly correlated. This is a purely statistical phenomenon, related to the definition of correlation.
6. Selection bias arises from differential selection or assignment of subjects to comparison groups.
7. Mortality is the differential loss of subjects from the comparison groups.
8. Interaction effects of the aforementioned.

In analyzing whether or not the independent variables (which may be organismic, or treatment(s), or differing conditions) have produced a change in the dependent variable, the investigator may confuse the effects listed above with those truly attributable to the study variables. *Confounding* occurs when the effects of one or more independent variables (which may be outside the study) cannot be disentangled from the effects of independent variables that are part of the study. This means one does not know which of several variables was "responsible" for the observed level of the dependent variable. Frequently, the main confounding effects are those of the researcher's unacknowledged interventions. *Cancellation of effects* occurs when the design fails to identify or isolate variables whose effects cancel or suppress each other; for example, some medical procedures involve drugs of such toxicity that it is difficult to decide whether the disease or its cure was the cause of death. *Multicollinearity* occurs when the variables used in the study are so highly interrelated that distinguishing the effects and allocating them to particular causal variables is impossible. You must be careful to avoid these errors.

The generality or representativeness of a finding is threatened by:

9. Interaction effects of selection biases and the independent variable(s).
10. Effects of pretesting or other preliminary procedures, which make a pretested population unrepresentative of the general population.
11. Reactive effects, arising from experimental or observational procedures including interviewing, which do not occur except in the study setting.

12. Multiple treatment interference, which takes place when the effects of prior experiences, treatments, or conditions persist and influence subsequent treatments or conditions.

Any of these may be present in studies of any type: you should carefully examine their influence before making any decision as to generalization of the findings.

Campbell and Stanley (1963) have analyzed a number of frequently used experimental designs according to how well they control unwanted variation; another attack on the same problem can be found in Ross and Smith (1968). Both these references are concerned primarily with experimental studies whose goal is to identify causal relationships. This material will be highly useful whether or not your study is experimental. A later work by Cook and Campbell (1979) focuses on sources of invalidity in so-called *quasi-experimental* research, in which the investigator has only limited control over when and to whom the treatment is administered, or to which condition or group a subject is assigned. Wiggins (1968) offers a thoughtful and thought-provoking discussion of four sources of unwanted variation in experimental studies, (the experimenter, the subjects, the manipulations, and the measurements) and three strategies for deling with them. Barber (1976) enumerates and illustrates several additional categories of unwanted effects, including those arising from the investigator, the data-analyst, and—not least—the choice of methodology. The main point of both Wiggins (1968) and Barber (1976) is that variation in the dependent (outcome) variable is more likely to be the effect of multiple independent variables than of a single one. The aim of design is to sort out the effects so the researcher can assess the respective variational contributions of the independent variables. Commonly overlooked are effects attributable to conceptualization; behavior or personal characteristics of the researcher or interviewer; subjects' motivation, history, and information or beliefs about research; situation realism; question form and sequencing; and the technical aspects of subject assignment and data-analysis.

Control of Variance

Let us now look at some of the techniques at the researcher's disposal to achieve internal and external validity. Design decisions concern the specifics of arranging observations and measurements so as to (1) provide (an) answer(s) to the research question(s), (2) maximize internal validity, and (3) maximize external validity. "The main technical function of research design is to *control variance* . . . the statistical principle . . . is: *Maximize systematic variance, control extraneous systematic variance, and minimize error variance.*"[16] By *control of variance* we mean taking into account all the factors which systematically contribute to the generation of individual differences in the outcome measures. A good design decision is one which incorporates a strategy that permits us to minimize risk in accepting an answer while maximizing payoff in utilizing the answer, where the possible "states of nature" have been identified.

It is obvious that in an experimental study you have much more latitude in controlling treatments and subject assignments so as to achieve these goals. However, even in quasi-experimental or nonexperimental studies it is possible to identify sources of variance; by incorporating suitable comparisons into the research plan you can greatly improve both internal and external validity. Hence, no matter what your proposed research type, the discussion that follows is important.

Systematic or experimental variance in the outcome is variance that can be attributed to the variable(s) associated with the research hypothesis. Control of this variance is accomplished by designing, planning, and executing the study so that the values of these variables are as different as possible on the comparison groups; thus, the importance of different values will be emphasized. Clearly, if you are able to manipulate or select treatments and conditions, you are more likely to be able to achieve control of systematic variance than if you have to take what you get in a "natural," "as is," or post facto situation; it is generally agreed that the manipulation or selection of treatments and conditions, and the presence of comparison groups, characterize an experimental study. For example, in a study of different methods of toilet-training young children, the adults must be carefully instructed and supervised so that each child receives only one clearly specified training, with no overlap. Because this is almost impossible to ensure in post facto situations—grandmothers *will* give advice!—such a study should be experimental.

Extraneous variance refers to unwanted systematic effects on the outcome, associated with variables whose effects are not the objects of the study. Six major techniques have been developed to reduce or eliminate extraneous variance.

1. Randomization in selecting subjects or units of study, and in assigning them to treatment or control groups, is a powerful technique which controls for all possible subject-related extraneous variance simultaneously. (It does not, of course, control systematic measurement, treatment, or experimenter error.) We will say a research plan has *strong control* if this technique is used, otherwise *weak* control; Campbell and Stanley (1963) refer to *true experimental designs* and *quasi-experimental designs*. The latter are those in which the

researcher can introduce something like experimental design into the scheduling of data-collection procedures but lacks strong control over scheduling of treatments. Spector (1981) points out that it is useful to think in terms of a continuum, from strict experimental designs to "as is" descriptive studies.

While randomization ideally permits you to ignore subject-related extraneous variance, it is foolish to assume that groups or subjects do in fact have a random distribution on all the variables in question. You must verify the assumption.

2. Holding the value of an extraneous variable constant means that the effect of that variable on the outcome variance will be the same across subjects, treatments, or whatever.[17] (In some sense, this is the opposite of randomization.) Thus, in an experimental study of different methods of toilet-training young children, you may suspect that the sex of the child affects the age of "success," so you would group the subjects by sex in calculating mean ages of success under different treatments. Of course, if all subjects are of the same sex, external validity is decreased.

3. Building an extraneous variable into the design (e.g., as a factor) allows you to inspect the effect of this source of extraneous variance. Thus, in the study mentioned above, you could make sex one of the independent variables.

4. Matching subjects on one or more variables you believe may cause unwanted effects is a commonly used method for controlling extraneous variance. This technique has several drawbacks. First, the choice of matching variables reflects a researcher bias, an a priori decision as to which variables are important, and thus introduces an additional untested conjecture. Second, successful matching requires a valid and reliable measurement of the matching variables. Third, a statistical regression effect may occur. Fourth, the need to discard subjects that do not fit the matching criteria may result in a costly sample. Even under relatively ideal matching circumstances, as in twin studies, it is still necessary to carry out random assignment to treatments or groups. (See Chapter 8, section on matched groups.)

5. Statistical control in the form of analysis of covariance, applied where subjects are selected and assigned randomly on certain specified variables, permits an analysis of effects with one or more other extraneous variables held constant. This technique (discussed in Chapter 12) combines the advantages of points 1 and 2 above. Thus, in the example mentioned above, handedness of child or age of mother might be used as a covariate.

6. Multiple measures of the outcome may be feasible. Multiple measures must have a high degree of intercorrelation and be comparably accurate. Once a proposition has been confirmed by more than one independent measurement, the uncertainty of interpretation is reduced. Multiple measurement is a powerful technique for exhibiting evidence in support of conclusions.[18]

Note that most of the preceding address extraneous variance due to subject variables. Further and more general discussion of sources of error can be found in Barber (1976), Plutchik (1974, Chapters 10 and 11), Wiggins (1968—strongly recommended), and Webb et al. (1966).

Error variance arises from random fluctuations including errors of measurement. Control of error variance can be accomplished by great care in carrying out procedures, use of properly valid and reliable instruments, meticulous regulation of conditions, and sample size sufficient to permit unpredictable errors to cancel each other. Unfortunately, if error variance is large it can drown the systematic variables just as static in a radio circuit drowns both the signal and any "hum."

Baseline measures of outcome obtained from a so-called control group to which no treatment has been applied make possible sharper comparisons of treatment effects. More generally, control of extraneous variance permits a clearer identification of treatment effects. While controlled designs are extremely powerful, they are sometimes restrictive and artificial so that findings are difficult to apply to a more complex reality. Nonetheless, controlled designs are the most desirable if the goal is the exhibition of clearly identified causal relationships: they typically incorporate clear comparison. Designs which reflect compromises in one or another aspect of control are widely used, particularly in field settings, whether for experimental or descriptive studies.

Good design makes possible the isolation of effects of the variables of interest." It is unrealistic to expect that a single piece of research will effectively answer all of the validity questions surrounding even the simplest causal relationship."[19] The presence of some confounding factors need not make your study entirely worthless, but rather suggests the need for caution in reporting and interpreting findings. References to earlier theoretical or empirical results may justify your confidence that one or more extraneous variables can safely be ignored. As a novice researcher, you may find it helpful to remember that design is simply a plan of study, and like any plan it represents an accommodation to practical exigencies. In general there is no unique correct design for the solution of a given problem. Moreover, many designs that look good in advance require modification while the study is in progress. The accounts in Hammond (1964), especially Coleman's, provide a number of examples, and the discussion is instructive.

We do not encourage an overemphasis on the formal aspect of the taxonomy of design.

The best way to approach design issues is to specify very clearly the theoretical basis for the study. The link between theory and research hypotheses is of the utmost importance: no design can be good, no matter how ingenious or elegant, if it is grounded in a muddle, nor can variables be specified if the underlying theory is confused.[20] Plan first, label afterwards; match one of the standard designs to your study (if possible), but never force your study to fit a standard design. Since you are the person most knowledgeable about the background of your problem-question and the variables to be considered, you are in the best position to decide whether your design will allow you to draw the conclusions you seek. At this stage it is important for you to exercise an informed judgment and to feel confident about your own decisions.

Common Sources of Invalidity in Practice[21]

The list of "limitations and delimitations" commonly found in a dissertation is an acknowledgment of possible sources of internal and external invalidity. While it is advisable to be straightforward in such matters, it is important to recognize that acknowledging an error is not the same as preventing or removing it.

Examples of errors that may intrude in all types of research include the following:

- Ineffectively operationalized constructs represent a great threat to the validity of results. Goodness of fit between constructs and operations, (see Chapter 4, section on operationalizing) is equally important in studies of all types. The quality of the observations and analysis are secondary to conceptualization of the definitions and the validity of the measurements.

- Incomplete or incorrect specification of plausible alternative (e.g., null) hypotheses will almost certainly cause difficulty in interpreting findings.

- Overreliance on the ceteris paribus ("everything else being equal") assumption. When control groups are not feasible, as in most descriptive studies, and the use of comparison groups cannot take into account all possible variables, it is necessary to exploit the ceteris paribus assumption. This may also permit extrapolation of the findings to situations other than that of the original study. Both internal and external validity are best ensured, however, by successive replications, particularly if similar groups are investigated by different researchers. Modifications of traditional experimental designs to the limitations of descriptive research are discussed at length in Cook and Campbell (1979).

- The nonrepresentativeness of "typical" cases can mislead the investigator into stereotyping the effects. This error may reflect improper selection of arena, or inadequate sample size, or incomplete randomization.

- Lack of base-line data makes meaningful comparisons impossible and may lead to artificial inflation or deflation of apparent effects.
- The Hawthorne effect occurs when the subjects respond not to the treatments but to novelty, the excitement or prestige of participation, experimental modification of the environment, or the knowledge that a study is being conducted. This last evidently can affect the outcome in a survey or field study. (Someone has observed that most progress in instruction and perhaps also in psychotherapy is achieved through the systematic exploitation of the Hawthorne effect!)
- The placebo effect arises when an inert stimulus elicits the same response as an active one; thus, the effects of an experimental treatment cannot be isolated. This effect arises mainly in experimental studies.
- Overfondness for a particular measuring instrument and its use for marginally appropriate research questions usually results in faulty studies. Measuring devices and design may require custom modification to suit the particular problem.
- The halo effect, a constant rating error, occurs when a subject consistently responds on the basis of a general impression or a vague attitudinal preset, rather than to the specific stimulus. This effect "is particularly strong in traits that are not clearly defined, not easily observable, and that are morally important."[22]
- Other rating errors may reflect the subjects' tendency to be consistently severe or consistently lenient.
- Poor mechanisms for recording evidence, sloppy or inconsistent coding, and other errors in handling data can seriously jeopardize an otherwise ingenious and important study.
- Failure to make appropriate modifications in standard data analysis procedures may give rise to false significance or false absence of significance, or erroneous parameter estimates.
- Post hoc errors, a form of faulty reasoning, reflect the assumption that because events occur in sequence they must be causally related.
- Without question, *you* pose a great danger to the validity of your own study. The "studying the researcher" effect is insidious and practically impossible to suppress once present. Investigator bias can create a self-fulfilling prophecy by affecting procedure or analysis in subtle ways. Prevention is the best strategy, and you will find an experienced researcher who is willing to look over your method and procedure to be your best ally.

In each research type, whether historical, descriptive or experimental, the researcher adapts the design criteria discussed in this chapter to the particular methods appropriate to the type. In the next chapter, we look at these types and their principal subtypes.

Notes

All studies referred to in this chapter can be found in the bibliography.

[1]"Many things difficult to design prove easy to performance." (Samuel Johnson, *The Rambler*, Chapter XVI).

[2]See Shulman's (1981) thoughtful and discursive essay, more general than its title.

[3]Such an error is reinforced by a misuse of such manuals of design as Winer (1971), or Myers (1979), which are concerned primarily with the statistical analyses that refer to various experimental designs.

[4]Two very simple but thought-provoking short essays are those of Stouffer (1970) and Zetterberg (1970).

[5]See Tukey and Wilk (1970).

[6]See Barnow (1973) or Bennett and Lumsdaine (1975, p. 314).

[7]W. N. Schoenfeld, Lectures, Queens College, City University of New York, 1974–1977; private communication, G. S. Fisch.

[8]Even though the term *treatment* originated in reports of experimental studies, it is widely used in more general contexts. We employ it to mean any condition, event, or experience which can be used to categorize subjects.

[9]This is not to be compared with the control of inquiry or observations, as discussed extensively in Nagel (1961); see our Chapter 1. Some authors prefer to speak of isolation of the study domain rather than the control of extraneous variables.

[10]See Zeisel (1968, p. 115) for comment on direct versus indirect control of treatment conditions. See also Barber (1976) for other discussions of problems arising in research with human subjects, and Simon (1978) for "obstacles in social science research."

[11]Nagel (1953, p. 502).

[12]This terminology was originally developed for the evaluation of experimental designs (see Campbell and Stanley, 1963, passim), but is no longer restricted to them.

[13]The following characterization reflects the point of view introduced in Chapter 4: The *internal validity* of a hypothesis is the number of its alternative hypotheses disproved. Hypotheses are disproved by observing the lack of association . . . between variations of the independent and dependent variables . . . The *external validity* of a hypothesis is the degree of similarity between the variation in the independent variables (and the interactions thereof) and the variation in the population variables. (Wiggins, 1968, pp. 390–391)

[14]Cook and Campbell (1979, pp. 83ff.) has a good discussion of this point, with examples.

[15]Campbell and Stanley (1963, pp. 5–6. Note these statements apply to historical and descriptive, as well as experimental, plans.

[16]Kerlinger (1973, p. 306; original emphasis).

[17]Langbein and Lichtman (1978) point out that so-called homogeneous grouping has serious hazards as a device for control of variance, mainly because of the difficulty of interpreting statistical findings. See especially pp. 39ff.

[18]Sullivan and Feldman (1979) is a useful introduction to the appropriate statistical procedures.

[19]Cook and Campbell (1979, pp. 82–83).

[20]The combination of faulty design with great care in sampling, measurement and analysis is often referred to as "the error of misplaced precision" or "Type III error."

[21]See also "Common Errors" section in our other chapters especially Chapters 2–4, and 6–9, and the "Mistakes Often Made" sections in each chapter in Borg and Gall (1979). Many of these are discussed in Barber (1976), Wiggins (1968), Webb et al., (1966—this is very entertaining as well as informative), Simon (1978), and Smith (1963).

[22]Kerlinger (1973, p. 549).

Additional Reading

Validity: Design
Considerations and General Issues

Barber (1976): sources of error, especially those attributable to the investigator's own intervention at the data-collection stage.

Borg and Gall (1979): sources of errors.

Campbell and Stanley (1963) and Cook and Campbell (1979): guidelines, clearly stated though perhaps rigid, for evaluating designs experimental and quasi-experimental.

Plutchik (1974): sources of error.

Ross and Smith (1968): classification of designs.

Wiggins (1968): many examples of studies seeking to describe error effects; superb bibliography.

Webb et al. (1966): many examples of reactive effects as sources of error.

Kerlinger (1973, pp. 382ff.): a good overview and summary of goals of design.

Kish (1959): interrelationship of problems of design and problems of data analysis; clear and simple.

Riecken and Boruch (1974): extensive discussion of treatment effects versus uncontrolled variance in Chapters 3–6.

Festinger and Katz (1953; 1966): readings on issues pertinent to research in a variety of settings.

Selltiz et al. (1976): Chapter 4 and Chapter 5 offer an overview of design considerations in both "causal" and "descriptive" studies.

Van Dalen and Meyer: general manual.

Fisher (1966)
Myers (1979) } manuals: designs and statistical modifications.
Winer (1971)

Cochran and Cox (1957)

Hersen and Barlow (1976), and Kazdin (1982): design issues in single-case studies.

Spector (1981): concise, highly readable summary of principles of experimental and nonexperimental design; description of widely-used designs.

Cox (1958): clear, nonstatistical; directed to experimentalists but of general interest.

6

Research Types

Introduction

This chapter provides an overview of each of the main types of research: historical, descriptive, and experimental. We will present a brief discussion of principal

1. characteristics,
2. subtypes, and
3. problems (pitfalls and errors)

of the types most commonly encountered in the social and behavioral sciences. The chapter also describes and compares

4. special procedures for data collection, and
5. special procedures for data analysis

associated with each type. Our goal is to orient you so that you can make efficient use of more detailed reference material. We make no effort to be prescriptive and no pretense to be exhaustive. Every social science discipline has manuals of methodology; excellent manuals are available for specific topics such as survey methods, interviewing, and questionnaire construction. See this chapter's reference list of additional readings, consult the bibliographies of recent publications, or consult your research mentor.

We also include suggested PERT-network sequences for planning the steps in descriptive and experimental studies. (For a longer detailed description of how to construct and use these PERT diagrams see Chapter 15, pp. 366–369.) Your individual needs will dictate appropriate modifications. We urge you to consider this framework for scheduling start times and deadlines.

In this chapter we also elaborate the classification scheme described in Chapter 5, by incorporating the goal of the study in addition to the nature of evidence and the possibility of control.

Nonexperimental Research Types: Historical

If the evidence you need to answer your problem-question is already in existence, then your research must be classified as *historical*. When a study is concerned with events of the past, this research type appears to be appropriate, but it is a mistake to suppose that the past must be far distant. Indeed, it is possible to investigate historically an occurrence at which one was actually present. The investigator does not intervene in these events, control, select, or manipulate them; does not observe them or measure them or in any other way, direct or indirect, participate in the generating of evidence.

Every study must contain to some degree an element of historical research in its review of the literature section. Therefore, all researchers must be at least minimally familiar with pertinent techniques. The fundamental purpose of all historical research is to reconstruct knowledge of the past systematically and objectively, by locating, collecting, evaluating, verifying, analyzing, and synthesizing evidence to establish facts and reach defensible conclusions in relation to particular hypotheses. Historical research resembles other types of research in that constructs must be formulated and operationalized; specific, testable hypotheses must be stated; conditions for acceptability (validity) of inferences must be specified, and all procedures used in data collection and analysis must be exhibited. Historical methodology concerns itself with the adaptation of these familiar steps to the particular subject matter.

The cliometric studies by Conrad and Myers (1964) of the profitability of slavery in the ante-bellum period, based on econometric analysis of contemporary records, provide an example of historical research. In *The Great Hunger* (1962), Woodham-Smith exhibited data collected from a wide variety of sources to support her implicitly stated hypotheses that the Irish famine and consequent social disorganization of the 1840s was more the outcome of deliberate British policy than of failure of the potato crops.

Evidence from historical sources may be of many kinds. However, we are primarily concerned with quantitative or quantifiable data to which statistical or deterministic analysis techniques can be applied. Written or printed documents may be official (e.g., government census data, birth records, student records, proclamations, minutes of proceedings) or personal (e.g., business records, letters, diaries). (Zweigenhaft [1970] used sign-out cards in a college library in his analysis of the relationship between signature size and status.) Photographs and audio and TV tapes constitute a growing wealth of material for researchers. Pictorial evidence, such as stamps and paintings, lies between documents and relics. The latter category includes a vast variety of "cultural debris" such as coins, utensils, machinery, human bones, monuments and buildings, and books inspected for form rather than content. Considerable ingenuity can be brought into play in discovering the existence and location of documents and in identifying potentially useful evidence, as in the analysis of composition of household garbage to infer patterns of food consumption.

No matter what the form of the evidence, it must be correctly identified as a *primary* or a *secondary source*. A document is a primary source if its author was the direct observer of the particular event, and a secondary source if the author is reporting the observations of others and so is one or more steps from the event. Primary sources may include official records, published statistical material, diaries, home movies, and artifacts of all kinds, whereas newspaper accounts based on interviews with eyewitnesses are secondary sources. Oral history, accounts by individuals of events they observed (or created), can be an excellent primary source. In general, secondary sources are less reliable, because at each removal from the event, there is an opportunity for biases and errors to enter, so the difficulties of evaluating validity and the danger of erroneous interpretations increase in proportion. Whenever possible, primary sources should be used. (This means documents should be studied in their original language.)

We assume that before deciding to undertake an historical study you will have acquired the necessary skills and will be sufficiently familiar with the area of investigation to decide, on a preliminary basis, what constitutes evidence. If you are completely untrained in historiography and have no access to training, it is unreasonable to expect to produce a respectable piece of research.

While this book cannot deal effectively with the range of techniques for collecting evidence, one aspect of procedure does deserve special mention: your records of sources. It is a matter of the utmost importance that your notes be complete and organized with sufficient flexibility, so that you can easily retrieve and rearrange information. Chronological sequences and logical sequences may differ. Items which are classified under several headings should be coded in such a way that their classification can be readily recalled. Set up your system before everything gets out of hand, and keep it up to date. Index if necessary. Do not count on being able to return to sources to check dates, etc. An experienced researcher can be very helpful in advising you.

The evaluation of historical evidence must be concurrent with its collection. There are two types of historical evaluation.

External criticism is directed towards the determination of authenticity, that is, validation of attribution. Such issues as assigning a correct author, place of origin, and date to a document or relic and identifying forgeries, restorations, and amendments come under this heading. Techniques as disparate as radioactive carbon dating of artifacts and linguistic analysis of typical naming, spelling, and grammatical forms may be brought to bear. Strong resemblances to already authenticated evidence, or corrobating information from other sources, are reassuring.

Internal criticism is concerned with the accuracy and relevance of the evidence, that is, validation of content. Acquire a judgment concerning the "author" of the evidence: his truthfulness, his biases, his possible motives, his level of prior knowledge or training, his competence as an observer or recorder; thus, an unskilled tool maker forms an object which gives a misleading impression of the level of technology. Internal criticism may address the accuracy and completeness of the reporting and recording of numerical data; unfortunately, it is very hard to evaluate old measurements. The usefulness of each piece of evidence as a basis for inference, that is, its validity, should be verified by every means available, before proceeding with any synthesis.

Identifying an individual, determining the occurrence of an event, and ascertaining appropriate context, will in general require both types of historical criticism.

It is important to keep in mind the role of sampling. Many aspects of conventional sampling procedure are out of the question in historical research: the sampling frame must be inferred (indeed, that may be the goal of the study); the surviving documents or objects may be seriously nonrepresentative of the population (this is true of diaries, which are written by literate individuals, or clothing, which tends to be preserved only if it is valuable, i.e., expensive and made for special occasions); in general, very complicated self-selection processes take place before you gain access to the evidence.[1] You must be aware of the biases that may be introduced simply by differential survival rates. On the other hand, where large masses of documents or phyical debris or records of many individuals or material spanning a period of years are available, you may be able to develop and follow a sampling procedure which will ensure that the items you select are representative of the populations from which they are drawn.[2] Your best source of guidance will be discussion with an experienced researcher.

It is useful to point out that not all historical research deals with the distant past. Carr-Hill and Stern's study, *Crime, The Police and Criminal Statistics* (1979), applies econometric methods to official data collected during 1961, 1966, and 1971. Most of the demographic studies of factors affecting mortality rates and increased life-span such as that of Lyon et al. (1978) are based on recent census or life-insurance company data. Warner's (1962) analysis of the growth of Boston 1870–1900 makes use of sources including local, state, and federal statistics. Much work in econometrics, sociometrics and quantitative political science is essentially historical, according to the classification model we are using. Researchers in these fields must utilize quantitative data already gathered by others, such as government agencies; cliometricians then subject these data to sophisticated statistical and mathematical analysis. If conditions as to the level of measurement, number of items, etc. are met, then any of the usual descriptive statistics such as measures of central tendency, dispersion, and association can be computed, and both tabular and graphical displays can be prepared. Regression equations can be computed if appropriate. The difficulty lies in interpretation and in any inferences, such as predictions or projections. The kinds of extrapolations from sample to sample or from sample to universe which are an almost inevitable part of the statistical analysis of experimental data must be done with the greatest caution: uncertainties as to reliability of historical evidence, presence of bias, etc. diminish the precision of any estimate. Any conclusion as to the existence of a strong functional relationship must be qualified in two ways, first by an acknowledgment of the limitations of the evidence, and second by an explicit statement of the ceteris paribus assumption.[3] Since the researcher has no power to control variables or conditions except, perhaps, statistically, his/her only recourse may be to assume they have no significant effect.

In our classification, studies which use the historical method but are not further differentiated are labeled *historiographical*.[4] This category includes a wide variety of research problems and constitutes the bulk of the historical literature.

In *causal-comparative* studies the strategy is to "tease out" possible causal relationships by identifying the existence of effects and then searching back through the data for plausible causal factors. Such a study is called (ex) post facto because the data must be taken as found, that is, after the fact, with no opportunity to arrange conditions or manipulate variables. Perhaps the best-known example of a causal-comparative analysis of available data is Durkheim's study of suicide. More recent examples include Lyon et al.'s analysis (1978) of Utah deaths attributed to several categories of cardiovascular disease, and Farley and Hansel's (1981) test of the Gibbs-Erickson model of urban crime rates. The analysis by Jacobson (1978) of campaign finance records and available interview data led to an elegant regression analysis and a clear functional relationship. To reach sound conclusions, the investigator must consider all the other plausible rival hypotheses which might account for the identified effects. In such studies there is a real danger of confusing correlations with causality.

Another type of study which properly comes under the heading of the historical method is *content analysis*.[5] A representative sample of documents (or other material) is selected and examined for similarities and differences in substance, style or symbolic content. Originally developed for investigations of mass communications, content analysis is adaptable also to the study of linguistic forms, responses to projective tests, characteristic features in artifacts, etc. Note also that interview data can be treated as historical for purposes of content analysis. Systematic sampling and classification are crucial in content analysis. Examples are a recent study of racism and sexism in history textbooks,[6] Dziurzynski's (1977) classification of advertising appeals in TV commercials, and Sedelow's (1967) analysis of two differing English translations of a Russian work on military strategy.

Replicability in historical research does not refer to the replication of events (as in an experimental study), which is usually impossible, but to the replication of procedures and analysis. Evidence must be preserved and the basis for its classification made explicit: notes must be made in such a way that another researcher can identify the characteristics subjected to analysis, and all findings and conclusions must be clearly referred to the data on which they were based.

In view of the foregoing, the criteria of internal and external validity can be applied to research using available data.[7] Here, *internal validity* means that the evidence makes alternative hypotheses implausible; an important consideration in evaluating internal validity is the quality of internal and external criticism. *External validity* is reflected in the effectiveness of the conjecture to predict subsequent or current effects, or effects in other places or with other subjects.

The remark, usually attributed to Santayana, that those who do not learn from history are condemned to repeat it,[8] implies that by understanding the past we will be better able to predict and modify future events. However, the analysis of historical evidence can be a scholarly end in itself, whether or not the conclusions have predictive power.

Errors in historical studies commonly reflect one or more of the following: (These are, of course, not unique to such studies.)

1. Insufficient evidence available to provide an adequate test of the conjectures.
2. Excessive reliance on secondary sources.
3. Inadequate internal or external criticism: overlooking such issues as inspection of terminology, definitions, limitations in the collection of the original material.
4. A poorly defined problem or weak formulation of hypotheses; vagueness or excessive breadth of scope.
5. Intrusion of personal research bias.
6. Categorization of statistical data which is incompatible with the analysis.[9]
7. Overall lack of skills in the component tasks or inadequate resources (time, money, personnel) to carry them out.

Planning the sequence of steps required for a historical study can be particularly difficult because of the well-known tendency for an item of evidence to lead in an unanticipated direction, so you may be unable to assess time requirements in advance. It is wise to over- rather than underbudget time, and to allow generously for delays in gaining access to documents and other evidence.

Nonexperimental Research Types: Descriptive

If the evidence you need does not already exist, but the problem does not permit either strong or weak control of conditions and groups, (i.e., you cannot assign subjects) your only choice is a descriptive study. *Descriptive* (nonhistorical, nonexperimental) research has as its goal the investigation of the characteristics of a given "as is" universe or sample of interest. The researcher seeks such measures as parameter values, distributions of attributes, differences between groups, associations between variables, and communality or clustering of variables. Descriptive studies are rarely definitive, but they often exhibit important patterns or relationships.

Throughout this section we list examples drawn from many areas of the social and behavioral sciences.

The term *descriptive* can be used in its literal sense: describing situations or events, without any except incidental inferences or predictions. A study so labelled would be unlikely to use data collected by others except as a basis for comparison of findings. Some authors broaden the term, as we do, to include all but historical or experimental research. Others regard *descriptive* as synonymous with a particular method such as survey research. The survey method is used for a large proportion of all descriptive research. *Survey research* is characterized by the collection of evidence from a carefully selected sample of the population under study using interviews, usually structured by an instrument of some kind such as a schedule, form, or scale, and/or questionnaires. While available evidence (e.g., records and observational techniques) are also employed, the heaviest reliance is on self-report data. Uniformity of procedures and meticulousness in record-keeping are essential, as are a flexible approach to data-analysis and a reasonably cautious interpretation of findings.

> The survey or field method studies the effects of manipulations of social forces not under the control of the investigator. The major controls are statistical rather than experimental. In this approach, sample design is a crucial factor; otherwise there is little basis for the interpretation of the statistical evidence. Moreover, the measurement of many more factors is necessary than in laboratory experimentation. The laboratory can exclude or hold factors constant by direct manipulation. The field study cannot and so must be able to factor out the effect of a large number of potentially relevant variables. . . .Thus, survey methodology includes any set of quantitative measurements taken of people in their natural habitat.[10]

We will consistently use the term *descriptive* in its broader meaning. We distinguish four main categories, with several subheadings, within the descriptive research type:

1. *Longitudinal studies*: time is an independent variable and changes over time in other variables are the object of investigation:

    A. Panel, intracohort trend or follow-up studies
    B. Cross-sectional studies
    C. Projection studies
2. *Case and generalized case studies*: these are comprehensive and/or intensive investigation of one, or a few disaggregated, individual(s) or social situation(s):
    A. Individual case studies
    B. Group and community studies
    C. Ethnographic studies
3. *Correlational studies*: these exhibit and analyze concomitant variation in subjects selected as representative:
    A. Imputed variable studies
    B. Functional relations studies
4. *System studies*: these make comparisons and identify patterns in subjects selected as representative:
    A. Process analyses
        i. Activity analyses
        ii. Time, method, and motion studies
        iii. Operations research
    B. Structure analyses
        i. Evaluation studies
        ii. Component analyses

This classification is based on the purpose or object of the study, not on methodology. We introduce this vocabulary to suggest that each of these approaches is more or less useful in answering a particular research question. As we have stated before, a proper formulation of the problem is essential before an appropriate research design can be selected. By examining the purposes and special features of each research subtype we may shed some light on your decision.

1. LONGITUDINAL STUDIES

When the purpose of the research is to investigate patterns and sequences of growth and/or change as a function of time, it can be classified as longitudinal.[11]

A. *Panel or intracohort trend studies* begin with a sampling of specific population (cohort) of subjects and follow them over a long period of time. A good example of a panel study is the research of White (1952) who has studied "lives in progress" of several Ivy League graduates over a period of years. Vaillant (1979) has studied the same group of Harvard men at intervals for nearly 40 years, concerning himself with the relationship between their mental and physical health. Terman (1975) has followed the development of exceptionally bright children into adulthood, for more than 40 years. The study of Thornton and Freedman (1979), described in Chapter 2, followed a panel of adult women over the period 1962–1977. A related subtype samples repeatedly over time from the same population: the study of help-seeking behavior, by Veroff et al. (1981) is an example of this. *Follow-up studies* examine a set of subjects and then examine them again at a specified place and time. (Sometimes the follow-up was not designed as a part of the original study.) Typical are the studies carried out by colleges in which a follow-up of graduates, after five or ten years, is conducted to see how "success" is related to performance in earlier course work and to expressed attitudes and goals. Many investigations of the outcomes of instruction, of medical treatment, or of catastrophes have a follow-up component to permit an assessment of long-term effects, for instance, examinations of soldiers exposed to Agent Orange in Vietnam. The recent *Middletown Families* (Caplow et al. 1982) is an example of a follow-up community study. *Follow-up studies* are typically used in the process of test-construction in order to establish predictive validity: subjects may be given an aptitude test in computer science, then taught selected computer skills and given an opportunity to practice. The subjects are then tested, after some interval, for mastery. If those who scored high in aptitude also score high in mastery, and vice versa, we say the first test is valid.

By their nature, panel or cohort studies (these labels reflect differences in the sampling approach,[12]) are generally unsuitable for doctoral dissertations, because they require a long period of time and frequent re-interviews or observations.

B. *Cross-sectional studies*[13] start by specifying a sequence of steps or stages in a process. Different cohorts are sampled, usually at the same point in time, to provide information about the respective stages; this means that a longitudinal study is "collapsed." Typically more subjects can be included but fewer factors can be investigated than in a panel or cohort study. Gould's (1978) analysis of adult life stages is based on cross-sectional interviews.

C. *Projection studies* combine a longitudinal approach and reliance on historical data, and thus really lie halfway between historical and descriptive. Evidence concerning past events is collected, analyzed, and extrapolated to a prediction of present (and future) events.[14] This means that the populations sampled at different points in time are not necessarily the same. Typical of this class of study are the forecasts of demand in different industries, projections of future costs of hospital care, and predictions of urban growth based on a life-cycle theory of cities. Time-series analysis techniques may be very useful. Glenn (1977) points out that almost all panel or cohort studies require the use of some available data, at least for baseline purposes.

Certain difficulties are endemic in longitudinal research:

• The amount of time required in longitudinal research requires reliance on different observers and limits feasible samples; maintaining continuity can become a burden to the researcher.

- Study subject mortality may be high.
- Sampling from stable populations to avoid subject mortality frequently results in bias.
- Once a longitudinal study is underway, no improvements in technique can be made without damaging continuity; hence, emphasis on planning is very heavy.
- Cross-sectional and intracohort studies can confuse differences between stages due to development, and differences due to history variables.
- The base line information needed (e.g., for projection studies) may be unavailable.
- All these types are vulnerable to confounding (see Glenn 1979) and to unpredictable factors. They depend heavily on a ceteris paribus assumption. Nonetheless, if you are asking, What are the patterns of growth or change, their rates, directions, sequences and the interrelated factors that may affect these characteristics? longitudinal types are appropriate.

2. CASE AND GENERALIZED CASE STUDIES

When the goal of the research is to study intensively the background, current status, and environmental interactions of a particular unit, or of multiple disaggregated units, it can be classified as a case or generalized case study. The unit may be an individual, a group, an institution, a community, or an entire culture. It is useful to conceptualize a continuum of unit size, from the individual subject to the ethnographic study. Case and generalized case studies can be extremely useful as preliminaries to major investigations: because they are intensive, they may bring to light the variables, processes, and relationships that deserve more extensive attention. Often they are the source of hypotheses for further research. In addition, these studies provide anecdotal evidence to illustrate more generalized findings. Typically, an effort is made to maximize the number of variables under consideration. It is difficult to label as "experimental" any study with only one or two subjects because of the impossibilty of achieving strong control, notwithstanding the manipulation of conditions. Note that a collection of case studies is not, strictly, a case study. However, if the cases are not aggregated, it is convenient to place a study of several cases under this heading.

A. *Individual Case studies* involve the selection of a single subject and an in-depth investigation either of the entire life cycle or of a segment emphasizing specific factors. Often the individual case study, or a collection of case studies, is used to define the "typical" case.[15] Well-known examples of the former include Jones' (1924) classic laboratory study of deconditioning (extinction), Trinkhaus's (1982) study of a single Neanderthal skull, and Bachrach et al.'s (1965) study of an anorectic, and, of the latter, Piaget's (1969) investigations of cognitive growth and Levinson's (1978) studies of life stages. A case study should focus on a subject that is either very representative or extremely atypical.

B. *Group and Community studies* extend the case study to several subjects who can be classified together into a distinctive unit or group within the larger society. Examples of group studies include Rohrer et al.'s (1960) investigation of New Orleans Negroes,[16] Bernard's (1966) study of women faculty members, Helson's (1980) study of "creative" women mathematicians, and Crane's (1969) clever sociometric analysis of the "invisible college". Crucial to any successful group study is the definition of the group, which separates it from the general population in such a way that another scientist following the same criteria would arrive at the same group membership. Often, as in Rubinstein's (1973) study of an urban police force, there is an explicit statement of generalizability.

Community studies examine a complete social unit that functions within a culture. It may be regional, local, or institutional, or the community may be that of shared interests or concerns. Examples include Srole et al.'s (1977) study of mental health in Manhattan; Mayhew's (1851) classic work on the London underclass; Sternlieb et al.'s (1971) analysis of housing patterns in Princeton, N.J.; Poll's (1962) account of the Hassidim of Williamsburg; and last but not least, the Lynd's classic *Middletown* studies (1929, 1937) and their follow-up (Caplow et al. 1982). Once again, the specification of the community to be studied must be clear and replicable. The line between group and community studies may be blurred; we do not regard the distinction as particularly important here.

C. *Ethnographies*, or studies of entire cultures, are exemplified by such anthropological classics as Gorer's (1955) investigation of British character. Ethnic studies such as those of Billingsley (1968) and Sklare (1971) fall between this category and the one preceding.

In understanding any case or generalized case study it is most important correctly to identify the unit(s) of study and the characteristics, relationships, and processes that are to be investigated. The selection of the particular units is another issue needing serious attention. Frequently, the observer must become an active participant in the study unit, so participant-observer techniques are called for. In addition, many community and group studies make extensive use of available data, for base-line, comparison, or other purposes.

Typical errors and difficulties encountered in case and generalized case studies include the following:

- Cases are incorrectly identified as typical.
- Cases are incorrectly identified as atypical.
- The investigator, by his presence or actions, affects the behavior of the observed unit but does not allow for this in the report, or he interprets the observations while recording them.
- Observers are insufficiently trained, or their biases are intrusive, so observations are unreliable.
- Data are insufficient for reliable generalizations or conclusions.
- Baseline data are unavailable.

If it is understood that the findings will not be definitive (and may not have generalized applicability), but are the basis for conjecture and further research, the case study technique can be very effective. It often happens that there is no alternative: an examination of the Amish, for example, must be a community study in the field setting. Again, where very few units of analysis are available, the generalized case study is the only choice.

It is important not to confuse the choice of a case study, in which the characteristics of the particular individual or community are the issue, and the selection of an arena: Every study has to be conducted in some setting and with some population! Even if the case or set of cases is selected to be typical, the emphasis in the case study is on the characteristics of the particular case; thus, external validity is not of great importance. Compare, for example, a study of the so-called "Seven Sisters" women's colleges, and a study of a dozen independent women's colleges, selected to be representative, in which findings are expected to be generalizable.

The case-study type of research has a highly reputable history so you should have few qualms in exploiting such a design if it is permissible. Unfortunately many doctoral committees are strongly biased against the case study approach—perhaps because of the low external validity and the absence of inferential statistics—so you should check carefully with your mentors before undertaking even a preliminary proposal.

3. CORRELATIONAL STUDIES

Correlational studies are similar to causal-comparative studies except that the data do not already exist. If the purpose of the research is an examination of the extent to which variation in one or more factors is associated with variation in one or more other factors, and the nature of this association, then the choice should be a correlational study. The goal, ideally, is the construction of a model in which the values of certain variables, identified as dependent, are determined wholly or in part by the values of another set of (independent) variables. More generally, this category has as its goal the description of concomitant variation. The study is not necessarily correlational in our sense just because a statistical measure of association is computed.

The association may be incidental, that is, not the main interest of the investigator. Moreover, in longitudinal studies, elapsed time is always present as a variable and is usually associated with differences in the outcome variables, but these studies are not classified as correlational.

Two subtypes are commonly encountered.

A. *Imputed variable studies* attempt to relate the nature and strength of human behavior or perceptions to inferred (imputed) hypothetical construct variables. Examples abound in the marketplace. The color, size, and shape of a package were examined in Dichter's (1964) careful study of the relationship between these characteristics and the (imputed) desire to purchase the commodity. Also under this heading should be placed such work as Frieze's (1975) analysis of women's attitudes towards success and failure, Latané and Darley's (1969) investigation of bystander apathy, and Karacki and Toby's (1962) analysis of the possible causes of gang delinquency. The conclusion of an imputed variable study may be that some underlying variable must exist, or that such a variable, if already identified, is strongly associated with some observed effect. It seems to us that many scaling studies which create a measure of a hypothetical construct, fall into this class. (See Chapter 4, pp. 68–74 passim.) Once the hypothetical construct variable is shown to "exist", it can be used in a system analysis.

B. *Functional relations studies* have as their object ascertaining the precise form of the relationship between variables. Examples include the Gluecks' (1956) investigation of the association of physique and delinquency, several efforts to relate socioeconomic status to incidence of the chronic diseases,[17] Jencks' (1973) monumental survey seeking factors which contribute to social and economic inequality, Parson's (1982) analysis of factors which contribute to differences in mathematics achievement in boys and girls, and Bell et al.'s (1981) Kinsey Institute Study of the origins of sexual preference. Many investigators hope to use their findings predictively in planning social interventions, school programs, and so forth, as well as in understanding complex events.

Correlational studies may be concerned with the interrelationships between independent variables, and/or the degree of relationship and the percentage of dependence attributable to independent variables. They can handle typological variables, or several variables in a realistic setting. Longitudinal studies such as the Rosetta, PA investigation of factors in heart disease (Stout et al., 1964), may have a correlational analysis. By and large, statistical analyses make use of such multivariate techniques as multiple regression, factor analysis, canonical correlation and discriminant-function analysis. *Path analysis*, which strings together functional relations, is frequently applied, as in Parson (1982) and Bell et al. (1981), with the goal of identifying possible causal connections.

The major pitfall of all correlational studies is the confusion of correlation and causation. Spurious interpretations may be difficult to avoid; even a true functional relation need not imply causality; for instance, several highly correlated variables may have a common cause, unsuspected by the researcher, yet none of the studied variables will be a cause of the others. Typical errors found in correlational studies include:

- Study is designed to exploit available data rather than data which will answer a question of real interest, because the power of multivariate techniques is seductive.
- Conjectured functional relations and/or causal sequences are not based on sound theory.
- Imputed variables reflect lack of parsimony or other defects in theory or definition.
- Intuitively plausible variables are selected, but no theoretical rationale for the expected relationship(s) is developed.
- Different groups may differ in so many pertinent variables that comparison is meaningless.
- Number of subjects is insufficient for the number of variables.
- Subgroups may lack homogeneity.
- Significance or importance of a correlation is not established.
- Inappropriate correlational techniques yield misleading or even meaningless outcomes.

In Chapters 11–14 we discuss correlational and multivariate analysis of data, and their applications, at greater length. Correlational research is very popular, since with suitable measurements and sound theory, it offers the potential to identify the path of causality.

4. SYSTEM STUDIES

When the purpose of a study is to collect precise and detailed information; make comparisons; identify or justify current patterns, conditions or practices; and determine what others are doing or saying in the face of the same or similar problems, it should be classified as system research.

An interesting aspect of the systems approach is the underlying assumption that living and nonliving systems may exhibit goal-directed behavior and have the capacity to accept information in order to correct their performance (feedback); that is, decision making is identified as a process outcome. Nonetheless, the basic study method is most often a survey of the interrelated components and an examination of how they act together. Systems research thus includes both "static" and "dynamic" analyses.

Much of traditional descriptive research can be placed under the heading of system study; in particular, when the question is "how is the behavior of interrelated parts directed towards a goal? How does the system use information to redirect its behavior?"

There are two principal subtypes of system studies, each further subdivided:

A. *Process analyses* are concerned primarily with dynamic aspects of the system under study: for example, analyses of a sequence of planned changes in an organization, where the criteria for success of each step in the sequence are formulated in terms of the outcomes of the preceding steps. The essential difficulty to be overcome in a process analysis is that the characteristics of a process may not be directly observable but must be inferred from a sequence of observations each made at a fixed point in time.

i. *Activity analyses* study various activities of a group in order to determine how well the group meets its objectives for these activities. Examples are Leontieff's (1966) large-scale input-output analysis for the U.S. and other nations, which tells us which [economic] sectors must be enhanced in order to achieve targeted growth and permit balanced economic development; and the self-examinations carried out by many American universities in the 1970s to see whether programs and management were consonant with the objectives of contemporary higher education. Activity analysis has been extensively utilized in economics but little in other social science disciplines.

ii. *Time, methods, and motion studies* have as their objective the optimization of human energy expenditure in a production process. The popular conception of an efficiency expert, stopwatch and clipboard in hand, overlooks the wide use of such methods and procedures as interviews, questionnaires, and observational recording devices. The fundamental work on time, methods, and motions was done by Taylor (1911) and Gilbreth (1919); in recent years the profession of industrial engineering has exploited techniques of survey research.

iii. *Operations research* examines the operations of a system and identifies their optimal state. It is often used for maximizing profit or sales, minimizing costs, etc. Examples include Singer's (1972) study of the optimal number of organisms to occupy a specified environment, and an analysis of the best allocation of an advertising budget to the various media.[18] In Chapter 15 we discuss several of the mathematical techniques extensively used in this relatively new research approach, which remains underutilized.

B. *Structure analyses* seek to describe static aspects of the system under study: how the system fits together, which parts are connected to each. A study comparing friendship networks among urban and suburban women thus exemplifies the effort to relate variables associated with place of residence or lifestyle, and variables associated with personality traits or interpersonal behavior. Investigations of the *outcomes* of dynamic processes (rather than of the steps in the processes themselves) can properly be placed under this heading; in contrast, process analyses focus on the variables affecting the steps or their sequence.

i. *Evaluation studies* fall between activity and structure analyses. Evaluation studies assume the existence of specified precursor events whose outcomes or effects must be measured and evaluated; thus, they often (but not necessarily) accompany large-scale social programs. Federal and state agencies carry out such studies to determine impact and effectiveness of new regulations. Whatever the nature of the precursor event(s), three basic steps by the researcher are essential: (1) state the expected outcomes of the precursor event(s) in observable, that is, behavioral, terms; (2) specify the procedures and techniques designed to implement these outcomes; (3) specify outcome measures, feedback devices, and decision criteria which will permit assessment of actual outcomes in terms of expected outcomes.[19] A typical example of a descriptive evaluation study is Stanley's (1976) report on special fast-progress mathematics classes.[20] Note that if the precursor event utilizes weak or strong control, the analysis of outcomes, while it may use, for example, survey methodology, should be classified as experimental rather than descriptive research.

ii. *Component analyses* seek to solve the problems of how components of a system work individually and interactively. The arena for such a study can be the human body, an individual's personality, a family, an industrial payroll, a specified social group, a government agency, or the world economy. Examples that can be placed under this heading include Goode's (1956) study of divorce as an aspect of kinship systems; Coleman's (1961) and Gottlieb and Hodgkins' (1963) analyses of the structure and functions of high-school social groups; the many studies of illness behavior;[21] Yankelovich's (1981) analysis of the effects of recent social changes; the many efforts to identify and measure sources of stress;[22] Coleman et al's (1957) study of diffusion of medical information; Bott's (1955) analysis of urban family structure; Caudill and Plath's (1966) investigation of Japanese family structure based on sleeping locations; Duncan and Duncan's (1978) research in social roles and sex-typing; and various social stratification studies. Many component analysis studies effectively utilize survey research technique, in conjunction with deterministic or probabilistc data analysis procedures. Various analytic methods make it possible to describe the relationships of the system's component parts in mathematical form.

Sociometry, for example, is basically the application of the mathematical subspecialty graph theory to the study of social networks:[23] the set of interactions among members of a family, or between members of a teaching team, or among groups in society. Any of the data-collection procedures described in Chapter 7 can be used, but the focus is specific and the analysis is correspondingly directed.

Critics of structure analysis-oriented research have pointed out that it is difficult to give the findings a time and process perspective, stability and structure maintenance (i.e., the status quo) are overemphasized, and unsystematic effects such as deviance and conflict are overlooked or poorly dealt with.

Descriptive research must be carefully planned. The PERT network shown in Figure 6.1 can be utilized to make the many stages in a typical project much less onerous. (See Chapter 15 section on PERT networks for explanation of how to use these diagrams.)

By far the most serious error in descriptive research is the wholesale inclusion of large numbers of variables without a clearly stated rationale, on the assumption that the conjectures that guide the analysis will come out in the wash. As in all studies, there is no substitute for sufficient thought, far in advance of data-collection, directed towards the identification of important variables and the clear formulation of guiding hypotheses. The strength of descriptive research is the strength of social and behavioral science methodology in general: the possibility it offers for the investigation of very complex situations with many variables only a few of whose values can be controlled or assigned. So long as your goal is to exhibit patterns, differences, or comparisons, the descriptive type can serve you well. Unfortunately, exact formal models, whether of association or causality, are difficult to construct except on the basis of measurements obtained under controlled conditions. Thus, the experimental type is more likely to yield useful findings *if* it can be employed in your arena.

Experimental Research Types

If the goal of your study is the identification and investigation of possible causal relationships between variables, *and* if you can control by selection or manipulation the values of the variables whose effects you wish to measure and also assign subjects to different groups on which these variables have distinct values, then your choice may be an *experimental research* design. To many people, *science* means knowledge obtained using the experimental method. Characteristic of an experiment is that the investigator exposes one or more "experimental groups" to one or more values of the conjectured causal (independent) variable(s), while a "control group" is exposed to a baseline value; the groups are then compared on the measures of the conjectured effect(s) (i.e., dependent variable[s]). Thus, experiments are manufactured events and may be quite simple or extraordinarily complex. Causal inferences are based on evidence of concomitant variation,[24] absence of effects in the control group, and the rigid exclusion of other factors as possible determinants of the effects. Ideally, the experimenter is able to achieve a high degree of

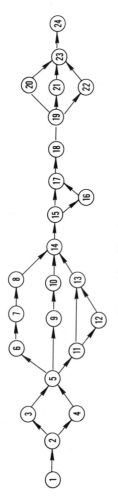

Event Identification

1. Start Project
2. Complete Objective
3. Complete Data Paradigm
4. Complete Hypotheses
5. Start Item Construction
6. Start Universe Definition
7. Start Sampling
8. Start Sample Selection
9. Start Tryout
10. Start Final Form
11. Start Interviewer Selection
12. Complete Administrative Procedures
13. Complete Schedules
14. Start Field Interview
15. Start Data Coding
16. Complete Follow-up
17. Start Tabulation
18. Start Statistical Tests
19. Complete Tests
20. Complete Interpretation
21. Complete Tables
22. Complete Charts
23. Start Narrative
24. Complete Narrative

FIGURE 6.1 Network for descriptive research project. (Source: Cook, 1966.)

control over sources of both extraneous systematic and random error variance; thus, conclusions can be strongly stated with great confidence. Effects attributable to each independent variable can be identified and interactions of selected combinations of independent and/or classification variables can be investigated with the help of statistical techniques (see Chapters 12–14).

In practice, the arrangement of experimental and control conditions, the selection and assignment of subjects, and the analysis of measurements on the classification, independent (manipulated) and dependent (outcome) variables, require a number of interlocking decisions. Trade offs involving internal validity (Did the experimental treatment make the difference in this specific instance?), external validity (In what ways is the conclusion generalizable?), and practical considerations are almost inevitable.

Unfortunately, there are many objections, both theoretical and practical, to the use of experimental methods in social and behavioral science research, and many impediments to their implementation.

- Almost every social science problem of interest involves too many variables to control feasibly, but the alternative, which is to restrict the number of variables, leads to an artificial situation which is neither useful nor interesting.[25]
- In effect, experimentalists are interested only in the variations they themselves create,[26] and the criteria they impose are confining and unproductively rigid.
- Ethical and political considerations may prevent the manipulation of conditions and assignment of subjects which are needed to isolate the effects under study.[27]
- In many proposed experiments, particularly those carried out in field rather than laboratory settings, the achievement of strong experimental control is impossible. Most authors identify random selection of subjects from the population to which extrapolation will be made, and the random assignment of subjects to treatment groups, as the sine qua non of the true (strongly controlled) experiment. To the extent that only weak control is possible, the resulting *quasi experiment* may lack internal validity, the task of the researcher is to separate the effects of treatment from those due to other (uncontrolled) independent variables.

  Keep in mind that true (strong) experimental designs lie at one end of a continuum, along which it is also possible to locate the various quasi- (weak) experimental designs, and, at the other end, the nonexperimental types. To some critics, being "quasi-experimental" is like being "a little bit pregnant." The label is much less important, however, than the extent to which safeguards on internal validity, in the particular study, allow the desired inferences to be made.[28]

- The agricultural models of experimental design, on which most statistical procedures are based, are basically unsuitable for social and behavioral studies, because the former make no allowance for canonical variables or dynamic processes, which may be crucial in the latter.

There is substantial difference of opinion among authoritative writers on the relative importance of artificiality and imprecision. In applications involving human subjects in the real world, the experimental approach is not often usable because of the restrictions on availability, cost, setting, time, behavior, etc. In the right circumstances, experiments are valuable, and large-scale experimental evaluations of social innovations can be most useful in determining future policy.

For analyses of the most widely used true experimental and quasi-experimental designs according to the internal and external validity criteria listed in Chapter 5, see the reference lists for Chapters 5 and 6. Some of this material is summarized in two charts (Figure 6.2 and Table 6.1); the first illustrates the eight best-known experimental designs, and the second systematically lists their potential weaknesses.

The literature of all the social and behavioral sciences is replete with reports of studies that use the experimental method.

- Sherif and Sherif's (1956) study of intergroup rivalry and level of conflict in a boy's summer camp.
- Isen and Levin's (1972) investigation of the relationship between a person's affective state and subsequent helpfulness to others.
- Travers and Milgram's (1969) network analysis of chains of acquaintance.
- Any F.D.A.-mandated studies of drug effectiveness and side-effects.
- Schachter and Singer's (1962) study of the response to a drug when information as to its possible effect is provided.
- Mithaug and Burgess's (1969) study of development of social cooperation.
- Coutts and Montgomery's (1980) study, described in Chapter 2, designed to test a proposed arousal model of interpersonal intimacy.
- The Transitional Aid Research Project which attempted to reduce recidivism in ex-felons in two Southern states by providing employment and support services.[29]
- Milgram's (1974) study of obedience behavior, mentioned earlier.
- Horner's (1968) analysis of "motivation to avoid success" (an imputed variable).
- Riecken and Boruch's (1974) *Social Experimentation* which contains in its appendix a large number of abstracts of experimental studies classified under nine different headings as diverse as fertility control, criminal reform, and problems of data-collection.

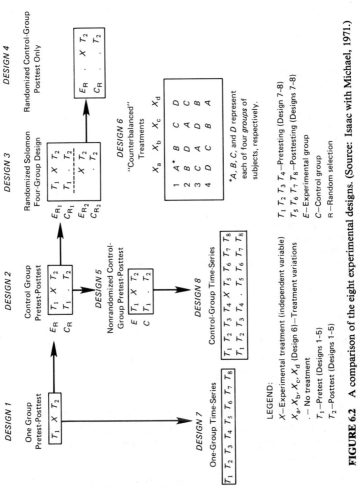

FIGURE 6.2 A comparison of the eight experimental designs. (Source: Isaac with Michael, 1971.)

DESIGN 1

One Group
Pretest-Posttest

| T_1 | X | T_2 |

DESIGN 2

Control Group
Pretest-Posttest

E_R | T_1 | X | T_2
C_R | T_1 | . | T_2

DESIGN 3

Randomized Solomon
Four-Group Design

E_{R_1} | T_1 | X | T_2
C_{R_1} | T_1 | . | T_2
E_{R_2} | | X | T_2
C_{R_2} | | . | T_2

DESIGN 4

Randomized Control-Group
Posttest Only

E_R | . | X | T_2
C_R | . | . | T_2

DESIGN 5

Nonrandomized Control-
Group Pretest-Posttest

E | T_1 | X | T_2
C | T_1 | . | T_2

DESIGN 6

"Counterbalanced"
Treatments

	X_a	X_b	X_c	X_d
1	A^*	B	C	D
2	B	D	A	C
3	C	A	D	B
4	D	C	B	A

*A, B, C, and D represent
each of four *groups* of
subjects, respectively.

DESIGN 7

One-Group Time-Series

| T_1 | T_2 | T_3 | T_4 | T_5 | T_6 | T_7 | T_8 |

DESIGN 8

Control-Group Time-Series

| T_1 | T_2 | T_3 | T_4 | X | T_5 | T_6 | T_7 | T_8 |
| T_1 | T_2 | T_3 | T_4 | . | T_5 | T_6 | T_7 | T_8 |

LEGEND:

X—Experimental treatment (independent variable)
X_a, X_b, X_c, X_d (Design 6)—Treatment variations
.—No treatment
T_1—Pretest (Designs 1-5)
T_2—Posttest (Designs 1-5)

$T_1 T_2 T_3 T_4$—Pretesting (Design 7-8)
$T_5 T_6 T_7 T_8$—Posttesting (Designs 7-8)
E—Experimental group
C—Control group
R—Random selection

TABLE 6.1

Factors Jeopardizing the Validity of Experimental Designs

	Experimental Designs[a]							
	Little control	Rigorous control			Partial control			
Sources of invalidity	1	2	3	4	5	6	7	8
Internal validity								
Contemporary history	−	+	+	+	+	+	−	+
Maturation processes	−	+	+	+	+	+	+	+
Pretesting procedures	−	+	+	+	+	+	+	+
Measuring instruments	−	+	+	+	+	+	?	+
Statistical regression	?	+	+	+	?	+	+	+
Differential selection of subjects	+	+	+	+	+	+	+	+
Experimental mortality	+	+	+	+	+	+	+	+
Interaction of selection and maturation, etc.	−	+	+	+	−	?	+	+
External validity								
Interaction of selection and X	−	?	?	?	?	?	?	−
Interaction of pretesting and X	−	−	+	+	−	?	−	−
Reactive experimental procedures	?	?	?	?	?	?	?	?
Multiple-treatment interference						−		

[a]Names of Designs 1 to 8 are:

1. One-group Prestest-Posttest
2. Randomized Control-group Pretest-Posttest
3. Randomized Solomon Four-group
4. Randomized Control-group Posttest only
5. Nonrandomized Control-group Pretest-Posttest
6. Counterbalanced
7. One-group Time-series
8. Control-group Time-series

Note: A plus symbol indicates control of a factor, a minus indicates lack of control, a question mark suggests there is some source for concern, and a blank indicates that the factor is not relevant.

Source: Van Dalen & Meyer (1966, p. 291).

- Bennett and Lumsdaine's (1975) *Evaluation and Experiment* which not only abstracts, analyzes, and rates a large number of field experiments, but includes papers discussing theoretical issues, such as the desirability of randomization, common errors, etc.

Experimentation is probably the most powerful strategy at the researcher's disposal in that, when used correctly, it can yield definitive findings. Note that experimental designs are not the only ones which permit causal inferences, though they may be the most efficient ones. Moreover, there are many common errors and pitfalls to be avoided in undertaking an experimental study:

- Uncontrolled or overlooked differences between treatment of experimental and control groups may result in systematically biased findings.

- Failure to decompose a large group into appropriate subgroups where a classifying variable is of potential importance may blur the effects.
- Subject responses may reflect the effects of the experimental procedure or environment rather than the effect of treatments.
- Control and experimental groups are matched on irrelevant variables.
- Attempts to control on too many variables will be unsuccessful and samples will thus be biased.
- Need for appropriate designs for sequential treatments may be overlooked or ignored.
- Potentially important variables are overlooked, or their values associated with those of other variables, so that appropriate control is not achieved.

Sometimes the labelling of a study as experimental reflects the illusion of control and the assumption of randomization.

In the final analysis, you may decide that the experimental type of research is not suitable for the solution of your problem because the need for controls is restrictive or artificial, or because the conditions of your study are beyond your—or anyone's—control. It is important that you consider these possibilities before coming to a decision. (See Phillips [1981] for an extensive discussion of the pros and cons of experimental studies in education.) Bear in mind also that some university doctoral committees and journal editorial boards reject any but "true" experimental and some quasi-experimental findings. Check carefully to find out what is acceptable before making the major commitment needed for a serious experimental research proposal.

The PERT network in Figure 6.3 may be helpful to you in planning an experimental or quasi-experimental study. (See Chapter 15, section on PERT, for a longer discussion of the construction and use of these diagrams.) The optimal use of time and effort can result in better implementation of any design, and PERT offers a framework within which this can be achieved. It will be most useful if you modify it for your particular project by including the specific tasks in your experiment such as equipment construction, treatment stages, and observational sequences.

Overlapping Research Types

Many problems are potentially suited to investigation by means of more than one research type, and in deciding which to use you need to consider both feasibility and the disciplinary framework. A few examples of research problems that can overlap two or more types are:

- Studies of crowding effects
- Studies of ingroup and intergroup traits and attitudes
- Studies of social networks
- Studies of disease transmission

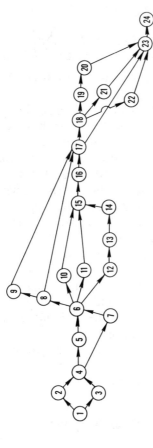

Event Identification

1. Project Start
2. Complete Theoretical Framework
3. Complete Literature Review
4. Start Objectives
5. Start Hypotheses
6. Complete Hypotheses
7. Complete Generalization Considerations
8. Start Method Analysis

9. Complete Decision Error
10. Complete Working Guide
11. Complete Treatment Definition
12. Start Sample Selection
13. Start Treatment Assignment
14. Start Pre-measures
15. Start Treatment Application
16. Start Post-measures

17. Start Data Summary
18. Complete Data Summary
19. Complete Interpretation
20. Complete Conclusions
21. Complete Tables
22. Complete Graphs
23. Complete Narrative
24. Complete Bibliography

FIGURE 6.3 Summary network for experimental research project. (Source: Cook, 1966.)

- Studies of student choices of programs and curricula
- Studies of consumer preference
- Studies of the effects of propaganda
- Studies of voter behavior
- Studies of stress

Pilot Studies

Every substantial research project should include a *pilot study*, which is basically a smaller-scale version or miniature walk through of the proposed investigation. Appropriately planned, a pilot study will almost certainly help you avoid most if not all of the common errors described earlier, or at least reduce them to a manageable minimum level. In the pilot, any or all of the sample, the data-collection procedure or the analysis techniques may be reduced or varied.

If properly conducted, the pilot study can accomplish any or all of the following:

- Sharpening the precision or specificity of the research hypotheses
- Suggesting relationships or approaches not previously considered
- Improving instruments and procedures for data collection; correcting defects in questions and instrument format[30]
- Checking reliability and validity of instruments
- Trying a variety of alternative measures
- Identifying sources of treatment errors
- Trying out a variety of alternative designs
- Trying out a variety of data analysis techniques
- Providing the investigators with practice in carrying out procedures
- Trying out sampling procedures; investigating population characteristics
- Checking coding procedures and verifying documentation
- Obtaining an estimate for population variability, on which estimates of the power of your proposed statistical tests can be based. (See Chapter 10, pp. 217–218).

Most important of all, your pilot study can inform you in advance that a full-scale study will be fruitless.[31] Many projects that appear very promising turn out to be impossible or not worth doing. This can be extremely disappointing, but in the long run the time and money you can save as a result of a careful pilot study, which suggests a different procedure or the complete abandonment of the project, will justify the effort the pilot requires.

Before undertaking a pilot study, you must have taken these steps in the research process:

- Identify and formulate the problem
- Survey the literature relevant to the problem
- Identify the critical variables
- Formulate hypotheses and alternative hypotheses
- Select a research design
- Select or develop instruments
- Select a small sample of subjects representative of those which will ultimately be used for the proposed full-scale study.

Remember in planning a pilot study that, unless procedures, population characteristics, and analysis are comparable to those in the full-scale study, they will provide no guidance for modifications or the making of conjectures. We also urge you to discuss your plans for a pilot study with your mentors, and to obtain their approval before you undertake this part of your project.

Summary

The information contained in this chapter is summarized in Figure 6.4. This diagram should enable you to identify key characteristics of your problem so as to help you choose a research design. It is in the form of a flow diagram and works like a decision-tree (see Appendix, pp. 5–7) even though the underlying taxonomy is neither perfectly exhaustive nor perfectly exclusive. The diamonds enclose questions, the ovals design types.

Notes

All studies referred to in this Chapter can be found in the bibliography.
[1]See Carr (1964).
[2]Compare items (6) and (7) p. 91.
[3]See Nagel (1961).
[4]For this usage, which is not standard today, see Gottschalk (1969).
[5]See Selltiz et al., (1976); Krippendorff (1980), Festinger and Katz (1953, 1966).
[6]Council on Interracial Books for Children (1977).
[7]See Cook and Campbell (1979, pp. 230ff.), "Limitations on Archival Data." It seems to us that in historical studies, seeking external validity is crucial (or why bother?) but this reflects a touching faith in the force of the ceteris paribus assumptions. Jacob (1984) has an extensive discussion, with numerous examples; he uses criteria of validity and reliability to evaluate published data.
[8]"Those who cannot remember the past are condemned to repeat it" (G. Santayana, *Introduction* and *Reason in Common Sense*; *The Life of Reason*, Vol. 1. New York: Scribners, 1905). Actually, those who do not learn from history are condemned to repeat other historians.
[9]Fischer (1970) contains an entertaining and informative discussion of errors of statistical reasoning in historical studies.

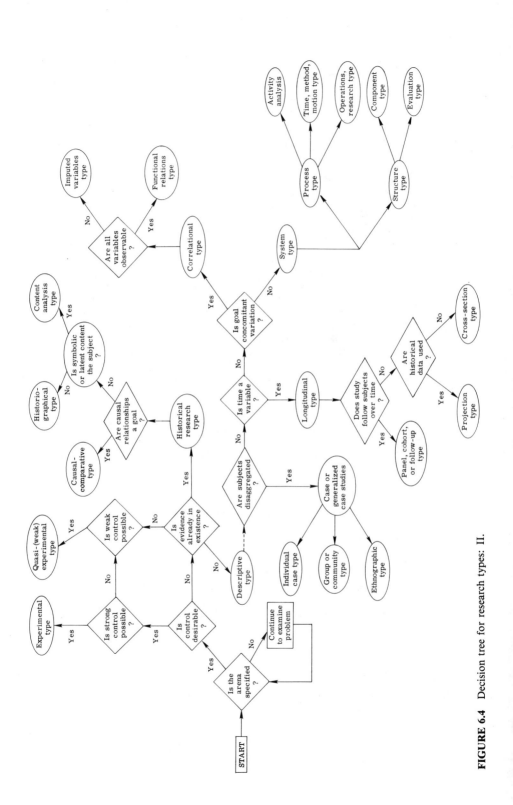

FIGURE 6.4 Decision tree for research types: II.

[10]Katz (1967, pp. 147–148).

[11]As stated in Chapter 5 (p. 89), the terms *developmental* or *progressive* are also used.

[12]See Glenn (1977); Babbie (1979), Goldstein (1979), or Markus (1979) for techniques of analysis.

[13]This term is used quite differently by Glock (1967) and by Babbie (1979).

[14]Many examples can be found in Glock (1967).

[15]Some interesting aspects of inference from case studies are discussed in Meehl (1954), also in Davidson and Costello (1969).

[16]Rohrer uses *Negro* to mean a Black with some white ancestry.

[17]See Mechanic (1968, pp. 259–266) for a review of this controversy.

[18]See Gensch, (1970).

[19]See Rossi et al. (1972) for numerous examples and discussion of problems and procedures.

[20]For numerous further examples and extensive discussion, see Bennett and Lumsdaine (1975) or Riecken and Boruch (1974).

[21]See Mechanic (1968; Chapter 4) for a review.

[22]See Dohrenwend and Dohrenwend (1974).

[23]For a brief introduction, see Selltiz et al. (1976, pp. 268–271); for examples of theory, applications, and analysis, see Leinhardt (1977); for analysis, see Knoke and Kuklinski (1982).

[24]See Plutchik (1974) and Sidman (1960). Although both these authors are experimental psychologists, and many of their examples are drawn from their own discipline, their general comments are interesting and valuable to every researcher in whatever area.

[25]See Greer (1969, pp. 114ff.) and Phillips' (1981) essay. Nagel (1961) also touches on this point.

[26]Cronbach, referred to by Shulman (1981).

[27]Riecken and Boruch (1974, Chapter 8).

[28]Spector (1981, p. 9 and Section 1 passim).

[29]Rossi et al. (1980)

[30]Pilot studies are sometimes used specifically to verify reliability and validity of instruments. See also Chapter 7, pp. 146 and 163.

[31]See, in particular, Sidman (1960) and Madge (1967); also for a general discussion, Medawar (1979) and Beveridge (1950); for piloting of surveys Babbie (1979, pp. 211–222).

Additional Reading

Choosing an Arena

Stinchcombe (1968, passim).

Riecken and Boruch (1974): Chapter 2 discusses the decision to experiment.

Hammond (1964, passim): informative accounts of arena decisions and many other aspects of study management.

Simon (1978): comparison of different research types and their advantages or disadvantages.

Pilot Studies

Plutchik (1974) }
Sidman (1960) } experimental emphasis.
Madge (1967): trying out interviewers.

Historical Research

There is no substitute for thorough training.
Carr (1964): what historians do, their role in "making history."
Madge (1967): Chapter 2 on documents.
Gottschalk et al. (1947): use of personal documents.
Festinger and Katz (1966): Chapter 7 on use of records, census materials, etc.
Jacob (1984): extensive discusion of problems in use of published data; examples.
Selltiz et al. (1976; 1959): Chapter 11 on available data.
Krippendorff (1980): state-of-the-art in content analysis, excellent.
Dollar and Jensen (1971): statistics for historical researchers.

Descriptive Research

Case and Community Studies

Jahoda et al. (1951): Chapter 3; emphasis on formulative aspect.
Goldstein (1979): compact discussion of design issues in longitudinal studies, with attention to sampling, measurement, and appropriate analysis.
Davidson and Costello (1969): inferential issues.
Festinger and Katz (1966): Chapter 2; emphasis on community studies, sources of respondents.
Blalock (1970): succinct discussion of participant observation.

Survey Research

Aside from the manuals we have cited so often, we find the following particularly helpful:
Glock (1967): many disciplines, superb references.
Lazarsfeld and Rosenberg (1955): theoretical problems.
Rosenberg (1968): analysis.
Madge (1967): full of profoundly useful comments.
Festinger and Katz (1966): Chapter 9 on group behavior.
Babbie (1979): thorough.
Leinhardt (1977), Proctor and Loomis (1951): sociometric analysis.
Backstrom and Hursh-Cesar (1981): practical.

Experimental Research

Field Settings

Madge (1967): Chapter 5.
Cook and Campbell (1979).
Riecken and Boruch (1974): excellent bibliography, chapters on many aspects of field experimentation.

Laboratory Settings

Plutchik (1974)
Festinger and Katz (1966): Chapter 4.

General

Kerlinger (1973).
Campbell and Stanley (1963).

7

Procedure: Measurement, Instrumentation, and Data Collection

Introduction

This chapter has two principal goals. First, it offers a brief general orientation to the philosophical and technical problems involved in measurement, and a description of the sorts of instruments most commonly used in social or behavioral science research. Second, it presents a summary description of the data-collection procedures most frequently employed in such research.

Investigators in every discipline tend to develop preferred techniques of data-collection which over a period of time come to characterize their respective fields. Like other decisions, the choices of instrumentation and, in turn, data-collection type, must take into account feasibility as well as other factors. The acquired know-how of your mentors and colleagues is an invaluable resource in choosing and using appropriate procedures; particularly for survey studies, excellent reference manuals are also available to provide guidance on technique and alternative approaches. (See the list at the end of this chapter.)

Measurement

"Measurement is the link between mathematics and science."[1] To formulate the design of your study you must transform your problem-question about the occurrence of events or the relationships among attributes into a testable hypothesis about measurements, their distributions, and the degree of association among them. In order to do this effectively, you must first have a clear idea of:

- what measurement is;
- how measurements are obtained; that is, what procedures are at your disposal and what their relative advantages are;
- what kinds of information the measuring procedures yield;
- what are some criteria for evaluating both measuring instruments and procedures for collecting measurements;
- what kinds of analysis are possible with different kinds of measurements.

Just as it is difficult to describe in a strictly logical way the most (apparently) elementary mathematical concept, namely counting, so it is challenging to specify exactly what is involved in measuring. Almost everyone takes both the process and its outcome for granted.

> The nature of measurement should . . . be a central concern of the philosophy of science. Yet, strangely, it has attracted little attention. If it is discussed at all . . . it is usually dismissed in a fairly short and standard chapter . . . : for the most part the logic of measurement has been treated, as though it were neither interesting nor important. Why this should be so, I do not know. Its importance can hardly be questioned: to understand how mathematics is applied is to understand the most significant feature of modern science."[2]

One ordinarily speaks of assigning measurements to phenomena. In fact, the sequence is more complicated, and can be shown as follows:

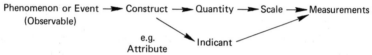

There is a persistent confusion between events and their associated constructs, and also between construct and quantity: *Quantity* means the implicit measurable aspect of a construct.[3] *Indicant* means something that signals the presence of something else: the something else is the construct. The algebraic equations or inequalities which describe differences or correlations state relationships between measurements, *not* between quantities or indicants. (It may be helpful to refer back to the section on operationalizing in Chapter 4.) We are primarily concerned in this chapter with the classification of scales and the accuracy of instruments.

Stevens' Classification of Scales

"In its broadest sense, *measurement* is the assignment, according to rules, of numerals [numbers] to objects or events." The specification of such a rule creates a scale.

> And the fact that numerals can be assigned under different rules leads to different kinds of scales and different kinds of measurements. The rules themselves relate in part to the concrete empirical operations of our experimental procedures which, by their sundry degrees of precision, help to determine how snug is the fit between the mathematical model and what it stands for . . . . Measurement is possible in the first place only because there is a kind of isomorphism [correspondence between structures] between: (1) the empirical relations among objects and events, and (2) the properties of the formal game in which numerals are the pawns, and operators the moves."[4]

(This isomorphism is, of course, incomplete, because not every attribute of the object or event is included in the model.)

The foregoing, which embodies a strongly operationalist point of view, suggests the basis for Stevens' classification of measurement scales.[5] In this system, scales are classified according to the empirical decision procedures which can be applied to the objects or events. The level of a variable is usually understood to be the class of the scale used to measure it.[6] Researchers continue to disagree deeply about the distinctions embodied in this classification scheme and, in particular, in Stevens' assertions concerning the choice of statistics. We present a summary of the controversies to help you decide which data-analysis procedures may be appropriate.

The *nominal scale* uses numerals as labels, and indeed any kind of label will do. Two examples are the classification of individuals by their stated religious preference as in census categories, and the coding of subjects by sex; in each class each member of the same class is assigned the same numeral. The purpose of the numbering is served just as well when the numerals are reordered. The underlying empirical operation is the determination of equivalence with respect to some criterion (equality is a special case), and the associated rule is: Assign the same numeral to equivalent objects and different numerals to objects which are not equivalent. Thus, when individuals are classified by sex, all males may be assigned numeral 0, all females 1; "equivalence" means "same sex." Forming classes, or defining equivalence, or establishing taxonomic standards, is a nontrivial empirical and theoretical problem, which must be effectively dealt with before a nominal scale can be introduced.[7] (See also the discussion of dichotomies, below.) Reynolds (1977) suggests that most nominal scales reflect measurement errors in that, if the researcher had better techniques he could operationalize the construct quantitatively, that is, using an interval scale. We find it hard to agree. Although some writers do not accept the nominal scale as true measurement, it certainly does satisfy Stevens' general definition of a scale.

The *ordinal scale* uses numerals to designate rank order or relative position in a sequence. One example is the familiar lower-class, lower-middle, upper-middle, etc. classification. Any measuring instrument whose scores reflect an empirical determination of greater or less (e.g., more or less favorable attitudes), in fact yields an ordinal scale, so that most scales widely used by behavioral and social researchers fall into this category. Any order-preserving transformation is permissible; thus all transformations by monotonic increasing functions (e.g., square, logarithm) leave the scale form invariant. In general, ordinal measurements permit a decision as to which objects possess more of the measured attribute. The differences between measurements are not informative, however, since ranks 4 and 2, for example, may differ by more—or less—of the attribute than do ranks 3 and 1 ("seeds" in a tennis tournament, or your own preferences in ice cream flavors, come to mind.) A modified form of the ordinal scale, the so-called ordinal-interval or ordinal-metric scale, permits comparisons of differences in ranks or relative positions (Coombs 1950). Researchers using ordinal scales should be careful to distinguish between true rank orders, and scores which reflect relative ranking with respect to some attribute. The latter can be transformed into true rank orders for the study population, and certain statistical procedures require this step. (See Chapters 11–14, discussion of nonparametric statistics.)

The *interval scale*, illustrated by the familiar Fahrenheit and Centigrade scales for temperature and by scales of calendar time, permits decisions as to the equality of differences in the measured quantity based on the equality of intervals or differences in the measurements. Numerals are assigned in order to achieve this correspondence between the measurement and the quantity. Evidently, decisions as to rank order are also possible, so that every interval scale is ordinal but not necessarily vice versa. Any interval scale is quantitative in the ordinary sense, so that addition of measures reflects increments in the property: for example, 40 units of temperature plus 10 units of temperature equals 50 units of temperature. Some caution is appropriate. The location of a zero point, or its absence, is a matter of convention or convenience; statements about proportion are in general meaningless. All linear transformations $x' = ax + b$ are scale-preserving but it is incorrect to infer that if two scales are related by a linear function, they must both be interval scales.[8]

"Most psychological measurement aspires to create interval scales."[9] Techniques have been developed which introduce transformations whose effect, it is asserted, is to replace ordinal scales by interval scales:[10] Intelligence is an example of an attribute whose measurement is so manipulated. These procedures yield gratifying results of great importance in both theory and application. One the other hand, aptitude scales (see pp. 146–148) can be very useful even when their classification as interval has not been established.

Ratio scales require for their construction the empirical determination of equality of ratios of measures, and in turn permit decisions based on equality of ratios. Operations must exist a priori for determining the relations of equivalence, rank order, and equality of intervals. In practice, these together with the determination of a zero-value ensure that a ratio scale can be constructed. The only permitted scale transformations are those in which each scale value is multiplied by a constant. Length and mass are familiar examples of quantities measured using ratio scales, as are income and age.[11] Differences between values on an interval scale can be regarded as measures on a ratio scale.

The foregoing has been the basic point of view on measurement for over 30 years. However, the working researcher needs to be aware of several criticisms:

1. The basic formulation, which involves the existence of "any rule" for the assignment of numerals to events, is too vague and does not make clear the role played by units, nor does it adequately account for the relationship of the scale and the particular empirical operation used to obtain the measure. We feel that Stevens' system is satisfactory in practice even though these primarily philosophical issues are not resolved.

2. "In practice it is extremely difficult to know whether or not we have an equal unit, interval scale. . . . Stevens gives . . . no formal rules for determining whether we have obtained such a scale or not. Guilford (1954) . . . points out that one way of determining whether or not an equal unit scale exists is by demonstrating additivity . . . However, Guilford notes that 'the property of additivity is rarely experimentally demonstrable, even in the physical sciences.' "[12] It is important to bear in mind that the emphasis on additivity, and even the assumption or forcing of this characteristic to satisfy the dictum that it is an essential for any measure, is quite unnecessary. You need not reject a useful measuring instrument just because you cannot verify that it yields interval-level data. The instruments of the physical scientists are in practice no more meticulously developed than those of the social scientists. However, sometimes scales are accepted as interval-level simply because their inventors assert firmly that such is the case. More frequently, data are analyzed using interval-level procedures, so later researchers assume the instruments do in fact generate interval-level measurements. Ordinal-level measurements and the inferences that can be drawn from them may be quite acceptable for your purposes.

3. Mathematical transformations can change a scale from a lower level to a higher level, so conceivably any kind of scale can be made into any other kind of scale. We find arguments such as those in Ferguson (1981) to justify this strategy very confusing in their logic, and the techniques based upon questionable assumptions. As Abelson and Tukey (1959) point out, moreover, in many situations more information about the variables is available than is reflected in the labels ("ordinal-level," etc.) alone, and this information can be exploited in interpreting the statistical findings, so strenuous efforts to change scale level are wasteful.

Other Ways to Classify Scales

A *continuous scale* is one in which the measure of a quantity (i.e., the numeral assigned to an object or event) may be any real number in some specified interval, or possibly any real number whatsoever, and in which every real number on the scale corresponds to some empirically determinable value of the quantity. In general, two subjects are not expected to have precisely the same value. Age and weight are examples of continuously measurable variables. In contrast a *discrete scale* is one containing at most a denumerable set of possible values, such as designated grade-level of a child or census categories for marital status. (One may argue that more refined measuring devices would permit either a larger number of categories or even use of a continuous scale.) Continuous scales lend themselves to certain procedures not permitted otherwise; hence, it is frequently convenient to treat a discrete scale as if it were continuous. Although this pretense may yield acceptable results, it is important to keep in mind that an assumption has been introduced. Conversely, grouping converts a continuous to a discrete scale: the underlying variable may be continuous but the measures (e.g. scores) may be discrete. A discrete ordinal scale can sometimes best be regarded as nominal: Kerlinger (1973, p. 438) refers to such scales with finitely many scores as quasi-nominal.

A *dichotomy* or *dichotomous scale* permits the assignment of every item in the universe of items to exactly one of two mutually exclusive categories that collectively exhaust the entire population; that is, the rule of assignment uses exactly two numerals. Some dichotomies (such as male–female) appear to be natural or real, while others (like guilty–not guilty at the outcome of a trial, or a median-split of scores) are arbitrary or artificial in that they reflect the computation of a break point. A dichotomy can be derived from an ordinal, interval, or ratio scale, whether discrete or continuous, by defining the categories according to a scale value greater than some specified number, or from a nominal scale by clumping categories together. For example, the rule "Class 1 consists of all individuals in the study population whose Stanford–Binet IQ exceeds 120; Class 0 consists of all other individuals" defines a dichotomy. Finding a breakpoint for the dichotomy involves all the difficulties encountered in deciding on any other taxonomic scheme: Such statistical techniques as cluster or discriminant analysis can be helpful. (It is also important to keep in mind that while any variable can be dichotomized, the procedures for analysis of relationships between that variable and others vary according to whether the underlying scale is continuous.)

Nominal and ordinal scales are often called *nonmetric*; continuous interval and ratio scales are called *metric* or *numerical* or *quantitative*.

Scales and Statistics

In the course of presenting his classification, Stevens writes "The nature of the invariance under permissible transformations of each class of scale sets limits to the kinds of statistical manipulations that can legitimately be applied to the scaled data. This question of the applicability of the various statistics is of great practical concern to several of the sciences."[13]

Stevens' assertions have stimulated a lively debate and some strong disagreements among authorities.[14] Typical is Kerlinger (1973):

> Strictly speaking, the statistics that can be used with ordinal scales include rank-order measures such as [Spearman's] rho, Kendall's W, and rank-order analysis of variance . . . How can statistics like r, t and F be used with what are in effect ordinal measures . . . without a qualm by most researchers [?] . . . [The usual argument is] a pragmatic one, that the assumption of interval equality works."[15]

Kerlinger suggests, however, that the researcher be alert to the possibility of gross departures from an interval scale. "Above all, we need to be particularly careful with the interpretation of ordinal data to which statistical analysis suitable for interval measurement has been applied."[16] An even more extreme position is expressed by Anderson (1961) as follows:

> Can the F test be applied to data from an ordinal scale? . . . The F test . . . can be applied without qualm. . . . The justification . . . is purely statistical and quite straightforward . . . the statistical test can hardly be cognizant of the empirical meaning of the numbers with which it deals. Consequently, the validity of a statistical inference cannot depend on the type of measuring scale used."[17]

Statements like the preceding leave the novice researcher in a cleft stick. On the one hand, it is important to use procedures which make sense and which reflect acceptable assumptions; on the other, it is necessary to exploit the data with as powerful techniques as possible. When authorities contradict each other and the research literature contains examples of all the stated positions, how can you decide what to do?

Our point of view in this controversy (incorporated in Chapters 11–14) is fairly conservative, agreeing more closely with Stevens'. It is quite true that numbers don't know what variables they are used to measure, and so can be manipulated freely. The decisions and inferences about the objects or events, of which these numbers are the measures, DO depend on how these numbers are obtained, that is, how the variables are defined and how well the instruments meet the criteria for measurements. Such considerations certainly affect the choice of statistics, which can permit conclusions no better than the weakest link, namely, the one between the event and the record of the event. A moderate position, very appealing because it combines caution and practicality, is that of Verba and Nie (1972), who suggest that the application of such parametric techniques as analysis of variance to ordinal data should be regarded as statistical exploration which can point to possible interactions of variables or other effects for future study. They warn, however, that computed "significance levels" should not be taken seriously.

Finally, measurements of relatively loosely defined attributes whose underlying constructs are not well specified, (even though the study as a whole may be potentially useful) yield at best numerical data which should be dealt with most gingerly and cautiously. Assumptions that the data are parametric or interval-scale should be avoided. It may even be impossible to be certain that a measuring instrument yields ordinal-level data, which will permit comparisons based on rank.[18] It is a serious error to suppose that an ordinal scale is easy to construct: the crucial issue is the demonstration that if measures $m_1 > m_2$ and $m_2 > m_3$ then $m_1 > m_3$ and the corresponding relation holds for the attribute being measured. This property of transitivity is not always present and is not easy to verify. Sheldon's (1940) somatotyping, for instance, does not readily lend itself to the establishment of an ordinal scale (although recently developed proximity measurement techniques might yield useful results).

Measuring requires instruments, and the development of an appropriate scale is a necessary step in the creation of an instrument. The next section describes the kinds of instruments in most general use in the social and behavioral sciences.

Instruments

By *instruments* we mean devices, in the most general sense, which are used for:

- The recording of evidence, that is, data-collection, under standard conditions.
- The assignment of measurements to the events, objects, or subjects involved in the study.
- The control or selection of the conditions of the study (*treatments*).

Thus, we would include such disparate items as instruction sheets distributed to participants, exercise machines, automated food-dispensing machinery, two-way mirrors, etc. However, we are mainly concerned with instruments used for the first two purposes mentioned. The choice of appropriate instruments is a crucial aspect of the design of your study. Such instruments:

1. should be consistent and accurate;
2. should yield measures suitable for testing your hypotheses, compatible with other design decisions;
3. should not be intrusive, that is, introduce extraneous effects.

Criteria for Item 1 above are formal and relatively specific, and are discussed at some length beginning on p. 156. Comments on Item 2 and related issues can be found in Chapters 4, 5, and 10. Item 3 represents a counsel of perfection: Any record of events is necessarily a sampling process, and so the collection of data intrinsically introduces new factors. For instance, it is not uncommon for an instrument or procedure to alter the event measured: in the videotaping of a group interaction, the acknowledged presence of the camera may cause the participants to modify their behavior.

Reactive research is that in which the subject is affected by some aspect of the research, such as measurement or selection procedures, rather than by the treatment. From the investigator's standpoint this may be undesirable. Knowledge of the purpose of a study may alter the subjects' "set" and thus their responses to an interviewer. A social psychologist may discover that subjects respond to receiving the attention of the observer, as much as to the controlled changes in the environment or group structure. (Many ingenious procedures have been devisd to distract subjects from the real purpose of a study.) The danger in all studies is that effects may be attributed to treatments but are in fact reactive effects, or that real effects may be mistaken for reactive ones and disregarded. It is important to be attentive to the potential of your instruments for introducing unhypothesized factors, and to make suitable efforts to avoid or control them.[19]

In the next several sections we present some of the principal types of instruments and data-collection techniques.[20]

DIRECT OBSERVATION

The basic procedure for research in the social and behavioral sciences is direct observation and measurement by an individual of subjects' behavior, which may be verbal (oral or written), and the preparation of a record of specified, that is, selected, aspects of that behavior. It may also be desirable to obtain observations of designated aspects of the environment ("was it raining?"), or other variables such as subjects' ethnicity.

Direct observation entails certain problems of reliability and validity of data:

- The observer's presence may affect the behaviors or events under observation.[21]
- The observer can, necessarily, only sample the behavior and so must make a decision as to which behaviors should be recorded as valid indicators.
- The observer, in classifying what is observed, makes an inference about the behavior. This inference is not necessarily correct. For example, in recording facial expressions or gestures in a culture not his own, the observer may label as "guilty" or "evasive" behavior which is intended to express respect or deference.
- The observer is not necessarily consistently accurate. Observer fatigue, sensory inadequacy, or bias may significantly affect the data as recorded. Also, a different observer might assign a different classification to observed events.

- If the observed behavior is complex or consists of many bits, both the recording and the analysis usually require special schemes for dealing with interactions because it is difficult to achieve agreement among observers. Techniques for this purpose include sociograms, Blumberg's matrix, etc., but others may have to be developed or modified for your purpose.

Direct observations can be combined with interviews and the use of questionnaires and accounts, prepared by subjects, to yield a very rich record of events and information on other variables. Ultimately, empirical science is inseparable from observation; *all* other procedures represent concessions to the difficulty or impossibility of making direct observations.

In order to be scientific, observation must take place in some framework as well as being systematically structured: This means that the usefulness of casual or scatter-shot "let's take a look" efforts are very limited. Even if the purpose of the observation is exploratory, it is essential to proceed in a clearly specified fashion in order to permit identification of variables and formulation of hypotheses.

EQUIPMENT

Observation and direct measurement may be difficult to accomplish, but mechanical, electrical, or electronic devices can come to your aid.

Two special categories of measuring equipment are widely employed. The first, which includes cameras (movie and still, color and black and white) and audio and video (TV) transmission and recording devices, appears to be able to preserve for some time interval, perhaps permanently, the events at which an observer would otherwise be present. Thus, (1) several observers can compare their recorded observations; (2) repeated observations of the same event can be made; (3) time constraints can be avoided or evaded; and (4) multiple or complex concurrent events can be recorded by a single observer. You should be aware that the use of these devices always involves a selection of events (whether because of the scope, focus, and sensitivity of the particular device, or because of the elimination of some variables accessible to a direct observer, such as smell); also, the presence of these devices is often a factor in the situation (very few people are oblivious of a visible TV camera). Hence, the analysis of such observations is not necessarily equivalent to the analysis of direct observations.

A second category of equipment includes devices which automate either the control or the record-keeping aspect of the observations, for instance printer-counters, reaction-time recording machinery, timers, and those which make it possible to observe and analyze body changes, such as polygraphs, blood-pressure gauges, specialized equipment for psychological or drug studies, growth measurements, etc. (see Chapter 9, section on process control). There are many such devices for specific purposes.

If your study requires the use of equipment of any sort (whether simple skin calipers or the most sophisticated stimulus generators), be sure you are familiar with its capabilities and its shortcomings. The required level of mastery must be achieved *in advance*. An efficient way to accomplish this is through an informal apprenticeship to a more experienced researcher such as an advanced graduate student working on a related problem. Your mentor should be able to suggest experts willing to guide you in acquiring the necessary skills.

QUESTIONS AND SCHEDULES

Much of the research in the social and behavioral sciences involves eliciting responses to questions addressed to the subjects. An enormous variety is possible in the types of questions and the formats or *schedules* in which they can be presented, as well as the procedures by which the responses can be gathered, so that both unstructured interviews and aptitude tests in questionnaire form can appropriately be included under this heading. One can adopt the point of view that all question-and-answer instruments are simply devices for carrying out observations of verbal behavior.

"Other aspects of . . . research are more technical, but writing the question is a combination of art and science, an understanding of subject matter and the specific population blended with experience in the subtleties of communication."[22] "The questions we ask determine the answers we get."[23] This means that no question can be effectively framed without a clear idea of what purpose(s) the response may serve. Your questions represent the operationalization of the constructs and the conjectures of your study: in other terms, a theory is always implicit in every question. It also means that unless carefully stated, the question "sets" or confuses the responders.

Questions can be classified into four types:

- Fact questions: seek background or demographic data.
- Information questions: seek data on knowledge and its sources.
- Opinion or attitude questions: seek data on feelings, beliefs, values, predispositions to act, ideas, opinions, preferences.[24] All such questions reflect an assumption: 'It is commonly supposed, although there is very little evidence to suggest such a supposition, that there exists a simple and logical relation between what a person says and what he thinks."[25] Schedules of questions of this type are sometimes called *opinionnaires*.
- Behavior questions: seek data on individuals' perceptions of their own and, perhaps, other's behaviors. These schedules are sometimes referred to as *perceptionnaires*.

Both the substance and the wording of questions present problems which if not resolved will effectively interfere with the usefulness of any data you may collect. The following criteria may help you to evaluate questions:

- Type of questions should be appropriate to the information you are seeking. (See later section on Questions, pp. 151ff.)
- Questions should be related to the problem and your objectives.
- Questions should permit only one interpretation.
- Questions should be clear.
- Questions should not be leading or sensitive.
- Questions should not ask for knowledge the respondent does not have.
- Questions should not be loaded to social acceptabililty.

A well-planned and -executed pilot study will make it possible for you to decide whether your questions are effective in obtaining the information you need.

Another set of problems arises when questions must be sequenced and compiled into working instruments such as interview schedules or questionnaires.[26] The questionnaire, whether it is an ad hoc survey schedule or an elaborately validated value scale, embodies the theories and hunches that guide the study. It also must be so designed that it is easy to use (by subject or interviewer) and easy to code and process.

The rest of this section deals with subcategories of question-and-answer instruments and data-collection procedures and with the relative advantages and disadvantages that have to be taken into account in choosing a particular method. The classification is not rigid and the terminology may reflect a usage different from that in your discipline.[27] The literature on this topic is extensive (refer to the technical manuals listed in the chapter references). It is important also that you have access to a knowledgable advisor who can help you identify technical problems and can point you to sources of know-how. There is no substitute for practice.

Interviews.[28] Interviewing is a widely used technique by which information can be obtained from one or several individuals; it is distinguished from other methods by its reliance on the subjects' self-reports. Thus, it offers the researcher the possibility of exploring internal phenomena such as anxieties, but at the same time it is susceptible to inconsistencies, biases, and other sources of invalidity.

The *face-to-face* or *personal* interview is the traditional form of survey research. It has unique and important qualities: It is flexible, adaptable, and usable where questionnaires are not (for instance, with children); the interviewer can repeat questions, make ongoing inferences about the respondent, and gain access to complicated or sensitive material through judicious probing. It can be combined with direct observation and with the presentation of displays to the subjects. On the other hand, the interview is expensive in time and (usually) money, and requires thorough training of interviewers and real skill in formulating questions. The potential for rapport between interviewer and subject may be advantageous, or quite the reverse.

Finally, the respondent and the interviewer have to be available for the interview at the same time and place.

There are many examples of studies whose data were collected in personal interviews. Lortie's (1975) analysis of the professional concerns and socialization of schoolteachers is one such. Another is the study by Veroff et al. (1981) on mental health help-seeking patterns (described in Chapter 2). The reports of both these studies contain their interview schedules. Bell et al?s (1981) investigation of the sources of sexual preference makes extensive use of open-ended questions: the report contains many illustrative answers.

The *telephone interview* permits a very wide geographical net and is typically fast and inexpensive; much less training of interviewers is required, and interviewers can be better monitored. Subject anonymity may reduce bias on both ends. The data are available for inspection and analysis as soon as the interview is completed. Unfortunately, a telephone call may be intrusive, and many low-income individuals do not have a telephone or the privacy to answer complicated questions at length. The *New York Times* weekly report of opinion on national issues is an example of results based on data obtained by way of telephone interviews.

The *questionnaire* is a *self-administered interview.* Questionnaires can be distributed in person to individuals or groups, or can be mailed to selected potential subjects. (In the first instance, respondents may feel coerced or exposed; while in the latter, the response rate may be very low and the returns very slow). Closed or fixed-choice questions are relatively easy to code but can be restrictive; in contrast, the subject may be reluctant to write long answers to open-ended questions, and in any event, no rephrasing or explanation of questions is possible. The greatest advantage of questionnaires is that they are the cheapest form of interview and the most likely to preserve subject anonymity. Their greatest disadvantage is that they require literacy in the respondent and demand exquisite clarity in the instructions and questions. Erbe's (1962) study, described earlier, is based on questionnaires distributed to a national sample. Coleman's (1961) well-known analysis of the social system of the high school makes extensive use of questionnaires as well as historical evidence in the form of student records. Let us not overlook, too, the U.S. Census.

Other forms of interview are in use or will soon be feasible, such as cassettes with taped questions and an answer sheet, or a CRT screen read-out and a recording of the spoken answer (already used for computer-assisted instruction and medical history-taking). Those mentioned above are by far the principal types in use at present.

Other ways of classifying interviews are based on the amount and kind of structure imposed on the range of acceptable responses, such as nondirective, focused, informal, and life history.

In planning your study, you will need to decide:

1. whether the evidence you want can be obtained by interviewing;
2. what type of interview will be most effective;
3. what type of questions (e.g., structured versus unstructured) will be most effective.

Your decision will be based on a knowledge of your research area, a familiarity with the population, and feasibility considerations. It should be evident, for example, that a widely scattered population may be reachable only by mail, or that constraints of time or money may eliminate the training or payment of interviewers. Likewise, you can use questionnaires advantageously to obtain "factual" background information; it may be hard to decide whether opinions, feelings, attitudes, intentions, and similar emotion-laden issues are better explored with the neutral questionnaire or the structured interview. It is also important to bear in mind that so-called opinionnaires are surveys of verbal behavior, and that their predictive use requires correlation of verbal and other behaviors.

Every schedule, whether it is used as a self-administered insrument or as an interview, needs preliminary piloting. (See Chapter 6, section on pilot studies.) This essential step permits you to de-bug the questions and also to determine whether the answers to the questions permit you to discriminate between different categories of respondents. If a pilot use is omitted, you may have a disagreeable surprise when the data are analyzed. As soon as you choose a research question, and whether or not you have access to expert guidance, you should also begin to accumulate a collection of schedules used in other related studies. Most researchers are willing to send you copies of their schedules even if these were omitted from their published report.

Finally, note that interviews serve a number of purposes in research. They may be exploratory, allowing the investigator to identify variables and their relationships; they may be the main instrument used in data-collection and the answers the principal evidence needed in the study; or they may supplement other procedures and provide incidental, specialized, or background information. Survey research, a powerful and useful tool, can be effectively utilized only if instruments capable of identifying and measuring the behavior of interest can be created. Thus problems of measurement can be the major inhibitor of success in using this method.

Our Additional Readings for this chapter include checklists both for question and schedule construction, and for interview and questionnaire administration technique.

Rating Scales and Tests.[29] The goal of your questions may be the identification and measurement of attributes in such a way that comparisons can be made of their intensity, degree, amount, or relative importance (rather than simply their presence or absence). You may need to use one or several such scores or ratings of the subjects to predict other scores or ratings; therefore, a necessary step in the analysis of the scores is an accurate estimate of the various sources of error. Above all, it is essential to be able to make an inference from the scores or ratings to the subjects' possession of whatever attribute is being measured, on the assumption that that attribute is an invariant of the subject. The responses ideally will be temporally, contextually, and situationally independent.

These considerations suggest that instruments developed to serve such purposes as those mentioned above should be:

- Objective: observer variance is as close to zero as possible, that is, disagreement among different users as to what measures are to be assigned is minimized, so that findings obtained by different observers are comparable.
- Normed and/or standardized: a reference group is specified to whose typical scores your subjects' scores can be compared or a typical pattern of scores is determined theoretically or empirically.
- Generalizable: the instrument is usable for other than the initial study population.
- Reliable: the ratings or scale scores are consistent both internally and across time.
- Sensitive: the instrument permits fine distinctions to be made.
- Valid: the instrument measures an attribute that is otherwise identified as present; to use the scale score as an operational definition of the attribute is hazardous.

While the last four requirements can reasonably be imposed on most if not all instruments, the first two typically apply only to tests and rating scales.

Hundreds of tests and rating scales have been devised for different purposes. Tests usually convey the meaning of competition and success or failure, whereas rating scales do not. We concern ourselves here with questionnaires, though other kinds of tests and rating scales are also in use. Many of these are obtainable from commercial publishers who also offer computerized scoring services.

Among the principal types of tests and rating scales are:

- Intelligence and aptitude tests: These are directed primarily to predicting achievement. Familiar examples are the Wechsler WISC-WAIS intelligence tests, the Scholastic Aptitude Tests, and various tests developed by the military for placement of personnel in specialized training programs.
- Achievement tests: These measure mastery of skills, proficiency and understanding of general or specific areas of knowledge, (e.g., standardized reading and mathematics tests); Educational Testing Service achievement tests; and licensing examinations in the professions.

- Personality measures, and value and attitude scales: These may be
  designed to identify and measure at least one of the following:
      Traits: Enduring characteristic responses of the individual, independent
  of the situation.
      Attitudes: Predisposition to behave, perceive, think, or feel toward a
  specified set of phenomena (Kerlinger, 1973); the degree of positive or
  negative affect associated with some "psychological object" (Thurstone,
  cited in Edwards, 1957).
      Values: "culturally weighted preferences for . . . modes of conduct and
  states of existence."[30] Examples are extremely varied and include the
  Minnesota Multiphasic Personality Inventory (MMPI), the Fennema–
  Sherman and Aiken–Dreger Scales for the identification of attitude
  towards mathematics learning, and the ATDP scale of Yuker, Block, et
  al. for the measurement of attitudes towards disabled persons; also
  Spielberger's State-Trait Anxiety Inventory, Adorno's Authoritarianism
  Scale, and Rokeach's (1960, 1968) dogmatism scale, the Coopersmith Self-
  Esteem Scale, and the Dubin et al. (1956) Central Life Interest scale for
  job involvement. All the instruments just mentioned were developed to
  measure hypothetical construct variables.
- Miscellaneous "objective" measures. These elude simple categorization.
  They can be extremely useful both for research and practical application.
  Examples include the Bem Sex-Role Inventory, the Strong–Kuder
  Vocational Interest inventory, the Likert Profile of a School, the Hemphill
  and Coons Leadership Behavior perceptionnaire, various social class
  scales, the Jennings measure of social distance (personal space), and
  confusability, similarity and proximity scales,[31] for example, in
  psychometric analysis of flavors.

Any of the foregoing can be unidimensional (measure a single attribute) or
multidimensional (measure a combination of attributes, assigning scores to
the attributes separately). They can possess subscales which permit
interpretation of scores as a typology. Also, they differ widely in the sorts
of questions they use to elicit the desired information. An inspection of the
instruments listed in Buros or other specialized indexes will give you an
impression of the variety at your disposal, so you can decide whether any
is appropriate for your study.

Indirect and Disguised Methods.[32] People are often reluctant to reveal
socially unacceptable attitudes, opinions on controversial topics, or intimate
information, and they are sometimes unable to give information about their
behavior or their responses. Hence, techniques may be needed that are
independent of the subjects' self-insight or willingness.

One approach to obtaining such information exploits the availability of
measurements for related variables by proposing theoretical relationships
between those variables and the attribute under investigation. For example,

the lie-detector or polygraph procedure is based on correlation of changed patterns of heartbeats and respiration with anxious, that is, "guilty" response to a question. Ideally, a group of substitute measures, each of which is relatively highly correlated with the attribute of interest, (but only negligibly with the others) should be combined to yield a sort of index for that attribute. The construction of Adorno's F-scale reflects this strategy.

A second approach involves the use of disguised tests, which appear to measure, say, information or reasoning, but in fact tap the respondent's attitudes. Examples may be found in Selltiz et al. (1976, Chapter 10). Schuman and Presser (1981) reverse the question and analyze "opinions" on an obscure bill and conclude that responses reflect an effort to interpret the questions meaningfully as well as the willingness to admit ignorance; consequently, they suggest that the "don't know" option should be incorporated into attitude surveys.

The third and most familiar indirect devices rely on so-called projective methods. These methods are based on the assertion that individuals project or express their internal states onto external objects, and that a useful inference can be made about the subject's emotions, motives, etc. by presenting an ambiguous stimulus and analyzing the response, and comparing it with a preconceived taxonomy of the meanings of possible responses. While this procedure can be flexible, imaginative, and potentially powerful, the problem of objectivity in scoring is serious, and validity or reliability may be questionable.

The projective tests and rating scales available at this time are numerous, and a variety of special techniques have been developed for the indirect analysis of behavior. Among those in general use are the Rorschach test, the Thematic Aperception Test (T.A.T.) and the Rosenzweig Picture-Frustration Test. Horner (1968) made use of a story-completion instrument in her well-known study of the association between success and anxiety in women.

Among the scaling and measurement procedures frequently used with projective tests are the following:

- *Q-Methodology*[33] is a scaling technique (see next section) in which the subject is asked to sort items into groups according to relative agreement or disagreement with some criteria (which may but need not be explicitly stated). Typically, the investigator seeks to measure differences between real and ideal types or to compare a subject's views about different ethnic groups.
- The relatively recent semantic differential technique attempts to elicit the meaning of a concept by asking the respondent to rate the concept on a number of bipolar scales such as fair–unfair, clean–dirty (these reflect *evaluation*; large–small, heavy–light (relecting *potency*); and fast–slow, hot–cold (reflecting *activity*). Note that the bipolar scales are quite irrelevant to the concept being rated. Evidently such scales have a

projective aspect, but they yield an easily computed numerical score; the proponents of this technique claim that it permits comparison of individuals according to the similarity or difference in the way they identify a given concept.[34] Despite considerable resistance to this technique because of its peculiar indirectness, it has potential for research use.

The researcher seeking a test or rating scale for the measurement of some pertinent variable may well begin to feel dizzy in the first encounter with this area of expertise. The sense of being inundated in a vast sea of technicality is entirely justified: The construction and evaluation of instruments is a specialty to which it is possible to devote an entire professional lifetime. You can, however, avoid drowning by adopting a few sensible strategies.

- Familiarize yourself with the basic vocabulary of test construction; most general research texts or manuals have a chapter on this topic. (We have a brief introduction, pp. 151ff.) Then, if your needs or interests make it desirable, consult one of the more specialized reference works dealing with the kind of instruments you plan to use.
- Make the acquaintance of several tests or rating scales related to the one(s) you may ultimately use. They may, for instance, measure different personality traits, or they may present so-called critical incident forced-choices, etc. Try to develop a feel for each of the instruments. The instrument you select should be the best available measuring device for the construct you are interested in.
- Develop a list of sources for instruments. See the references at the end of this chapter, and do not overlook the work of other investigators in your problem area.
- Before using any instrument, mentally rehearse the steps in administering it and in coding, scoring, and analyzing, and interpreting the responses. You must know what scores look like. In particular, check whether the scores are nominal, ordinal, interval or ratio-level. If any special safeguards are necessary to minimize sources of inaccuracy, or if background information must be collected at the same time, be sure to make the arrangements in advance. Keep in mind that specifying a measuring device is also describing a scoring system. Thus decisions about scoring are part of your instrument construction; changes in the scoring of already-existing instruments (for instance, for use in sociometric studies) may necessitate re-piloting as new validity issues emerge. Ignoring this possibility may endanger your entire study.
- If you use an instrument that has been developed in the course of some other research project, make certain it meets the usual criteria for sensitivity, validity, and reliability (see next section); *always* read the description of the procedures by which it was constructed and evaluated.

This is usually obtainable from the original researcher or from the publisher. It is unwise to depend on the summaries which appear in reports of later applications of the instrument.

The rest of this chapter is devoted to a brief introduction to some of the technical vocabulary of instrumentation and to the criteria for evaluating most available or researcher-made instruments.

Some Vocabulary[35]

It is important that you develop an acquaintance with the terminology used to describe tests and rating scales and, more generally, questions and schedules. Some of the terminology is probably already familiar.

QUESTIONS

Questions (items) can be

- Unstructured (free-response): The subject is invited to speak or write freely and at whatever length. These are useful for exploration or when a wide range of responses is anticipated, but they are hard to record and to classify or score.
- Structured (fixed-response): The subject is presented with a set of alternatives. These are easier to answer and to code and score, but critics assert they force artificial choices. There are many types of fixed-response questions and a large literature discussing their relative advantages and disadvantages. Some examples are

  - Dichotomous: agree/disagree, true/false.
  - Paired-comparison: "do you prefer
    (A)____ or (B)____
    (B)____ or (C)____
    (A)____ or (C)____
  - Rank-order: list 1, 2, 3, . . . in order of importance to you.
  - Multiple choice: which of the following would you choose first. . . .
  - Multiple choice Likert-type: agree strongly, agree somewhat, neutral, etc., on a (for example) 5-point scale. This is a type of weighted-response question.
  - Critical incident questions: short "story" followed by statements with which subject indicates relative agreement.

Depending on what data are sought, responses can be analyzed in terms of presence/absence, high/low frequency, high/low intensity, high/low degree of importance, positive/negative direction, and so on. Whatever item form is adopted, a scoring system must be so devised as to yield (numerical) data whose meaning can be interpreted: for example, presence (1) or absence (0) of an attribute. Statistical analysis of the scores may require modification for various item forms.

SCALING: CONSTRUCTING SCALES

Scaling may be usefully regarded as a form of data-reduction: A single number (unidimensional score) or a small set of numbers (multidimensional score) is assigned to a large set of numbers or other components, for example, responses to individual items, physical indicators, etc. For instance, the individual's score is the number of "true" responses on a true–false attitude inventory. Another point of view is that scaling is the operationalizing step in the measurement process: thus, a scale is an internally consistent and duplicatable plan for defining and/or developing a measure. The establishment of a scale may in itself serve a variety of purposes. For example, scaling five indicators in a newborn infant into the well-known Apgar model and then using this model to evaluate the relative fit of these indicators to the category "healthy" is basically a hypothesis-testing approach. Reducing a complex data (response) structure to a summary scale is a form of exploratory analysis, and the decision to scale along several dimensions[36] rather than a single one reflects an hypothesis about the nature of the attribute being measured and its relationship to other measures.

Scales may be applied to persons (e.g., a test rates individuals according to their relative knowledge of a political issue), to stimuli (e.g., a group rates listed qualifications of several candidates), or to responses. An example of the last, in which both persons and stimuli are the subject of the scale, is provided by an attitude scale in which respondents are asked to list the candidates in order of preference. Scaling models can be categorized by subject type (e.g., attitude or aptitude).

Three major types of unidimensional rating scales have been developed; all of these are in general use.[37]

- Summated-rating or additive scale: Each item has equal value, but respondent can indicate degree of agreement. Total score is obtained by summing. Likert-type scales fall into this category. Semantic differential scales (see above) can be used to yield an additive rating. Summated-rating scales, which allow intensity of attitude to be expressed, are probably the most widely used and are the easiest to construct. (In some sense, the familiar "1 point per correct answer," or even the "1/2 for partial credit" test-scoring schemes, represent a special case of this type, as do the scales in which the number of "agree" answers is added to yield the score.) Selltiz et al. (1976, p. 369) observe that the "Likert type scale does not claim to be more than an ordinal scale" but you will find that most statistical analyses treat the scores as interval-level if there are more than 10 items with 5 or more choices.

- Equal-appearing interval scales (Thurstone): Each item, usually in agree-disagree form, has a weight or scale value that reflects strength of attitude. (Ideally, the score values are so chosen that the possible total scores are equally spaced on the scale. Total score is obtained by adding the scale values of the "agree" responses.) Tests with weights assigned to different items resemble this type. These scales are more laborious to construct than the first type.

- Cumulative or Guttman scale: Items are relatively few in number and are all designed to measure the same attribute, chosen and ordered so that agreement—or a correct response—on one item is strongly associated with agreement—or correctness—on the preceding items. Thus, from the total score it is possible to predict with some accuracy the pattern of responses. Items are randomized for test administration. A familiar example is provided by an arithmetic test, where the individual who answers hard items correctly is very likely to have answered the easy ones correctly also, and contrariwise. A shortcoming of any Guttman scale is that the ordering of items is determined according to each population to which the test is administered, so the predictive usefulness can be much lower in another population.

These and many other scaling models can each be characterized by the curve that describes the relationship between the probability of specific response to a dichotomous item (e.g., "Do you feel nauseated before a math test?") and the attribute (e.g., mathematics anxiety) that the item supposedly measures. Such a curve is called a *trace line*. The scaling types described above have trace lines shown graphically in Figure 7.1.

If you know in advance which characteristic curve you prefer, you can select the appropriate scaling model; then, formulation of items varies according to the anticipated scaling model to be used.

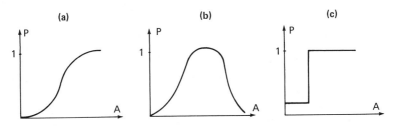

FIGURE 7.1. Trace lines of principal scaling types: (a) summated rating scale, (b) equal-appearing interval scale, (c) cumulative scale. P, probability of a "yes" response; A, attribute being measured, e.g., "math anxiety".

Frequently when responses to items on a multiple-item instrument are scrutinized using some clustering technique, such as factor analysis, the items can be assigned to two or more subscales. This means, in effect, that the instrument yields not a scalar measure but a vector (multiple component) measure. For instance, the Halpin–Crofts Leadership Behavior Description Questionnaire allows a leader to be rated in each of two dimensions, Consideration and Initiating Structure, which are independent. Similarly, Sheldon's (1940) somatotyping procedure leads to a three-dimensional typology with ecto-, meso-, and endomorphic components. Multidimensional scaling models (see below) thus assign to the object a point in multidimensional space, rather than a point on a line. A social class scale which combines dimensions of income, education, place of residence, and occupation, each of which is measured along a different axis and in different units, thus represents an effort to assign a single number (scalar) to a 4-component vector.

The term *multidimensional scaling* refers to a class of techniques. Input is a set of proximities, similarities, or dissimilarities between pairs of any kind of objects; output is a spatial configuration of points, with each point corresponding to one of the objects. These points are then clustered into families or "dimensions." Choice of particular clustering techniques depends on the type of data. For metric data, regression analysis and factor analysis are often used. MRSCAL is a computer program which can carry out several types of multidimensional scaling for metric data using different criteria such as smallest space or the method of steepest descent. MINISSA and MDSCAL are computer programs which can be applied to nonmetric data.

A wide variety of problems can be attacked by such methods. Included are the development of taxonomies based on pair-wise comparisons for "likeness," in biology, liguistics, and anthropology (see Note 31). Despite the technical difficulties, scaling techniques are the key to successful operationalizing of measurement and so occupy a crucial place in the development of any study. It is important at the very least to understand what scaling model is embodied in the instrument(s) you use.

INDEXES[38]

An *index number* is most simply described as a scale that assigns a single number not to objects but to n-tuples of other numbers (not necessarily in the same units) in such a way as to permit the computation of ratios with specified n-tuple called the *base*. In this way comparisons against a base, and comparisons of change in several different items relative to their respective bases, can be made. Consider some examples. IQ can be regarded as an index: ratio of mental age to chronological age. If the population of each of three suburban communities is recorded in 1950 as 2000, 3000, 4000; in 1960 as 7000, 10500, 14000; and in 1970 as 12000, 13000, and 14000, then using the 1950 populations as a base, the index values (also called *relatives*) are all 3 for 1960 but for 1970 are 6, 4.3, and 3.5, even though the absolute population increase has been the same over the 20-year period. Of course, we do not need the concept of index number in order to exhibit this relationship. Index numbers become more useful and also much more complicated in such cases as the familiar Consumer Price Index, currently based on the 1967 prices of a typical market basket of purchases; or an energy consumption index combines tons of coal, gallons of oil, and kilowatts; or indexes measuring quality of life, stress, and other social and psychological variables. Thus, an index may be used to indicate relative contribution of different groups of items in an aggregation (compared to a base mixture), or change in an aggregation over an interval (compared to the initial time).

An index number can be viewed as the outcome of what is intuitively a sort of averaging process applied to the index values of its components derived from sample data. Such an averaging process, while it smooths variation in individual component variables, must not completely suppress or cancel these variations. The crucial decisions in constructing an index are how to weight the components when there are two or more, and which averaging procedure to use. An introductory discussion of some of the alternatives can be found in Yamane (1976b), along with formulas for linking, splicing, re-basing, or chaining index numbers, and tests for evaluating the degree of bias that a given definition of an index may introduce.

Index numbers have been used mainly in economics but have many other potential applications in the social and behavioral sciences. Indexes are a powerful device to summarize diverse data into an index value formulated as a one-dimensional measure and thus permit effective comparisons.

NORMATIVE AND IPSATIVE SCORING

As noted earlier, statistical analysis of scores depends to some extent on item-form and the scaling model used. The distinction between normative and ipsative measures is also important in your choice of statistical analysis. When an instrument is scored *normatively*, the individual's score is referred for interpretation to the mean and standard deviation of the scores of all respondents in some group. In theory, since the scale items are independent, an individual can achieve any score. *Ipsative* scoring is appropriate when items are not independent: for example, in paired-comparison, rank-order, Q-methodology, and other forced-choice forms. Scores are in general not referable to the mean of the group and, inevitably, item scores are negatively correlated. It is important to remember not to use any statistical tests with ipsative data whose underlying assumptions include independence of item scores. (Rank-order statistics are often appropriate.)

Criteria for Evaluating Instruments

In order to be of value in research, instruments must yield accurate data; otherwise, no confidence can be placed in the conclusions drawn from those data. In this section we discuss some of the criteria for evaluating measuring instruments. Keep in mind that this is just touching the surface of a large and highly technical subject.[39]

There is virtually no disagreement among researchers that validity and reliability are essential characteristics of a good instrument; in addition, sensitivity and standardization are important considerations. Other attributes may be determined by the needs of the particular problem area; for example, data of a specified level may be necessary to permit certain types of analysis.

Checklists included in the Additional Reading of this chapter should be helpful in evaluating your proposed instruments and data-collection procedures.

VALIDITY

An instrument is valid when it measures what it is intended to measure. (It may measure something else quite well, but fail to be valid for the intended use: A mathematics achievement test is not valid as a measure of mastery of computer programming skills.) Alternatively, an instrument is valid if the systematic error of its measurements is small. "The subject of validity is complex, controversial, and peculiarly important in behavioral research. Here . . . the nature of reality is questioned. It is not possible to study validity, [unlike reliability], . . . without sooner or later inquiring into the nature of one's variables."[40]

Recall that the scientist is interested in obtaining knowledge about objects, individuals, and events—and depends ultimately upon observations and measurements—but the properties of objects are neither observed nor measured: The existence of a property (or characteristic) is inferred from an indicant (see p. 134). Certain verbal behaviors, for instance, are indicants of the constructs we call attitudes such as bigotry or tolerance. The indicants are measured, and an inference is then made about the constructs or variables. It is important to keep in mind that almost all the important variables of social and behavioral research, such as intelligence, achievement, attitude, self-concept, social class, personality (traits), preference, kinship, mental health, etc., are constructs. Constructs can be defined in two ways:

- A *constitutive* definition specifies the construct in terms of other components.
- An *operational* definition specifies the construct by specifying either how to manipulate it or how to measure it. (See Chapter 4, sections on definitions and operationalizing; it should be evident that validity is a formulation of goodness-of-fit or epistemic correlation.)

An example which illustrates the distinction just mentioned is that of social class. "The term 'social class' . . . is used . . . to refer to the horizontal stratification of a population by means of factors related in some general way to the economic life of the society."[41] Warner, for instance, bases his research on the concept of a status group whose ranking is determined by judgments of members of the society, incorporated into an instrument (Index of Status Characteristics or ISC) which measures six characteristics: occupation, education, income, source of income, house type and dwelling area. Thus, social class can be defined operationally by the clustering of scores of individuals who respond to the ISC. Constitutive definitions of social class are elusive, because the core concept is the pattern of social relationships in which members of the society engage. Gordon (1958) discusses at some length the difficulties in formulating a constitutive definition, the failure of various authors to agree on a meaning for the term "social class", and the resulting lack of precision in its use.

We now look at the notion of instrument validity bearing the preceding in mind. Several somewhat differing criteria for validity have been proposed.

- An instrument possesses *content validity* if it provides an adequate sample of the universe of content or substance of the property being measured, that is, of everything that can be said or observed about the property. As phrased, this definition poses a theoretical problem impossible of solution. In practice, content validation requires that competent judges use their experience and expertise to evaluate the items and the instrument as a whole, and that their independent judgments be pooled. The judges must be given as clear as possible a description of the universe of content as well as specifications for what they are judging. It may be difficult to find experts and to evaluate the extent of agreement among them. Nonetheless, every instrument should undergo at least content validation. A common mistake is regarding instruments, for example, achievement tests, as "self-validating."
- An instrument possesses *criterion-related validity* if the measurements it yields correlate strongly with the measures of one or more external variables (criteria) which are known or plausibly believed to be associated with the construct being studied. Scores on your instrument should allow you to discriminate between those individuals who possess the criterion

property and those who do not. For example, scores on a test for aptitude in computer-programming can be correlated with some measure of success in a computer course (*predictive* validity), or with measures on performance or aptitude instruments in logic or problem-solving (*concurrent* or *discriminant* validity). It may be difficult to find suitable criterion variables or to find valid measures for them.

Predictive validity evidently assumes great importance when the measurements (scores) are used to make decisions about a possible course of action. You can easily appreciate that an aptitude test with poor predictive validity is useless, or worse; the predictive or concurrent validity of various measures of economic activity can be significantly reflected in the success or failure of certain government policies. In general, if your main interest in research lies in application of your results to practical problems, you may want to concentrate your attention on achieving predictive validity in your instruments; if, on the other hand, your primary concern is with developing new theory, criterion-related validity (predictive or concurrent) is inappropriate.

- *Construct validity* is set apart from other types of validity by its concern with the theoretical context within which the construct being measured is hypothesized as relating to other constructs. The process of construct validation, in effect, calls for validating the theory underlying the instrument. It requires:

1. Identification of theoretically plausible constructs accounting for the measures assigned by this instrument (e.g., test scores). The techniques of factor analysis are frequently used to identify clusters of items that suggest the definitions of new constructs. Path analysis can be employed to assess the relative importance of these factors.
2. Formulation of hypotheses describing the conjectured relationships between the measured construct and the other identified constructs (or clusters of constructs). These hypotheses are derived from theory involving the constructs.
3. Empirical testing of alternative hypotheses, to establish convergence (evidence from different sources, gathered in different ways, must all point to the same or similar meaning of the construct) and discriminability (it is possible empirically to differentiate the construct from other constructs that may be similar, and to identify what is unrelated to the construct).

Even from this brief description you can see that construct validity is a very sophisticated and demanding requirement on an instrument, and that the processes of defining the construct and developing of the measure require a systematic scientific research project in themselves. Construct validation employs procedures designed to increase our confidence that something is actually being measured and that the measures permit meaningful inferences to be made. Construct validity is the only suitable type for an instrument to be used in basic or even applied research.[42]

Interesting examples of problems of construct validation can be found in the literature dealing with social class measurement scales.[43] For instance, factor analysis of responses to interview questions concerning a large number of variables may help the researcher to identify factors to be incorporated into a scale; then, analysis of correlations of scale scores with other indicators theoretically associated with social class can support the selection of these factors.

RELIABILITY

An instrument is reliable if it yields measurements which are:

- consistent and predictable (repeated measurements are strongly correlated)
- accurate and precise (measurements are close to the "true" values)

or more precisely, if the random or error variance of the measurements is small compared to the total variance (this ratio is called the *error of measurement*).

Even if the error variance is small, the systematic error, or *bias*, can be large. Systematic error concerns the issue of validity (see above); hence, an instrument can be reliable without being valid. On the other hand, it is hard to imagine assessing the validity of an instrument if it is not reliable.

The reliability coefficient of an instrument is defined theoretically as the ratio of the true variance of the measurements to their total variance; that is, the proportion of total variance not attributable to errors of measurement. In practice it must estimated by one of several procedures, each of which reflects a slightly different point of view.

- *Test–reliability*: The instrument is administered to the same sample on two different occasions, and the Pearson product-moment correlation between the two sets of measures is computed. The reliability coefficient describes *stability*.
- *Internal-consistency reliability*: The instrument is administered once; scores on all possible subtests (subsets of test items) and all intercorrelations are computed; the mean intercorrelation, corrected by the Spearman–Brown formula, is a measure of internal consistency. High reliability by this criterion, which is a sort of generalization of the so-called split-half method, means each subset ranks the subjects in the same order; low reliability implies this is not so.

- *Item-reliability*: On the assumption that all the items measure single trait, Kuder and Richardson obtained formulas which take into account the proportion of correct responses to a given question; the formulas are simplified if all items are of equal difficulty.
- *Equivalent forms reliability:* Two forms of the instrument, judged to be equivalent, are administered and the correlation coefficient of the two sets of scores is calculated. Reliability is interpreted as *equivalence.*

Each of these techniques has advantages and disadvantages, for which you would do well to consult the technical literature. The use to which you will put your measurements, together with the circumstances in which you apply or administer it, suggest which of the above criteria of reliability is most appropriate. If your project requires personal interviews, your concerns may involve the external conditions of measurement as well as the internal consistency of the instrument. Since the technical aspect of reliability assessment is well-presented elsewhere, we do not discuss it in further detail here.[44]

It is important for you to check on the original validity and reliability studies in preparing to use any already developed instrument. As you can see from the two preceding sections, it is also important that you understand *what kind* of validity and reliability were established, because, for example, predictive validity may be inappropriate or inadequate for your purpose, or test–retest reliability may be meaningless or irrelevant for your population.

A widely accepted way to increase accuracy is to carry out multiple measurements of the same construct when possible, using either different instruments, or repeated applications of the same instrument. Since the "noise" components probably differ in each measurement, one can have strong confidence in the outcomes if they are consistent. This strategy embodies the notions of validity and reliability. Thus, improvement in the validity and reliability of a question-and-answer instrument can be facilitated by:

- Writing the items unambiguously. Differences in interpretation permit increases in error variance.
- Adding items of equal kind and quality, such as several questions on the same issues. Where there are more items, a random error is more likely to be balanced by another random error with opposite sign.
- Clarifying and standardizing instructions, and carefully controlling the conditions of administration.

Finally, keep in mind that so-called objective tests (standardized and scored) represent an effort to identify some invariant in the individual; whereas, other instruments may seek contextual, situational, or temporally dependent responses. Hence, the traditional formulations of reliability may be inappropriate or inapplicable in some cases, for instance, for certain survey instruments.

STANDARDIZATION

In order that an instrument may be useful in research with a particular set of subjects, it may be desirable to compare the measurements obtained from these subjects and those obtained by known subjects. The process of carrying out preliminary studies of the way the instrument works—in order to obtain a basis for comparison—is called *standardization*; it requires administration of the instrument under controlled circumstances to a well-defined group and the careful specification of performance records, called norms, for this group. (Do not confuse this with the issue of normative versus ipsative scoring, above.) The selection of the so-called norm group can be crucial, especially for achievement and aptitude tests, because of the need to make inferences about measurements from later study populations. The norm group should be one for which other measures, such as those with which you expect yours to be correlated, are available. The group must be large enough to permit statistical conclusions about validity and reliability, and it must be representative of the populations to which the instruments will later be applied. The standardization of administration also requires attention to uniformity of instructions, and so on. A well-known example of normed instruments are the Wechsler intelligence tests.

Standardizing an instrument, whether it is an interview schedule, a device to measure reaction-time, an objective test, or any one of a variety of expressive or projective techniques, is a highly technical enterprise. When properly done it constitutes a substantial research project in itself. (See later section in this chapter: Problems of Developing Your Own Instrument.)

SENSITIVITY AND DIFFERENTIABILITY

The instrument should be able to distinguish sufficiently small differences in the attribute you want to measure, so that subjects are assigned different measurements in an appropriate way. Moreover, the break points in the patterns or clusters of responses at which different measures are assigned should be plausible in view of what is known about the measured attribute. For instance, a performance test designed to measure manual dexterity and used as a predictor of success in a training course for small-parts assembly workers should not only identify those possessing high dexterity but should distinguish various degrees of dexterity in a realistic way to permit placement of workers. As another example, a projective test intended to assist child therapists in diagnosing their patients' problems should differentiate categories of the patients' responses.

To achieve these characteristics of sensitivity and differentiability, good judgment and thoughtful analysis of the attribute to be measured are needed. Statistical procedures, such as cluster or discriminant analysis of the responses, may make it easier to find the break points between assigned numerals.[45]

THE ROLE OF MEASUREMENT AND INSTRUMENTATION

[O]perationalization of independent variables is essentially the statement of procedures used to create their levels. Choice of instruments is as important as any step in an investigation, but too often little attention is given to instrumentation. . . . Too often an investigator spends much time and energy developing a complex manipulation for the independent variable, but only spends a few moments creating self-report items of unknown reliability and untested validity to measure the dependent variable.[46]

Weaknesses of instrumentation constitute the most serious problems in the research projects undertaken by novices. Likewise, one of the most difficult tasks confronting any investigator is constructing a suitable instrument and establishing its validity and reliability for the purpose(s) of the research at hand.

Problems of Developing Your Own Instrument

Beginners seriously underestimate the difficulty of developing an instrument, which also necessarily means selecting a measure. Needless to say, you must have at the outset some kind of intuitive feeling for the attribute to be measured, that is, a good understanding of the construct in question. Let us look at the different types of measuring devices and the characteristic pitfalls in their construction.

If you do not already possess, and cannot acquire, mechanical or electrical/electronic know-how, there is no question of your developing your own equipment. Your task will be to find a competent technician, describe your specifications as clearly as possible, and wait. If you are fortunate, it will be possible to adapt a more-or-less standard item to your needs; if not, what you want will have to be built from scratch, and the expense in time and money may be considerable. Remember, the machine will not be able to read your mind, so any capabilities not built in will not be available.

Interview schedules and self-administered questionnaires can usually be developed by the researcher, but it is not a job to be undertaken casually. Resources are available in most universities in the form of experts, files of previously-used questionnaires, courses in interviewing, and reference literature. It is very helpful to ask an experienced researcher in an area related to yours to look over your questionnaire. Instructions for administration and the items themselves should be phrased unambiguously; ideally, each item should involve only one bit of information or opinion. A careful analysis of your problem-question should help you to anticipate the range of possible responses and/or the acceptable responses to each item. Remember that any information you fail to elicit from your subjects will be unavailable for later analysis, so that a comparison of your questionnaire with your hypotheses (or problem statement) may prevent grief later on. The responses should be easy for you to classify and code.

It is essential to pilot test your instrument and your instructions, with a group of subjects genuinely comparable to the subjects you will use for your research, because you must determine whether the instrument discriminates between the categories covered by your hypotheses. If not, it is useless. (See discussion of pilot studies in Chapter 6.)

The problems of developing objective tests and rating scales are far more complex, because of the need to establish reliability and validity, as well as (often) to define the construct. In fact, carrying out the procedures—which require a theoretical rationale, a suitably specified and selected norm population, repeated administration of preliminary and final versions of the proposed test and of related instruments, and a sophisticated data analysis—constitutes a respectable research project in itself. Some studies develop a construct and an instrument more or less simultaneously. This is a particularly difficult and delicate enterprise and requires a great deal of careful thought in order to avoid circularity, weakness in validity, or a shallow definition. There is nothing standard or mechanical about such a project. Attitude, value, and personality scales are particularly difficult to validate, and may have low reliability. A number of special techniques have been developed for the construction and scoring of such instruments. (See Oppenheim [1966] and Schuman and Presser [1981].) Consequently, our advice to you if you are considering developing objective tests and rating scales is DON'T!

What are your options in planning instrumentation?

- Unless the goal of your study is the development of the measure, make every effort to find a suitably validated instrument appropriate for your needs. (It is possible to make minor changes in a test or scale and to check the new version for validity and reliability with relatively little difficulty.) Verify copyright status and permission requirements of any instrument you plan to use.
- If you have no choice, seek an expert in test construction. Ordinarily, a graduate department in psychology or educational psychology will be able to recommend one. Be prepared to learn a great deal of new, highly specialized technical material.
- Prepare yourself also for a long delay before you can take up the part of your study that uses the test, because many months are usually needed

to carry out the steps described above even if you have the services of a skilled and interested consultant.

> Measurement is never better than the empirical operations by which it is carried out, and operations range from bad to good. Any particular scale, psychological or physical, may be objected to on the grounds of bias, low precision, restricted generality, and other factors, but the objector should remember that these are relative and practical matters and that no scale used by mortals is perfectly free of taint.[47]

And keep in mind that measurement involves both philosophical and practical issues, as we have repeatedly emphasized; neither can be disregarded. Your choice of variables and the nature of your conjectures, the setting in which you plan to carry out your study, and such constraints as time, money, and available personnel, will in part determine both instrumentation and procedures for data-collection.

Another set of decisions involving many of the same considerations lead to the selection of a suitable study population. The next chapter addresses these.

Notes

[1]Ellis (1968, p. 1). Our introductory section strongly reflects the viewpoint of Ellis and is largely based on his discussion. The concepts may be difficult to follow. Press on regardless: the later sections of his book offer a practical and straightforward discussion of important issues.

[2]Ellis (1968, p. 1).

[3]See Ellis (1968, Chapter II) whose main point is "operational significance can be given to quantify names without describing any measuring operations," (p. 38). Ellis observes (p. 31) that fairly rigid criteria can be formulated for the existence of quantities independent of measurement or calculation, but that while these criteria work well for physical quantities, they would exclude many psychological and social ones. He then admits it is probably impossible to set out criteria which will be both interesting and sufficiently inclusive. A real question in the social and behavioral sciences is often whether there is in fact a quantity to be measured. It is, however, hard to contemplate a discussion of test validity in the absence of the attribute!

[4]Stevens (1951, pp. 1-2). Stevens' formulation is generally accepted today: "A rule for the assignment of numerals (numbers) to aspects of objects or events creates a scale."

[5]Campbell (1957) attempted to classify scales according to the procedures used in setting them up. *Fundamental* or direct measures are those which do not depend on prior measures, whereas *derived* measures are obtained by the application of mathematical functions to other measures. The former are exemplified by length and weight, the latter by density and velocity. The classification was developed in the context of the scales used in physics, and although the ideas are important—as are Ellis' (1968) criticisms and amendments (pp. 74-127)—they are less pertinent to the social and behavioral sciences.

[6]Scales can also be classified according to permissible applications of arithmetic, so that for a nominal scale a $\neq$ b, for an ordinal scale, a $\gtreqless$ b etc. See Ellis (1968, pp. 58-61 and 63-67).

Alternatively, we can say that measurements on an ordinal scale are transitive and asymmetric, while those on an interval scale are also additive.

[7]Mezzich and Solomon (1980).

[8]See Ellis (1968, pp. 58ff.), which also includes a well-presented example.

[9]Stevens (1951, p. 27). See also Blalock (1960, Chapters 1 and 2).

[10]Abelson and Tukey (1959), Lodge (1981).

[11]"Numerosity" is a further example mentioned by Stevens but Ellis objects (Ellis, (1968, Chapter X). There is a misleading resemblance between counting and measuring: it is appealing but incorrect to think of measurement as involving the cardinality or numerosity of a bunch of units.

[12]Plutchik, (1974, p. 263). Compare, however, note 8 above. See also Campbell (1921, p. 121).

[13]Stevens (1951, p. 23). For more detail see Chapters 10, 11, and 12–14.

[14]For examples of the interchange, and a reprint of the crucial portion of Stevens' essay, see Steger (1971, pp. 6–52) or Haber, Runyon and Badia (1970, pp. 1–63, Block 1).

[15]Kerlinger (1973, pp. 430–440).

[16]Kerlinger (1973, p. 441). An instructive simulation of the way use of ordinal data as interval can distort the outcome of a t-test, introducing either α (Type I) or β (Type II) errors, is reported by Trachtman, Giambalvo, and Dippner (1978). Also pertinent are Townsend and Ashley (1984), and Moses et al. (1984).

[17]Anderson (1961), reprinted in Steger (1971, p. 28).

[18]Blalock (1960, Chapters 1 and 2).

[19]A variety of suggestions for measurement without the awareness of the subject can be found in Webb et al. (1966) and Wiggins (1968). See also Plutchik (1974, Chapter 14).

[20]A comprehensive list of data-gathering techniques and many references on the use of various instruments can be found in Kerlinger (1973, Chapters 28–30). This is a useful introduction to the field of instrumentation. "Get your facts first and then you can distort 'em as much as you please" (Mark Twain).

[21]There are many studies in which the investigator becomes a participant as well as an observer. An anthropologist collecting information, whether from an isolated tribe or an urban subculture, as in Wallace's study (1965) of Skid Row, must in some way interact with the subjects. A military historian may find himself actively involved in the battle that he was brought along to observe. The opportunity for bias is obvious, but what to do about it is much less obvious. An extensive literature on the pitfalls of participant-observation has developed in recent years; see Selltiz et al., (1976), for an introductory discussion of hazards and safeguards. See Denzin (1978) for a discussion of participant-observation (field methods) and associated validity issues. The latter have recently (Winter, 1982–1983) captured public attention in connection with the early work of Margaret Mead.

[22]Backstrom and Hursh-Cesar (1981, p. 119). This section draws heavily on this important manual (which is very practical) with useful instructions, examples, checklists, and excellent references on all aspects of question-writing (not just survey questions). Also many sections on pre-testing, training interviewers, mailing, etc.

[23]Backstrom and Hursh-Cesar (1981, p. 121).

[24]For the distinctions, see Backstrom and Hursh-Cesar (1981, pp. 125ff.) and Kerlinger (1973, pp. 495–499).

[25]Roethlisberger and Dickson (1939), cited in Madge (1967, p. 154).

[26]Backstrom and Hursh-Cesar (1981, Chapter 4).

[27]We are following that of Kerlinger (1973); Babbie's (1979) is often in conflict, for example, in the use of *scale*.

[28]See Backstrom and Hursh-Cesar (1981, pp. 20ff.: Chapter 5 [conducting interviews] and Chapter 4 [questionnaires]). Special issues related to telephone interviews are discussed in Groves and Kahn (1979); this book is very thorough and helpful, includes mention of costs, sampling, form of questions, etc. *ISR Interviewer's Manual* (1976) is generally useful. Converse and Schuman (1974) discusses problems of survey research from the interviewers' standpoint. Presentation of

some of the arguments for a "participatory" or "intimate" interview strategy can be found in Oakley (1979, 1981). The latter has an excellent bibliography. Gorden (1975) emphasizes communication rather than "information gathering" and provides many exercises and discussion of specific techniques for special types of interviews.

[29]The terminology and to a certain extent the classification used in this section follows that of Kerlinger (1973, Chapters 29–30), which we recommend for an overview and for specialized references. However, Kerlinger emphasizes the objectivity of tests and scales (in contrast to interviews), whereas we feel the distinction between them and, say, ad hoc opinion or fact questionnaires should be based on other criteria. Selltiz et al. (1976, Chapter 10) provides an accessible and very thoughtful introduction to the construction of scales as rating devices.

[30]Kerlinger (1973, p. 499).

[31]Special analytic methods, designed to map the underlying space on the basis of "distance" data, include multidimensional scaling. See Kruskal and Wish (1978), Schiffman et al. (1981), and Shepard et al. (1972); for a brief discussion, see section on scaling, this chapter. An interesting example of scaling of geographical preferences can be found in Gould and White (1974), especially Chapter 2.

[32]See short section Selltiz et al. (1976, Chapter 10) and Kerlinger (1973, Chapter 30).

[33]Kerlinger (1973, Chapter 34).

[34]See Selltiz et al. (1976, pp. 380–383) and Kerlinger (1973, Chapter 33).

[35]This section follows Coombs (1964) and McIver and Carmines (1981).

[36]Compare, for example, Gordon (1958) and Coleman and Rainwater (1978). For a related discussion of the psychophysical model for scaling in the social sciences, see Lodge (1981).

[37]See Carmines and Zeller (1979), Lodge (1981), and McIver and Carmines (1981) for relative advantages and disadvantages of different types. See also Backstrom and Hursh-Cesar (1981, pp. 128–139).

[38]The use of this term here is as in economics; Babbie (1979) has a different usage.

[39]In particular, see Kerlinger (1973) (whose terminology we use), Guilford (1954), and Nunnally (1973); Roscoe (1975) has a brief but informative summary; Plutchik (1974) has a thoughtful discussion.

[40]Kerlinger (1973, p. 456).

[41]Gordon (1958, p. 3). See also note 36.

[42]For thorough discussion of construct validation, see Cronbach and Meehl (1956). See also Zeller and Carmines (1980) and Kerlinger (1973, Chapter 27).

[43]Gordon (1958) reviews the development of several social class scales.

[44]See Kerlinger (1973, Chapter 26), Guilford and Fruchter (1973; 1977, Chapters 17 and 18), Carmines and Zeller (1979), Zeller and Carmines (1980), Selltiz et al. (1976, passim), Plutchik (1974), and Backstrom and Hursh-Cesar (1981) for issues relevant to survey questionnaires.

[45]Mezzich and Solomon (1980).

[46]Spector (1981, p. 20, original emphasis).

[47]Stevens (1951, p. 30).

Additional Reading

References on theory of measurement will be found in the Notes: We particularly recommend: Blalock and Blalock (1968, Chapter 1), Blalock (1960, 1st ed., Chapters 1 and 2), Ellis (1968), and Coombs (1950, 1952a, b, 1964). None of these is very easy but all are thought-provoking and worth the effort. Coleman (1964, Chapters 1–4) offers an interesting discussion of the role of measurement in theory-building.

Scale Construction

Rozeboom (1966): nice elementary tone.
Carmines and Zeller (1979); clear elementary introduction to reliability and validity issues.
Thorndike (1971); educational measurement: authoritative.
Guilford and Fruchter (1973, 1977) ⎫
Anastasi (1976) ⎪ validity and reliability from a
Kerlinger (1973) ⎬ technical viewpoint.
Nunnally (1973) ⎭
Zeller and Carmines (1980) ⎫
Cronbach (1971) ⎬ construct validity
Cronbach and Meehl (1956) ⎭
Combs (1950, 1952b), Edwards (1957): attitude and other psychological scales.
Stevens (1972): very informative; psychometric viewpoint.
Lodge (1981): psychometric orientation.
Stouffer et al. (1950): many general issues on scaling, plus specific methodological discussion.
Selltiz et al. (1976): Chapter 6 introduces validity and reliability; Chapter 12 discusses attitude measurement.
McIver and Carmines (1981): unidimensional scaling very clearly presented.
Kruskal and Wish (1978): multidimensional scaling clearly introduced.
Bloom (1956): helpful for achievement or performance tests.
Sullivan and Feldman (1979): multiple indicators.

Questionnaires and Interviews

Backstrom and Hursh-Cesar (1981): generally useful on all aspects of survey research.
ISR Interviewer's Manual (1973): guidelines and know-how.
Payne (1951): very detailed on form of questions.
Babbie (1979): standard.
Oppenheim (1960): question form and sequencing; attitude questionnaires; practical.
Webb et al. (1966): nonreactive interview and questionnaire techniques.
Schuman and Presser (1980): reports of experimental studies of form and other aspects of questionnaire construction and administration.
Schuman and Presser (1981): construction of questionnaires on attitudes.
Kahn and Cannell (1957): very thorough; applications to medicine, social work, etc.; also have a chapter in Festinger and Katz (1966).
Simon (1978): advantages and disadvantages of different data-collection techniques.
Bailey (1982): ditto.
Madge (1967): superb, very practical.
Groves and Kahn (1979): techniques for telephone surveys.
Merton et al. (1956) ⎫ interview techniques, from
Stewart and Cash (1974) ⎬ the formal survey to the
Gorden (1975) ⎭ open ended probing.
Sheatsley (1951) and Kronhauser and Sheatsley (1976): interviewing and schedules.
Rosenberg (1968): thoughtful pre-analysis; *not* a how-to book.

All of these are rich in further references. All emphasize the importance of know-how, and the role of experience.

Participant-Observation, Nonreactive Research, Related Topics

Madge (1967): Chapter 3.
Madge and Harrison (1938): the horse's mouth.
Kerlinger (1973): pp. 539–549.
Webb et al. (1966): the low profile; using "stooges"; wonderful references; nonreactive questionnaire and interview techniques.
Jacobs (1970): participant-observation.
Oakley (1981): nontraditional interview situations.

Sources of Instruments

First and foremost—other reports on related problems may suggest sources.

Buros (1965, 1972, 1978)
Miller (1970)
Robinson and Shaver (1969)   } Buros reviews tests and other instruments for their research suitability. All contain lists.
Shaw and Wright (1967)
Thorndike and Hagen (1961)

Sidman (1960): equipment.
Chun et al. (1975): sources and citations, emphasis on psychological measures.

8

The Study Population: Sampling

Introduction

Imagine that a physician is visited by a patient complaining of breathlessness, chronic fatigue, a general lack of energy, and persistent drowsiness. The patient appears listless and pale. The physician may suspect anemia, a condition characterized chiefly by a deficiency in the number of circulating red (oxygen-carrying) blood cells. The physician knows that the red cell counts of 99.73% of "normal" individuals of specified sex, age, height, and weight fall within certain limits, establishing a confidence interval. Thus, to test the hypothesis of low red count, the physician must ascertain the number of red blood cells in the patient's body. She could draw out all the patient's blood for the count but, while this procedure would permit confirmation or rejection of the hypothesis, its effect on the patient would be more damaging than that of an untreated anemia. It is preferable that the physician draw a sample of blood, small enough to avoid injury to the patient's health but large enough to permit an informative cell count.

The foregoing illustrates a situation in which sampling offers the only possibility of obtaining certain information. By *sample* is meant a subset of the *universe* or *population* we want to know something about. A count of the entire universe; for example, all the red cells, is called a *census*. A complete and accurate census is always preferable to the use of a sample, but in some cases a census is impossible. Where a census would require examination of the whole of a large population in a very short time interval, a sample may yield comparably accurate results. For instance, the U.S. population count is designed to be carried out on a specified day; the errors involved in counting more than 200 million persons are no less difficult to deal with than those which might arise from a well-constructed sampling procedure applied to this universe.

Sampling is a highly technical subject, and it is important for you to be familiar with its basic terminology. The first step in a discussion of sampling is the identification of the target population or universe (these words are used interchangeably) from which a sample is to be drawn. A population is the totality of all the cases, called *population elements*, or *units*, that meet some designated set of specifications. When one population is included in another, the former is called a *subpopulation*, or a *stratum* (pl. *strata*). It is essential that the population units be clearly definable. Identifying the population properly can be a difficult problem in itself.

An interesting illustration of some of the problems encountered in using a census is provided by the study (Lyon et al., 1978) of cardiovascular mortality 1969–1971 in Utah. In order to test the conjecture that mortality from ischemic heart disease would be lower among Mormons (who neither drink nor smoke) than among non-Mormons, it was necessary to carry out a proper classification of death certificates so as to identify and locate the Mormons; this was possible because of the availability of extensive and up-to-date records maintained by the Mormon Church (The Church of Jesus Christ of Latter-Day Saints). (Findings strongly supported the conjecture.)

While hypothetically the universe can be infinite (e.g., the set of all positive integers), in practice it is always finite (e.g., the set of all patients in a certain institution, children in a certain class, or all female holders of a doctoral degree). If samples are repeatedly drawn from a finite universe, and the units are not replaced (sampling without replacement), the universe will eventually be exhausted. In contrast, if the units are replaced after inspection (sampling with replacement) the number of units in the universe remains the same. Then, in effect, the universe is infinitely large, since it is not diminished by the removal of a finite subset. Mathematically, the analysis of sampling with replacement from a finite universe approximates that of sampling from an infinite universe.[1] Under appropriate assumptions, the same statement holds where a sample (which may be large) is small in proportion to a very large-but-finite population.

We choose a sample from a universe because we are concerned with some specified characteristic of this universe. For example, we may be interested in hospital patients for a study of response to different types of nursing care, in brands of soap for a study of consumer behavior, or in religions for a study of the relationship of religious affiliation and community activism. Thus, the characteristic(s) we are interested in determine(s) our unit of analysis. The *unit of analysis* is, roughly, the portion or subset of the population about which you seek to obtain information so as to make descriptions or comparisons. Treatments, illnesses, durations, and classes represent aggregates of individuals: Select as the unit of analysis the smallest aggregate unit that makes sense to your study. In studying hospital patients who may be suffering from different illnesses for varying lengths of time and receiving different treatments, the individuals are the units of analysis. In contrast, a study of methods of instruction may have classes as the units of analysis. We may be examining several characteristics of the unit of analysis such as the cost of the soap, the color of the package, the size of the bar, etc. From the foregoing, it should be evident that the target population is implicit in your choice of arena for your study, and the unit of analysis is determined by your conjectures.

An example of a study whose report reflects some confusion concerning the unit of analysis is that of McMillan (1977) concerning possible effects of effort and feedback on student attitudes. Although the author uses students as the units of analysis, he states as a limitation (!) that in fact classrooms should have been the units since the students are not assigned randomly.

In any study, the choice of sample will determine the generalizability of the results. This means you can make statements only about the populations your sample represents.

To be useful a sample must satisfy three criteria:

- The sample must represent the population.
- The sampling procedure must be efficient and economical.
- The estimates of population characteristics (e.g., income, religious affiliation, sexual preference) obtained from the sample must be precise and testable for reliability.

The basic distinction in sampling is between probability and nonprobability samples. A *probability sample* is one in which the probability that any element of the population will be included can be specified; in the simplest case each element is equiprobable, but this is not necessary. It is only necessary that the probability of inclusion be knowable. For example, if you have a mixture of 10 rough and 20 smooth chips and choose one in a blind draw, each rough chip has a 10/30 probability of being selected and each smooth chip a 20/30 probability of being selected. In contrast, the probability of any element's inclusion in a *nonprobability sample* is unknown. Hence the typicality of the sample cannot be assessed. Despite this drawback, nonprobability sampling has a place in research, particularly when the goal is not to generalize.[2] When based on good judgment, a meaningful quota, or even a serendipitous hit or miss technique, a nonprobability sample can permit data to be gathered that would otherwise not be available. The researcher may get ideas and insights; in some cases volunteer subjects, the probability of whose inclusion is not at all knowable, result in more sensitive data collection (e.g., in clinical studies). It is unlikely that a doctoral committee, a government evaluation panel, or a scientific review committee will approve a study whose sample selection method is nonprobabilistic unless the problem is of such importance that there is no other choice. For example, the collection of moon rocks was not a probability sample, because the cost of a true probability sample would have been indeed astronomical.

Sampling: Advantages and Disadvantages

The major advantages of sampling are:

- It is cheaper to sample than to take a census of a population.
- Information can be gathered more quickly.
- A sample can be examined more thoroughly than a census; hence, more comprehensive or more detailed data can be obtained.
- Sampling permits acquisition of data not otherwise available because of, for example, the destructiveness of the measurement procedure (as in our blood count example).
- If sampling procedures are carried out in such a way that suitable assumptions apply, estimates of probable error and a confidence level for specified precision can be established. Exactly stated, "precision" = confidence coefficient (expressed as the z associated with the specified probability) $\times$ standard error of the statistic. This identity makes it possible to feel comfortable with the generalizability of results.
- In a properly devised sampling plan, repeated samples yield findings which "would not differ from true population figures by more than a specified amount in more than a specified proportion of the samples."[3]

On the other hand, sampling does have limitations, among which are:

- It is not feasible in any situation where knowledge of each unit of the population is required (for instance, the IRS won't allow a sample of records to justify deductions);
- Sample findings may contain errors whose sources and effects cannot be accounted for;
- The sample(s) may not be representative if the units to be measured are rare and variability is great;
- Sampling permits only a probabilistic inference from findings, whereas a census establishes a comparative certainty (subject to measurement and procedural errors).

Nonprobability Sample Types

Although nonprobability samples have serious drawbacks when incorporated into a research plan, they may be your best or your only choice. Several types are in common use.

The *judgment* or *purposive sample* is the principal form of nonprobability sample. On the basis of experience or the outcome of previous research, the investigator can in effect hand-pick the cases to be included in the sample. Provided that the selected cases are actually typical of the population,[4] or at least, that the atypical cases counterbalance each other, such a procedure will often be quite satisfactory: the difference between the universe parameters and results based on the sample may be less than one percent. Interviews with so-called opinion makers, tribal elders, or student leaders are examples, so also are the physician's blood sample or the chef's sample taste. Unfortunately there is really no systematic way to verify the assumption of typicality, or to know the probability of the subjects' possession of any attributes other than those for which they [the subjects] were selected.

The *quota sample* is another widely used nonprobabilistic form. An educational researcher, lacking a comprehensive list of teachers of learning disabled children, may suggest that a quota of, say, two from each of a sample of schools be interviewed. A market researcher may instruct each member of the survey team to stand on a corner and stop 50 men and 50 women, half (apparently) over 35.

Quota sampling may be satisfactory if there are enough cases from each population stratum to make possible an estimate of the population stratum value, and if we know (or can estimate with reasonable accuracy) the proportion that each stratum constitutes in the total population. (Easier said than done!) The cost of this sampling procedure is lower than that of more probabilistic samples, because elaborate procedures for assuring typicality (such as travel, consulting census data, etc.) are avoided and thus larger samples can be obtained. However, there is no way to measure sample errors or to correct them in the course of data analysis.[5]

A third form of nonprobability sampling is the *hit or miss* technique. An example is the use of street-corner interviewers who stop passersby. Sciences such as archeology, astronomy, and medicine often depend on so-called accidental samples. Historical studies, which must depend upon the chance survival of documents or artifacts, are ultimately based on accidental samples. (See also Chapter 6, section on historical research types.) Researchers investigating sexual behavior often make use of "snowball" samples in which subjects are recruited through an expanding network of acquaintances. There is no way to evaluate the biases arising through such accidental samples. Accidental sampling is a last resort in any sort of scientific research.

We do not recommend that you rely on a nonprobability sampling plan. First, it may destroy the replicability of your study and thus defy a fundamental principle of science. Second, your study can be challenged because of the lack of known sampling error. Third, reputable scientists may not take any aspect of such a study seriously. Nonetheless, the need for information on certain pressing problems may leave you no alternative but to resort to one of these techniques. If so, emphasize your theory as the more important aspect of the research, which may compensate for some of the flaws of your sampling plan.[6]

Estimation Based on Probabilistic Sampling

Most sampling procedures are expected to yield a good estimate of some population parameter(s), such as the mean value of some variable or a correlation between two measures. When a statistic is computed using data collected from a sample and used to estimate a population parameter, it is called an *estimator* for that parameter. Any sample procedure you use carries with it a sampling error,[7] but the precision[8] of estimates from so-called probability samples can be specified in advance.

Different estimators of a population parameter may not be equally desirable; for example, a sample mean and a sample median can both be used to estimate the population mean. How can we decide which is better? Criteria for goodness of estimators can be defined, permitting an ordering of preference for one statistic over another. A good estimator is (1) unbiased, (2) consistent, (3) efficient, and (4) sufficient.

In general, when the expected (mean) value of the statistic used as an estimator, averaged over all samples selected by a given procedure (assuming identical measurement processes, of course), is equal to the actual population parameter, the estimator is said to be *unbiased*. In the case of a sample mean $\overline{X}$, we have $E(\overline{X}) = \mu$, that is, the expected value of the sample mean is the universe mean, whereas if the variance for a sample of size n is defined as $\frac{1}{n}\Sigma_i(\overline{X}_i - \overline{X})^2 = s^2$ we have $E(s^2) \neq \sigma^2$, the population variance, but rather $E(s^2) = \sigma^2 \frac{n}{(n-1)}$. In general if Θ is an estimator for a parameter γ and $E(\Theta) = \gamma + a$, a is called the *bias*[9] of the estimator Θ, that is, a is the difference between the parameter value and the expected (mean) value of the estimator.

When an estimate, such as $\overline{X}$, approaches the population parameter to be estimated, in this case μ, as the sample size increases, it is said to be a *consistent* estimator of the parameter.[10] This means if we take larger samples a consistent estimator should give us improved estimates of the population parameter.

The criterion of efficiency permits a comparison of different estimators for the same universe parameter. Imagine that values of some estimators are computed for all possible samples of fixed size. These values cluster around the true universe parameter; their dispersion can be measured by the variance. An estimator having the smallest possible (minimum) variance is the most *efficient* estimator; thus the values it yields will lie in a closer cluster around the parameter than those obtained using other estimators.

Finally, we say an estimator is *sufficient* if all the measurements used to calculate the value of the estimator affect the estimate. No data are lost in the calculation of a sufficient estimator. Thus in our example above the mean is sufficient but the median is not.

Parametric estimators will be unbiased, consistent, efficient, and sufficient. Nonparametric estimators will typically be lacking in one of these characteristics, usually efficiency or sufficiency. Therefore, parametric estimators are more desirable than nonparametric estimators when both are available and a choice is feasible.

With an appropriately selected estimator and a suitable sampling procedure, you can arrive at conclusions of the following form, for example: the population mean falls between 90 and 110, with probability .95, or, the confidence interval for the population mean is (90, 110) at the 95% confidence level.

Determining a Sampling Procedure: Initial Steps

If your study appears to call for a sample, your first step is to determine as precisely as possible the universe to be examined. A *sampling frame*, which is a list or file of all sampling units in the statistical universe, must be developed. (Differences between the sampling frame and the true universe will result in biases.) Specification of the sampling units must be sufficiently exact to permit anyone carrying out the sampling to identify the sampling unit and distinguish it from other objects. This specification should be written so that a reader could replicate the sampling unit; otherwise, your results will not be verifiable. The time and administrative elements in your study should also be enumerated: include such items as (1) maps available, (2) survey personnel available (3) money and time available, and (4) data processing available.

Two factors should emerge from this list, the first being the degree of precision desired. Precision can be expressed in terms of permissible error (tolerance) and acceptable risk (confidence). Their values will depend on your study. For example, a lower permissible error is desirable when sampling the population for veneral disease (S.T.D.) than when sampling for IQ. On the other hand, the acceptable risk or confidence should be about the same in each case.

The second factor that should emerge when you examine your sampling frame is the sampling procedure most appropriate to your study. Many sampling procedures are available to the researcher and the brief descriptions of the principal ones that follow should guide you. However, you should refer to one of the many excellent manuals and, preferably, consult with a statistician (see Chapter 10, sections on Experts and Using a Consultant) in choosing a sampling plan, because mistakes can lead to losses in time and money and diminish the value of your findings.

Sampling Types

SIMPLE RANDOM SAMPLING

Probably the most familiar type of sampling involves the simple random sample. Statistical inference based on simple random sampling reflects the assumption that each sampling unit[11] has the same chance of selection for the sample. The procedure requires a complete list of all sampling units in a clearly specified population and the absence of interaction among all or some of the units. A random number table can be used to ensure equiprobability.[12] Statistics computed from simple random samples without replacement are excellent estimators of population parameters. It is also possible to calculate the precision of these estimates.

Despite the simplicity of the sample selection process and the neatness of the statistical conclusions, simple random sampling presents the researcher with several difficulties. A population frame or list in the desired form may be unobtainable. (The list should not be arranged in order of magnitude on any variable you wish to study.) Fairly large samples are needed to achieve good precision, so that more time and money may be needed to carry out the study than is available. Finally, the assumption that the population elements are statistically independent ("no interaction") may be inapplicable. It may therefore be inappropriate or unfeasible to attempt to use a simple random sampling plan for your study.

STRATIFIED SAMPLING

When a universe consists of a number of subgroups, simple random sampling may be too cumbersome in that too large a sample may be needed to guarantee that all groups are represented. For example, suppose you wish to sample a prison or hospital population which contains several categories, or *strata*, each of which has a separate universe list or sampling frame. When a simple random sample is drawn from each stratum, the total sample is called a *stratified random sample*. The sampling procedure can be carried out in several different ways.

If the strata consist of equal numbers of elements, we would wish to draw a simple random sample of the same size from each stratum. If, however, the numbers of elements in different strata are different, the selection of equal size samples from each will yield a disproportionate stratified random sample and calculation of statistics should incorporate weights in accord with the number in each stratum. For instance, mean blood pressure reading or mean amount of food consumed for each category would be weighted by the number of patients or prisoners in each category, summed over all categories and divided by the total number in the institution to get the mean. On the other hand, if a random sample is drawn from each stratum, then in effect the same sampling fraction is used for each stratum. This procedure is called *ratio* or *proportionate stratified random sampling.* For example, our adult hospital patients are classified as male versus female and as surgical (S) versus medical (M) versus psychiatric (PS) and these categories contain numbers and percentages of patients as shown in Table 8.1. A 10% sample would then contain 20 female psychiatric patients, 48 male medical, and so forth. If one or more strata are very small, it may be desirable to use a larger sampling fraction from those strata, lest a proportionate sample yield inadequate information about that group.

TABLE 8.1

Sampling Frame for Ratio, or Proportionate Stratified Random, Sampling

Sex	Type of Problem	No. of Patients	% of Total
M	S	160	8
F	S	240	12
M	M	480	24
F	M	800	40
M	PS	120	6
F	PS	200	10
		2000	100

A quite different procedure, when information is available concerning variability in the different strata of the characteristics under study, is to sample proportionately to the relative variability. As Sudman and Lazerwitz[13] both observe, this ensures the greatest possible precision in the estimate calculated from the sample. Obtaining this information may be an important goal of a pilot study.

As the preceding brief description of a few of the alternatives available for sampling a stratified population suggests, a number of procedures are at your disposal. All take advantage of the homogeneity within strata to reduce error; thus, smaller sample sizes than for simple random sampling yield comparable precision. The procedures' disadvantages include the need for accurate sampling frames for all strata and increased complexity of the formulas used for calculation of estimates. Your choice of one of these sampling methods must take into account realistic feasibility issues as well as the desired degree of precision.

SYSTEMATIC SAMPLING

Systematic sampling involves the following procedure: Decide how large a sample size n you need to draw from a population of size N and calculate the sampling fraction $\frac{1}{i} = \frac{n}{N}$. Using a table of random numbers, select one of the first i units, and thereafter select every ith unit. For example, if $n = 200$ and $N = 2000$, then $i = 10$, so we choose one of the first 10 at random, say the 7th, and the sample consists of the 7th, 17th, 27th, etc. units in the universe.

Systematic sampling can be much easier and thus more practical to use than simple random sampling. Project staff members can learn more quickly to select every ith unit from a list than to use a table of random numbers. This procedure is frequently used to obtain a sample of student records or other documents for analysis.

Measures of central tendency in systematic samples yield unbiased estimates, since the units are equiprobable. If periodicities are present in the list, systematic samples are contraindicated. Moreover, the variance can be biased, so if measures of dispersion are crucial to the study some other procedure should be employed.[14]

CLUSTER SAMPLING

For some populations, it may be more practical to group the elements, for listing purposes, into clusters which you have reason to suppose are heterogeneous. After the clusters are listed and a random sample of clusters is selected (these are primary or first stage sampling units), then within each of the selected clusters a random sample of individuals (the secondary or second stage sampling units) can be chosen to be interviewed or observed. The number of stages can be increased according to the nature of the study. There are many variations on this procedure, with associated complications in the statistical analysis.

A relatively simple example can be seen when a population can be specified geographically, but no single list of households in the community is available. Suppose a map of the area exists with the city blocks identified. Select a sample of blocks at random (first stage). From each selected block choose lot numbers at random (second stage); from among housing units on these lots, select a sample at random (third stage). Persons occupying these units are included in the study.

Cluster sampling can effect enormous economies in time and money. It makes possible studies involving, say, a probability sample of the entire adult U.S. population. Its most important disadvantage arises from the homogeneity of particular locations (or whatever clusters) in class, race or marital status; that is, the last-stage sample is not randomly selected on all variables, especially those which *may* be strongly correlated with the study variables. This homogeneity will affect the variance of the estimated mean, so that the probability of error will be increased.

Ideally, all later stage clusters contain equal numbers of final sampling units, but in practice this is rarely the case. Differences in sampling ratios in the secondary or later clusters may create biases in estimates of population parameters such as means, proportions, and variances. Techniques to achieve equiprobability for all sampling units, and to modify statistical calculations, depend on specific situations.[15] Consult with an expert, such as your statistical consultant or the committee overseeing the project.

MATCHED SAMPLES

The use of matched samples to form pairs for later comparison is a popular study design, because it allows one or more variables to be controlled and eliminated from the analysis. A variety of statistical techniques have been devised to permit comparison of differences in the data obtained from matched pairs. The sampling procedure, which still requires random assignment of subjects to treatments or groups, presents certain special problems. These include:

- On which variables should subjects be matched?
- Can units in matched samples be assigned randomly to groups?
- Will statistical "regression" errors bias the results?
- Are discarded subjects representative of the universe?

Because of these and other problems, matching subjects to form pairs may create more difficulties than it removes. Two alternatives worth considering, using the matched sample concept, are twin studies with random assignment, and matched groups.

Twin studies are best conducted using identical twins, because "Nature" has provided an excellent control for each subject. If a supply of twin pairs is available, by all means try to make use of it; unfortunately, the relatively low incidence of twins in most populations makes it impractical to rely on a sufficient number to serve as subjects.

For a matched groups design, subjects are assigned to treatment blocks on the basis of their homogeneous responses on some independent variable(s) in the absence of treatment effects; compare this with the expected heterogeneous responses of subjects selected completely at random. The advantage of matched over randomized groups lies in the smaller mean square error term for the analysis of variance.

TWO-PHASED SAMPLING

Double or two-phased sampling is an excellent technique to use when no information on the universe is available. First, a large sample is selected at random and the needed descriptive data are collected such as distribution of age, sex, ripeness of fruit, etc. Second, a subsample, designed to reflect the proportions on the variables identified in the first step, is selected for the study. For example, a sample of 10,000 questionnaires can be used to determine population characteristics and a comprehensive questionnaire on attitudes on a specific topic can then be sent to 1,000 of the 10,000 when these characteristics are used as a basis for stratifying the subsample.[16]

This procedure provides otherwise missing information about the universe, but it is important to keep in mind that the accuracy of a statistical estimate of a parameter is only as good as the large first sample from which it was generated.

SEQUENTIAL SAMPLING

Consider the problem of predicting, as early as possible after voting begins, the outcome of an election in which A and one or more others are candidates. Each voter leaving the polling booth is interviewed and the number of votes for A is tallied cumulatively against the number of voters interviewed. We select a level of confidence, such as 95%, and prepare a graph in which the X-axis is labelled for the number of voters interviewed and the Y-axis for the cumulative number of votes for A. Two parallel lines are drawn on the chart: The upper line corresponds to a cumulative vote for A which permits the decision "A will win" with 95% confidence, while the lower line corresponds to a cumulative vote permitting the decision "A will lose" with 95% confidence. We locate the recorded cumulative totals on the graph and so long as the points lie between the lines we continue to sample the votes. As soon as the points cross one or the other line we stop and draw the appropriate conclusion with the stated level of confidence. This is an example of *sequential sampling*.

Sequential sampling is commonly used in acceptance sampling for quality control purposes, but as our example illustrates, it has many other applications. Sequential sampling graphs, and the tables on which they are based, are difficult to construct: you will need either the assistance of a competent statistician or access to a good reference[17] in sequential trials. Despite this difficulty, the technique minimizes sample size, which is a great advantage. Needless to say, it cannot be used unless the sampling units can be meaningfully ordered.

INTERPENETRATING REPLICATE SUBSAMPLING

Since replicability of results is an essential aspect of most research that qualifies as scientific, an investigator may wish to determine whether the study will yield the same results if it is done again. Tukey and Deming developed an ingenious method that, in effect, permits an ongoing replication of the study by the original investigator. So-called interpenetrating replicate subsamples allow the data of various enumerators to be checked against each other, and also make possible the simplification of formulas for calculation of sampling variance (error) in certain complex types of samples. The method,[18] very briefly, involves the separation of the whole sample into overlapping subsamples and the comparison of the several estimates from the subsamples. The mechanics of the procedure are complicated, as are formulas for parametric estimation of mean, etc. However, the outcomes of greater precision and increased assurance concerning the results may justify the additional effort required.

OTHER SAMPLING TYPES

Many sampling types do not fall readily into any of the categories we have mentioned. A large literature on sampling is available for further reference. A basic orientation can be achieved through reading Sudman (1976), Stephan and McCarthy (1963), Blalock and Blalock (1968) and other handbooks of social research. Sudman (1976) is particularly practical and addresses feasibility issues with common sense and humor.

Determining Sample Size

The question, "How big a sample do I need?" is an irksome one for all researchers, and especially so for the novice. Sample size depends on several inter-related factors, which include (1) the variability, known by experience, of the population being sampled, (2) the population parameters to be estimated, (3) the confidence level selected, (4) the precision required in the estimates of population parameters, (5) the sampling method being used and (6) the estimating procedure or method of statistical analysis to be employed.[19] Most of these in turn reflect the design of the study and, ultimately, the purpose of the study and the research problem as stated. Thus sample size is one of the last decisions you make about the design. (Also to be taken into account are the traditions of your area of research and various feasibility considerations.)

Unfortunately, there is no simple answer, nor is any definitive answer easy to find. A number of authoritative reference books are available (see Additional Readings), but there is no real substitute for the advice of a well-trained and experienced consultant. Elementary and intermediate level texts often contain simple formulas in the sections dealing with sampling or estimation (e.g. Roscoe (1975), etc.) but these may be more confusing than helpful because so many of the terms are unknown before the study is carried out, or require familiarity with the research area to evaluate. A pilot study is usually needed to provide information about these unknown terms.

In many cases, tables can be extremely useful. Imagine a state of affairs in which you expect half the universe to have an attribute of interest to the researcher ($p = 0.5$). For instance, if half the sample population for a study was male and half female, and you now ask: is half the (universe) population female? You want to be able to decide if the proportion p is actually .5. First, a decision must be made as to the confidence level desired in the results: If you choose 95% confidence ($\alpha = .05$) you use Table 8.2A, and if you choose 99.7% confidence you use Table 8.2B. Next, we consider the percentage error we will tolerate: Both tables allow an error of from ±1% to ±5% in estimating our universe parameter, namely, the proportion with the attribute; in addition, Table 8.2A allows an error of ±10%. We enter the appropriate table depending on the selected confidence level, and read down the stub to a population size approximately the same as the size of our universe. Finally, we read across the table to the column headed by the selected precision. Thus for 99.7% confidence and ±3% precision, Table 8.2B tells us that a universe of 9000 requires a sample size of 1957.

Inspection of these two tables suggests that sample size decreases as we relax the precision and the confidence level. Also notice that smaller proportions of large universes are needed in sampling these universes.

Tables comparable to 8.2A and 8.2B can be drawn up for $p = .3$ or .4, that is, where the expected proportion of the universe having a specified characteristic is 30% or 40%. The Readings at the end of this chapter suggest an approach to constructing such tables.

Suppose our research problem is to estimate accurately the proportion p of a universe which possesses some characteristic, for instance, the proportion of adults with 4 or more years of post-secondary schooling. Table 8.3 assumes we are willing to accept a 95% level of confidence and a 5% error in precision (this means our estimate must fall within $p \pm .05p$ with probability .95). To use the table we must guess the value of p we expect to find, and we must also know the approximate size of our universe. Thus for a universe of 1000 and a (guessed) 30% occurrence of the specified characteristic we need a random sample of 790 to achieve 95% confidence and 5% error in a calculated estimate[20] that $p = .3$, whereas if our universe is 10,000 we need a sample of 2700.

It is important to keep in mind that each estimator, such as population mean, variance, chi square, etc. that you may need to use, would require a different table. Such tables may not be available but the formulas for calculating minimum sample sizes can be found in such references as Cohen (1969).

The great variety of study designs, sampling types, and statistical procedures entails a corresponding complexity in decisions concerning sample size. It is tempting to rely on rules of thumb for minimum permissible numbers of

TABLE 8.2

Sample size for specified confidence limits and precision when sampling attributes in percent. This table is for true $\pi = 50\%$

A. 95% confidence interval (p = 0.5)[a]

Population size	Sample size for precision of					
	+1%	+2%	+3%	+4%	+5%	+10%
500	b	b	b	b	222	83
1000	b	b	b	385	286	91
1500	b	b	638	441	316	94
2000	b	b	714	476	333	95
2500	b	1250	769	500	345	96
3000	b	1364	811	517	353	97
3500	b	1458	843	530	359	97
4000	b	1538	870	541	364	98
4500	b	1607	891	549	367	98
5000	b	1667	909	556	370	98
6000	b	1765	938	566	375	98
7000	b	1842	959	574	378	99
8000	b	1905	976	580	381	99
9000	b	1957	989	584	383	99
10000	5000	2000	1000	588	385	99
15000	6000	2143	1034	600	390	99
20000	6667	2222	1053	606	392	100
25000	7143	2273	1064	610	394	100
50000	8333	2381	1087	617	397	100
100000	9091	2439	1099	621	398	100
∞	10000	2500	1111	625	400	100

B. 99.7% confidence interval (p = 0.5)[a]

Population size	Sample size for precision of				
	+1%	+2%	+3%	+4%	+5%
500	b	b	b	b	b
1000	b	b	b	b	474
1500	b	b	b	726	563
2000	b	b	b	826	621
2500	b	b	b	900	662
3000	b	b	1364	958	692
3500	b	b	1458	1003	716
4000	b	b	1539	1041	735
4500	b	b	1607	1071	750
5000	b	b	1667	1098	763
6000	b	2903	1765	1139	783
7000	b	3119	1842	1171	798
8000	b	3303	1905	1196	809
9000	b	3462	1957	1216	818
10000	b	3600	2000	1233	826
15000	b	4091	2143	1286	849
20000	b	4390	2222	1314	861
25000	11842	4592	2273	1331	869
50000	15517	5056	2381	1368	884
100000	18367	5325	2439	1387	892
∞	22500	5625	2500	1406	900

Source: Yamane (1967a).

[a]Proportion of units in sample possessing characteristic being measured = p; for other values of p, the required sample size will be smaller.

[b]In these cases 50% of the universe in the sample will give more than the required accuracy. Since the normal distribution is a poor approximation of the hypergeometric distribution when n is more than 50% of N, the formula used in this calculation does not apply.

TABLE 8.3

Sample Size Needed to Estimate Percentages (error not to exceed 5% in 95 out of 100 samples)[a]

Number of units in universe	Size of sample needed to yield error of 5% or less in 95 out of 100 samples, if percentage of occurrence is:												
	1%	5%	10%	20%	30%	40%	50%	60%	70%	80%	90%	95%	99%
50	50	50	50	50	50	49	49	48	47	45	39	32	12
100	100	100	100	99	98	96	94	92	87	80	64	45	14
200	200	199	198	194	190	184	178	168	154	132	93	58	15
500	499	492	485	465	440	415	380	337	285	218	128	70	16
1000	994	967	940	860	790	700	610	507	398	278	146	75	16
2000	1975	1872	1760	1520	1300	1080	880	678	496	323	158	78	16
5000	4841	4270	3700	2800	2100	1600	1200	851	582	357	166	80	16
10000	9384	7449	5800	3900	2700	1900	1400	930	618	370	168	81	16

Source: Slonim, 1960, p. 78.

[a]It is important to recognize that the 5% error limit specified here refers to a relative rather than absolute percentage error. For example, if the percentage of occurrence is 20%, a 5% relative error limit would signify that our range of tolerance is 20% ± 5% of 20%, or 20% ± 1%. If we were concerned with a 5% absolute error (i.e., 20% ± 5%) our table of sample sizes would be entirely different from the one above.

subjects when such statistics as analysis of variance and chi square will be used; however, these rules frequently derive from the approximations used in the analysis and do not reflect questions of precision. Moreover, decisions about appropriate subsample size in multi-stage sampling, and the related modifications that may be necessary in the statistical tests, require a high degree of expertise. In this, as in other sampling issues, seek advice and guidance. (See the section on Experts in Chapter 10.)

All the foregoing discussion has emphasized the importance of selecting a sample, or samples, of suitable size if you want to be able to generalize your sample results to the universe. Given a desired precision, confidence level, universe size, and known variability of a characteristic in the universe you can calculate the minimum required sample size. A smaller sample may result in a loss of external validity, so that you will be unable to make inferences about the universe on the basis of sample data. (On the other hand, it is better to use a smaller sample and qualify your results, than to overreach and end up with sloppy measurement or poorly trained interviewers.) Researchers very commonly draw conclusions about a universe from inadequate samples; hence, many findings are not replicable for the specified universe. It is wise to limit generalization of findings only to the universe(s) that the study has in fact adequately sampled. Your statement of delimitations serves to alert your reader. There is no shame in describing outcomes as suggestive rather than asserting they are definitive.

In spite of care, some sampling errors may persist.

Sampling Errors To Avoid

The most common sampling errors fall into three categories: (1) formulation errors, (2) process errors, and (3) measurement errors.

Formulation errors arise from faults in a sampling design, and hence may be difficult to discover. One principal type of formulation error arises from mis-specification of the variables. Suppose that for a study of job satisfaction we interview a large sample of employees of Mobil Oil and A.T.& T. We would not be able to generalize to all workers, but only to those in these two organizations. Comparison of the two organizations would be appropriate, but even a generalization to large communications or oil companies would be dubious: The sampling frame is too limited. This is an example of mis-specification. The second main type of formulation error is caused by unsuspected or overlooked relationships between variables. For example, if we wish to examine the incidence of gout in a certain ethnically specified population, we may select a large sample consisting of equal numbers of men and women and determine a rate per 100,000 of this disease in the general population. However, previous large-scale studies have shown that gout occurs preponderantly in males, with a ratio to female sufferers of 19:1, so that our ignoring the sexual bias results in a serious underestimate of the incidence of gout in those who are at greatest risk.

Process errors can be illustrated by the example of nonresponses.[21] The bias introduced into a study by the failure of a number of selected subjects to respond may be substantial and cumulative, because there is in general no way to know whether whatever causes a subject to respond also distinguishes that individual from the rest of the population. A nonresponse may reflect one or more of such factors as absence from home, lost questionnaires, or incapacity, as well as outright refusal. Nevertheless, those who do respond may be a special subset of the whole universe.[22] Corrections for nonresponse can be developed using various methods. However, the preferred way is to make repeated trials to obtain responses from some nonrespondents. The responses from the sample of nonrespondents should then be compared statistically to the responses from respondents to determine whether the groups are essentially the same.

Measurement errors can seriously distort any conclusions based on sample findings. To collect data with care and precision, but within a framework of faulty design, invalidates the findings and wastes the painstaking effort that goes into any study. Likewise, measuring the variables with inadequate precision or with a faulty instrument (such as an unreliable test or an unvalidated questionnaire) yields information that could be misleading or just plain incorrect. Errors of this sort can be avoided by a careful analysis of the research problem and the use of appropriate instruments and procedures.

Sampling and Studying Human Populations

Sampling human beings involves special philosophical and moral considerations, many of which are beyond the scope of this book. A number of scholarly associations have taken the position that no human being should be the subject of a research study without his or her knowledge and expressed consent to act as a subject. Further, the researcher is under obligation to inform a potential subject of the risks, if any, to mental or physical well-being, and to preserve the anonymity and confidentiality of subjects with scrupulous care. Whenever the expected outcome of the research will not be damaged by the explanation of its purpose, this must also be explained to the participants. (These safeguards virtually guarantee the impossibility of carrying out any study which requires truly naive subjects.) Deceit of any kind therefore requires elaborate justification.

Issues associated with the withholding from human beings of a treatment that might be successful, or with the use of placebos, have also been discussed at length in the literature;[23] we will not reiterate them here. However, questionable practices to be avoided include invasion of privacy, imposition of constraints, manipulation of behavior, and the withholding of benefits (even if compensatory benefits are provided). Particular caution must be exercised in dealing with subjects who are children or otherwise incompetent. Not being in a position to protect their own interests, and in the absence of caring individuals to look after them, such subjects can all too easily be victimized.

Sampling and External Validity: A Concluding Note

The purpose of sampling is to permit generalization to a larger population. Generalizability, often called *external validity*, can be jeopardized by a number of factors (see section on Sources of Invalidity in Chapter 5). To improve the generalizability of results, keep the following in mind:

- Avoid sampling bias by ensuring representativeness in the selection process by whatever means are feasible, for example, probability versus nonprobability procedures.
- Select subjects from a more aggregated sampling frame rather than a simpler frame, where possible.
- Use larger samples: large sample statistics involve smaller sampling errors and greater reliability, and increase the power of the statistical test applied to the data.
- Calculate the marginal cost of a sampling unit; that is, the cost of adding a unit to your sample. If the benefits greatly exceed the costs, it is worthwhile to enlarge the sample.
- Select a sample of treatments, because variation of the treatments may display the treatment effects more forcefully than exact replication of treatments. This is mainly an issue in experimental studies[24] where such statistics as mixed or random model n-way ANOVA are called for.

Since sampling so strongly affects the generalizability of a study, the sampling plan involves many of the researcher's most important decisions. Help from any knowledgeable source is extremely valuable to new researchers. Your sampling plan, procedure, and appropriate statistics must all mesh together, and attention to them early on will be repaid in the greatly increased value of your findings and results.

Notes

[1]An example familiar to many statistics students is the use of the normal distribution to approximate the binomial distribution arising from independent trials, where

$$\min (Np, Nq) > 10.$$

[2]See discussion in Chein (1959, pp. 538–544).

[3]Chein (1959, p. 512).

[4]"If I am only for myself, what good am I?" (Hillel).

[5]See Sudman (1976, pp. 191–196).

[6]Following the classical advice to young lawyers: if the evidence is weak, argue the law; if the law is weak, argue the evidence; if the law and the evidence are both weak, yell like hell and pound on the desk.

[7]"Round numbers are always false." (Samuel Johnson).

[8]Slonim (1960, p. 14): "The accuracy of an estimate [is] the degree to which it approximates the *true* figures. The precision measures the degree to which it approximates the figure that would be obtained from a [census] if identical methods of data gathering were used." Chein (1959, p. 513n.) observes "accuracy," "dependability," and "precision" are frequently used as synonyms.

[9]The term *bias* is used more generally to refer to any source of measurement or sampling error. See Plutchik (1974, 2nd ed., Chapter 10), and Williams (1978, §6.1), which discuss sources of bias.

[10]Formally, $\lim_{n \to \infty} \overline{X} = \mu$ and, in general, $\lim_{n \to \infty} \theta = \gamma$.

[11]In addition every combination of 2,3, . . . units has the same chance of selection as every other combination of the same size.

[12]Use of a random number table is described clearly in Backstrom and Hursh-Cesar (1981, Chapter 2, p. 87).

[13]Sudman (1976, §6.3) and Lazerwitz (1968, pp. 294–295: "optimum allocation").

[14]See Sudman (1976, pp. 56–57) for other drawbacks.

[15]Sudman (1976, Chapter 4) is very informative. For a helpful introductory presentation of cluster sampling, see Lazerwitz (1968, pp. 298–326); Stephan and McCarthy (1963, pp. 194–210, 418–424) for both mathematical and practical considerations; and Kalton (1983).

[16]Slonim (1960) and others call this double sampling. It is not the same as a form of acceptance sampling with the same name. Acceptance sampling involves quality control. You may sample a specified number of units and inspect them for defects. If more than a stated number have defects, you can reject the whole lot *or* you may wish to draw another (double sample) and inspect these additional items for defects, according to the decision rule you are using.

[17]See Armitage (1960).

[18]For a short but clear description see Slonim (1960, Chapter XI, pp. 60ff.).

[19]You may note the omission from this list of the "obvious" item, the proportion of sample size to universe size. The variability of the sampling distribution is by far the most important consideration. When the population (universe) is very large, the so-called sampling fraction has only a very small effect on precision and can safely be ignored in formulas. When the population is finite, increasing sample size and thus the sampling fraction, can markedly decrease the sampling error. See Sudman (1976, Chapter 5) and Plutchik (1974, 229ff.); for formula modifications, any standard text, for example Lapin (1980).

[20]This means we will have $.30 - .015 < p < .30 + .015$ with probability .95.

[21]Other examples involve careless tabulation of responses, poor supervision of enumerators, improper selection of subjects in quota samples, and so forth.

[22]Compare with some of the criticisms, such as Madge (1970), of the Kinsey et al. (1948, 1953) studies on human sexual behavior. A discussion of the nonresponse problem can be found in Namboodiri (1978, Chapter 11).

[23]See Riecken and Boruch (1974, Chapter 8), Denzin (1978, Chapter 13), Selltiz et al. (1976, Chapter 7), and Miller (1972). General issues concerning the regulation of research with human subjects are discussed in Gray (1975).

[24]See Plutchik (1974, Chapter 4, and pp. 83ff. concerning sampling of *conditions*.

Additional Reading

The discussion of sampling in most general statistics texts is not very useful. We therefore suggest that you consult any of the following:

Slonim (1960): very simple and non-technical.

Chein (1959), (1953) ⎫
Kish (1953, 1966) ⎬ These are extremely thorough for their length and give a good overview of various sampling procedures.
Lazerwitz (1968) ⎭

Sudman (1976): comprehensive and practical.

Cohen (1969): concerned mainly with beta-error, power-efficiency, and sample size.

Kalton (1983): very clear; emphasizes sampling in survey research

Namboodiri (1978): emphasis on problems of non-response.

Backstrom and Hursh-Cesar (1981): how-to-do-it for survey sampling.

Yamane (1967a): thorough, clear.

Williams (1978): simple insight into the mathematics of sampling and estimation.

Stephan and McCarthy (1963): serious and thoughtful, discusses many issues arising from empirical studies based on sampling.

Cochran (1953): still good.

Neter et al. (1978): general text, useful for discussion of sample size and Bayesian decision-making.

Lindner (1979): general text, useful for sample size and power.

Cox (1958): useful discussion of randomization, number of observations and choice of units; nontechnical and clear.

9

Role of Computer in Research

Computer Processing of Data

The computer is an important member of almost every research team; its role in processing and analyzing data may be crucial in the completion of a study. In the past, it was frequently necessary to limit the scope and complexity of a research project in order to conform to limitations on data handling imposed by slow mechanical devices. Research methodology that involved time-consuming computation was underutilized because of high costs and the lack of timely results; complex calculations and elaborate sorting schemes needed for sophisticated and delicate analysis were simply impossible to carry out within a reasonable time. In recent years, fast and accurate computing and information retrieval have made data analysis vastly easier, and has led to the extension and development of new applications. Now neither costs nor timeliness of computation should be a limiting consideration in the choice of research design. It is important, however, to recognize that the availability of data processing at low cost can easily lure you into requesting information that may be trivial or useless. Moreover, carrying out data analysis irrelevant to the soundly formulated research design can be counterproductive, in that large amounts of your time must be wasted in sifting through the computer-generated output, and in discussing or trying to interpret information that should never have been reported.

For pilot results, day-to-day monitoring of data, and calculations involving data from small studies, you may find a programmable hand or desk calculator[1] very convenient, perhaps indispensable. The instruction manuals are extremely well prepared and easy-to-read, and address the concerns of users, so the equipment can be mastered in a matter of hours. A machine that prints out the results of calculations will provide you with a permanent record. The cost may range from 30 to several hundred dollars. There is, of course, no comparison between a hand or desk calculator and a computer in their capacity for data analysis.

The capability to carry out computer-controlled experiments can often make possible a creative and fruitful approach to the solution of a problem. While the use of computing facilities for data processing is fairly well understood, the procedures for so-called automated data acquisition are not nearly so well-known. We examine this topic briefly later in this chapter and in Chapter 15.

The design of the study is the starting point for planning data analysis. Examine the variables and the possibilities for coding the data you anticipate. If the data will be too numerous or too complex, or if you have chosen a method of statistical analysis which involves too many steps for economical and timely hand-calculations, then a computer will be useful, if not essential, to the research project. Your next step is to locate computer facilities.

Some Basic Computer Terminology

Processing of data: sorting, tabulation, and display of data; computation of (statistical) measures; computation and statement of probability estimates for statistical tests.

Hardware: the computer parts themselves, the machinery and circuitry. Hardware is classified as mainframe, mini, and micro (personal), but the precise distinction is not very important for you to know.

Interface liaison: the person who can translate the problem into a set of instructions readable (acceptable) by the machine.

Software: the instructions to the computer which make it do what you want it to do, for instance, carry out a sequence of steps in some procedure.

Language: the symbolic representation of the steps actually followed by the computer; vocabulary and syntactical rules which can be read (interpreted) directly or indirectly by the machine.

Program: procedure prepared by the user, a set of steps to be followed by the machine.

Package: procedure or collection of procedures available to the user, generally prepared by someone else.

Routine: set of instructions constituting a subprogram.

GIGO: garbage-in garbage-out; the output can never be cleaner or more precise than the input.

User-friendly: designed for easy use, requiring a minimum of background or special training.

Hard copy: printed out versions of data, computations, graphs, or routines.

Support: acceptability of the software to the computer installation on which you plan to use it.

Access to Computing Facilities

Computers can be found in any one of three places: a university, a commercial data processing facility, and (more recently) the home or private office. Where you go to use the computer will depend on how much time and money you have available.

· Universities generally make computer resources available to students and faculty on a subsidized basis. University faculty members devote much of their time to research, and the National Science Foundation was in the past extremely generous in funding the acquisition of suitable computer equipment; consequently, university computer facilities are usually extremely well-suited to an investigator's needs for data analysis. Costs are (relatively) low, power and speed of computation are high, and hardware is suitable for most research purposes. At university computer centers you can usually find people, typically undergraduate or graduate students, with computer and statistical expertise.[2] Therefore, the center will be an excellent place to obtain a consultant, if you need one. Some universities maintain and subsidize staff consultants, or have faculty members whose assignments include these responsibilities. University computer centers are also likely to have large libraries of software particularly suited to data processing for statistical analysis and automated experiments. If you are fortunate, you will have access to an interactive terminal, that is, one on which you can in effect carry on a conversation with the machine concerning your procedure.

On the other hand, access is frequently difficult because of the heavy demand by other users, some of whom have priority, so that timeliness may be a problem. Also, the center itself may be inefficiently designed and poorly staffed, organized, and managed. Data loss is a not-infrequent problem, so you must prepare for that contingency by maintaining a duplicate set of records.

Commercial data processing centers are usually more efficient in their operations than university connected centers. Thus you can plan on a shorter response time. On the other hand, the charges are unsubsidized, so they will be higher than those in university centers; in addition, you are likely to be billed for time spent talking to a consultant as well as for machine time.[3]

The cost of data acquisition will probably account for the largest chunk of your research budget, and making these data *machine-readable* (that is, understandable to the computer) will probably be the largest of your data-processing costs. If you reasonably expect the total cost of coding and processing the data to exceed $2500, you may be better off purchasing a personal computer (PC). You should consider such a purchase only if you intend to continue your involvement in research, and if you are willing to devote a large amount of time to the care and feeding of the computer: The substantial investment in time needed to become familiar with it can slow down your project. Your decision should take into account convenience, economy, and time available for the mastery of new skills. Keep in mind the potential usefulness of both text editing and graphics capabilities in a PC. Do not undertake the purchase of a PC unless you have consulted with an expert (or plan to become one yourself).[4]

Another possibility to be considered is the purchase of an input/output device (e.g., terminal). This may be economical for you if you anticipate a large amount of data input and/or output. Prices start at about $300[5] for new equipment and substantially less for used equipment (and will probably continue to fall in the near future).

Some terminals also have enough intelligence to do some statistical calculations and may use canned packages for the purpose. If it is to be useful, the terminal must be able to communicate with the computer by telephone. Some terminals have a built-in *modem*, a device that sits between the terminal and the telephone; if not, a suitable one must be bought or rented. In any case, this item as well as both the telephone connection and the use of a mainframe must be included in your cost estimate.

Who Processes Your Data?

If you have no access to "free" data processing by subsidized staff members, you may find it economical in time or money to hire someone to do your data processing. Unless your university (or department) disapproves, this can be a reasonable choice. We discuss issues involved in choosing and using an expert in Chapter 10.

The alternative is to learn to do the job yourself. This task is made easier by the existence of so-called canned programs, prepared in advance and available at most computer facilities, which can be used free of charge or at minimal cost. Canned programs will indeed save you many hours and many dollars, but you must make an investment in learning the language required to utilize the package. Most of the statistical and mathematical procedures used in empirical research have been canned, and the language is generally simple and well-documented: Nonetheless, access to an individual who will answer questions on the program and/or language is an absolute necessity for you. The language used for the program may differ from the one used by the operating system to put your program and its data into the job stream of the computer center. Thus you will also have to master an interface or Job Control Language (JCL).

Fortunately, there are courses, self-teaching texts, libraries, computer-assisted learning devices, and other resources for learning computer languages, available at most universities at minimal cost. Locating these, fitting them into the time you have available, and planning for their use must all be carefully worked out if delays in processing are to be avoided. Forewarned is forearmed: we strongly recommend that a course in computing be part of the background of everyone who contemplates pursuing an advanced degree or a career as a researcher in whatever setting. Be sure the course you take is appropriate for your needs: Fortran is the most widely used language for data analysis;

Algol, PL1 and Pascal are reasonable alternatives though not as widely used in statistical research.

Computer Costs

Computer-related costs can be classified under four headings: interface liaison, hardware, software, and supplies or special equipment.

Most persons who act as interface liaison are extremely skilled and can command high rates (approximately $25 per hour). Students with these skills constitute a cheap source of labor; using them will cut your costs in half or less. It is important to make certain that the people you employ are responsible and conscientious as well as competent; ask for references and check them.

Hardware is such that the bigger the computer, the lower the costs. The mainframe computer carries out calculations at high speed and relatively high cost, at most a few seconds for typical studies in the social sciences. On the other hand, the machine may require a large amount of time to read the data, using a so-called peripheral device at low cost. Hence total hardware costs are dramatically lower for social science than for other kinds of data processing (e.g., engineering, which requires extended calculations). A typical statistical procedure (for example, producing contingency tables on 10,000 records) should cost no more than $50 in all for the hardware use.

Software costs are those ascribed to getting the machine to do what you want it to do. If an appropriate canned subroutine or program exists, costs may be negligible; however they can become astronomical if you need a program written specifically for the analysis of your data. The writing of instructions will average $10 per instruction[6] and hundreds are needed to utilize the computer. It is obvious that whenever possible the use of canned programs (existing instruction sets) is the way to go.

Finally, you may need special supplies, such as address labels, optical scanning sheets, tapes, disks, etc. While many computer centers may have such materials on hand you will be charged for their use as well as for the printer. It may even be necessary for you to order and purchase them from the manufacturer, so you will first have to investigate how and where to get these items.

Timely Processing

While it is true that computer calculations take microseconds, you cannot conclude that the total data processing time will be matter of minutes. The use of a computer in research is only part of a complex procedure; Figure 9.1 shows all the steps in the process. After the data are recorded on a

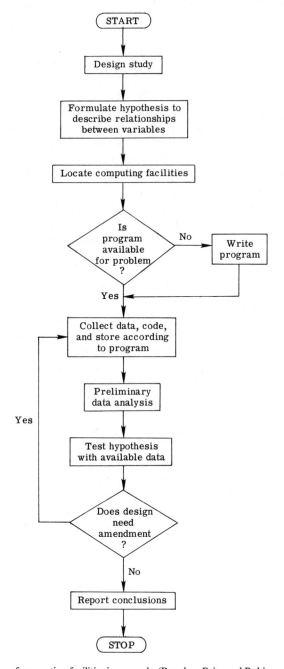

FIGURE 9.1 Use of computing facilities in research. (Based on Brier and Robinson, 1974, p. 107.)

machine-readable device (cards, tapes, disks, etc.), a few weeks to a few months—at a minimum—will be required to analyze them completely. Plan your deadlines accordingly. You can certainly expect that an allowance of a few days for processing research data will be inadequate.

Some of this time can be compressed by careful planning of the research design. The use of PERT methods (see Chapters 6 and 15) can be effective.

Coding and Documentation

Modern research not uncommonly generates thousands of data items. It should be obvious that the value of your conclusions depends heavily on two aspects of data handling: categorization and record-keeping, usually referred to as coding and documentation.

Coding[7] is the procedure by which raw data are transformed into symbols, to be tabulated, counted, and otherwise analyzed; every response or observation must be assigned to appropriate categories. Errors can enter at several levels:

- Data collection can be careless; interviewers or observers fatigued or poorly trained.
- The categories can be poorly defined, or not exhaustive or mutually exclusive.
- The responses may be illegible, incomplete, or otherwise uncodable.
- The coders can be inadequately trained, and make erroneous or inconsistent assignments.
- Coding of responses to open-ended questions requires special techniques; unless these are mastered, data cannot be analyzed.

Tabulation by hand may suffice if the number of items is small, but in general a machine is fast and untiring, and exploits the coding once it is completed. A computer incorporates the tabulation procedure into the calculation of various statistical measures. It is therefore desirable that you discuss coding with your computer consultant, or refer carefully to your computer's manual, before data collection, so as to be able to make this part of your project as efficient as possible.

The data should be processed in such a way as to yield a frequency distribution of all codes, called an *edit run*. If a nonexistent code value appears, you know at once that there is an error in the data entry. When the computer counts, it must "see" only those codes which have been established; otherwise, the calculations will be incorrect.

You can utilize the computer to recode the data if you wish to aggregate (i.e., sort or group) data in another manner, so it is desirable to code initially at the lowest level of aggregation (i.e., with the least possible grouping).

The computer can also be so programmed that when it prints data on a set of codes it can convert the code back to the English equivalent. This allows the tables to be used in the printout form as part of the final report on the research.

Documentation makes it possible for you to keep track of what you are doing in a complicated multiphase project, and also goes a long way to ensuring replicability. The outcome of this nuts-and-bolts activity includes:

- Clear definitions of all technical terminology.
- Explicit statement of all assumptions.
- Statement of data-collection procedure (who, when, where, how; instrumentation.)
- State of data-classification procedure (coding guides).
- Statement of data processing and analysis (programs, location, particular algorithms or modifications).
- Statement of sampling procedure.
- Description of all sources of materials, special equipment, training routines, etc.

Needless to say, a statement of your hypotheses, the rejection-retention criteria, the underlying theory, the findings, and your generalizations are an intrinsic part of the documentation of your study.

Computerizing Input Information

The first step in computer processing of information is the translation of this information into machine-readable form. Prepared data are then stored using one of several different devices such as punched cards, optical scanning sheets, disks, tapes, or terminal and real memory storage.

To utilize any of these efficiently, you must encode the data in alphabetic or numeric characters. In some cases, you will need to code the data even further, to save storage space and ease processing. For example, a male subject John Smith may be a member of your sample; if sex is a variable for your study but the specific names of subjects are unimportant, you may decide to give Smith a case number and to code all males "1" instead of using the label MALE. Such a procedure requires the preparation of a so-called code book so you can retranslate data for later use.

In choosing a device to translate your information into machine readable form, consult the computer center you intend to use. Most computer centers will be able to handle a standard card of 12 rows and 80 columns, punched in Hollerith code. Likewise, most centers whose computer can communicate by telephone can accept data by telephone from another terminal. Not all centers have every device: Disks, tapes, and optical scanning devices have such variations in types that only by careful checking in advance can you avoid the considerable expense of translating from one to another (even if you find appropriate machinery to do this job!).

Verification of Input Information

After preparing the data for machine readability, and before undertaking their analysis, you should verify that they are correct: This will save much grief later on. Historically, the rate of error in recording data on machine-readable media is between 5 and 2%. This means that if a significance level of 5% is used, the alpha-error could, hypothetically, be entirely accounted for by recording error. Verification of input data is a necessity.

The traditional method of verifying input is to arrange for two different people to enter the data independently, then to resolve any discrepancies.

An amusing account of an input error is the statistical detective story of Coale and Stephan (1962). The 1950 U.S. Census report showed an unexpectedly large number of teenaged widowed males and an implausible excess of Indians in regions where the Indian population is small. These authors deduced (from circumstantial evidence) that systematic errors were made in punching the Hollerith cards, so that middle-aged males became teen-agers by a column displacement, and white children of heads of household likewise became Indians. While the Bureau of the Census has shifted to magnetic tape, comparable errors can creep into any data-processing or recording procedure.

Security of Machine-Readable Information

It is a wise precaution to create a duplicate set of your machine-readable files, to be stored on magnetic tape, on floppy disks, or on cards. The availability of valid back-up information can protect the investment you have already made in creating your own file. Your choice of medium for both sets is governed primarily by what is available at the computer center. However, if magnetic tapes or floppy disks are to retain the information, they must be stored under fairly constant environmental conditions, (e.g., temperature, pressure, etc.). Cards cannot be exposed to high humidity for long periods, nor can they be bent or mutilated without losing their readability.

A printout (so-called hard copy) of your data set may be a worthwhile, though substantial, investment. All duplicate files and hard copy must be kept in a safe place.

Automated Data Acquisition and Process Control

In some studies it is desirable or necessary to input data to the computer simultaneously with the events. In a certain maze experiment, rats were expected to press one of several bars to open a door. The researcher needed to know which bars the rat actually pressed before achieving success. A human observer, watching the rat, could record the sequence, but such work is tedious and subject to substantial error. An alternative is to have each bar press recorded by a computer: the information is then available at once for retrieval and analysis.

The computer can also be used to pick up a signal for the completion of some event, and to return a signal setting off the next event in a sequence (e.g., in the foregoing, to reset the bars, relock the door, or vary the reward either at random or in a regular pattern). This kind of data acquisition is called *process control*. Process control experiments require special computer circuitry (often called "breadboards") and hardware. Technical advances in recent years have made experiments possible that would have been out of the question in the past. In effect the computer conducts the experiment or the survey in an unbiased way at electronic speed.

If you take advantage of an automated data acquisition procedure, we strongly advise that you arrange to have a printout or a hard-copy data set, which can be stored securely.

Data-Base-Management (Management Information) Systems and Computer Simulation (Automated Data Generation)[8]

One of the more productive approaches to computerizing your data is a Data Base Management System (DBMS), often called a Management Information System (MIS). Most large- or medium-size organizations today keep data files on the computer in a DBMS, permitting addition and deletion, and providing easy access to data-analysis programs frequently used to generate reports. An MIS/DBMS transforms data into information (useful output).

The use of an MIS/DBMS may be most helpful in social and behavioral science research projects. If data are appropriately organized, you may be able to predict what additional data will be needed; in any case, a study on many variables which spans a long time interval typically yields a huge number of data items, so that efficient organization of data can mean the difference between an easy analysis and a frustrating muddle.

Many MIS/DBMS packages have the capacity to answer "what-if" questions. For example:

- What if wage increases are granted: What will be the effect on productivity?
- What if a new doctoral program is offered: Will it encroach on enrollments in already-established programs?
- What if a larger proportion of registered Democrats vote: Will increased local school budgets be more likely to pass?

Such questions attempt to identify potential consequences of future actions, decisions, or conditions. To answer them, the MIS/DBMS must contain programs that permit manipulation of some of the parameters built into the report-generating (data-analysis) routines. For example, you can exploit information already obtained about population characteristics to make projections to the effects of a shift in population proportions. Many what-if questions thus fall into the general category of computer simulation.

"*Computer simulation* is a procedure that attempts to recreate a problem situation under study by developing a computer model of the process."[9] The researcher carries out an experiment in which the computer itself is the laboratory and both generates and analyzes the data. Such a formalized trial-and-error technique can be appropriate for studying complex problems whose many possible options for input and output make such methods as linear programming unfeasible.

A typical queueing or waiting line problem (see Chapter 15) lends itself to computer simulation. Arrival times, queue discipline, number of service facilities, and service times, can be modelled by a set of equations; the number of arrivals, for instance, might be described by a Poisson distribution, and service time by a normal distribution. The computer can generate random events and, using the equations, can calculate the values of the variables which describe the simulated flow of "customers." The behavior of the system can be evaluated by averaging these simulated data for a series of repeated events in which variations are assumed to be random. Without the many years of experimentation and observation which would be needed in the "real world," it is possible to determine whether a single waiting line at a bank or lines at the several windows will minimize the average waiting time.

While a computer simulation may not give you an optimal solution to a problem, it can identify better and good outcomes in the light of the what-if. You must, of course, use judgment in selecting values of parameters to be investigated. Simulation is especially useful when the process under study has random parametric or nonparametric continuous variates. In this case, most of the variables can be generated by a random number selection from a specified distribution. It is also suitable for discrete variables. Most important is that a model has been formulated algebraically or logically, so that a computer program can be written easily and at low cost.[10]

Von Neumann and Ulam have termed simulation methods the *Monte Carlo technique*. Comparison of observed events and the computer simulation can be made to determine the capacity of the model to predict reality. Languages especially amenable to use in simulation studies include GPSS and SIMSCRIPT. Imaginative applications will permit the rapid analysis of a wide variety of possible situations: simulations can be an extremely powerful and useful research tool for the social sciences. They should be increasingly exploited in the future.

Your Own Software

It may happen that no computer software exists to do precisely the job you want done. If all else fails, you will be forced to write a software package in order to obtain a solution to your problems.[11] (There are, in fact, sociograms or particular tests for which already existing programs do not suffice.) As we have indicated earlier, this is a large task. Such work should be undertaken only by an expert: find one and contract the job. Usually the programming of a computer application is extremely expensive. If you undertake to develop the necessary software yourself, you must also consider the expenditure of time. Only the most experienced programmers can produce effective and timely results with minimal costs. In any case, you must seriously question whether or not you can afford to pursue the problem.

If a software package is available, evaluate the pros and cons of using it as opposed to writing your own software (assuming costs are potentially within your budget). Take into account both positive and negative factors which may be present: Positive Factors include lower cost, less duplication of effort, faster implementation, better documentation, staff freed for other work, and better support by your hardware. Negative Factors include possible inefficiency, weak documentation, inflexibility, need for tailoring, and lack of acceptance at the computer installation.

Computer Packages for the Social Sciences

We strongly recommend the use of a software package if a suitable one is available. Our major argument in support of this position is the high quality of existing software packages for the social sciences: they are extraordinarily flexible, universally available, cheap to use, and reliable in their results. Almost every commonly used statistical or mathematical procedure can be obtained in canned form.

The best-known computer packages in the social sciences are Statistical Package for the Social Sciences (SPSS), Biomedical (BMDP), Statistical Analysis System (SAS), and the International Algorithmic Statistical and Mathematical Library (IASML). Many other packages exist and are widely available.

SPSS, the most widely-used statistical package, includes software for many procedures, classified under various subprograms. Among these are most of the familiar techniques for classification, graphing, and statistical analysis (parametric and nonparametric) of data. The manual is extremely informative, well-written, explicit, and thorough. Periodically, new procedures are added to SPSS. With a little skill in Fortran or some other language you can add programs of your own design. Recent updates have addressed many problems present in the earlier versions. SCSS is a scaled down, interactive version of SPSS and, if available, may be both convenient and suitable for your purpose.

BMDP, Biomedical Data Processing System, is very much like SPSS. It has file creation and file management capabilities, as well as the capacity to transform all kinds of variables. The package of statistical routines is very extensive; it contains a few items not available in SPSS. It is also more sophisticated mathematically. BMDP is written primarily for use in biostatistics. Documentation of the system is quite good; most novices can read the instructions and make use of the system with minimal computer background. It is a relatively inexpensive system to run, and user costs are thus low. However, if you do use it you must cite the system and the U.S. Government grant number under which it was developed. If SPSS is not your first choice, BMDP is probably your best alternative.

The Statistical Analysis System (*SAS*) is similar to the aforementioned packages. Its major advantages are in the system's file handling capabilities and ease in attaching BMDP routines. SAS is produced by the SAS Institute, which publishes a users' and programmers' guide. Subroutines in languages such as Fortran or PLI can easily be added; thus you can modify the package to suit your own particular needs. A standard set of statistical routines is available with the system. SAS suffers from lack of clarity in its documentation; some sophistication is required to read and understand the various instructions. Overlap in routines between SAS, SPSS and BMDP is extremely high. The latter two are probably easier for the novice to use.

IASML is a system of subprograms to be used with a Fortran program. A knowledge of Fortran and subprogram use is required. Besides the familiar statistical measures, this package has mathematical routines such as integration, the simplex method, approximate solution of differential equations, and many other numerical procedures for solving deterministic problems.

All the packages listed above are available at any university computer center and at many research computer centers. A good computer center library has many others as well, some designed in response to special data analysis situations, such as MDSCAL and its relatives for multidimensional scaling. Always inquire as to what is available for your purpose. A fee may be charged for the use of packages such as these. Before deciding on a suitable package, it is important for you to consider carefully issues of precision, flexibility in use of subroutines, and ease of interpretation, as well as costs and availability of tests. *It is essential to select a package which can be supported by your computer*: no matter how powerful and appropriate the routines, they are of no use if they can't be carried out.

Computer Graphics

In the past few years, computer graphics techniques have developed rapidly and an extraordinary variety is now available for visual data display. For example, many desk-top devices suitable for home or office use (in fact, all but the simplest CRT's) can be modified to produce not only standard items such as line plots but an ever-expanding list of other graphics as well. SPSS and SAS both have graphics packages which will produce line, bar, and pie charts (including cumulatives); in addition, versatile specialized graphics packages are available which, with relatively minor modifications, will accept data in various standard file formats and thus can be interfaced with SPSS. Some universities have extensive graphics facilities associated with their computer science departments. Finally, certain commercial vendors can supply graphics services, tailor-made for the needs of the user. Among the most striking are maps of many kinds.

If you are interested in exploring the potential application of this part of technology to data display for your project, it is essential that you seek out an expert who can advise you on what is possible and what is appropriate. Since this is a state-of-the-art field, it is impossible for us to indicate here what your choices may be a year from now; moreover, the use of computer graphics is susceptible to all the hazards of any computer techniques, mainly, the GIGO problem together with those of any graphics or tabular display[12]—they provide an immediacy which can be easily misleading.

It is important to inquire about available graphics early in your project planning, because whatever computer center you select for data processing must have appropriate hardware and software.

Text Editors

Most computers (personals, minis, or mainframe) allow the user to interact with the machine to gather and process output information: the software used to accomplish this is called a *text editor* or word processor. The text editor permits manipulation of various types of text such as computer programs, manuscript, and letters; its interactive capabilities allow the user to create a text; change and correct the text by backspacing, retyping, deleting, inserting, and rearranging pieces; and search and display the text. The editor, a user-friendly piece of software, will allow you to re-try commands, it will prompt you to give it information needed for a valid command or another line of text, and it will announce the presence of an error in a command. When the execution of your command could effect a significant change in your work, it may indicate what the change will be and ask you to okay it.

Text editors can be extremely useful in calling up the programs to run a SPSS, BMDP, SAS etc., job. It goes without saying that they can be most helpful in preparing your thesis or report because of the many revisions that are involved. In addition, questionnaires, test banks, and all manner of verbal and numerical material that change frequently lend themselves to text editing.

There are as many text editors as there are different types of computers, but they all have similar features. If you plan to use computers interactively, we suggest you learn to use their text editors. Some commonly used text-editors are CMS, WORDSTAR, WYLBUR and SCRIPT, but learning one without establishing that your machine will support it may be a waste of time: check this in advance. It is wise to plan to use as few different text-editors as possible, because you may find the shift from one to another quite confusing.

Keeping Data Records (Archiving)

Most research records or materials should be kept for 3 years after publication. (After 3 years, most data are obsolete for further research purposes.) Primary records, such as hard-copy data, or files should be protected against loss during this period. All records should be dated, particularly computer output which is often duplicated with only minor modifications. Binders are available so that storage of computer printouts, photocopies, pertinent photographs, and machine readable data can be neat and convenient. Archiving your material can be a major undertaking if you have a mass of newly-discovered documents or artifacts. A librarian knowledgeable about your discipline can be an effective consultant on how best to do this.

Complete records include the items mentioned in the section on Documentation (above). Intermediate results should be retained, dated, and archived: the purpose is to permit you to recapture your procedure, identify possible sources of error, and pursue additional lines of analysis later on.

On occasion you may be asked to release your data to others. Take care that doing so does not violate any agreements you have made with subjects or sponsors of your research. It is usually wise to delay such release until your study is complete.

Notes

[1]Such as Texas Instruments' TI-59C or Hewlett-Packard's HP-19C (as of early 1984); these machines are quickly replaced in the product line.

[2]If you are employed by a company which maintains a research department of its own, you may well be in a situation comparable to that of a graduate student so far as access to computing facilities and personnel are concerned. A computer consultant may be available to you as one of many resource staff, such as statisticians, reference librarians, experts in conducting surveys, etc. Before undertaking your project, be sure to find out what assistance is available in-house, because budget, time, and other planning decisions will be affected.

[3]Cost figures (1985, New York City) assuming minimal consultant use. Costs for an analysis of variance procedure at a commercial center are likely to fall between $50 and $70; compare this with $10–$20 at a university center.

[4]McWilliams (1982, 1983) may be helpful. See also Schrodt (1984).

[5]New York City prices, 1985.

[6]New York City prices, 1985.

[7]An excellent summary can be found in Selltiz (1976, Chapter 13). Backstrom and Hursh-Cesar (1981 pp. 309–335) is a good source of know-how on coding and data compilation.

[8]We recommend reading Anderson et al., either (1976, Chapters 13 and 18) or (1978, Chapters 16 and 19).

[9]Anderson et al. (1976, p. 438).

[10]Problems modelled by such techniques as Markov processes, queueing, PERT, and parametric programming are often examined by simulating the data. See Chapter 15 (sections on each of these topics).

[11]The steps involved are given in Woolbridge (1973).

[12]Garbage-In-Color-Garbage-Out!

Additional Reading

The following deal with various aspects of computer use in social science research:

Barcikowski (1982).
Brier and Robinson (1974).
Moore (1978).
Woolbridge (1973).
Heise (ed.) (1981).
Hy (1977).

For both the descriptions of the statistical procedures and the details of the particular programs, the SPSS and BMDP manuals are essential. Both are clear and generally informative.

McWilliams (1982, 1983): introductory guides for selection and use of personal word processing and computing equipment.

Schrodt (1984): emphasis on methods usable with personal computers.

10

Techniques for Analysis of Data

Introduction

The principal purposes of data analysis are (1) to reveal patterns, differences, and relationships which might not be evident from direct inspection of the data and (2) to permit you to decide whether observational evidence supports your hypotheses. Your most important task in data analysis is to decide which technique will do the best job for you, but before you can make this decision you must first be clear about two things: The nature of your problem and the nature of your conjectures.[1] The choice of an appropriate statistical technique is then largely determined by the specific questions you are trying to answer (for example, by the relationships you want to exhibit), and by the sort of data you have.[2]

Many beginning researchers may be apprehensive about planning the statistical portion of their projects, but familiarity with the range of available techniques can dispel some of these terrors. These preliminary steps will help you feel more comfortable with statistical analysis:

- Review your notes and other resource materials, to refresh your recall of the vocabulary and your understanding of the various possibilities. While you should have had at least a year of introductory statistics, additional course work is desirable, particularly if you plan to use a multivariate analysis. Do not overfocus on formulas or on the mechanics of their application. Formulas for computing and strategies for modifying them are available in handbooks of statistics for researchers. Look for the explicit statements of the assumptions (mathematical and other) underlying each statistical procedure. Devote most of your attention to the special applicability and special weakness of each technique and to comparing it with related techniques.
- Seek out a knowledgeable resource person. It is easy to become confused when confronted with several dozen alternatives: a statistical "consultant" can assist you in planning your statistical anaysis and in interpreting the results. (See later sections on choosing and using experts, this chapter.) In general, this individual will not be as well-informed in your particular domain of research as you are, so it will be your responsibility to describe clearly and succinctly the theoretical frame of reference for your study,

all instruments and the sorts of data they yield, and what you hope to establish. If you are a graduate student or are associated with a research institution, one or more of the staff members will probably perform the function of statistical consultant; otherwise, it may be necessary for you to budget the expense of this service.

- Remember that data analysis is part of your overall research design. DO NOT PROCEED with any data collection unless and until you are fairly clear in your mind about what numerical criteria must be met to permit you to draw your conclusions. Under no circumstances should you delay planning statistical analysis until after the data have been collected. If you incorporate the statistical design into your plan of other aspects of the study you will be much more secure in working through the details of data analysis and interpretation and presentation of your findings; these procedures will be a natural, organic part of your argument.

- "[data analysis] should aid in the clarification of meaning. . . but the production of a statistical summary in some impressive and elegant form should never be the primary goal of a research enterprise. If no inferential statistical techniques are available to fit the problem, do not alter the problem in essential ways to make some pet or fashionable technique apply. Above all, do not "jam" the data willy-nilly into some wildly inappropriate statistical analysis simply to get a significance test; there is little or nothing to gain by doing this. Thoughtless application of statistical techniques makes the reader wonder about the care that went into the [study] itself. A really good [study], carefully planned and controlled, often speaks for itself with little or no aid from inferential statistics."[3]

A Note on Word Usage

Statistics has several different meanings. It refers to the portion of applied mathematics that deals with the theory and application of techniques for reduction, display, and analysis of quantitative data, and also to a particular computed value or values, (e.g., the mean, the F-ratio, the correlation coefficient). In this book, we use both and trust the usage is clear in context.

Questions That Data Analysis
Can and Cannot Answer

Statistical techniques permit you to summarize many kinds of numerical data, and to describe in a neat and mathematically manageable fashion certain kinds of relationships or comparisons among two or more sets of data. You may be able to assign values to parameters in functions used for description or prediction, or to make inferences about the larger population from which were drawn the samples that you observed. Techniques serve their useful purpose if, and only if, in the company of appropriately formulated hypotheses, they assist you to reach a decision about the compatibility of your observations and the propositions you seek to establish. Your decision or inference may be *probabilistic* in the sense that the conclusion will always be associated with a probability estimate of error. (Refer to Chapter 4, sections on hypothesis testing and decision rules.)

Data analysis never "proves" and never "finds." Deductive validity, familiar from the example of proofs in elementary geometry, cannot be established statistically. No inferences are possible as to the validity of statements that are normative or judgmental, or concern action to be taken, or involve relationships among variables not studied. Strictly speaking, neither causality nor direction of effect can be "proved" statistically: It is only possible to assign a probability to each of several alternative statements describing the strength of association among observed variables.

Statistical techniques will not draw conclusions for you, or interpret themselves. No matter how sophisticated, they cannot remedy incorrect theoretical formulations, weaknesses in design, researcher's bias, or failure to collect sufficient data. They cannot replace experience and judgment on your part.

Every technique, no matter how carefully chosen, presents certain hazards. The most general and insidious are the following:

- Failure to exploit the available data. For instance, in computing a moving average, the first few time intervals are lost, but the pattern in the later intervals is revealed. It is up to you to decide on the proper balance between precision sacrificed and clarity gained.
- Improper choice of statistical procedure. It is important to consider the type of measurements, sampling, and other aspects of design. Even though some statistics are robust in that certain of their underlying assumptions can be violated without serious damage, caution is necessary: whenever possible, verify the applicability of the ones you use. Avoid statistical fads (such as multiple regression or loglinear procedures), even if they promise powerful results, unless they suit your design.
- Failure to modify techniques to reflect peculiarities of design. On the other hand, "bending the study" to conform to standard design models may also weaken statistical conclusions.
- Overreliance on numerical pyrotechnics. Many perfectly good studies do not lend themselves to statistical analysis at all, or to any but a very simple-minded descriptive treatment. This in no way diminishes their value.[4]
- Misinterpretation of numerical results. This may be due to ignorance, carelessness, or stubborness (or perhaps wishful thinking) on the part of the researcher. Data do not lie, but they can—and do—mislead.

For instance, *probability pyramiding* (repeating tests on the same data) can suggest the presence of effects, whereas all you are seeing is the effect of the α-error.

Experts

In our experience, novice researchers most commonly seek an expert's technical help with one or another—but we hope not all—of the following: question and schedule construction, reliability assessment, sampling, computer use, statistical analysis.

By *consultant* we mean any knowledgeable individual who acts as a resource person to assist you in some specialized aspect(s) of your research project. Such an individual may be one of your mentors, perhaps even a member of your dissertation committee, another member of the faculty or staff who by assignment or on an informal basis is available for consultation; a fellow researcher, a friend who has special know-how, or a skilled and experienced practitioner whose expertise you have arranged to buy.

You must find out whether your committee or department maintains the position that every doctoral student must proceed as if shipwrecked alone on a desert island (i.e., must possess all relevant skills); if so, you will be most unwise to anticipate seeking advice from a paid consultant. Even if this is the case, much of what we have to say about your role in working with a consultant applies equally well to in-house and informal resource persons.

CHOOSING AND USING
A STATISTICAL RESOURCE PERSON OR CONSULTANT

There are many good reasons to seek knowledgeable assistance with your statistical work. There are also some very poor reasons. Advice at the planning stage from someone experienced, interested, authoritative, and somewhat detached from your particular study can be very useful. You will have to make your proposed research understandable, and in the process clarify your own ideas. Your resource person may be able to think about the problem in a fresh way and see it from a different point of view. A good consultant is familiar with many statistical techniques, some of which may not have occurred to you. Working with him or her should give you increased confidence in your own judgment and your skill in using statistical procedures.

Do not seek a consultant with your data in hand, in the hope that some magical bail-out operation can salvage a poor design or remedy oversights in data collection. Likewise, do not expect to be relieved of your responsibility for making decisions: the study is, and remains, yours. However, the information and self-confidence you acquire should make you a better advocate for your own position in case a supervisor or a member of your committee is giving you a hard time about your choice of analysis.

There are certain criteria to guide your selection of a consultant, once you decide to seek assistance. Their relative importance will depend on your own temperament and your particular needs. Remember, no consultant will be able to work with you in an effective way unless you know what you expect him/her to do.

1. Appropriate knowledge and skills: Whatever the formal credentials, the person you choose must be familiar with a wide variety of different statistics and the advantages and shortcomings of each. A good consultant should possess both an understanding of the theory underlying the various techniques (so as to be able to modify them when necessary) and a facility in applying them. Some consultants are stronger in mathematics. Others have greater intuitive "feel" for statistical analysis. Your consultant's specialized skills must be compatible with your needs. It may be inadvisable, for example, to choose one who is an authority on agricultural experimentation, if your work will involve survey studies of urban ethnic groups, unless you can be reasonably certain he/she is informed and open-minded about social research.

2. Willingness to learn about your problem and what it entails: an individual who comes to a conclusion after too brief a discussion of your problem and its special aspects may mislead or, more likely, frustrate you. Since no one can be an expert in every field within the social and behavioral sciences, a good consultant must be curious, capable of asking pointed questions, and willing to accept the assumptions of your discipline. One who adopts a "my way or no way" attitude leaves you between Scylla and Charybdis. Try to find someone who is able to be flexible and to entertain plausible alternatives. (Be patient while he/she reflects on them.)

3. Extensive experience: Statistical consulting is a line of work in which book learning is emphatically not sufficient. Your consultant should have participated in research projects in several different fields, using different methodologies and many different data analysis techniques. Any serious limitation in his/her experience should be revealed to you as well.

4. Accessibility: Your consultant should be easy for you to reach, in person or by telephone. Someone whose base of operations is very far from yours, or who is so busy that you have to make appointments weeks or months in advance, will be of limited usefulness.

5. Congenial personal style: It is important that you enjoy working with your consultant. You have every right to seek out an individual whose personality meshes comfortably with yours. If you feel ill-at-ease, foolishly ignorant, or overwhelmed, something is wrong. Keep looking.

6. Other considerations: Find out if your consultant has access to computer facilities. The best possible situation would be one who can also function as a computer consultant. (See next section.)

Any consultant necessarily performs a teaching function. Yours must be able to tell you which texts are appropriate, and be willing to explain the basis for any suggestions and give thoughtful answers to your questions. If possible, he/she should be capable of giving you an overview of design and analytic procedures so that in future studies you will be better equipped to work on your own.

Finding such a paragon is far from simple. You are indeed fortunate if a member of your committee or department meets these requirements. A realistic assessment of your own strengths and weaknesses will help you decide which of the attributes listed above are the most important for you. Members of any university faculty can suggest possible consultants but, unless they are themselves actively engaged in research, are apt to place too much weight on formal credentials and too little on experience or the other considerations we have listed. More advanced doctoral students or recent degree recipients can usually give you additional names. Knowing someone who has worked with the consultant allows you to get a preliminary impression of his/her style and special interests. You are certainly entitled to interview a person whom you will be paying and who will work with you over a period of weeks or months.

Finally, do not permit yourself to be intimidated by the notion that the statistical consultant possesses arcane knowledge which you can never master but of which you must always stand in awe.

CHOOSING AND USING A COMPUTER RESOURCE PERSON

For many researchers the processing of data will be a concern that begins and ends with the choice of a computer consultant. If you are a doctoral candidate, your department or university computer center may have on staff individuals whose assignment includes assisting faculty and students in their computer use or, in some cases, taking responsibility for all data processing. This is ideal from a cost point of view, but timeliness and individualization of attention paid to your problem may suffer from the many demands made on a limited staff. Again, you need a clear understanding of the consultant's job: to process data, not to design the study, not to select the statistical methods, nor to interpret or write up the results of processing. A computer consultant is an interface with the machine, someone you can talk to about the data, who can translate for the "black box" that the computer represents for many people. He or she must be generally knowledgeable and highly skilled in the area of data processing and should have

1. a good reputation,
2. experience with the hardware to be used,
3. familiarity with the research area,
4. a history of selecting appropriate software,
5. a professional, well-organized approach to the job, and
6. a proven record of completing work on time.

The consultant should be able and willing to

1. understand what it is you are doing and why you are doing it,
2. talk to you in standard English and avoid the excessive use of jargon (you will, however, need to master some jargon yourself if you are to communicate effectively), and
3. clarify results, if necessary.

Such individuals can be found through most university computing centers and sometimes through private consulting firms that have a statistical department.[5]

Classification of Data Analysis or Statistical Techniques

Statistical techniques—statistics—are commonly classified according to the purpose they serve (descriptive versus inferential), the necessary assumptions about the data to which they are applied (level of measurement; parametric versus nonparametric), or the number of variables whose distributions or relationships they analyze (univariate, bivariate, and multivariate). A less-familiar classification is based on the type of model (deterministic versus probabilistic) on which the analysis is based.

- The categories of descriptive versus inferential reflect the main purpose of the statistical technique. So-called descriptive statistics are primarily procedures for data reduction and display. They permit you to see what you have more clearly than you could from inspection of all the data. It should be evident that this involves a trade-off: loss of completeness or precision, to be balanced against a gain in clarity or conciseness. Included under the heading *descriptive* are the following:

  descriptors of cross-breaks: for example, frequency tables, percentages;
  descriptors of central tendency: for example, mean, median, mode;
  measures of dispersion: for example, quartiles, percentiles,
      variance, standard deviation, coefficient of variation;
  measures of the shape of the distribution: skewness, kurtosis;

measures of disparity of your distribution from one specified a priori: chi square;

measures of disarray (ordinal data): D, S; Kendall's W;

measures of association between two sets of data: various correlation coefficients, for example, Pearson, Spearman; Phi, Eta, Yule's Q, odds ratio, etc.;

descriptors of linear or other functional relationships: for example, regression equations,

procedures for identifying clusters, factor and discriminant analysis, multidimensional scaling;

procedures for graphical presentation of data.

- *Inferential statistics*, on the other hand, enable the user to decide how much to rely on data from a sample (that is, how typical these data are); to extrapolate to larger or different populations, or to compare data from different samples. The underlying mechanism is that of probability theory. Every inferential application of a statistic uses a sampling distribution to find the probability that the observed value has occurred by chance alone. This means that you can evaluate, within specified limits, the extent to which the values of obtained descriptive measures depend on the particular sample. Thus, the line between descriptive and inferential statistics is not a firm one. Too often, "data reduction" versus "inferential" is a difference without a distinction. The distinction where it exists depends on your purpose.

- Classification of data analysis techniques into parametric versus nonparametric is based upon the characteristics of the data to which the statistical techniques are being applied. Parametric statistics are useful only under the following conditions:

1. Data are interval- or ratio-scale and continuous. Thus, arithmetic procedures needed to calculate mean, variance, etc. are meaningful.

2. The sample (or samples) is (are) drawn from a population in which the variables being measured are normally distributed. If the parent population is not expected to have a normal distribution, large samples are essential.

3. When two or more samples are being compared for difference of means, variances are homogeneous, that is, not statistically different.

In certain situations these assumptions can be relaxed without major damage to the validity of the technique. (This will be discussed in the context of the specific procedure.) Parametric procedures have the advantage that they permit you fully to exploit the mathematical consequences of probability and integration theory. Decision making based on these powerful parametric techniques can be very precise, perhaps misleadingly so, in that it is easy to overlook uncertainty introduced in the design or the nature of the variables. Extensive tables of the parametric distributions are available in most standard texts.

Nonparametric or distribution-free statistics are appropriate[6] when you are dealing with:

1. Data that are ordinal or nominal. Thus, no assumption as to additivity of measurements is incorporated into the procedure. (See our discussion of differing viewpoints on this issue in Chapter 7.)
2. Small samples from populations in which distribution of the variable under study is known to be nonnormal, or not reasonably assumed to be normally distributed.
3. Inhomogeneity of variance in two or more samples.

The advantage of the nonparametrics is, primarily, relative simplicity. They are a must for small sample studies. They are quick and easy to compute, good for preliminary estimates, and reflect the honest recognition of the nature of your measures.[7] These procedures are mathematically based on combinatorial (counting) arguments. Many of the sampling distributions can be approximated by familiar parametric distributions. The major disadvantages are less power (see next section), and their waste of information when used on interval data. Also, no analogous nonparametric methods are at present available for certain kinds of analyses, notably, multivariate interaction effects.

Because of the unfamiliarity of many researchers with nonparametric methods, as well as the intrinsic limitations of these methods, there is a great temptation to use parametric techniques with ordinal data, with coded nominal data, or when the necessary assumptions are not verified. Until recently, not many computer programs were available for nonparametric procedures, but this omission has been remedied and several major packages (e.g., BMDP, SPSS) have routines for the most widely used procedures.

Here are some examples of analyses inappropriate for the level or other characteristics of the data.[8] McMillan (1977) investigated the relationships of effort and feedback with the "cognitive and affective attitudes" expressed by college students towards two course assignments in educational psychology. The study used an analysis of variance procedure, treating continuous ordinal data obtained from a Likert-type summated rating scale as if it were continuous interval. This study has other shortcomings (unit of analysis, operationalizing, nonrandomization) mentioned elsewhere. Moyer's study (1981) of police disposition of a suspected offender uses a 5-category dependent variable, and three nominal independent variables: race, sex, and demeanor. Again, an analysis of variance procedure is used, and although the author acknowledges that an *F*-test does not apply, she reports findings in terms of percentage of variance explained. ANOVA requires a continuous interval dependent variable.

- Finally, statistical procedures are classified as univariate, bivariate, or multivariate, according to whether they are applicable to data for one, two, or more variables. The mean and variance are univariate statistics. Spearman rank-order correlation is bivariate. Factor analysis is multivariate. Multivariate methods look computationally complicated, and explanations in reference books usually assume familiarity with terminology and with simpler strategies. Do not be discouraged. Calculations can, and should, be done by machine. The potential for drawing sophisticated conclusions from data is so great that it makes your efforts to develop a comfortable understanding of these methods well worth your while.

- A classification of statistical techniques can be based on the underlying model. This requires a brief digression to review terminology:

    "[A]ny system A is a model of a system *B* if the study of A is useful for the understanding of B without regard to any direct or indirect causal connection between A and B . . . . [W]hen one system is a model of another they resemble one another in *form* and not in content."[9]

Thus, a *mathematical model* can be thought of as an hypothesis concerning two or more variables, in which the solution of the problem and the relationships between the variables are expressed in the language of formal mathematics.

For example, the problem of describing disagreement between rankings by two or more independent judges, can be approached using several models. One model is Kendall's coefficient of concordance W,[10] associated with which is a distribution, that is, set of probabilities of occurrence. Another model[11] is based on the notion of "distance" between the two rankings, and seeks to develop a measure of disagreement which will have the familiar properties of distance in geometry. Loosely speaking, a model is *deterministic* if, by having sufficient information about precursor events, one can predict future events, whereas if one can only predict probabilities of future events, the model is *probabilistic* or *stochastic*. Another formulation of this distinction reflects the fact that in a deterministic model once the parameters for the model are specified, the outcome (solution) is entirely determined or forced by the mathematical relationships and rules built into the model. In contrast, a probability function is part of a probabilistic or stochastic model, so the solution may be of the form: where X has value x, there is a probability p that the value of Y will fall between y_1, and y_2. This is the case even when the parameters are specified. Thus, your data can be used to decide which member of a family of models is to be used to make a deterministic prediction, to decide what probabilities are associated with each of several possible outcomes, or both.

- One additional classification is that of exploratory, as opposed to confirmatory, data analysis techniques.[12] We will have relatively little to say about these, although they can be an important aspect of formulative studies. The pattern of relationships reflected in data obtained from a pilot study may need exploration before hypotheses for the main study can be formulated. Similarly, data from large surveys with many question items may be sorted out more efficiently by making use of these strategies. The uncovering of unexpected relationships can greatly enrich the discussion of your expected findings.

In the next four chapters, we list and describe the most commonly used statistical techniques and point out problems characteristic of each. Our concern will be for their relative appropriateness for different purposes. Since we are assuming you have access to a computer to do the numerical calculations, we will describe and in many cases exhibit sample computer printouts. In view of the wide availability of excellent texts and manuals, we will make no attempt to recapitulate standard formulas, their derivations, or schemes for computational shortcuts. If you need such information or techniques other than those listed you can find an annotated reference bibliography at the end of each of the next two chapters.

Evaluating Competing Procedures

The selection of a statistical procedure will, of course, depend ultimately upon what kind of decisions you want to make about your data and what kind of data you have. The choice must make sense, and must be compatible with your design and method. If two procedures are available to do the same job, and both appear equally suitable to your purpose, you will have to choose between them. The following considerations will help you make your selection.

- The *power* of a statistical test is the probability that it will correctly reject a false hypothesis. It is defined as $1 - \beta$ where β is the Type II error (see Chapter 4, section on Type II error) associated with the particular sample size. In general, for a given sample size, choose the test with greater power.
- The *power-efficiency* of a statistical test, relative to some other test, is a measure of the sample size needed to achieve a specified power.[13] If

U and V are statistics which require samples of size N_u and N_v, respectively, to achieve power P, then the power-efficiency of U relative to V is defined as N_v/N_u. (This is sometimes converted to a percentage.)

So for example, the Kruskal–Wallis nonparametric one way analysis of variance test has power efficiency .955 relative to parametric one-way analysis of variance; hence, a sample of 955 is needed to achieve the same power in the ANOVA as a sample of 1000 in the Kruskal–Wallis. In general, if it is desirable to control sample size, choose the more power-efficient test.

- The relative ease with which the test can be carried out is important. If no computer program is available, or if extensive preliminary preparation of data is necessary, you may be better off with a somewhat less powerful or efficient test. Some tests are more expensive to run, so check costs before you make your final choice.

Computer Use

Modern statistical techniques depend for their usefulness on readily accessible computer facilities. Otherwise the analysis of large masses of data is unfeasible. Ready-made programs and statistical packages (as described in Chapter 9) permit you to sort and group data, to carry out lengthy and complicated computations, and to prepare tables, graphs, and other displays. Procedures which were unimaginable or prohibitively expensive a few years ago, are now routine.

There is, however, a concomitant hazard. Even those who are thoroughly comfortable with statistical packages and warmly enthusiastic about their use express the need for caution in their application:

[S]tatistical systems like SPSS can be important tools in the research process . . . . However, precisely because of their power they may be easily abused. . . .

1. *Ease of access often means overaccess.* Modern computing packages have made it so easy to produce large amounts of information on a single pass of a data file that even the experienced researcher is tempted to go on 'grand fishing expeditions,' substituting the crudest form of empiricism. In the careful interaction of concepts, hypotheses, and data analysis . . .[the] best rule-of-thumb is to request only those tables, coefficients, etc., for which you have some theoretical expectations based upon the hypotheses in your research design.

2. *Uninformed use of the available statistical techniques.* . . . There is little doubt that social scientists are using complex statistical techniques, and there is equally little doubt that in many instances these techniques are being utilized by both students and researchers who understand neither the assumptions nor their statistical or mathematical bases. There can also be little doubt that this situation leads to some "garbage-in, garbage-out" research ("GIGO"). The [packaged] statistical

procedures . . . have little ability to distinguish between proper and improper applications . . . . They are basically blind computational algorithms that apply their formulas to whatever data the user enters . . . .

The general rule is that a user should never attempt to use a statistical procedure unless he understands both the appropriate procedure for the type of data and also the meaning of the statistics produced."[14]

Decision Trees for
Choosing Statistical Procedures

In the next two chapters we repeatedly emphasize the importance of choosing a suitable procedure for the statistical analysis of data, where determination of suitability—as described earlier in this chapter—involves criteria including measurement level, parametricity, sample size, number of treatment groups, and number of variables, that is, problem characteristics. In addition, you need a properly formulated question about the data, such as, "How strong is the association between these two sets of measurements?" or "How probable is the observed difference in mean scores between these two groups?" Your decision as to which statistical procedure can be used, or which among several may be the best for your purpose, therefore requires repeated choices or, more specifically, a systematic sorting of alternatives. To guide you in making these choices in an orderly way, we will make extensive use of decision trees in our presentation. The plums are labelled by the usual terminology for statistical procedures. We also include short sections discussing special aspects—strengths, shortcomings, etc.—of the several procedures.[15]

You may wish to refer back to the section on Decision Trees in the Appendix.

Chapter 11 deals with (probabilistic) techniques for analysis of data in one or two variables; Chapters 12–14 with multivariate techniques suitable for data with two or more variables. (Deterministic data analysis techniques are discussed in Chapter 15.) Within each chapter, we indicate which descriptive measures reflect various aspects of the data, and then discuss related significance tests and inferential procedures. You will find nonparametric techniques placed alongside their parametric counterparts. The emphasis throughout is on identifying both the purpose for which each technique is best adapted, and its limitations and possible pitfalls in application. Your awareness of the classifications and your thoughtful selection of an appropriate technique will greatly simplify all your statistical work and will help you avoid the wasteful buckshot style that appears all too frequently in reports of research.

No matter how many alternatives are available, it is finally possible that none is exactly right for your purpose. Your judgment and scholarship ultimately justify your choice and permit interpretation of your findings.

Notes

[1]Although we are assuming that you expect to test already stated hypotheses, we urge you to read Tukey and Wilk (1965) which emphasizes the experimental or exploratory aspect of data analysis. This point of view can be very helpful in any study.

[2]This and the next three chapters are written on the assumption that the mechanics of data analysis, that is, the arithmetic, can be carried out with the assistance of a computer or, in simple cases, an appropriately selected hand calculator.

[3]Hays, W. L., (1973, pp. 518–519). Barber (1976) observes that excessive preoccupation with positive results can lead to fudging in data analysis. See also Davis (1958; Chapter 8 in Morrison and Henkel [1970]) and Babbie (1979, Chapter 16, "Proper Uses of Statistics"). It should not be said of any researcher "He uses statistics as a drunken man uses lampposts—for support rather than illumination" (Andrew Lang). Some editorial boards unfortunately insist on statistical analysis of data, or, worse, on the use of particular techniques.

[4]See Achen (1982, pp. 7–30). This reference also contains (pp. 44–51) an interesting discussion of evaluating substantive significance.

[5]If you hire an expert, some cost considerations are important. Statistical consultants usually charge on the basis of time expended: $50 per hour (New York City, 1984–1985) is not untypical. Try to get an estimate of probable total cost in advance. Although somewhat expensive this expertise is an excellent investment. It will save you time, inconvenience, and perhaps money, later on. An experienced and qualified computer consultant will probably estimate costs at $20–100 per hour in setting a price. This estimated cost may be large; on the other hand, if you have stringent time constraints and your self-confidence is low, the cost is likely to seem reasonable. Any consultant should:

- work on the basis of a fixed price per job rather than a time charge;
- give you an explicit estimate of the costs;
- sell his/her services rather than an ancillary product or service such as software;
- write and sign a contract based on your agreement (if time is crucial, deadlines should be specified in the contract).

You should be made aware of examples of earlier consulting assignments, and given references if you ask for them. Check the references!

[6]An amusing and forceful presentation of the arguments in support of the appropriate use of distribution-free statistics, making clear the difference between "nonparametric" and "distribution-free" can be found in Bradley (pp. 13ff.). For an extended interchange on misuse of the chi-square, see Steger (1971) or Haber et al. (1970).

[7]Conover (1980) remarks that nonparametric methods offer approximate solutions to exact problems, rather than the exact solution to approximate problems.

[8]Trachtman et al. (1978) have carried out an ingenious analysis of computer-generated data sets illustrating both Type I and Type II errors which arise from the use of the t-test rather than the Mann-Whitney.

[9]Kaplan (1964, pp. 263ff.).

[10]See Daniel (1977), or Chapter 14.

[11]Kemeny and Snell (1972, Chapter 6).

[12]Tukey (1977); also Hartwig and Dearing (1979), Mosteller and Tukey (1977), and Ehrenberg (1982).

[13]For discussion of Asymptotic Relative Efficiency and a comparison table showing many nonparametric procedures, see Bradley (1968, pp. 56–62).

[14]Nie et al. (1975), SPSS Manual, (2nd ed., p. 3). "Statistics are no substitute for judgment" (Henry Clay).

[15]See Andrews et al. (1981). So-called expert systems are currently (1985) under development to assist both students of statistics and advanced users in their selection of appropriate statistical procedures. See Gale and Pregibon (1985) for example. These interactive packages include questions that permit identification of problem and data characteristics, and incorporate decision trees whose "plums" are standard methods, suggestions for modification, or the statement that no analysis is available. A readable description of such a system can be found in Schaffner (1983).

Additional Reading

For further reading on the topics touched upon in this chapter, see:

Achen (1982): neatly stated summary of the proper task of statistical analysis in social science research.

Babbie (1979, Chapter 16): overview of descriptive versus inferential use of statistics in the analysis of survey data; discussion of statistical versus substantive significance.

Bradley (1968): gives an overview and a (not truly elementary) clarification of the distinction between distribution-free and nonparametric; this author is a strong proponent of the use of appropriate statistics.

Jacobson (1976): organization is excellent, though we do not always agree with this author's "flexible" view of levels of measurement.

Fitzgibbon and Morris (1978): very elementary presentation of the classification scheme.

Festinger (1951): sorts out the alternatives for statistical analyses.

Willemson (1974): reassuring.

Stock and Dodenhoff (1972): classification based on data types.

Andrews, Klem, et al. (1981): decision trees for choice of statistics; includes many special techniques and citations of technical discussion. Also indicates which computer packages include each procedure.

Elementary probability can be reviewed using:

Hays (1973): good coverage of essentials.

Arthurs (1965): simple, clear, basic.

If your mathematics preparation includes calculus, and you have time to invest in learning some probability:

Pfeiffer (1978): many examples from applications.

Uspensky (1937): oldie but goodie.

Phillips (1982) and Moore (1979) emphasize statistical sophistication and statistical thinking and may be useful for preliminary review or overview.

11

Probabilistic Methods:
Univariate and Bivariate Statistics

Introduction

It is the rare graduate student who has escaped a course in statistics early in the course sequence. Most likely, however, you have been concentrating on other matters for a year or more, so that your recollection of details or even of general strategies may be dim. The purpose of this chapter is to remind you of what you already know in such a way that you will be able to look up appropriate specific procedures. Our emphasis is heuristic rather than formal.

The particular goals of this chapter are:

- to describe tabular and graphical techniques for the display of data;
- to describe univariate (one variable) analysis of distributions of all levels of data, whether parametric or not;
- to describe measures of difference between two groups (for all types of univariate data);
- to describe measures of relationship for all types of bivariate (two variable) data, whether parametric or not;
- to set out the decision process for selecting a particular statistical technique. Decision trees are used to present this process graphically.

No attempt is made to exhibit algorithms or formulas. Only the more commonly used techniques are presented, together with their interpretations when appropriately applied. Advantages and disadvantages of competing procedures are also discussed.

Techniques for analyzing data containing more than two variables (multivariate) or obtained from more than two groups will be presented in the next chapter.

Graphs and Charts

The essence of a well-executed study can almost always be displayed in simple tabular or graphical form. A large part of the statistician's work is to design tables or graphs that clearly communicate outcomes. These devices are trusted by the reader because of their apparent simplicity, so they can be extremely useful or, potentially, disastrously confusing and misleading.

The effect of well-planned and well-designed visual aids is enormously more forceful than that of any amount of numerical or text material. Whether you address your results to a general audience or to the most sophisticated fellow researcher, graphical devices can be both accurate and convincing; their uses for clarification or emphasis are manifold.

Since the goal is communication, the potential value of any visual device depends on the relationship that is being illustrated. For two variables, a graph is a picture that can be clearer and more informative than the proverbial thousand words; for more than two variables, however, a table is usually better than a graph because the latter may be too complicated to draw.

Many graphing techniques are available to the researcher. A conventional vocabulary is employed in creating and describing a chart or graph. The first essentials are a chart number and a chart title. Most graphs have a set of X (horizontal) and Y (vertical) axes, which should be labelled with variables and units of measurement. Guidelines make the graph easier to read and should appear on both axes. The chart should be followed by a source, and footnotes if needed.

Computer technology can make charting very simple through the use of color or black and white cathode ray tube (CRT) terminals and printing devices. You should inquire whether the computer center you use has appropriate software and hardware.[1] The entire field of computer graphics is undergoing rapid expansion and development at this time, so almost any description we might give here would be obsolete by the time you read this. (See also Chapter 9, section on computer graphics.)

Some of the standard graph types and their appropriate uses are listed below. This listing is not exhaustive but rather exemplary of the possibilities for data presentation. For other examples, we recommend that you look at the charting literature.[2] All illustrations in this chapter are computer output, to give you an idea of the capability now available.

BAR CHARTS

Conventionally, bar chart data are discontinuous on the X axis but continuous on the Y axis. Rectangles are drawn for a given interval on the X axis, with height corresponding to the Y value. Rectangles never butt each other when the value of the X variable changes. (Bars can be horizontal: Simply reverse role of X and Y [Figure 11.1].) Bar charts can also be *clustered*, to show Y values for two or more categories of subjects with the same X value, or *layered*, to show how a total Y value decomposes as a sum for two or more categories with the same X value, or both (Figure 11.2A).

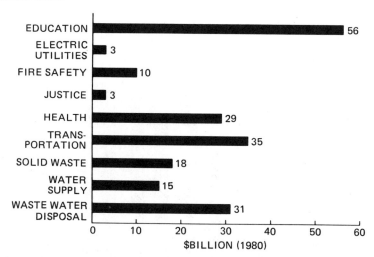

FIGURE 11.1 Bar chart: estimated value of selected rural community facilities, by type of facility.

The *histogram* is a variant of the bar chart. Data must be continuous in both the X and Y variable; the Y variable usually measures frequencies. Data points are draw as butting rectangles, each centered at the midpoint of a given interval on the X axis. If these intervals are of different lengths, the heights (Y values) should be so adjusted that the area of each bar reflects the proportion of the population that falls into the base interval.

Pictograms include bar charts in which appropriate pictures or symbols replace the bars (see Fig. 11.2B) The report of a census of pets preferred by school children might employ columns of cats, dogs, fish, and birds; research examples are usually less whimsical. Also classified as pictograms are illustrations of housing starts using houses of different sizes, money bags to show changes in the national debt, and so forth.

LINE PLOTS OR LINE CHARTS

In *line plots* or *line charts*, data should be continuous in both the X and Y variable; the usual Cartesian coordinate rules apply. Line segments are drawn connecting successive data points. When appropriate, points are located at the midvalues of class intervals. If the Y variable measures the number of cases or frequencies, the chart is called a *frequency polygon* (Figure 11.3), as in this illustration, which also shows the histogram for the same data. The areas covered by the frequency polygon and histogram are equal. Line charts can be clustered to show frequency data for several populations with the same range of X values. *Layered line charts* (also called *surface charts*) show the

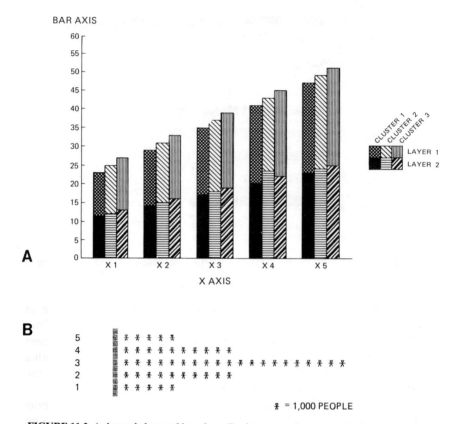

FIGURE 11.2 A, layered clustered bar chart; B, pictogram: elevator use by elevator number.

Y variable broken into subclasses so several curves appear that accumulate into the highest curve (Figure 11.4). The width of the strip describes the value of the Y subclass. There are several types of surface charts.

A *time series chart* is a special form of line plot used when both variables are continuous and one variable represents time. The time variable is most often plotted on the horizontal X axis (Figure 11.4).

Ogives are a variant form of line chart used when the Y variable is measured cumulatively from top to bottom (in the more-than ogive) or from bottom to top (in the less-than ogive) (Figure 11.5). Both variables should be continuous. Ogives are useful for showing cumulative distribution functions.

Semilog and *log-log charts* (Figures 11.6 and 11.7, respectively) can be used to display a functional relationship more forcefully and therefore are particularly useful for exploratory data analysis. Charts of this type require that both variables be continuous. In effect, the graphing procedure introduces a transformation of the variables.

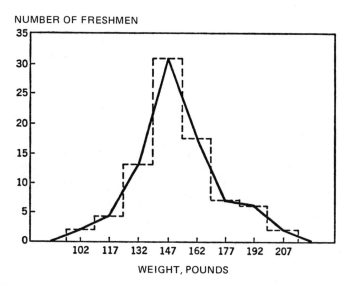

FIGURE 11.3 Frequency polygon: weights of freshmen.

The semilog chart has one axis marked in logarithm units, so pairs (X, Y) are replaced by pairs (X, log Y) or (log X, Y), and an exponential function appears linear. The log-log chart shows (log X, log Y) instead of (X, Y), so a power function appears linear. Both axes must avoid a zero point.

SCATTERGRAMS

Scattergrams require two continuous variables that have simultaneous measurements in X and Y for each observation. The data are plotted as dots on a Cartesian plane but are not connected. Scattergrams are used to exhibit bivariate relationships (see page 262), rather than univariate distributions.

PIE CHARTS

A pie chart is a circle subdivided into fractions corresponding to the proportional value of the dependent variable. One variable is usually discrete or nominal, the other is unrestricted (Figure 11.8).

EXPLORATORY GRAPHING TECHNIQUES

Box-and-whisker plots (Figure 11.9), which exhibit the interquartile mass together with the span and endpoints of the range of observations, and *stem-and-leaf* plots (Figure 11.10), which combine a frequency distribution and a histogram, can be extremely useful in a preliminary inspection of data. Additional techniques permit you to look at residuals after "data smoothing." Dendrograms (see Gordon [1981] or Aldendorfer and Blashfield [1984])

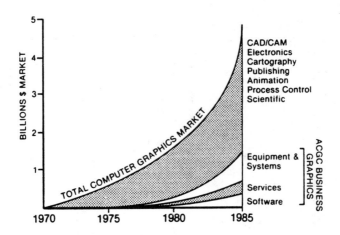

FIGURE 11.4 Layered (surface), time series chart: Abt Computer Graphics Corporation's market.

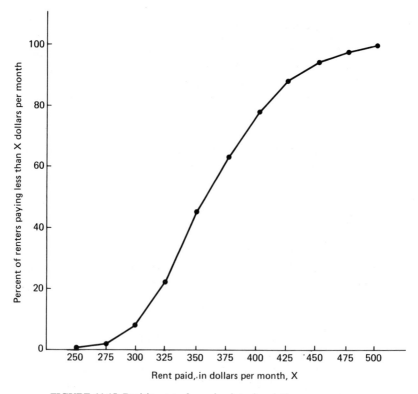

FIGURE 11.15 Decision tree for univariate descriptive measures.

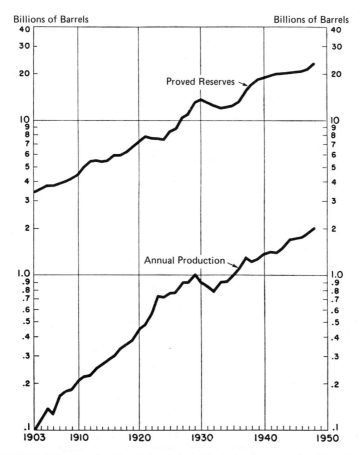

FIGURE 11.6 Semilog chart (vertical scale logarithmic; horizontal scale arithmetic): rate of growth in petroleum production and crude reserves.

facilitate the inspection of clustering patterns. It is possible to make a good case for the point of view that all graphs are exploratory in that their visual impact emphasizes aspects of the data that might escape your attention in tabular or other numerical form. Tukey (1977) contains an extensive discussion; computer programs, such as SPSS MANOVA, are available for rapid preparation of displays.

STATISTICAL MAPS

Statistical maps show the location of a specific measure, for example, degrees of temperature, growth rate, etc. Computer graphics techniques allow incorporation of elaborate statistical data into map format, such as before-

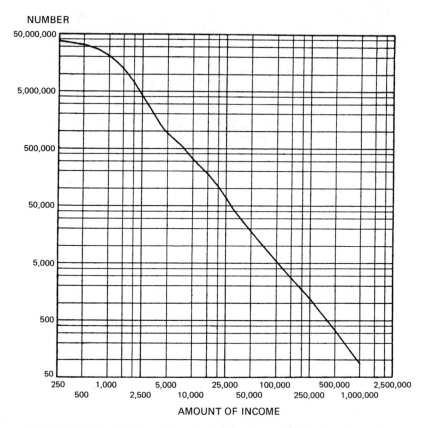

FIGURE 11.7 Log-log chart: Pareto curve of cumulative distribution of annual incomes of 37,334,766 single individuals in the United States receiving $250 or more.

and-after fatality reports (Figure 11.11), median household incomes, and so on. Whenever data involve a spatial variable, or the analysis suggests aggregation by region, a map may be the best form of display.

MISCELLANEOUS SCHEMATIC GRAPHS

Miscellaneous schematic graphs can be very useful for the communication of conclusions or patterns. A specimen is shown (Figure 11.12). They are hazardous to interpret because of distortion and omission of scale, but they can be extremely forceful.

Tables

The standard techniques and nomenclature of table construction are relatively easy to learn. You should utilize them in order to introduce uniformity of style into your research report.

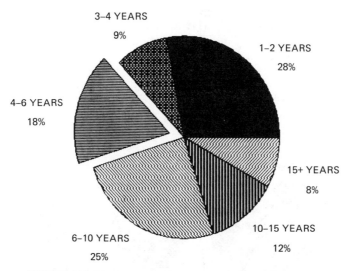

FIGURE 11.8 Pie chart: company staff by length of service (years).

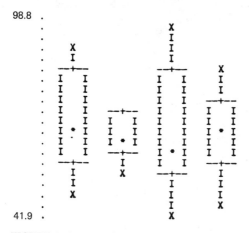

FIGURE 11.9 Box-and-whisker plot: variable test scores.

Tables are useful for both exploration and display of data and can facilitate the study and analysis of relationships. In particular, they:

- support statistical analysis of relationships, like chi-square or phi;
- display trends and patterns of relationships by exhibiting frequencies and percentages;
- exhibit study design, for example, different levels of the variables, interaction effects;
- expose spurious relationships and design defects.

```
4 . 257
5 . 02345667889999
6 . 01445567
7 . 0011568
8 . 4555
9 . 1359
```

FIGURE 11.10 Stem-and-leaf plot: variable test scores.

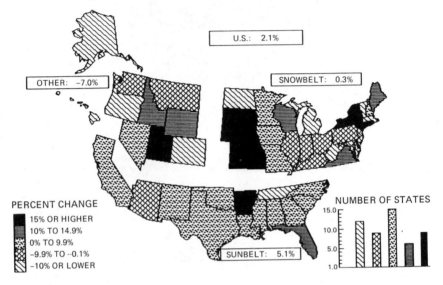

FIGURE 11.11 Statistical map: percentage change in fatality rate by state and region, 1979–1980.

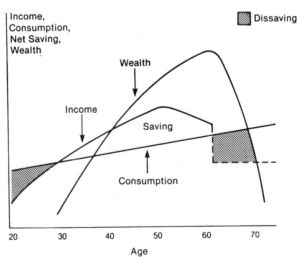

FIGURE 11.12 Schematic graph: typical life-cycle pattern of income, consumption, saving, and wealth accumulation.

A table is called *n*-fold or *n*-way if *n* is the number of variables; thus, a three-fold table displays three variables. Each variable may have many levels (subclasses). One of the simplest tables has two variables with each variable having two levels. It is called a 2 × 2 ("two-by-two") table. Likewise, a 4 × 2 × 2 table has three variables, the first variable having four levels, the second two, the third two. Thus the familiar univariate frequency distribution with, say, 10 classes, yields a 10 table, 1-fold, using this notation, (or 10 × 1). The number of cells (locations) in the table is calculated by carrying out this "multiplication", so a 2 × 2 table has 4 cells, and a 4 × 2 × 2 table has 16 cells.

Decisions concerning number of variables, levels of each variable, and population size are properly made at the design stage of your study. In arriving at such decisions, and in classifying continuous data already collected, it helps to bear in mind the rule of thumb that the number of cells in the resulting tables should be, on average, one-tenth the total number of cases, otherwise many cells will be empty, or so small as to make further statistical analysis meaningless. Empty cells detract from simplicity and ease of understanding, and limit the computational usefulness of the table. Ready access to computers offers the temptation to produce more tables of extreme complexity, with low cell frequencies. This usually wastes time and money.

Percentages

Percentages can be useful measures because they compare a measurement to a suitably chosen base. Thus, they are sometimes called relative frequency data. Misused percentages can distort results, so whenever necessary for clarity, both percentage and absolute data should be reported. A percentage in a cell is impossible to interpret unless its base is specified. For example, percentages can be calculated for a row based on row totals, or for a column based on column totals, or for either based on grand totals.

Decisions as to how to present percentages reflect the (1) purpose of data analysis; (2) preliminary analysis of relationships in the data.

Percentages can be interpreted as (contingent) probabilities, but they must be tested for significant differences if effects are to be compared. For grouped interval data, a cumulative percentage distribution may be an informative adjunct to the frequency distribution.

Cross Sorts and Cross Breaks

The tabulation of the subclasses of one variable against one or more other variables, also broken down into subclasses, is called a cross sort or cross break. The purpose of such a cross tabulation is to exhibit a relationship between the variables. Data of any level, nominal, ordinal, interval, can be cross tabulated. Column or row totals in cross sorts are referred to as marginal distributions and can be useful for an understanding of the subclasses of the variables. As indicated earlier, n-way tables can be confusing. However, cross tabulations can be used effectively in the analysis of differences between subclasses and quantitative relationships between variables. We will discuss this statistical material later in this chapter and the next.

Choices of the layout of a cross tabulation are based on decisions as to the relative importance of the effects of different variables. Guidance in both the construction and preliminary analysis of such tabulations can be found in Davis (1971, 1963), in Rosenberg (1968), and in Zeisel (1968).

To illustrate the terminology and other aspects of the foregoing, we examine a simple table (Figure 11.13) prepared using SPSS program CROSS-TABS (see Chapter 9, section on computer packages). The table illustrated in Figure 11.13 is one level of a 3-way table (see Figure 12.3, in section on multivariate displays). The variables are chest pain (Var 46), reported as yes–no; age (Var 76) and weight (Var 13) each classified and coded[3]. The table shown displays value 1 (yes) of Var 46. The total number of cases $N = 93 = 100\%$ is shown in the lower right corner.

The table heading consists of the number and title. The table number permits later reference to it in the text or index. Just below is a short title (usually under 50 characters), which ought to do the following:

- Identify the problem area
- Specify dependent and independent variables
- Identify target population
- Identify quantity units employed

An effective title is clear, concise, and communicates forcefully. Each cell (box) in the table body, numbered i, j by its row and column location, contains four numbers. To the right of each row is the row total, R_i and, beneath it, R_i/N expressed as a percentage. Likewise, at the bottom of each column is the column total C_j and, below it, C_j/N. The top number in the i, j cell is the number n_{ij} in that cell, the second is n_{ij}/R_i expressed as a percent, the third n_{ij}/C_j, the fourth n_{ij}/N. Thus, for instance, in the cell corresponding to weight 151–165 pounds, age 50–59 years, 11 subjects report chest pain; these individuals constitute 45.8% of the total in the same weight class, 32.4% of the total in the same age class, and 11.8% of the grand total of 93 reporting chest pain. The weight class contains 24 subjects, 25.8% of the total; the age class contains 34, or 36.6% of the total.

Below the table, the SPSS program CROSS-TABS points out the values of several statistical measures of association, which are shown in Figure 11.14 and described later in this chapter.

TABLE HEADING {

Table I

Subjects Reporting Chest Pain, Classified by Age (Var 76)a and Weight (Var 13)

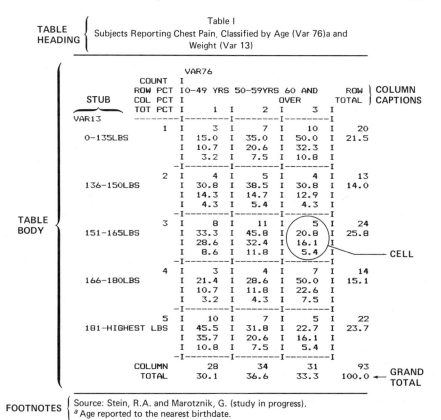

FOOTNOTES {
Source: Stein, R.A. and Marotznik, G. (study in progress).
[a] Age reported to the nearest birthdate.
}

FIGURE 11.13 A simple table.

Univariate
Measures and Techniques

In any statistical analysis it is essential to determine the basic distributional characteristics of each variable. The first step is to ascertain the level of each variable, that is, nominal, ordinal, interval, ratio, and whether it is discrete or continuous. The next step, providing a variable is at least interval level, is to determine whether the data are parametric or nonparametric.

Basically, statistics offers a mechanism for organizing and summarizing information. It can be shown mathematically that if the mean, standard deviation (or variance), moment coefficient of skewness, and moment coefficient of kurtosis of a continuous closed distribution are known, the distribution can be reconstructed. If, moreover, the distribution is normal,

```
************************ C R O S S T A B U L A T I O N   O F ************************
     VAR13     WEIGHT                              BY VAR76    AGE
CONTROLLING FOR..
     VAR46     CHEST PAIN        VALUE..    1  YES
************************                                               ************************ PAGE  1 OF  1
```

		VAR76			
COUNT ROW PCT COL PCT TOT PCT		10-49 YRS	50-59YRS	60 AND OVER	ROW TOTAL
		1	2	3	
VAR13					
0-135LBS	1	3 15.0 10.7 3.2	7 35.0 20.6 7.5	10 50.0 32.3 10.8	20 21.5
136-150LBS	2	4 30.8 14.3 4.3	5 38.5 14.7 5.4	4 30.8 12.9 4.3	13 14.0
151-165LBS	3	8 33.3 28.6 8.6	11 45.8 32.4 11.8	5 20.8 16.1 5.4	24 25.8
166-180LBS	4	3 21.4 10.7 3.2	4 28.6 11.8 4.3	7 50.0 22.6 7.5	14 15.1
181-HIGHEST LBS	5	10 45.5 35.7 10.8	7 31.8 20.6 7.5	5 22.7 16.1 5.4	22 23.7
COLUMN TOTAL		28 30.1	34 36.6	31 33.3	93 100.0

```
5 OUT OF    15 ( 33.3%) OF THE VALID CELLS HAVE EXPECTED CELL FREQUENCY LESS THAN 5.0.
MINIMUM EXPECTED CELL FREQUENCY =   3.914
RAW CHI SQUARE =    9.36909 WITH      8 DEGREES OF FREEDOM.   SIGNIFICANCE =   0.3121
CRAMER'S V =   0.22444
CONTINGENCY COEFFICIENT =   0.30253
LAMBDA (ASYMMETRIC) =   0.10145 WITH VAR13    DEPENDENT.          =   0.15254 WITH VAR76    DEPENDENT.
LAMBDA (SYMMETRIC) =   0.12500
UNCERTAINTY COEFFICIENT (ASYMMETRIC) =   0.03193 WITH VAR13    DEPENDENT.      =   0.04609 WITH VAR76    DEPENDENT.
UNCERTAINTY COEFFICIENT (SYMMETRIC) =   0.03772
KENDALL'S TAU B =  -0.15648.        SIGNIFICANCE =   0.0382
KENDALL'S TAU C =  -0.16996.        SIGNIFICANCE =   0.0382
CONDITIONAL GAMMA = -0.21323
SOMERS'S D (ASYMMETRIC) = -0.17049 WITH VAR13    DEPENDENT.          = -0.14361 WITH VAR76    DEPENDENT.
SOMERS'S D (SYMMETRIC) = -0.15590
ETA =   0.19463 WITH VAR13    DEPENDENT.          =   0.29157 WITH VAR76    DEPENDENT.
PEARSON'S R = -0.18825 SIGNIFICANCE =   0.0354
```

FIGURE 11.14 Measures computed with SPSS program CROSS-TABS: age and weight.

only the mean and standard deviation are needed, since for such a curve moment skewness is 0 and moment kurtosis is 0. It follows that these four measures or moments are the most economical and efficient storage for a closed distribution of data obtained from a large population and measured on a continuous interval scale. Of course, individual data points cannot be recaptured from the moments.

For summarizing open-ended distributions or discrete (discontinuous) data no such efficient and universal techniques exist. Indeed, the moment measures listed above may be entirely inappropriate for application to nonparametric distributions. It is necessary to explore other measures such as the mode, median, range, quartiles, etc. Descriptive statements about the class or type of variable (e.g., the observation that a distribution is bimodal) may have inferential value to the investigator.

Most computer statistical packages have the capacity to generate these measures. For example, the SPSS routine, FREQUENCIES, will calculate the values of several statistics for ratio or interval data, appropriate for closed parametric distributions. It will also carry out the same calculations blindly for ordinal or coded nominal data. It is up to you to decide which among the many descriptive measures may be suitable for your data and your purpose. To help you, we have prepared Figure 11.15 in the form of a decision tree. The accompanying Table 11.1 lists the best-known descriptive statistics, their uses, limitations, and interpretations.[4]

To illustrate the calculation and evaluation of these measures, we consider three of the variables involved in the study described earlier (see note 3). A portion of the printout generated for each of three variables by SPSS program FREQUENCIES is displayed.

We look first at Figure 11.16, resting heart rate (Var 16). Each observed value is listed, along with absolute frequency, *relative frequency* (as percentage of total number of cases), *adjusted frequency* (as percentage of total number of valid cases), and *cumulative frequency* (as percentage of valid cases). At the end of the frequency list, we see there are 258 valid cases and 16 missing cases. The computed summary statistics offer an insight into the shape of the distribution of this variable. The mean of 74.112 and median of 72.67 suggest that the hump in the curve is to the left; while, the standard deviation of 14.863 and range of 151 suggest that the curve is spread out compared to the normal. The impressions are confirmed by skewness value 3.466 which tells us the tail is to the right, and kurtosis value 25.326 which indicates that the curve is very peaked: Evidently the distribution departs substantially from normality. Even so, the standard error 0.925 can be used to estimate the mean of the population from which this sample is drawn: There is 68.37% probability it lies in 74.112 ± 0.925 and 95.45% probability it lies in 74.112 ± 1.850.

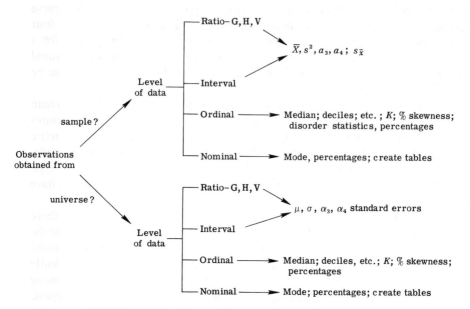

FIGURE 11.15 Decision tree for univariate descriptive measures.

```
SPSS BATCH SYSTEM
11/15/XX              FILE - CDIC      - CREATED 11/15/XX

VAR16      RESTING HEART RATE
```

CATEGORY LABEL	CODE	ABSOLUTE FREQ	RELATIVE FREQ (PCT)	ADJUSTED FREQ (PCT)	CUM FREQ (PCT)
	45.	1	0.4	0.4	0.4
	48.	2	0.7	0.8	1.2
	51.	1	0.4	0.4	1.6
	52.	3	1.1	1.2	2.7
	.	.	.	.	.
	.	.	.	.	.
	.	.	.	.	.
	85.	12	4.4	4.7	84.5
	.	.	.	.	.
	.	.	.	.	.
	.	.	.	.	.
	178.	1	0.4	0.4	99.6
	196.	1	0.4	0.4	100.0
	0.	1	0.4	MISSING	100.0
	999.	15	5.5	MISSING	100.0
	TOTAL	274	100.0	100.0	

MEAN	74.112	STD ERR	0.925	MEDIAN	72.667
MODE	75.000	STD DEV	14.863	VARIANCE	220.909
KURTOSIS	25.326	SKEWNESS	3.466	RANGE	151.000
MINIMUM	45.000	MAXIMUM	196.000		

VALID CASES	258	MISSING CASES	16

FIGURE 11.16 SPSS program FREQUENCIES: resting heart rate (Var 16).

TABLE 11.1
Univariate Descriptive Measures

Measure and notation	Uses	Limitations	Interpretation	Comments
		CENTRAL TENDENCY		
Arithmetic mean μ for universe $\bar{x}$ for samples	Measures central tendency of any closed, continuous, interval or ratio level distribution. Called the "first moment" of a variable. Excellent measure of the center of an approximately symmetric distribution.	Sensitive to extreme values; distorts central tendency in very skewed or asymmetric distributions. Cannot be calculated if distribution is open-ended or incomplete. Meaningless if data are ordinal or nominal level.	Will always be closer to the tail of a skewed distribution. Sum of deviations from the mean is zero, as negative and positive values cancel each other. If weights correspond-ing to frequencies are distributed along a lever, the mean corresponds to the location of the fulcrum; hence, the mean is the center of gravity of a distribution. Also, the sum of squares of deviations from the mean is a minimum.	Best single estimator of any value in the distribution. In a sample or universe that is parametric or closed it is the expected value (best estimate) of the center of distribution. This is true for normal, binomial, Poisson and all other parametric distributions.
Median $\tilde{x}$ for samples (symbol not used uniformly)	Measures central tendency in skewed, open or incomplete distributions of ordinal, interval or ratio-level data.	Insensitive to large clusters of values at the extremes of distributions. For normal distributions, coincides with mean. Calculation requires an array (arrangement of data by magnitude).	Geographical center of the distribution, dividing it into two parts of equal area. Sum of absolute values of devia-tions from the median is a minimum. Always lies be-tween mean and mode.	In a skewed or open-ended sample or universe, it is an excellent measure of central tendency. The median together with average devia-tion from the median give an excellent picture of the center of a curve.

(continued)

TABLE 11.1 (*continued*)

Measure and notation	Uses	Limitations	Interpretation	Comments
Mode Mo (symbol not used uniformly)	Measures central tendency as the most common value in ordinal, interval or ratio-level distributions.	Distributions may have two modes (bimodal) or many modes (polymodal). Mode coincides with mean and median in normal distributions.	Modal value(s) occur(s) most frequently; mode corresponds to maximum point on the curve of the distribution. Always further than mean or median from tail of skewed distribution.	Useful when most frequently occurring value is important, e.g. body measurements in determining clothing size; preferences in marketing strategies.
Geometric mean G	Measures central tendency for ratio-level data.	Inappropriate for nominal, ordinal, or interval data. Geometric mean is always less than or equal to arithmetic mean.	Used to obtain an average rate of change. Defined as nth root of product of all values.	Suitable for averaging sets of ratios, or year-to-year percentage changes in a variable.
Harmonic mean H	Measures central tendency for ratio-level data where reciprocals have been calculated.	Harmonic mean is always less than or equal to geometric mean. Useless except for ratio-level data.	Defined as the arithmetic mean of the reciprocals of the values.	Will not distort the averaging of (equally-weighted) items. Convenient for averaging speeds and other ratios. Does not have a suitable measure of dispersion.
Quartiles Q_1 1st quartile Q_2 Median Q_3 3rd quartile	Separate distribution into 4 equal classes. Measures central tendency for ordinal, interval, or ratio data.	Relatively insensitive; quartiles mask marked fluctuations in frequencies. Calculation requires an array.	25% of distribution (area) falls below Q_1 Q_2 is median 25% of distribution (area) falls above Q_3	Useful when sensitive measure of central tendency is unnecessary, e.g. location in school classes.

Deciles D_1 1st decile D_2 2nd decile D_9 9th decile	Separate distribution into 10 equal parts. Measures central tendency for ordinal, interval, or ratio data.	Deciles may mask location of marked fluctuations in frequencies. Calculation requires an array.	10% of distribution falls below D_1 20% of distribution falls below D_2 10% of distribution falls above D_9	Useful to define location within distribution, e.g. description of test scores.
Percentiles $P_1, \ldots, P_{99}$	Separate distribution into 100 equal parts. Applicable to ordinal, interval, or ratio data.	Useful only where fine descriptions of locations in distribution are necessary.	1% of distribution lies below P_1 2% of distribution lies below P_2 1% of distribution lies above P_{99}	Most sensitive descriptor of location of value in the distribution.
Root mean square, quadratic mean RMS	Interval level only. Avoids negative values, locates data on a positive scale. Used to calculate dispersion.	No direct interpretation.	Mean of sum of squares of all values in the distribution.	Useful in calculation of variance (below).

DISPERSION

Range	Difference of highest and lowest values, or these values themselves.	Not useful when extreme values are present. Not calculable for open-ended distributions.	Domain of values present in the distribution.	Range of heights, weights, etc., in two populations allows rough comparison of "spread."
Mean (absolute) deviation, average deviation MD	Average absolute difference of data points, from either mean or median.	Distorted by extreme values in asymmetric distributions. Not calculable for open-ended distributions.	It is $\approx 4/5\ \sigma$ for a normal distribution.	Approximately half the distribution lies between one average deviation above and one average deviation below the median.

(continued)

TABLE 11.1 *(continued)*

Measure and notation	Uses	Limitations	Interpretation	Comments
Semi-interquartile range *or* quartile deviation	Defines the average interval containing 25% of the data points.	Distorted by extreme values and non-symmetric distributions.	50% of the data-points lie between Q_1 and Q_3, so the semi-interquartile range is the average interval containing a quarter of the distribution. It is $\approx 2/3$ σ for the normal distribution.	
Variance σ^2 for universe s^2 for sample	Most widely used measure of dispersion: larger variance means more dispersion. Useful when samples are combined or pooled.	Not meaningful for nominal or ordinal data. Grouping of data causes error.	Square of the standard deviation. Variance, sum square deviation from the mean, is the minimum among all sum square deviations from a fixed value. Larger the variance, the more dispersion.	Defines total variation in a distribution. Susceptible to extreme values, hence can be misleading in skewed distributions.
Standard deviation σ for universe s for sample	Defines an interval for any distribution: the mean $\pm$ 2σ includes at least 75% of all cases.	Not meaningful for nominal or ordinal data. Grouping of data causes error.	For normal (bell-shaped) curves, the interval: $\mu \pm \sigma$ contains 68.27% of the distribution; $\mu \pm 2\sigma$ contains 95.45% of the distribution; $\mu \pm 3\sigma$ contains 99.73% of the distribution.	Standard measure of dispersion for any continuous distribution; interval $\mu \pm k\sigma$ always has $1 - \frac{1}{k^2}$ proportion of the entire distribution, when $k > 1$.

242

Measure	Description	Data level	Interpretation	Uses
Standardized variable z	Transforms a variable into standard dimensionless values.	Not meaningful for nominal or ordinal data.	Each value in the distribution is given as a fraction or percentage of a standard deviation, hence is expressed in standard units.	Indicates relative distance of each value from the mean, in units that can be used for comparison purposes.
Coefficient of variation V	Measures dispersion relative to the mean. Useful in comparing dispersions of two or more distributions.	Defined only for ratio level data.	The value of V is a fraction or percentage. The larger the V the more spread out the distribution.	Applicable when several distributions in which measurements are recorded in different units must be compared.
SKEWNESS				
Pearson's skewness	Measures the symmetry of a distribution. Zero skewness means perfectly symmetrical.	Not defined for nominal data; weak measure for ordinal level data.	Percentage departure from symmetry, measured in terms of σ. Positive sign means a tail to the right, negative a tail to the left.	Where mean, median and/or mode has been calculated, any difference(s) can be used to measure skewness.
Percentile measure of skewness	Same	Particularly useful for ordinal data; weak measure for interval or ratio-level data.	Same, except percentage is relative to area of whole distribution.	Where percentile markers have been calculated for the distribution.
Moment coefficient of skewness α_3 for universe a_3, for sample	Same	Not meaningful for nominal/ordinal data. Particularly useful for moment-generating functions.	Same information as from Pearson's measure.	Can be calculated directly from a given mathematical distribution (moment-generating function).
KURTOSIS				
Percentile Measure K	Measures "peakedness" of a curve.	Useless for nominal data. Better for ordinal data.	Positive value means curve is leptokurtic, pointed at top. Negative value means curve is platykurtic, flat on top. Normal or mesokurtic curve has value of .263.	Can be calculated easily from interquartile range and deciles.

(continued)

TABLE 11.1 *(continued)*
Univariate Descriptive Measures

Measure and notation	Uses	Limitations	Interpretation	Comments
Moment coefficient of kurtosis α_4 for universe a_4 for sample	Same	Useless for nominal data; not easily used for ordinal data.	Usual measure of kurtosis is $K_4 = a_4 - 3$; hence mesokurtic curve has measure 0 (normal). $a_4 < 3$ for platykurtosis, $(K_4 < 0)$. $a_4 > 3$ for leptokurtosis, $(K_4 > 0)$.	Can be calculated from a moment-generating function.
STANDARD ERRORS				
Standard error of a mean $\sigma_{\bar{x}}$ universe $s_{\bar{x}}$ sample	To construct confidence intervals within which mean will fall, with associated probabilities.	Formulas must be modified for finite universes, and if population σ must be estimated. Not useful for very small samples, $N < 30$	Distributions of means must be normal. Standard error of the mean serves purpose of standard deviation of sample means. $\mu_{\bar{x}} = \mu$.	Useful in obtaining an interval estimate, with a probability, for locating a universe mean based on a sample mean.
Standard error of a proportion σ_p universe s_p sample	To construct confidence intervals, with probabilities, within which proportion will fall.	Not useful for very small samples. Must be modified for finite universes.	Distribution of proportions will be normal. Measure serves as standard deviation of distribution of sample proportions. $\mu_p = p$.	Useful in obtaining an interval estimate, with a probability, for locating a universe proportion.
Standard error of a standard deviation σ_s	To construct confidence intervals, with probabilities, within which the standard deviation will fall. Slight modification makes it useful for variances as well.	Useful only for large samples. Formula changes for parametric and non-parametric samples.	Distribution of standard deviation is approximately normal for $n \geq 100$. Measure serves as standard deviation for a distribution of σ's $\mu_s \approx \sigma$.	Useful in obtaining an interval estimate and a probability for locating a universe σ.

Standard error of a median σ_{med}	To construct a confidence interval, etc. as above, for a median. Slight modification of the basic formula makes it useful for deciles and quartiles.	Useful only where N ≥ 30 and the population is approximately normal.	Distribution of median is approximately normal for $n \geq$ 30. Measure serves as standard deviation of a distribution of medians. $\mu_{med} = \mu$.	Useful in obtaining an interval estimate and a probability of locating a universe median.
Standard error of interquartile range σ_Q	To construct a confidence interval etc, for the interquartile range.	Useful only where $n \geq$ 30 and the population or sample is normally distributed.	Measure serves as a standard deviation for an approximately normal distribution of semi-interquartile ranges.	Useful in obtaining an interval estimate of the universe interquartile range.
Standard error of coefficient of variation σ_v	To construct a confidence interval etc, for the coefficient of variation.	Useful only for $n \geq$ 100 and if the population sample under study is normally distributed.	Measure serves as a standard deviation for an approximately normal distribution of coefficients of variation.	Useful in constructing an interval estimate of the universe coefficient of variation.

The distribution of age (Var 76) shown in Figure 11.17 is nearly normal. Minimum value is 21.0, maximum is 79.0, for a range of 58.0 which is close to six times the standard deviation of 11.165. Mean 51.720, median 52.118, and mode 52 based on 257 cases, suggest an almost symmetrical curve: Indeed skewness is −0.297 and kurtosis is −0.132, so departure from normal is negligible. Thus we can predict that 68.37% of the cases lie in the interval 51.720 ± 11.165 and 95.45% in the interval 51.720 ± 22.330. (This distribution may be misleading, because the subjects include both males and females.) From the standard error of 0.696 we can predict that in the population from which the sample is drawn, the true mean lies in 51.720 ± 0.696 with 68.73% probability and in 51.720 ± 1.392 with 95.45% probability.

Finally, to emphasize the basically mindless operation of the computer, we inspect Figure 11.18, the calculations performed for sex (Var 77). For 257 valid cases, the mean of 1.222 tells us that 22.2% of the cases are in category 2; the mode 1.00 tells us there are more males than females. No other statistics are meaningful, because this is a nominal-level variable.

The Measurement of Difference

Your research problem may require that you compare data obtained from two groups on a single variable or from a single group at two different times. You may also need to evaluate data obtained from a single group, so as to decide whether it can be part of a larger (observed or hypothesized) population. If such comparisons employ a test of significance they fall within the scope of this chapter. (Comparisons of results from more than two groups will be examined in the next chapter.)

Statistical measures of difference and their associated probability values allow you to decide whether your data support the assertion that the difference between the groups is greater than that which might be predicted to arise through chance variation among subjects. Procedures employed in this analysis are classified according to whether the data are interval, ordinal, nominal, dichotomous, continuous, discrete, parametric; the size of the groups, whether we are comparing two groups or one group to a universe, and whether the groups are matched.

Difference testing is conventionally based on a simple four step logic. It starts with the tentative assumption that the conjectured result of your study will not occur. Hence, the first step is formulation of a null hypothesis, in terms of the statistic you are interested in (for instance, the difference of means of two samples). Next, it is necessary to examine the graph (distribution) of the results of many such studies; this graph is obtained from the mathematical theory of your statistic. The second step, thus, establishes a universal

```
SPSS BATCH SYSTEM

11/15/XX            FILE - CDIC      - CREATED 11/15/XX

VAR76      AGE
                                        RELATIVE   ADJUSTED    CUM
                          AGE   ABSOLUTE  FREQ       FREQ      FREQ
CATEGORY LABEL           CODE    FREQ    (PCT)      (PCT)     (PCT)
                          21.      1      0.4        0.4       0.4
                          22.      2      0.7        0.8       1.2
                          25.      1      0.4        0.4       1.6
                           .       .       .          .         .
                           .       .       .          .         .
                           .       .       .          .         .
                          72.      1      0.4        0.4      98.4
                          74.      2      0.7        0.8      99.2
                          79.      2      0.7        0.8     100.0
                           0.     17      6.2      MISSING   100.0
                                ------  ------     ------
                        TOTAL    274    100.0      100.0

MEAN        51.720   STD ERR     0.696      MEDIAN      52.118
MODE        52.000   STD DEV    11.165      VARIANCE   124.663
KURTOSIS    -0.132   SKEWNESS   -0.297      RANGE       58.000
MINIMUM     21.000   MAXIMUM    79.000
```

FIGURE 11.17 SPSS program FREQUENCIES: distribution of age (Var 76).

```
SPSS BATCH SYSTEM

11/15/XX            FILE - CDIC      - CREATED 11/15/XX

VAR77      SEX
                                        RELATIVE   ADJUSTED    CUM
                               ABSOLUTE   FREQ       FREQ      FREQ
CATEGORY LABEL           CODE    FREQ    (PCT)      (PCT)     (PCT)
      MALES               1.     200     73.0       77.8      77.8
      FEMALES             2.      57     20.8       22.2     100.0
                          0.      17      6.2      MISSING   100.0
                                ------  ------     ------
                        TOTAL    274    100.0      100.0

MEAN         1.222   STD ERR     0.026      MEDIAN       1.142
MODE         1.000   STD DEV     0.416      VARIANCE     0.173
KURTOSIS    -0.187   SKEWNESS    1.347      RANGE        1.000
MINIMUM      1.000   MAXIMUM     2.000

VALID CASES    257   MISSING CASES    17
```

FIGURE 11.18 SPSS program FREQUENCIES: distribution of sex (Var 77).

population (sampling distribution) and its probability function, derived from the null hypothesis. The third step is computation of the statistical result for your study. This value is located on the graph of the sampling distribution. As a final step, the question is posed "How likely is your result?" or "What is the probability associated with the value of the statistic so located in the sampling distribution?" If the value you obtained in your study has low probability, that is, is unlikely, you can conclude that your null hypothesis is untenable. This conclusion is usually stated in the form "The statistic is significant at [probability] level."[5] A typical application of this logic is the test you should always conduct to determine whether or not your data are parametric: Your study results must be compared to a universe of possible values obtained from parametric samples of the same size, using a goodness-of-fit difference test such as chi-square (χ^2) (see Chapter 14).

If the given distribution involves interval or ratio-level data, it is important to correctly identify the distribution of sample means, in order to be able to determine confidence intervals and their associated probabilities. The decision as to which distribution to use to evaluate the statistics you compute from your sample depends on your answer to each of four questions:

1. Is the universe finite or infinite? If the former, use correction factor
$$FPC = \sqrt{\frac{N_p - n}{N_p - 1}}$$

2. Is σ given or assumed, or must the sample be used as a basis for estimating σ?
3. Is the universe normally distributed?
4. What is the sample size?

The distribution may be normal (z), t (with $df = n-1$), or it may have to be analyzed by nonparametric procedures.

In all distributions of sample means, we use $\mu_{\bar{x}} = \mu$; where necessary $df = n-1$.

Figures 11.19 and 11.20 illustrate the decision process that you should follow in order to select a suitable test for your purpose. Table 11.2 lists the most widely-used tests along with their uses, limitations, and interpretations. Additional tests can be found in such texts as Daniel (1978); Jacobson, (1976), and Bradley (1968). Andrews et al. (1981) is useful for sorting alternative procedures.

To illustrate tests of differences between groups, we offer two examples using data from the study described in note 3.

1. (Figure 11.21) Resting heart rate (Var 16), is measured for two groups: group 1 consists of 188 males and group 2 of 53 females (Sex is Var 77). Var 16 is continuous ratio-level data. The means, standard deviations, and standard errors of each group are shown first. The F-value for a test of difference of variances between the two groups is then calculated: $F = 3.12$. We ask if the means 74.0745 and 74.3774 differ significantly. The probability that this value occurs by chance is 0.000, hence we conclude that the variances of the groups are significantly different. Two t-values are computed. One uses a pooled variance estimate and is based on the assumption that the groups are correlated; the other uses a separated variance estimate and is based on the assumption that the groups are uncorrelated. The latter requires an approximation to t and a noninteger df:[6] In view of the fact that the groups are male and female, this is the appropriate one for our purpose. Note the

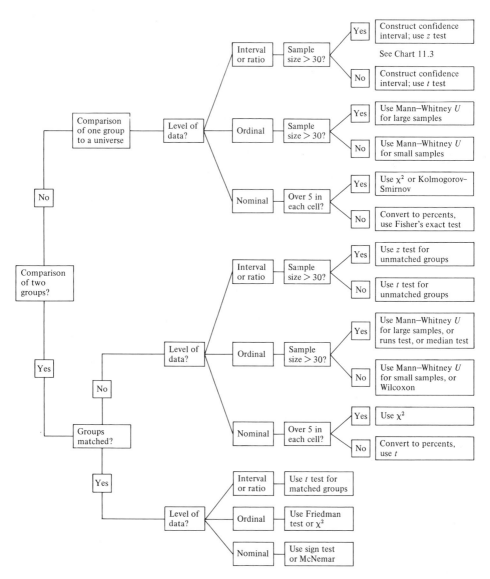

FIGURE 11.19 Decision tree for difference measures.

t value -0.17 has probability 0.862, so we conclude the difference between group means is not significant, even at the .10 level. (This routine prints 2-tail probabilities.)

    2. (Figure 11.22) Sex satisfaction (Var 124) is measured by an instrument whose "scores" should be regarded as continuous ordinal-level data. Again, two groups, 49 males and 9 females, are to be compared. Since the groups

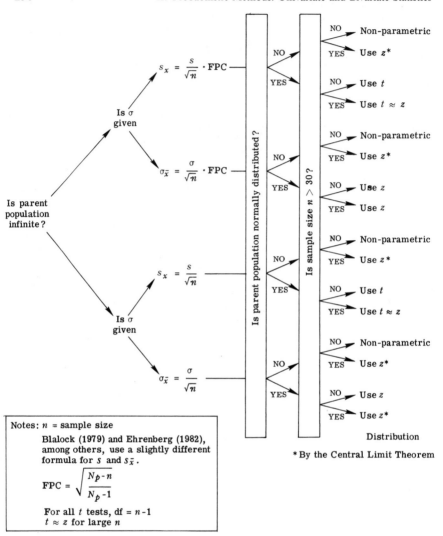

FIGURE 11.20 Decision tree for distribution of sample means.

are independent, the Mann-Whitney test is selected in the SPSS program NPAR TESTS, the scores are ranked and mean ranks (corrected for ties) are computed. Both the Mann-Whitney U and the Wilcoxon independent sample W are calculated, and since total $N > 20$, the Z value of $-.1076$ corresponding to $U = 208$ is obtained. Since the probability of this value is .9143, we cannot conclude that one group contains higher scores than the other, that is, the mean ranks differ significantly. Thus any conjecture that males report greater satisfaction than women cannot be supported, nor can its opposite. This finding may surprise you.

TABLE 11.2

Difference Tests—Comparison of Two Groups or One Group to Universe

Test (statistic)	Uses	Limitations	Interpretation	Comments
Students' t	Used to decide if difference between two means is statistically significant. One mean refers to a sample, the other either to a sample or a universe. t is a family of distributions, with df as the parameter. (degrees of freedom)	Usable only for interval-level, parametric data. For very large samples ($n > 60$), the t-distribution approximates the normal. Formula for the t-value of a difference must be modified if samples involve correlated measures. df must be modified if two samples differ greatly in size.	Ignore negative sign: if absolute value of computed t exceeds tabled value at .05 or .01 level, interpret difference of means as significant. Sample size(s), α error, number of tails, and correlation of variables, must be evaluated before test can be carried out and interpreted.	Test of following null hypothesis: $\bar{X} = \mu; \; s$ known, $df = N - 1$. $\bar{X}_1 = \bar{X}_2; \; s_1, s_2$ known; samples uncorrelated, $df = N_1 + N_2 - 2$. $\bar{X}_1 = \bar{X}_2; \; s_1, s_2$ known; samples correlated, $df = N - 1$. For formulas, see any standard text.
Normal z	Used to decide if difference between two means is statistically significant. One mean refers to a sample, the other either to a sample or a universe.	Useful only for interval or ratio-level, parametric data where $n \geq 30$ and σ is known. Formula must be modified if samples involve correlated measures.	Ignore negative sign: consult table of areas of normal curves to obtain probability associated with computed z. Sample size(s), α error, number of tails, and correlation of variables must be considered before test can be carried out and interpreted.	Test of following null hypothesis: $\bar{X} = \mu; \; \sigma$ known. $\bar{X}_1 = \bar{X}_2; \; \sigma_1, \sigma_2$ known, samples correlated or uncorrelated. For formulas, see any standard text.
Chi square	Used to decide if measures of an observed variable are distributed as expected or assumed. Also used to decide if two samples are statistically independent. Chi square is a family of distributions with df as the parameter.	Nominal (categorical) data. Useful only if number of cases is sufficiently large for the number of cells specified by the test: if cell values are less than 5, test is suspect. Observations are assumed independent. Categories must be exhaustive and non-overlapping.	Chi square is a tabled statistic. For each df, critical values and associated areas (probabilities) are given.	Test of goodness of fit between any observed and theoretical distributions. Test of independence in 2-way tables; should be followed by a test of strength of association. For formulas and procedure, see any standard test for extended discussion.

(continued)

TABLE 11.2

Difference Tests—Comparison of Two Groups or One Group to Universe

Test (statistic)	Uses	Limitations	Interpretation	Comments
Median test	Used to decide is two samples came from the same universe.	Ordinal data. Useful only if $n > 30$; otherwise, use Fisher's exact test.	Basically, a chi-square test of whether data are above or below the pooled median.	Test of null hypothesis of no difference between samples. For procedure, see text.
McNemar	Used with paired samples, to decide if number or proportion of cases in two categories are significantly different.	Nominal or ordinal, dichotomized, data. Must introduce Yates correction for continuity. If number of changes is <10, use binomial test.	Basically, a chi-square statistic.	Commonly used to test significance of direction of change between members of matched pairs. Strategy is to determine if cell frequencies (absolute or relative) in a 2×2 table differ significantly. Generalizes to Cochran's Q; see Chapter 14.
Runs test	Used to decide whether the pattern of runs of 0's and 1's represents significant departure from randomness.	Nominal data which can be dichotomized '0' and '1'. Meaningful only if order in sequence can be recorded.	Tabled values for small samples. For larger samples, test results in a 'z' value with known one or two-tailed probabilities.	Tests the hypothesis that a sample from a dichotomized universe is random: attention is directed to the sequence rather than the frequency of observations. For formulas and procedure, see text.
Binomial test	Used to decide whether the proportion of '0's and '1's is compatible with a random selection of the sample.	Nominal data which can be dichotomized '0' and'1'; known or assumed proportion of each in the universe.	For $n < 30$, use exact table of the binomial, for $n \geq 30$, consult normal tables to determine probability for the obtained z value.	Tests the hypothesis that a sample from a dichotomized universe is random: attention is directed to frequency of observation. Excellent for 2×2 tables with small samples. For formulas and procedure see text.

	Used to decide		
Fisher exact test	Used to decide, whether proportions of '0's and '1's in two independent samples differ significantly.	Nominal data, two categories, coded '0' and '1'. Two samples: thus, good only for 2 × 2 tables. Suitable for very small samples.	Exact probability, based on hypergeometric distribution, can be computed by formula.	Test the (null) hypothesis that the proportions in the two samples are the same. For formulas and procedure, see text.
Sign test, one sample	Used to decide if a sample was drawn from a population with a hypothesized median.	Ordinal data. Result misleading for small samples.	Based on the binomial; count scores above and below median, eliminate ties. For $n \geq 12$, can use a normal approximation.	Tests the hypothesis that in the sample, as many scores lie above as below the median, permitting inference as to location of population median. For procedure, see text.
Sign test, two sample	Used to decide whether direction of differences in scores of matched pairs is significant.	Data must be ordinal, and amenable to ranking in matched pairs. Assign + to pair where first is larger, − where first is smaller. Eliminate ties. Result is misleading if number of ties is excessive. Sample should exceed 30 pairs.	Based on the binomial. Distribution of signs approaches normality, so for large samples can use the normal table in the usual way, assuming α-error and number of tails.	Tests the hypothesis that the median of the population of differences is zero. For procedure, see text.
Kolmogorov-Smirnov	Used to decide if a sample distribution is equivalent to a known theoretical distribution. Can also be used to compare two independent samples.	Continuous ordinal, interval, or ratio data. The test distribution must be specified in advance. Use with the Poisson distribution requires caution because of possible inaccuracy. Special procedures for ties between samples.	A K-S z is calculated by measuring distance between observed parameters and theoretical parameters such as mean and standard deviation. z has a known two-tailed probability function.	Tests goodness-of-fit between observed data and the uniform, normal, binomial, Poisson, etc. Two sample form tests the hypothesis that the distribution functions of the samples differ significantly. For procedure, see text.

(continued)

TABLE 11.2 (continued)

Difference Tests—Comparison of Two Groups or One Group to Universe

Test (statistic)	Uses	Limitations	Interpretation	Comments
Mann-Whitney	Used to compare two independent samples for location parameters.	Ordinal continuous data; ties and unequal sample sizes can be handled. Important to use formula appropriate for small or large sample.	Exact two-tailed probability, corrected for ties, that the two groups come from the same universe. When both samples are ≤20, use tables values of test statistic. When both samples sizes are large, distribution of an adjusted test statistic approaches normality.	Used to test the hypothesis that the two samples are drawn from the same universe. For formulas and procedure, see text. The Kruskal-Wallis test represents a generalization of the Mann-Whitney to 3 or more samples. See Chapter 14.
Wilcoxon signed-ranks test	One sample test used to decide if sample is drawn from universe with specified median. Two sample test used to compare two matched samples for location parameters.	Two related samples with matched paired subjects, or one sample vs. universe. Ordinal metric data required, that is, absolute differences between paired ranks or between ranks and hypothesized median, can also be ranked.	Signs are attached to differences and sums for positive and negative differences are calculated. Tabled values for samples ≤25; for large samples, adjusted test statistic approaches normality. Consider magnitude of differences as well as sign. Yields a confidence interval for the population median.	Used to test the hypothesis that one sample is drawn from a universe with a hypothesized median, or that the differences in paired ranks obtained from two matched samples are significantly different. One and two-tailed tests possible. Experiments with controls are a common research design for this test. For formulas and procedures, see text.
Friedman	Used as a non-parametric analogue of the parametric two-way ANOVA for matched groups or a repeated measures design. Primarily a multivariate method.	Ordinal data (continuous), 2 or more related samples. It is assumed there is no "interaction" effect between blocks and treatments; all blocks have same number of data-points.	Scores are ranked, mean rank for each group and a χ^2 statistic are computed. Table values for small samples and few groups, otherwise use standard χ^2 tables with appropriate df. One and two tailed tests possible.	Used to test the hypothesis that mean ranks of the groups are significantly different. For formulas and procedures, see text. See also Chapter 14. Very useful if mean ranks have an interpretation in the context of the research question.

```
SPSS BATCH SYSTEM
- - - - - - - - - - - - - - - - - - - - - - T - T E S T - - - - - - - - - - - - - - - - - -

GROUP 1 - VAR77    EQ       1. MALES
GROUP 2 - VAR77    EQ       2. FEMALES

                                                             *  POOLED VARIANCE ESTIMATE  *  SEPARATE VARIANCE ESTIMATE
                      NUMBER          STANDARD   STANDARD     *     F   2-TAIL  *    T    DEGREES OF  2-TAIL  *   T   DEGREES OF  2-TAIL
VARIABLE            OF CASES   MEAN   DEVIATION   ERROR       *  VALUE  PROB.   *  VALUE   FREEDOM    PROB.   * VALUE   FREEDOM    PROB.
                                                             *                 *                            *
VAR16    RESTING      HEART RATE                             *                 *                            *
     GROUP 1   188   74.0745   16.366    1.194               *  3.12   0.000   *  -0.13     239      0.898   * -0.17   151.06    0.862
                                                             *                 *                            *
     GROUP 2    53   74.3774    9.272    1.274               *                 *                            *
```

FIGURE 11.21 *t*-Test of differences between groups: resting heart rate, by sex.

```
SPSS BATCH SYSTEM

FILE   CDIC      (CREATION DATE = 11/15/XX)
VARIABLE              N         MEAN     STD DEV      MINIMUM        MAXIMUM

VAR124               58       35.138      9.271       23.000         89.000
VAR77               257        1.222      0.416        1.000          2.000
 - - - - MANN-WHITNEY U - WILCOXON RANK SUM W TEST
    VAR124         TOTAL SATISFACTION
 BY VAR77          SEX

      VAR77   = MALES    1          VAR77   = FEMALES    2
      MEAN RANK       NUMBER        MEAN RANK       NUMBER
        29.40            49           30.06            9

                                      CORRECTED FOR TIES
          U               W            Z          2-TAILED P
        215.5           270.5       -0.1076        0.9143
```

FIGURE 11.22 Mann-Whitney U and Wilcoxon Rank Sum W tests of differences between groups: sex satisfaction, by sex.

For further discussion of the distinctions between W and U, see Bradley (1968), Chapter 5.

Note also that in the NPAR TESTS program of SPSS the user must specify the test and correctly identify the groups as correlated or independent. Moreover, if the t-test had been used on these ordinal data, we would have been testing the groups for difference in mean scores: This would be either irrelevant or incorrect.

Measurement of Relationships
and Strength of Association

After examining the distribution of each variable separately, you may want to examine the data for relationships between pairs of variables. Note also that measures of difference and measures of relationship are connected, in that if a measure reveals that values of two variables are strongly associated, we can conclude that differences between two sets of values of one variable can be used to predict differences between corresponding sets of values of the other variable.

This section deals with one of the most confusing aspects of data analysis. There are literally dozens of competing procedures for measuring strength of association; to the novice several may appear equally applicable (and may even be so). The type of analysis you choose will depend on the characteristics of the variables under investigation. Proper identification of data levels is crucial. You must once again ask the following questions about the data:

1. Are the variables discrete or continuous?
2. What is the level of measurement?
3. What type of distribution has been found?

If all variables are discrete, your best procedure may well be to compute a two-way to n-way cross-tabulation table, that is, a joint frequency distribution for two or more classifying variables. This often permits you to identify relationships whose significance you will need to test statistically.

Figure 11.23 is a decision tree designed to help you decide which among the many measures of relationship is appropriate for your data. The accompanying Table 11.3 summarizes the properties of the most powerful and thus most widely-used statistical measures of association. Column (1) specifies the level of measurement needed to apply the statistic. (Note that ordinal or interval data, once classified, may be treated as nominal.) Column (2) indicates whether a significance test for the statistic is available. If no such test, (i.e. a probability estimate arising from the distribution of the statistic) is available, then your obtained value of the statistic can be compared only to other values of the same statistic for other tables of the same kind. This limits the usefulness of the statistical measure. In Column (3), upper and lower boundary values for each statistic are given. If the statistic has no negative boundary, you can conclude only that the relationship is strong, but not whether its direction is inverse or direct.

Column (4) of Table 11.3 tells you whether the statistic is based upon dependence between the variables. If so, and if you cannot exhibit dependence, using χ^2 or some other measure, then the use of this statistic is inappropriate. Column (5) indicates whether the statistic can be used to partial out some other independent variables to give only true two-way relationships; thus, a multiply-determined variable could be measured in terms of the effects of a single independent variable. Column (6) tells you whether tie values are taken into account in the calculation. Finally, comments on possible uses of the statistic appear in Column (7).

In certain studies involving several variables, it is helpful to examine the bivariate relationship of all pairs of variables. We might also want the means and standard deviations of the variables based on all valid cases; in addition, we may want the cross-product deviations and covariance for each pair of variables. The PEARSON CORR program of SPSS will compute these quantities and organize the data in a matrix format that makes inspection and interpretation easy.[7] This program will not compute coefficient of determination, intercepts, slopes or standard errors of estimate, nor will it print out scattergrams. We recommend that you use the SCATTERGRAM program unless you have many variables but do not intend to carry out further multivariate analysis such as multiple regression or factor analysis, followed by the test of a null hypothesis $r = 0$.

It is important to be alert to the possibility that many of the computed correlation coefficients may have no meaning, if they involve variables below interval level, for example, racial designation and religious preference. The computer will compute all statistics without regard to meaning.

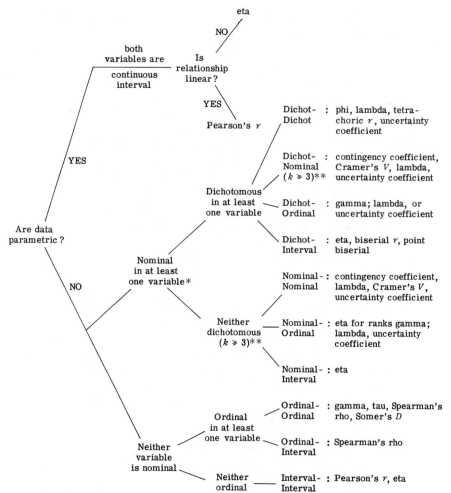

FIGURE 11.23 Decision tree for bivariate measures of relationship.
*Once ordinal or interval data are classified, they can be treated as nominal (dichotomous, or $k \geq 3$) or as discrete ordinal.
**k = number of values of the nominal variable.

PEARSON CORR can be made to print or avoid printing means and σ's as well as variance-covariance, at the option of the user. It can also produce output in a medium suitable for input to a multivariate analysis.

The use and interpretation of the output of SPSS program SCATTERGRAM is illustrated in Figure 11.24 using the variables VO2 (Var 4) and age (Var 76) for 244 cases from the study described in note 3. First, we see a plot in which the X axis is used for Var 76 and the Y axis for Var 4; each case (pair of values) is marked by an asterisk and repeated pairs are indicated by the appropriate multiple, for example, two cases have

TABLE 11.3

Measures for Association[a]

Statistic	Level of measurement[b] (1)	Significance test (2)	Boundaries[c] (3)	Dependence assumed (4)	Defined so as to partial out the effect of other variables (5)	Ties considered (6)	Comments (7)
Phi ϕ	any; 2 × 2 tables (dichotomous)	Yes	$0 \leq \phi \leq 1$	No	No	No	Can be defined for dimensions >2 but value can exceed 1: not useful. Often used with χ^2. Weak for interval and ratio level (classified) measures.
Cramer's V	any; $n \times n$ tables	No	$0 \leq V \leq 1$	No	No	No	Weak for interval and ratio level measures.
Contingency coeff. C	nominal; $n \times n$ tables	No	$0 \leq C \leq .707$ for 2×2	No	No	No	Upper-bound depends on dimensions of table. Weak for interval and ratio level measures.
Lambda λ asymmetric	nominal or classified ordinal or interval	No	$0 \leq \lambda \leq 1$	Yes	Yes	No	Measures reduction of error in prediction of specified variable.
Lambda λ symmetric	nominal or classified ordinal or interval	No	$0 \leq \lambda \leq 1$	No	No	No	Average of asymmetric λ's.
Uncertainty coeff. U asymmetric	nominal or classified ordinal or interval	No	$0 \leq 0 \leq 1$	Yes	Yes	No	Measures proportional reduction in uncertainty of a specified variable.

(continued)

TABLE 11.3 *(continued)*

Measures for Association[a]

Uncertainty coeff. U symmetric	nominal or classified ordinal or interval	No	$0 \leq u \leq 1$	No	No	No	Average of asymmetric U's
Eta η	one nominal, one ordinal or interval (continuous)	Yes	$-1 \leq \eta \leq 1$	Yes	No	No	Measures variance in dependent variable[d] accounted for by in-dependent variable. Useful in non-linear relationships. Many special formulas available, e.g. for analysis of variance.
Kendall's tau b, τ_b b	discrete or continuous ordinal-ordinal	Yes	$-1 \leq b \leq 1$	No	No	No	Good only for $n \times n$ (square) tables
Kendall's tau c τ_c c	discrete or continuous ordinal-ordinal	Yes	$-1 \leq c \leq 1$	No	No	No	Good for any rectangular table
Somer's D asymmetric	discrete or continuous ordinal-ordinal	No	$0 \leq D \leq 1$	Yes	Yes	Yes	Most useful for ranks
Somer's D symmetric	discrete or continuous ordinal	No	$0 \leq D \leq 1$	No	No	Yes	Only for ranks
Goodman-Kruskal's Gamma γ	ordinal-ordinal (discrete) or ordinal-nominal	No	$-1 \leq \gamma \leq 1$	No	Yes	No	Can "partial out" effects of one or more variables; inter-pretation difficult except in ordinal-ordinal application. Sign depends on coding in the table being analyzed.

Spearman's rank correlation coeff. rho or r_s or ϱ	ordinal (discrete or continuous)	Yes	$-1 \leq \varrho \leq 1$	No	No[e]	Yes	Useful for values coded to ranks
Pearson product-moment correlation coeff. r	(interval or ratio) vs. (interval or ratio)	Yes	$-1 \leq r \leq 1$	No	No	No	Used in term analysis where right or wrong classification is correlated against total scores.
Biserial correlation r_{bis}	one artificial dichotomy (continuous data) one interval (continuous)	Yes	$r > 0$; may be > 1	No	No	No	Used in item analysis where right or wrong classification is correlated against total scores.
Point biserial corr. r_{pbis}	one true dichotomy one continuous interval	Yes	$0 \leq r \leq 1$	No	No	No	Useful in item analysis. Lower than r or r_{bis} for positive values.
Tetrachoric corr. r_t	both artificial dichotomies on continuous interval data	Yes	$0 \leq r \leq 1$	No	No	No	Extremely useful for nominal dichotomies; extends r_{bis}.

[a] A variety of measures such as Yule's Q, odds ratio, Cronbach's α, rank biserial correlation, etc. are not listed.

[b] Many of these involve generalizations from data levels of original definition. It is advisable to exercise caution in using these extensions. See Jacobson (1976: passim).

[c] For any measure of association where values fall between 0 and 1, or -1 and $+1$, the square of the measure is referred to as a *coefficient of determination*.

[d] Eta is described in the SPSS Manual (Nie et al., 1975) and in standard texts as a measurement of the strength of a (nonlinear) association between nominal and interval-level variables. Jacobson (1976) offers a modification of the definition which permits the calculation and interpretation of eta for nominal and ordinal level variables. Welkowitz, et al. (1982) have a formula based on the Kruskal-Wallis H (p. 304). A few other authors refer to eta for ranks as theta. (The SPSS program will use ordinal scores as if they are interval.) Significance test can be found in Guilford & Fruchter (1973), 288ff., and in Welkowitz et al. (1982).

[e] See section on Multiple Regression in Chapter 12 for further discussion.

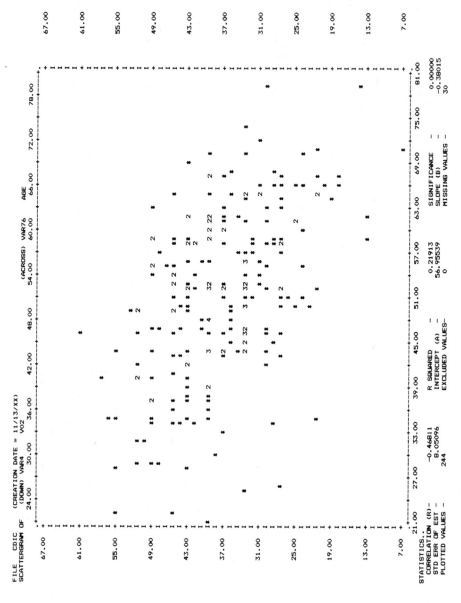

FIGURE 11.24 SPSS program SCATTERGRAM: VO2 (Var 4) and age (Var 76).

Var 76 = 37, Var 4 = 49. The choice of axes is determined by our intention to predict VO2 from age.

The Pearson correlation r is computed to be −.46811. Since r is negative, we infer there is a moderate inverse relation: When values of one variable increase, those of the other decrease, and vice versa. r^2 = .21913 so the linear relation between the two variables accounts for 21.913% of the variance in each one. This means that if we display the variances schematically using two congruent circles, the first overlaps 21.913% of the second (Figure 11.25). The computed significance value 0.00000 tells us that if the "true" population correlation is zero, the probability of a sample correlation of −.46811 with N = 244, is less than 0.00005. Therefore, while the computed r is not strong, we can comfortably interpret it as probably not due to random error.

The best linear equation, based on the least squares criterion, is $Y = -.38015X + 56.95539$, or VO2=(−.38015 × age) +56.95539, where the two numerical values are respectively slope and intercept. This equation can be used to predict VO2 value for an individual from his or her age. The computed value for the standard error of estimate is 8.05096, which tells us for cases in the population from which the sample was drawn, it is 95.45% probable that VO2 lies between [−.38015 × age] + 56.95539 ± (2 × 8.05096), that is, between lines parallel to the best line and 16.10192 above and below them.

Thirty cases in the overall study did not have valid data on these two variables and were thus omitted from the analysis.

Our illustration is a reasonably "clean" one. More generally, there is a wide range of possibilities; for example, if the data points cluster tightly around a line which slants upward from the left, we expect a positive slope and a strong positive correlation. If the data points are totally scattered in a circular or oval pattern, we infer a lack of relationship between the two variables. Curvilinear relationships are not immediately discernible by eyeballing the scattergram unless a particular kind of curvilinearity is expected, as, for example, if we believe that the dependent variable is determined by the logarithm of the independent variable. Accurate guesswork in selecting a curve will reflect your experience, your expectations, and an appropriate choice of scale or of transformation.

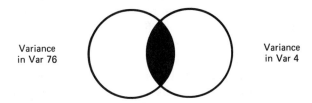

FIGURE 11.25 Schematic display of variances of the variables VO2 (Var 4) and age (Var 76).

Nonparametric Relationships

When the data under consideration are not at least interval level, or fail to be normally distributed, the use of Pearson Product Moment correlations is inappropriate. For data which are ordinal in scale and numerical in type, other statistical measures of relationship can be calculated: Spearman's coefficient *rho* and Kendall's coefficient *tau* are the most familiar.

SPSS subprogram NONPAR CORR will compute rho and/or tau for specified pairs of variables. The program will, if necessary, replace measured values with ordinal rankings; tied ranks are issued for data points whose ordinal positions are identical. Rho and tau differ chiefly in that tau tends to be more meaningful when there are many ties. Absolute values of tau may be smaller than those of Pearson's *r* when both are computable. In general, both statistics permit the same inferences of significance, etc. The program will output the correlation coefficient(s), the statistical significance level of the correlation (α-error for the null hypothesis that the correlation is zero), and the number of cases used in the calculation. Output from NONPAR CORR will be in the same format as that from PEARSON CORR. Output matrices tend to be more readable when a large number of variables is involved.

To illustrate some of the nonparametric measures of association, we once again turn to the variables of the study described earlier (see note 3).

Look first at Table 11.1, which shows 93 individuals reporting chest pain, classified by age and weight. Figure 11.14 displays the printed values of a variety of statistical measures. The chi-square value of 9.36909 with df = 8 has probability 3.121, which suggests no significant relation between rows and columns. Also, the program has calculated expected cell frequencies; and 33.3% of all cells have expected frequency less than 5, so the value of χ^2 is really uninterpretable. Both the contingency coefficient and Cramer's V are obtained from the chi-square, so they will simply reflect the weakness of the relationship. Moreover, they work best for truly nominal data.

Two values of lambda (asymmetric) are provided. They measure the improvement in a prediction of the value of Var 13 (weight) when the value of Var 76 (age) is known, and vice versa: The values are small (nearer zero than one) which suggests a weak association; lambda symmetric is a sort of average. Lambdas are best used when the classification variables are truly nominal, whereas here they are ordinal discrete (age and weight categories). No significance values are available for the lambdas.

If we shift our viewpoint and look at the classes based on Var 13 and Var 76 (grouped) as ordinal measures, the next set of computed statistics are appropriate. All of these in effect rank each subject on Var 13 and Var 76 and measure the discrepancy between these rankings (in different ways, allowing for ties, table size, etc.). As you can infer by consulting Table 11.4,

TABLE 11.4

SPSS Program NONPAR CORR: Spearman Correlation Coefficients

VARIABLE PAIR	Coefficient	N	SIG
VAR114 WITH VAR115	0.1686	59	.101
VAR114 WITH VAR116	0.2888	59	.013
VAR114 WITH VAR117	0.3577	59	.003
VAR114 WITH VAR118	0.4646	59	.001
VAR114 WITH VAR119	0.3298	59	.005
VAR114 WITH VAR120	0.1805	59	.086
VAR114 WITH VAR121	0.2106	59	.055
VAR114 WITH VAR122	0.1960	59	.068
VAR114 WITH VAR123	0.2647	59	.021
VAR114 WITH VAR82	-0.0877	56	.199
VAR115 WITH VAR116	0.2781	59	.016
VAR115 WITH VAR117	0.2250	59	.043
VAR115 WITH VAR118	0.0762	59	.283
VAR115 WITH VAR119	-0.0301	59	.411
VAR115 WITH VAR120	0.0940	59	.239
VAR115 WITH VAR121	-0.1987	59	.066
VAR115 WITH VAR122	-0.1895	59	.075
VAR115 WITH VAR123	-0.0072	59	.478
VAR115 WITH VAR82	-0.3175	56	.009
VAR116 WITH VAR117	0.5917	59	.001
VAR116 WITH VAR118	0.2085	59	.057
VAR116 WITH VAR119	0.5004	59	.001
VAR116 WITH VAR120	0.4383	59	.001
VAR116 WITH VAR121	0.2555	59	.025
VAR116 WITH VAR122	0.2371	59	.035
VAR116 WITH VAR123	0.1280	59	.167
VAR116 WITH VAR82	-0.0881	56	.259
VAR117 WITH VAR118	0.3498	59	.002
VAR117 WITH VAR119	0.3094	59	.009
VAR117 WITH VAR120	0.1088	59	.206
VAR117 WITH VAR121	0.2030	59	.062
VAR117 WITH VAR122	0.2944	59	.012
VAR117 WITH VAR123	0.1142	59	.195
VAR117 WITH VAR82	0.2372	59	.039
VAR118 WITH VAR119	0.3586	59	.003
VAR118 WITH VAR120	0.2536	59	.026
VAR118 WITH VAR121	0.2450	59	.031
VAR118 WITH VAR122	0.2404	59	.033
VAR118 WITH VAR123	0.2324	59	.038
VAR118 WITH VAR82	0.0716	56	.300
VAR119 WITH VAR120	0.4905	59	.001
VAR119 WITH VAR121	0.2939	59	.012
VAR119 WITH VAR122	0.2322	59	.038
VAR119 WITH VAR123	0.1545	59	.121
VAR119 WITH VAR82	-0.0595	56	.332
VAR120 WITH VAR121	0.4226	59	.001
VAR120 WITH VAR122	0.2826	59	.015
VAR120 WITH VAR123	0.3757	59	.002
VAR120 WITH VAR82	-0.3220	56	.008
VAR121 WITH VAR122	0.6089	59	.001
VAR121 WITH VAR123	0.6028	59	.001
VAR121 WITH VAR82	-0.0691	56	.306
VAR122 WITH VAR123	0.5326	59	.001
VAR122 WITH VAR82	-0.0062	56	.482
VAR123 WITH VAR82	-0.2012	56	.069

A VALUE OF 99.0000 IS PRINTED IF A COEFFICIENT CANNOT BE COMPUTED.

all of the computed values for tau b, tau c, gamma, or Somer's D suggest a weak association between the two variables; moreover, significance of the tau's at the .05 level suggests that this association is not trivial.

Finally, eta regards Var 13 as dependent (ordinal), Var 76 as independent (nominal) and then vice versa. The values .19463 and .29157 can be interpreted as proportion of variance in the dependent variable accounted for by variance in the independent variable. Again, the association is very weak. Pearson's r between these 2 attributes is $-.018825$ which confirms the impression of a weak association and again, this is unlikely to be the effect of chance as $p = .0354$.

In all the foregoing, we have used weight and age which have been classified for illustrative purposes. In practice, you may find it more suitable to use them as the continuous variables they naturally are. Note that although the program computes and prints a variety of measures, their use need not be appropriate, because of either the level of measurement or the size of the table.

As part of the study, subjects were administered 10 scales, measuring satisfaction under the headings marriage, physical condition, leisure, friends, family, sex, financial status, intelligence, personality, and coping. (A total satisfaction score was also computed but not analyzed here.) Because the scores must be interpreted as ordinal level, it is appropriate to compute Spearman correlations rho for each pair, and for each variable with income (see Table 11.4). Also printed are the N for each pair and the significance level. Observe, for instance, that sex satisfaction with income yields rho $= -.0595$ with significance $= .332$, so sex satisfaction is negatively related to income, but the value is likely to arise by chance approximately $1/3$ of the time; financial satisfaction with income yields rho $= -0.3220$ and significance $= .008$, so this negative relationship, while only moderate, is highly significant. The latter suggests that larger income tends to be associated with less financial satisfaction. Sex satisfaction and financial satisfaction are positively correlated, rho $= .4905$, and the value is significant ($p = .001$). Food for thought, perhaps?

Afterword

In using any measure of relationship for research, you must be concerned with three major considerations:

- Be sure that the designation of variables as independent or dependent is clear and justified by your theoretical rationale. The correlation coefficient will not change, regardless of which variable is called dependent. In contrast, the function that best fits a set of data will change; in the simplest case of a linear equation, the slope and intercept are likely to be different if the variables are interchanged. Constantly question whether the correlation (or other association) is "spurious." (The terminology is standard but unfortunate: The interpretation of the correlation is spurious, not the correlation.) A relatively high positive correlation, which implies that the variables covary together in the same direction, can arise when both variables are dependent on a third but not on each other. It can also arise through chance and coincidence. Spurious correlation is minimized by a sound theory underlying measurement, data collection, and choice of statistical procedure.

- Bear in mind that correlation (more generally, association) does not establish causality. The case for causality cannot be based on the mathematical rationale of the statistical technique, but must be made from the theory underlying the overall study design.

In the next three chapters, we describe and compare the multivariate statistical procedures most widely used in social and behavioral science research.

Notes

[1]In particular, SPSS Graphics and other software packages will prepare a variety of line, bar, and pie charts. Many personal computers have very impressive graphics capability.

[2]For example, Schmid and Schmid (1979), Tufte (1983); see also Chapter 5 in Tukey (1977).

[3]Earlier we indicated that computer printouts will be exhibited for a number of the statistical procedures described in Chapters 11–14. The data base for the calculations is part of a study in progress concerning the possible effects of an exercise training program on a large number (254) of physiological, psychological, and social variables. The 274 subjects were drawn from two subpopulations: (1) Individuals who had recently experienced a myocardial infarct and were referred by their physician at a New York City hospital; and (2) individuals who responded to a newspaper advertisement for volunteers and to other recruiting efforts. We are using a small subset of the variables, for illustrative purposes only, in all subsequent tables and printouts in this chapter and Chapters 12–14.

The study was conducted by Richard A. Stein, M.D., and Gerald Marotznik, who have generously permitted us to make use of their data set. For your convenience, the variables we will use in our examples are listed below:

Var	4	VO2 (an aerobic measure of maximum oxygen volume in the blood)
Var	7	maximum heart rate
Var	8	maximum blood pressure
Var	9	systolic depression; a measure of blood pressure change
Var	12	height (in.)
Var	13	weight (lbs.)
Var	14	resting blood pressure
Var	16	resting heart rate
Var	17	cholesterol (this is measured by an interval scale)
Var	18	triglyceride (this is measured by an interval scale)

Var   19   glucose (this is measured by an interval scale)
Var   20   pulmonary function capacity (pfc)
Var   21   full exhaling volume (fev)
Var   46   chest pain reported: label 1 = yes, 2 = no
Var   49   smoking: label 1 = yes, 2 = no
Var   76   age (years)
Var   77   sex: label 1 = male, 2 = female
Var   78   marital status: married, single, divorced or separated, widowed
Var   82   income: grouped, useable as discrete ordinal data
Var 114   marriage satisfaction ⎫
Var 115   physical condition satisfaction
Var 116   leisure satisfaction
Var 117   friends satisfaction   Each of these
Var 118   family satisfaction   is scored on
Var 119   sex satisfaction   a 5-choice
Var 120   financial satisfaction   Likert scale,
Var 121   intelligence satisfaction   hence is
Var 122   personality satisfaction   discrete
Var 123   coping satisfaction ⎭   ordinal
Var 124   total satisfaction (We will regard this as continuous ordinal)

All the preceding are pretest variables. The ones below are posttest variables.

Var 173   VO2
Var 176   maximum heart rate
Var 177   maximum blood pressure
Var 183   resting blood pressure
Var 185   resting heart rate
Var 186   cholesterol

---

[4]We have used the word *parametric* to mean normally distributed, but more generally, a parametric distribution function is one determined by the values of one or more (independent) parameters, such as the binomial, the Poisson, etc.

[5]See discussion of α error, Chapter 4.

[6]See Nie et al. (SPSS Manual, 1975, pp. 269-270).

[7]So-called intercorrelation matrices are used in many multivariate procedures: see Chapters 12 and 13 passim. See also Gould and White (1974, Chapter 2) for an intriguing and understandable application in the analysis of geographical preferences.

Additional Reading

Tables

Davis (1963, 1971): useful and thought provoking.
Rosenberg (1968): general guidance in analyzing role of variables.
Zeisel (1968): entertaining as well as informative.

Graphs

Croxton and Cowden (1967): classic.
Fisher (1966, 1970, 1973): graphs as a source of insight into patterns in the data.
Tukey (1977): Chapter 5 is very helpful in "seeing" your data.
Tufte (1983): "theory and practice in the design of statistical graphics."
Spear (1952): common-sense, straightforward, explains the alternatives.
Schmid and Schmid (1979): "social statistics in a visual manner."

Graphs and Tables

Morris and Fitzgibbon (1978): Chapter 4 is practical and very simple.
Ehrenberg (1982): generally useful advice on display of findings.

How to Calculate

Fitzgibbon and Morris (1978): work sheets and decision-trees, very clear and elementary.

General Statistics
(Elementary to [Low] Intermediate)

Take your choice:
Croxton and Cowden (1967): classic.
Edwards (1976): clear and simple.
Freedman, Pisani and Purves (1978): clear, intelligent discussion, no formulas, emphasis on heuristics.
Nie et al. (1975): SPSS Manual for formulas and short exposition.
Glantz (1981): very informative and concise; good-humored.
Guilford and Fruchter (1973, 1977): thorough
Hays (1973): thorough; repays close attention; Bayesian material pp. 856–858 (see also our Chapter 4).
Jaeger (1983): elementary, user-friendly.
King and Julstrom (1982): emphasizes and illustrates computer use for all statistical procedures.
Kurtz (1983): nice integration of nonparametric and parametric discussion.
Lapin (1980): straightforward.
Lapin (1983): good on time series analysis, Bayesian analysis.
Levine (1981): good exposition.
Lutz (1983): many procedures, good references, well-organized.
Snedecor and Cochran (1967): classic.
Spiegel (1961): also includes time series and index numbers (very clear).
Walkowitz, Ewen, and Cohen (1982): clear, well-organized exposition.
Walker and Lev (1953): thorough.
Yamane (1967b): thorough; has proofs.

Nonparametric

Daniel (1978) } easy to follow, many examples; helpful
Siegel (1956) } format.

Conover (1980): indeed practical; good discussion of advantages and disadvantages.

Bradley (1968): much more technical; superb bibliographies; emphasis on distribution-free interval level procedures.

Reynolds (1977a,b): specialized, thorough; good references.

Mathematical Statistics

Hoel (1971): not elementary.

Mood and Graybill (1963): not elementary.

General Reference

Jacobson (1976): encyclopedic, evaluation of competing techniques; organized by data levels; especially good for nonparametric.

Andrews et al. (1981): classification and short exposition, evaluation of competing techniques; many special procedures.

Roscoe (1975): a good "cookbook."

Liebetrau (1983): detailed but readable comparison of measures of association.

12

Probabilistic Methods: Multivariate Statistics I

Basic Strategies

Introduction

In this book *multivariate analysis* means any statistical analysis involving more than two variables[1], or more than two groupings, even if only one dependent variable is being considered at a time. We examine several multivariate techniques in this chapter and the two which follow. These include multiple regression analysis, the analysis of variance, covariance analysis, factor analysis, discriminant function analysis, canonical correlation, chi-square, Cochran's Q, Friedman's two-way analysis, and the Kruskal-Wallis test.

Most of the techniques just listed involve great computational complexity, as well as rigorous mathematical justification, and require both training and know-how for successful application and interpretation. We assume you have been exposed to some instruction in a sample of these procedures, but we do not expect you to be able to carry them out. As in the previous chapter, we will not be concerned with the algorithms or equations underlying the multivariate approaches (although a few are inescapable), but rather with their typical applications in a research problem. Our interest lies in strategy rather than tactics: when to choose which procedure.

As a researcher who needs to analyze data, you must offer a rationale for any choice among alternative methods. You should consider:

1. The purpose of the investigation—the nature and formulation of the research question; that is, what you are trying to discover or establish.
2. The mathematical characteristics of the variables, that is, continuous, discrete, interval, ordinal, etc.
3. The distributional assumptions made about the variables, that is, parametric, distribution-free, nonparametric, etc.
4. The sampling procedure used in data collection.

A rough guide to help you choose is given in Table 12.1. It gives the name of each of the most widely-used methods of analysis, the classification by type (e.g., ordinal, continuous) of independent and dependent variables for which the method of analysis is appropriate, and also a brief description of its purpose and use. Our table includes the techniques you are most likely to need.[2] We have omitted some specialty items—such as nominal partial regression analysis and time series decomposition—that might be useful under extraordinary circumstances. We have also omitted most of the extensions to three or more samples of such nonparametric procedures as Kolmogorov–Smirnov (see, e.g., Conover, 1980). While you should be able to make a basic choice of method for your statistical analysis, you will be well-advised to check both your decision and the application of the method with a professional statistician (see Chapter 10, section on using an expert).

Charts and Tables for Three or More Variables[3]

By far the greatest emphasis in standard texts is given to the techniques for presenting charts, graphs, and tables for univariate and bivariate data. It is easy to understand why: A sheet of paper presents a two-dimensional surface, and therefore considerable ingenuity may be required to deal with three or more variables. The possibilities for graphing and charting are very severely limited.

Certain techniques developed by cartographers[4] may suggest a useful approach when at least two of the variables are continuous interval level. Among these is the notion of level curves, which are incorporated into weather maps as isotherms. As an example of their use, suppose a curvilinear regression equation $Y = aX_1^2 + bX_2^3 + c$ has been fitted to data. For each selected fixed value of $X_2 = X_{2,0}$, the level curve $Y_0 = aX_1^2 + (bX_{2,0}^3 + c)$ is a parabola in the two variables X_1 and Y_0. By choosing a suitable sample of values for $X_{2,0}$, say -2, -1, 0, 1, 2, and drawing these five curves on the same set of X_1, Y axes, we can obtain some insight into the family of level curves associated with the three-dimensional surface with equation $Y = aX_1^2 + bX_2^3 + c$. With experience, it is possible also to develop a reliable intuition as to the characteristics of the surface. By and large, however, the science of graphing k-variable data is still in a rudimentary state.[5] We anticipate that with the rapid development of computer graphics techniques, new resources will become available to the researcher and data analyst; you will do well to inquire either at your university or commercial computer center, in order to keep aware of the state-of-the-art.

TABLE 12.1

Multivariate Methods

Name of method	Classification		General purpose
	Dependent variable	Independent variable	
Multiple Regression Analysis	One continuous interval	Classically, all continuous interval. In practice any type is used.[a]	To describe the extent, direction, and strength of the (linear) relationship between several independent variables and a continuous dependent variable.
Analysis of Variance	One continuous interval	All nominal	To describe the extent of the relationship between a continuous dependent variable and one or more nominal independent variables.
Analysis of Covariance	One continuous interval	Control variables continuous interval; others nominal[a]	To describe the relationship between a continuous dependent variable and one or more nominal independent variables, controlling the effect of one or more continuous independent variables.
Discriminant Analysis	One nominal	Classically, all continuous interval. In practice a mixture of types is used so long as some are continuous[a]	To determine how one or more independent variables can be used to discriminate among different categories (values) of a nominal dependent variable.
Factor Analysis	Variables are not classically identified as dependent or independent. Can be continuous interval or any other type[a]		To construct, or identify, a set of variables, called *factors*, each defined as a linear combination of other initially selected variables. Thus the factors are new composite variables.

(continued)

TABLE 12.1 (*continued*)

Name of method	Classification		General purpose
	Dependent variable	Independent variable	
Canonical Correlation	Several continuous interval	Several continuous interval	To describe the extent, direction, and strength of the relationship between a set of dependent variables and a set of independent variables.
Chi square	Nominal one or more	Nominal one or more	To determine the dependence or independence of a set of variables.
Categorical Data Analysis (Linear)	Nominal	Usually nominal; may be ordinal	To describe the relationship between a nominal dependent variable and several nominal or ordinal independent variables.
Cochran's Q	Dichotomous	Nominal	To test whether three or more related samples differ significantly in proportions or frequencies. Extension of McNemar test.
Friedman two-way	Ordinal continuous	Nominal	To describe the relationship or independence of one variable and k related samples. Data must be made ordinal to test whether rank orders in 3 or more related samples differ significantly.
Kruskal-Wallis	Ordinal continuous	Nominal	To test whether all k samples are drawn from the same population. Data must be made ordinal. Extension of Mann-Whitney.
Multiple Median	Ordinal	Ordinal	To test the difference among k medians.

[a]Dichotomized variables can legitimately be treated by these procedures if appropriately coded. Data at other levels of measurement are, strictly speaking, not useable; their analysis entails severe problems of interpretation.

Table construction presents less complex problems, although it is easy to make yourself dizzy trying to figure out what to do if variable A has four levels (A_1, A_2, A_3, A_4), variable B has two levels and variables C and D have two and three respectively. The table format shown in Figure 12.1 may do the trick for you.

In each cell you should enter the number of data-points which fall in that cell; for example, the number five entered in the table in Figure 12.1 indicates that five subjects have measures (A_2, B_2, C_2, D_1). The key to laying out such a format is deciding which variables and their possible relationships you wish to display most forcefully: In this example B versus D has higher priority than comparisons with A and C. This simple fourfold table can be collapsed into a set of four threefold tables by looking at the levels of A one at a time, or into a set of two threefold levels of C one at a time (Figure 12.2).

A	B	D_1	C_1 D_2	D_3	D_1	C_2 D_2	D_3
A_1	B_1						
	B_2						
A_2	B_1						
	B_2					5	
A_3	B_1						
	B_2						
A_4	B_1						
	B_2						

FIGURE 12.1 Sample table format.

Indeed, the three-dimensional tables can be collapsed further, but it is very confusing to make intelligent guesses for distribution patterns or interaction effects on the basis of an assortment of bivariate tables.

Your best strategy involves: (1) thinking through carefully which effects you wish to emphasize and which are secondary; (2) familiarizing yourself with research reports that contain a large number of multivariate tables (foremost among these is the US Census Abstract, but other examples are the Kinsey studies, recent Yankelovich and other public opinion surveys, and reports of agricultural experimentation. Consult the literature of your own field); (3) laying out several trial formats so you can see which variables are interactive,

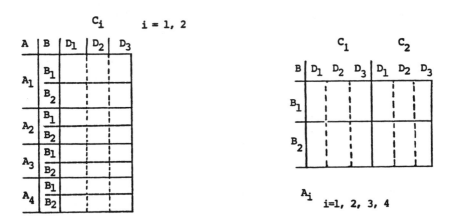

FIGURE 12.2 Alternative table formats, respectively emphasizing variables *A* (left) and *C* (right).

which subgroupings are contrasted, and what a reasonable cell size would be. Label rows and columns, include percentage columns and marginal totals where pertinent; then, pick the format(s) that suit your purpose(s) best.

The SPSS subroutine CROSSTAB will construct nested tables of *n* variables at a time, in specified order, for *n* as large as 999. It will also compute appropriate marginal totals and percentages. It will not make decisions about what is important!

> It must be noted that there is no table arrangement which will make small differences any bigger or trivial findings substantively important. Nevertheless, as we have seen, . . . the presentation of percentage data is only partly a statistical procedure. It is also a form of communication by which the analyst can facilitate or frustrate his reader and thus succeed or fail in his ultimate task of adding to the store of available knowledge.[6]

Figure 11.13 is one level of a tabulation of the variables age (Var 76), weight (Var 13) and chest pain (Var 46) from the study described in Chapter 11. Figure 12.3 shows both levels.

Multiple Causality

At the heart of the use of multivariate analysis is the notion of multiple causality. Both the theoretical foundation and the practical application or interpretation of every technique reflect an attempt to formulate this notion in a systematic and mathematically manageable way. On the other hand,

```
* * * * * * * * * * * * * * * * *  C R O S S T A B U L A T I O N   O F  * * * * * * * * * * * * * * * * * * * * * * *
   VAR13    WEIGHT          BY   VAR76         VALUE..  1  YES          VALUE..   2  NO
CONTROLLING FOR..                              AGE
   VAR46    CHEST PAIN                                                                    PAGE  1 OF  1
* * * * * * * * * * * * * * * * * * * * * * * * * * * * * * * * * * * * * * * * * * * * * * * * * * * * * * * * * * *
```

VALUE.. 1 YES

	VAR76			
COUNT ROW PCT COL PCT TOT PCT	10-49 YRS 1	50-59YRS 2	60 YRS AND OVER 3	ROW TOTAL
VAR13				
0-135LBS 1	3 15.0 10.7 3.2	7 35.0 20.6 7.5	10 50.0 32.3 10.8	20 21.5
136-150LBS 2	4 30.8 14.3 4.3	5 38.5 14.7 5.4	4 30.8 12.9 4.3	13 14.0
151-165LBS 3	8 33.3 28.6 8.6	11 45.8 32.4 11.8	5 20.8 16.1 5.4	24 25.8
166-180LBS 4	3 21.4 10.7 3.2	4 28.6 11.8 4.3	7 50.0 22.6 7.5	14 15.1
181-HIGHEST LBS 5	10 45.5 35.7 10.8	7 31.8 20.6 7.5	5 22.7 16.1 5.4	22 23.7
COLUMN TOTAL	28 30.1	34 36.6	31 33.3	93 100.0

VALUE.. 2 NO

	VAR76			
COUNT ROW PCT COL PCT TOT PCT	10-49 YRS 1	50-59YRS 2	60 YRS AND OVER 3	ROW TOTAL
VAR13				
0-135LBS 1	5 50.0 8.8 4.1	4 40.0 10.0 3.3	1 10.0 4.0 0.8	10 8.2
136-150LBS 2	5 31.3 8.8 4.1	4 25.0 10.0 3.3	7 43.8 28.0 5.7	16 13.1
151-165LBS 3	13 44.8 22.8 10.7	10 34.5 25.0 8.2	6 20.7 24.0 4.9	29 23.8
166-180LBS 4	10 37.0 17.5 8.2	12 44.4 30.0 9.8	5 18.5 20.0 4.1	27 22.1
181-HIGHEST LBS 5	24 60.0 42.1 19.7	10 25.0 25.0 8.2	6 15.0 24.0 4.9	40 32.8
COLUMN TOTAL	57 46.7	40 32.8	25 20.5	122 100.0

FIGURE 12.3 Crosstabulation of age (Var 76), weight (Var 13), and chest pain (Var 46).

implicit or covert assumptions about causality constitute a hazard for the researcher. They show up, often unidentified as such, in the initial choice of independent versus dependent variables, and again in the interpretation of findings. Many of the problems we have in talking about causal relationships are a reflection of inadequately operationalized definitions, as well as a basic difficulty in obtaining agreement among scientists as to what *cause* and *effect* really entail. (See section on Causality in Chapter 1.) Here, we will rely heavily on common usage.

A variable X_1 is said to be a direct cause of a variable X_2 if and only if change in the value of X_1 alone, where all other variables are controlled or do not vary, is associated with change in the value of X_2, and if X_1 precedes X_2. In most circumstances a third variable X_3 is present, and change in X_1 "causes" change in X_3 which in turn has a direct effect on X_2. The introduction of X_3 gives rise to different types of causal structures, such as those schematically illustrated below:

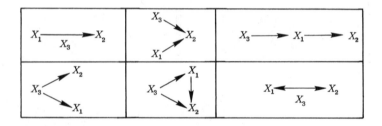

Larger chains can be constructed as more variables are introduced.

Examining the hierarchy of cause and effect leads us to the idea of *causal order*. A variable higher in the order cannot be affected by variables lower in the order. A strong or total order is one in which every variable can be causally compared to every other variable; if a variable can be unrelated causally to other variables, or only partially affect another variable, the causal order is called weak or partial. The first chain above illustrates asymmetric causality (X_1 causes X_2 but not vice versa); the last shows symmetric causality (X_1 and X_2 are each partial cause and effect). (See also Chapter 4, pp. 67–69.)

The phrase *causal closure* refers to a situation in which all the variables in a causal order chain (such as one shown above) are known.

Another schematic illustration of causal relationships is through the use of Venn diagrams. We look first at the case of two variables. If they are causally independent, the diagram shows disjoint circles:

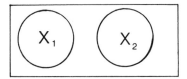

In contrast, if X_1 and X_2 are equivalent, so each variable is both the cause and the effect of the other, the diagram shows them as coincident:

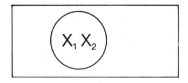

If a part of X_1 causes all of X_2, that is, a part of the change in X_1 accounts for all change in X_2, the illustration is:

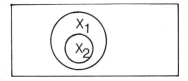

whereas if only a part of X_1 causes only a part of X_2, the diagram is:

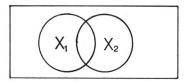

This also illustrates the cases in which X_1 is partially caused by a part of X_2, or X_1 and X_2 are each partial cause and effect of the other. It may be helpful to write $X_2 = f(X_1)$ and to analyze the functional relationship in the foregoing terms.

It can also be helpful to conceptualize the circle labelled X_1 as the variance of X_1 (or any other suitable measure of variation), so that the overlap of circles shows the part (proportion) of the variance of X_1

accounted for by the other variable(s). This gives you a pictorial interpretation of $r^2_{x_1x_2}$ in the bivariate case as the familiar[7] coefficient of determination

$$r^2_{x_1x_2} = \frac{s^2_{x_1} - s^2_{x_1 \cdot x_2}}{s^2_{x_1}} = \frac{SS_{reg}}{SS_{tot}}.$$

We next take up the case of three variables. An enumeration of possibilities is instructive in itself and helpful in understanding multiple regression analysis. To fix our ideas, we consider the following example: Research in the sociology of education suggests that family social class level and parent's education determine the child's success in school. Family income X_1 measures social class, number of years X_2 of father's schooling measures parent education, and high-school grade average Y measures success in school, for a randomly selected sample of students. Several Venn diagrams for the configurations of these three variables are possible, including:

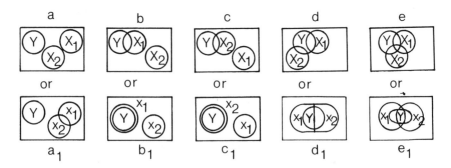

Corresponding interpretations can be stated if we assume the existence of a functional relationship of the form

$$Y = f(X_1, X_2). \qquad [\S]$$

In case (a) Y is independent of X_1 and X_2 which are, in turn, independent of each other, while in (a_1) Y is independent of X_1 and X_2 which are causally related. In these cases, the relationship [§] does not hold, since any such relationship must describe or measure the extent of "overlap" of Y with X_1 and/or X_2. In (b) and (b_1), Y is independent of X_2, so X_2 will not appear in the functional equation; similarly for X_1 in (c) and (c_1). Cases (b_1) and (c_1) show Y entirely caused by X_1 and X_2 respectively, while the effects are only partial in (b) and (c).

In (d) and (d_1) both X_1 and X_2 meet Y but are independent of each other. The functional relationship in (d_1), is "perfect", since Y is entirely accounted for with no overlap of the effects of X_1 and X_2.

Cases (e) and (e₁) involve an overlap of X_1, X_2, and Y, and so present the problem of determining how to assign the causality arising from X_1 and X_2 together. There are three solutions: One is to assign the effect entirely to the first independent variable in the functional equation; another is to assign the effect to the variable which overlaps Y the most (accounts for the greatest proportion of variation in Y); the third is to split the effect and assign equal parts to each independent variable. Unless the extent of overlap of X_1 and X_2 is only minimally significant—or not significant at all—the functional equation [§] may not be very useful.

Diagrams (b), (c), (d) suggest the need for a more general functional form, because not all the variation in Y is accounted for by the independent variables. Such a form as

$$Y = f(X_1, X_2, \ldots, X) + \epsilon \qquad [\S\S]$$

incorporates ϵ as an error term related to the unexplained portion of the dependent variable Y. Here there are independent variables.

Before proceeding, it will be helpful to formulate more precisely the notion of *proportion of variance* explained by the effects of two or more independent variables.[8] We will assume for the moment that, as in our example, the use of the product-moment correlation coefficient is appropriate. Look again at case (e).

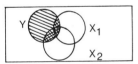 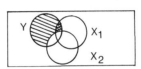 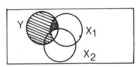

- The question, What proportion of the variance of Y is accounted for by X_1 and X_2? can be answered by comparing the portion crosshatched XXXXX to the total hatched \\\\ in the first diagram. The square of the multiple correlation coefficient $R_{Y.X_1X_2}$ provides a technical answer, under certain assumptions as to the nature of the functional equation.
- The question: if the portion attributable to X_2 is removed from the variances of both Y and X, the question, What proportion of the remaining variance of Y is accounted for by the remaining variance of X_1? can be answered by comparing the portion cross-hatched XXXXXX to the total hatched \\\\ in the second diagram. The square of the partial correlation $r_{YX_1.X_2}$ provides a technical answer.
- The question: if the portion attributable to X_2 is removed from the variance of X_1, the question, What proportion of the variance of Y is accounted for by the remaining variance of X_1? can be answered by comparing the portion-cross hatched XXX to the total hatched \\\\ in

the third diagram. The square of the semipartial or part correlation $r_{Y(X_1.X_2)}$ provides a technical answer.

Partial and Semipartial (Part) Correlation[9]

The researcher's effort to control sources of extraneous variance (see Chapter 5, section on internal and external validity) may lead to one of the following situations:

- The relationship between two variables must be accurately measured, but to do this the possible "contribution" of some set of intervening variables not under the researcher's control must be measured and removed. This is very common in surveys or other studies of intact groups.
- Subjects are assigned randomly to groups, but it appears that the groups may differ significantly on one or more control variables.

In both cases control can be accomplished by a statistical procedure which is a systematic exploitation of the idea illustrated in the Venn diagrams of the preceding section. The fundamental notion is the existence of some joint space (variance) where two variables overlap, and which is also overlapped by a third—and possibly fourth, etc.—variable. We want to quantify the association between the two variables of interest in such a way that the measure of relationship is not confused by their association with third (etc.) variable (*spurious correlation*).

In the first diagram, the variables X_1 and X_2 overlap each other and each overlaps Y; the multiple correlation coefficient $R_{Y.X_1X_2}$ (see next section) can be interpreted as a measure of the association between the variable Y and the pair of variables X_1, X_2. It does not, however, give us the information we want now, namely, the association between Y and X_1, when X_2 is held constant. The device of holding all but one (independent) variable constant is called *statistical control*, as distinguished from experimental control.

Partial correlation is a technique that handles this case extremely well. It is illustrated in the second diagram: X_1 is reduced by its joint space with X_2, and Y is reduced by its joint space with X_2, so we now have, in effect, two new variables no longer containing any joint space with the control variable X_2. A measure of association between these new variables is free of any intervening effect of X_2.

In our earlier example (p. 280) we looked at the association of child's success in school (Y) and family social class (X_1). Since parent's education (X_2) is plausibly related to each of these, it is desirable to control for this variable, that is, to "partial out" its effect.

Partial correlation statistics have been developed for several types of variables. Where all are interval level, we use the partial (Pearson) correlation coefficient. Where all are ordinal (or interval convertible to ordinal), we use Kendall's partial tau (rank order correlation) or partial Spearman's rho. We can use partial gamma when all variables are ordinal or nominal convertible to ordinal; other measures of association such a lambda can be partialled. Complex configurations in which three or more independent variables are involved, can be described using higher-order partial (and semipartial, see below) correlation coefficients. It is also possible to define multiple-partial correlations to measure the association between a dependent variable and two or more independent variables, while controlling for still other (independent) variables. The concept of partial variance can be useful as well.

Notation for partial measures is not entirely uniform across references, but the symbol $r_{12.34\ldots n}$ is widely employed; r stands for the coefficient, gamma, tau, or whatever. The 1 and 2 refer to the variables whose association is in question; the controlled variables are any and all those whose labels follow the dot. Thus $r_{1Y.2}$ is a first-order partial in which, say, the effect of X_2 is controlled in both X_1 and Y, whereas $r_{1Y.23}$ is a second-order partial in which both X_2 and X_3 are controlled, etc. (In our example, X_3 might be mother's education.) The range of values for the partial is the same as for the zero-order coefficient, typically between -1 and +1, and the interpretation is the same as for the simple bivariate measure.

Semipartial or part correlation should be distinguished from partial correlation: It does not measure the same thing. Here a variable X_1 is reduced by its joint space or covariance with the control variable X_2, and the part correlation measures the association of this new reduced variable and the dependent variable Y. Thus, the effect of X_2 is removed from X_1 but not from Y. The notation for the case described is $r_{Y(1.2)}$ and the corresponding illustration is the third diagram in the preceding section. Part correlations are particularly useful when there is covariance between independent variables, and information is needed about separate effects of the independent variables on the dependent variable. Multicollinearity occurs if the part correlations are large, and seriously interferes with the applicability of the linear (regression) model (see next section).

Referring again to our earlier example, $r_{Y(1.2)}$ allows us to measure the association between child's success in school, and the family's social class, where the effect of father's education has been controlled in the latter. $r_{Y(2.1)}$ measures association between child's success and father's education, where the effect of social class is controlled in the latter.

Multiple Regression Analysis

In order to decide how well a functional equation fits a set of data, it is necessary to express [§§] much more precisely, and to make explicit our assumptions about the class of functions in which we are interested.

The unifying theme of the first part of this chapter is that of the general linear model. In our example, the equation [§§] is assumed to have the form $Y = b_0 + b_1 X_1 + b_2 X_2 + \epsilon$; X_1, X_2, Y as before, and the parameters b_0, b_1, b_2 must be estimated. A straightforward interpretation of these is possible: The value b_0, often called the Y intercept, is the value of Y when X_1 and X_2 are zero; the values b_1, b_2 indicate the increments to be expected in Y corresponding to increments of 1 in each of X_1 and X_2 respectively.

More generally, the form [§§], assumed to be linear in the k independent variables $(X_1, X_2, \ldots, X_k)$ can be written:

$$Y = b_0 + \sum_{i=1}^{k} b_i X_i + \epsilon \qquad\qquad [\S\S\S]$$

Each of the n individuals in the sample has a set of measurements

$$(Y_j, X_{1j}, X_{2j}, \ldots X_{kj}) \qquad j = 1, \ldots, n.$$

Thus [§§§] gives rise to the system of equations:[10]

$$Y_j = b_0 + \sum_{i=1}^{k} b_i X_{ij} + \epsilon_j, \ 1 \le j \le n.$$

There are many ways to fit a linear function of the kind described above. The procedure used in most cases is Least Squares regression: It will yield an estimate of Y intercept (b_0) and slopes (b_i) that minimize the sum of squared deviations of the data points (observations) from the "line"

$$Y^c = b_0 + \sum_{i=1}^{k} b_i X_i$$

We use the Y^c to remind us that this equation predicts values of Y and does not state an actually existing relationship. Slope terms may be positive or negative, and indicate the change in Y effected by a specified X_i where all other X_i are held constant. In this formulation, the multiple correlation $R_{Y.12\ldots k}$ is simply r_{YY^c}.

The Least Squares strategy minimizes or maximizes sum square differences of data points from a proposed "best" model of the form [§§§]. The procedure rests upon a number of assumptions. If these are not met, estimates of the parameters b_0 and b_i will be inaccurate.

LEAST SQUARES ASSUMPTIONS

1. There are no specification errors:
   a. The relationship between $\{X_i\}$ and Y is linear.
   b. All relevant independent variables are included.
   c. All irrelevant independent variables are excluded.
2. All values of X_i and Y are free of errors in measurement.
3. The error term (residual) ϵ must have:
   a. The expected mean value $E(\epsilon_j) = 0$ and the expected variance of the error terms is 1.
   b. The distribution of ϵ_j is normal.
   c. Homoskedasticity or homogeneity of variance: $E(\epsilon_j^2) = \sigma^2$ where σ^2 is the variance error of estimate.
   d. Successive error terms must be uncorrelated:

$$E(\epsilon_{j_r}\epsilon_{j_s}) = 0 \text{ for } j_r \neq j_s$$

   e. The independent variables are uncorrelated with the error term: $E(\epsilon_j X_{ij}) = 0$.
4. The effects of the independent variables are additive.
5. Sample sizes must be adequate for the number of variables and observations.
6. Variance in the independent variables should be sufficiently large to accommodate variance in the dependent variable.
7. Intercorrelations between the independent variables are low and multicollinearity is avoided.[11] In practice, many of these assumptions[12] are violated; special variations of the least squares analysis are needed to develop unbiased estimates of the b_i. These modified models require an expert to utilize them effectively. There are differing views as to the robustness of regression analysis:[13] Some assumptions, such as that of normality when the sample is large, can be violated without harm to the conclusions; whereas others, such as absence of specification errors (e.g. exclusion of a relevant variable) are essential. Babbie (1979, Chapter 17) and Cohen and Cohen (1983) encourage general use of regression analysis, even where technically inappropriate, to help "understand the data"; we urge great caution in interpretation.

As listed, the least squares assumptions evidently refer to continuous interval or ratio variables. The extension of the general linear model to noninterval (nominal or ordinal) variables is fairly controversial; nevertheless, such variables are frequently incorporated into a regression framework through the technique of *dummy coding*.[14] A dichotomy can be treated as an interval variable with the two values 0 and 1. A nominal or (discrete) ordinal variable with multiple categories, say n in number, is represented by n-1 dummy variables. *The technique is unsuitable for continuous ordinal variables.* Choice of the values to assign these dummy variables, corresponding to each of the categories, will depend upon whether they are independent (orthogonal case) or not. Orthogonality permits a convenient decomposition of the form

$$R^2_{Y.123...k} = \sum_{i=1}^{k} r^2_{Yi},$$

since all intercorrelations are zero. The studies of Thornton and Freedman (1979) in changes in sex-role attitudes over a 15 year period, and Jacobson (1978) in campaign spending, both described briefly in Chapter 2, illustrate the use of coded variables in a regression analysis. The latter employs an elegant step-in procedure.

Significance tests (against the hypothesis that the true values are zero) and interval estimates are available[15] for R, b_o and b_i. Calculations are carried out routinely by computer on any multiple regression program.

The least squares procedure just described can be utilized in modified form to estimate:

1. nonlinear regression coefficients;
2. interactions among independent variables and the dependent variables;
3. the effect of known disturbances represented by a dummy variable, such as seasonality, cyclicality, etc.;
4. path analysis coefficients of a sequential variable.

An effective approach to these problems often requires that the data be transformed before the regression procedure is applied. We recommend that you check the model being utilized with a statistical consultant before proceeding.

Most multiple regression models yield the same output. Our illustration (Figure 12.4) of a multiple regression procedure is a printout of the SPSS program REGRESSION using variables obtained from the study described in Chapter 11 (note 3). The dependent variable is Var 4 (volume of oxygen, an aerobic measure of response to a stress test). The six independent variables are physiological measures. We are interested in ascertaining how well their values can be used to predict the value of Var 4. The first item on the printout—after the procedure statements—is the list of variables, their means, standard deviations, and number of cases; next, the matrix of correlations is calculated.

The program we have selected carries out the regression stepwise, entering first the variable whose correlation with Var 4 is greatest, namely Var 7. The correlation, its square, its value adjusted for *df* and number of cases, and standard error are computed. (The corresponding analysis of variance appears to the right.) This is a bivariate analysis because only one variable has been stepped in so far. Below, we see the coefficients of the regression equation: Var 4 = (0.2278396) (Var 7) + (-1.070159) or, standardized, $z_4 = 0.58612Z_7$. Under the heading "variables not in the equation" we see the values of the beta-weights each of these variables would have if they were included in the standardized regression equation, and their respective partial correlation coefficients. For example, $r_{\text{Var 4 Var 9.Var 7}} = -0.09951$, $r_{\text{Var 4 Var 76.Var 7}} = -0.20736$, etc. (Note that F-ratios are computed but significance levels must be looked up if needed.) Since the latter is the largest partial among those tested, Var 76 is the variable entered on step number 2.

In step 2, both Var 7 and Var 76 are used as independent. The multiple $R = .60972$, which we see is larger than the value 0.58612 obtained at step 1. The standardized equation $z_4 = 0.47213Z_7 + (-020303)z_{76}$ has as its beta for the new variable the "beta in" value computed at the previous step. We also see that for Var 14 the "beta in" value is -0.07426 and the partial correlation $r_{\text{Var 4 (Var 7 Var 76).Var 14}} = -0.08927$ is the largest of those listed, so it will step in next.

The outcome of the sixth and last step of this procedure is a multiple correlation value of .62093, whose square is .38556, which we interpret to mean 38.56% of the variance in Var 4 is accounted for by these six variables. The regression coefficients beta for the linear equation are given, together with B's, standard errors, and F ratios.

The summary table includes much of the preceding information. In addition, the column headed RSQ Change tells us what improvement in R^2 (coefficient of determination) is achieved at each step. We can infer that only the first two variables Var 7 and Var 6 account for a significant amount of variance in Var 4.

NONLINEAR REGRESSION:
TRANSFORMING (RE-EXPRESSING) VARIABLES[16]

If you have reason to believe that a linear function is not the most appropriate way to express the relationship between your independent and dependent variables, it is most unwise to attempt to force your data into a linear model, no matter how powerful the techniques which would then be at your disposal. Inspection of a bivariate scattergram plotted on standard coordinate axes may reveal a cluster of points which lie along an up-and-down roller coaster or a U shaped curve; on the other hand, the theory on which your study is based may predict logarithmic, power,[17] or other nonlinear relationships.

VARIABLE	MEAN	STANDARD DEV	CASES	
VAR4	37.2874	8.9965	261	VO2
VAR7	168.5532	23.1436	269	MAX HEART RATE
VAR9	0.7677	1.0480	269	ST DEP
VAR14	130.6926	19.2375	270	RESTING BP
VAR17	252.6978	48.0626	139	CHOLESTROL
VAR20	10.7168	6.2583	143	PFC
VAR76	51.7198	11.1653	257	AGE

CORRELATION COEFFICIENTS
A VALUE OF 99.00000 IS PRINTED
IF A COEFFICIENT CANNOT BE COMPUTED.

LOWER TRIANGLE: CORRELATION COEFFICIENTS
UPPER TRIANGLE: N OF CASES FOR CORRELATION

	VAR4	VAR7	VAR9	VAR14	VAR17	VAR20	VAR76
VAR4	261.	261.	261.	260.	134.	139.	244.
VAR7	0.58612	269.	269.	268.	139.	143.	252.
VAR9	-0.28986	-0.36656	269.	267.	139.	142.	252.
VAR14	-0.08453	0.05633	0.08512	270.	139.	143.	253.
VAR17	-0.21059	-0.18450	0.10149	0.00434	139.	83.	130.
VAR20	0.14827	0.11125	-0.06250	-0.04755	-0.26455	143.	130.
VAR76	-0.46811	-0.56147	0.46743	0.21528	0.27530	-0.13456	257.

********************** VARIABLE LIST 1
REGRESSION LIST 1

M U L T I P L E   R E G R E S S I O N   ********************

DEPENDENT VARIABLE.. VAR4   VO2
VARIABLE(S) ENTERED ON STEP NUMBER 1.. VAR7   MAX HEART RATE

MULTIPLE R	0.58612
R SQUARE	0.34354
ADJUSTED R SQUARE	0.33543
STANDARD ERROR	7.33400

ANALYSIS OF VARIANCE	DF	SUM OF SQUARES	MEAN SQUARE	F
REGRESSION	1.	2279.98992	2279.98992	42.38882
RESIDUAL	81.	4356.78753	53.78753	

------ VARIABLES IN THE EQUATION ------

VARIABLE	B	BETA	STD ERROR B	F
VAR7	0.2278396	0.58612	0.03499	42.389
(CONSTANT)	-1.070159			

------ VARIABLES NOT IN THE EQUATION ------

VARIABLE	BETA IN	PARTIAL	TOLERANCE	F
VAR9	-0.08666	-0.09951	0.86564	0.800
VAR14	-0.11792	-0.14531	0.99683	1.726
VAR17	-0.10606	-0.12866	0.96596	1.347
VAR20	0.08411	0.10317	0.98762	0.861
VAR76	-0.20303	-0.20736	0.68475	3.594

****

VARIABLE(S) ENTERED ON STEP NUMBER 2.. VAR76   AGE

MULTIPLE R	0.60972
R SQUARE	0.37176
ADJUSTED R SQUARE	0.35606
STANDARD ERROR	7.21930

ANALYSIS OF VARIANCE	DF	SUM OF SQUARES	MEAN SQUARE	F
REGRESSION	2.	2467.31890	1233.65945	23.67039
RESIDUAL	80.	4169.46094	52.11826	

------ VARIABLES IN THE EQUATION ------

VARIABLE	B	BETA	STD ERROR B	F
VAR7	0.1835274	0.47213	0.04163	19.437
VAR76	-0.1635908	-0.20303	0.08629	3.594
(CONSTANT)	14.85083			

------ VARIABLES NOT IN THE EQUATION ------

VARIABLE	BETA IN	PARTIAL	TOLERANCE	F
VAR9	-0.02860	-0.03157	0.76568	0.079
VAR14	-0.07426	-0.08927	0.90780	0.635
VAR17	-0.07324	-0.08877	0.92290	0.627
VAR20	0.06983	0.08721	0.98003	0.605

****

VARIABLE(S) ENTERED ON STEP NUMBER 6.. VAR9 ST DEP

			ANALYSIS OF VARIANCE	DF	SUM OF SQUARES	MEAN SQUARE	F
MULTIPLE R	0.62093		REGRESSION	6.	2558.85838	426.47640	7.94822
R SQUARE	0.38556		RESIDUAL	76.	4077.92146	53.65686	
ADJUSTED R SQUARE	0.33705						
STANDARD ERROR	7.32508						

------ VARIABLES IN THE EQUATION ------   ------ VARIABLES NOT IN THE EQUATION ------

VARIABLE	B	BETA	STD ERROR B	F	VARIABLE	BETA IN	PARTIAL	TOLERANCE	F
VAR7	0.1871520	0.48145	0.04380	18.261					
VAR76	-0.1145394	-0.14215	0.09931	1.330					
VAR14	-0.3537783D-01	-0.07565	0.04424	0.640					
VAR17	-0.1220866D-01	-0.06522	0.01808	0.456					
VAR20	0.7593419D-01	0.05282	0.13454	0.319					
VAR9	-0.2624687	-0.03058	0.88279	0.088					
(CONSTANT)	18.80013								

STATISTICS WHICH CANNOT BE COMPUTED ARE PRINTED AS ALL NINES.

***** MULTIPLE REGRESSION *****   VARIABLE LIST 1   REGRESSION LIST 1

DEPENDENT VARIABLE.. VAR4 VO2

SUMMARY TABLE

VARIABLE		MULTIPLE R	R SQUARE	RSQ CHANGE	SIMPLE R	B	BETA
VAR7	MAX HEART RATE	0.58612	0.34354	0.34354	0.58612	0.1871520	0.48145
VAR76	AGE	0.60972	0.37176	0.02823	-0.46811	-0.1145394	-0.14215
VAR14	RESTING BLOOD PRESSU	0.61382	0.37677	0.00501	-0.08453	-0.3537783D-01	-0.07565
VAR17	CHOLESTEROL	0.61827	0.38226	0.00549	-0.21059	-0.1220866D-01	-0.06522
VAR20	PFC	0.62036	0.38484	0.00258	0.14827	0.7593419D-01	0.05282
VAR9	ST DEP	0.62093	0.38556	0.00071	-0.28986	-0.2624687	-0.03058
(CONSTANT)						18.80013	

FIGURE 12.4 Multiple regression analysis: volume of oxygen (Var 4) and six independent variables.

Obviously, none of the procedures such as Pearson-product-moment correlation or linear regression and its elaborations (e.g. discriminant analysis) are applicable without modification, because their common foundation is the assumption of linearity. This means that any probabilistic arguments you may need to invoke for purposes of hypothesis testing, may require modification as well.

Three major issues must be considered:

- How should one go about deciding which family of functions may best describe the relationships between your variables?
- How does one identify the best fitting function in that family? How does one measure strength of association in nonlinear relationships?
- How does one test the proposed best fitting function or index of association for significance? What (probabilistic) inferences can be made?

We take up these issues briefly, in turn.

Let us set aside the case in which the theoretical rationale for your study specifies the form of the function to which you will try to fit your data. Your first and most important step should be to LOOK AT YOUR DATA. A variety of approaches have been developed to make insight into patterns easier, the simplest and most familiar being a scattergram or two-dimensional graph. This can be tedious to construct if you have many points, but it will give you an impression of the "shape of the relationship." Guessing the category of functions which best describes that shape requires a combination of art and science, (and luck). Drawing the scattergram on log or log-log paper may suggest a transformation (re-expression) of your variables, for example, replacement of X by $X' = \log X$ or $X'' = \sqrt{X}$. Certain transformations are well-known to reduce outliers, flatten distributions, or whatever: The procedures described in Hartwig and Dearing (1979) and in Tukey (1977) represent, despite novel terminology, a useful distillation of experience. It may be quite difficult to decide between certain power functions and certain exponential functions, because they may happen to agree closely in values over the range within which the measures of independent variables happen to lie. In general, this aspect of data handling is very challenging (we suggest that you refer to the relevant technical literature), but the clarity achieved is worth the effort.

The least-squares criterion can be exploited to find the best-fitting quadratic or higher-degree polynomial, or exponential or logarithmic function. In the latter case, it may be most efficient to transform one of the variables first and then proceed as if for a linear regression equation: Mathematically, this follows from the equivalence of $(\text{Log } Y) = a + bX$ and $Y = Ae^{bX}$ where $A = e^a$. Calculations can be carried out by computer and involve a multistep process, the first (several) steps involving—for instance, to obtain the best cubic—such transformations as $X_2 = X_1^2$, $X_3 = X_1^3$, etc., and the last step, a multilinear regression. (See SPSS Manual, Nie et al. (1975) Chapter 21.)

It is important not to use the ordinary (Pearson) correlation coefficient unthinkingly. If you have any doubt as to linearity, you will be wise to employ the correlation ratio η (eta), as indicated in our Table 11.3.

Finally, the F-test can be used to test the significance of higher-order polynomial terms; in other special cases where interval estimates and similar bases for inference are required, we advise that you consult a statistician with a strong mathematical background.

PATH ANALYSIS[18]

As we have suggested earlier, possible causal relationships can more readily be identified and analyzed when evidence is generated in an experimental study. When the researcher must deal with evidence obtained in studies in which either control of conditions is limited (or impossible), or randomization is absent, the task is more complex because, typically, a large number of extraneous variables may be operating. It is not, however, hopeless. In the past 20 years, a variety of techniques and approaches collectively referred to as *path analysis* have been developed to analyze so-called *causal models:* that is, to test hypothesized causal relationships as linear equations involving the relevant variables. They are based on a suitable definition of causality (typically that of Simon [1957, 1977]), a set of computed part and partial correlation and regression coefficients of various orders for all the variables of interest, and a path or causal diagram translated appropriately into equations. The details are technical but not difficult, as they involve primarily manipulation of the coefficients already mentioned; the interesting and challenging aspect is the formulation of the causal conjecture, which must clearly indicate the roles played by all variables. Needless to say, no "proof" of causality is possible, but it *is* possible to achieve greater confidence in the likelihood of such a directional relationship, and a clearer understanding of the role of mediating variables. In any proposed application of these techniques, it is essential to keep in mind that the analysis of the problem comes first: The *path diagram* is simply a sort of graphic organizer for the theoretical model. The numbers won't generate this, only provide support.

Researchers in a number of disciplines have greeted these developments with enthusiasm. The most familiar example of their application is the (controversial) Jencks (1973) study of the effects of schooling. Another, more recent but also controversial, is Bell et al.'s (1981) investigation of factors determining sexual preference in both men and women. This report also contains a section explaining in very elementary terms the construction and interpretation of path diagrams.

The Analysis of Variance (ANOVA)

When data are interval or ratio level, and we wish to compare simultaneously three or more sample means, the method of choice is the *analysis of variance*. Usually the several means are calculated from groups that have been categorized (labelled) by values of a nominal or discrete ordinal variable. In the latter case, trend analysis can also be useful.

Let us suppose that in connection with the study described in Chapter 11 (note 3), we would like to ignore the variable of marital status (Var 78) in analyses of the variable VO2 (Var 4). To put this another way, we need to know whether VO2 varies with marital status.

The dependent variable (VO2) is interval (in fact, ratio); these are the so-called scores of the respective subjects. The classifying variable (marital status) is nominal. In other examples, such discrete ordinal classifying variables as income class (i.e., low, lower-middle, middle, upper-middle, high) can be incorporated appropriately in the analysis of variance.

As we have suggested in Chapter 11, we formulate our conjecture as a *testing of differences* problem. Difference testing procedures start with a statement of the hypothesis to be tested: Denote the (true) subpopulation means μ_1, μ_2, μ_3, μ_4 for the four classes of marital status; then write the null hypothesis $H_0: \mu_1 = \mu_2 = \mu_3 = \mu_4$ and the alternative, its logical negation $H_1 = \mu_1, \mu_2, \mu_3, \mu_4$ are not all equal. Our decision will be based on the following: If the observed differences among the subsample means $\overline{X}_1$, $\overline{X}_2$, $\overline{X}_3$, $\overline{X}_4$ are statistically significant, that is, too great to be attributed to chance variation, we will reject H_0 and "accept" H_1, otherwise we will "accept" H_0 and reject H_1. (Recall that *accept* means *fail to reject*!).

The situation we have just described leads to the simplest type of analysis of variance, the so-called fixed-effects *one-way* because only one classifying variable is used. (*Fixed-effects* means, roughly, the values of the variables of classification are the only relevant values of interest, whereas *random-effects* means the values of the variables of classification represent a random sample drawn from a finite or infinite universe of possible values of interest.) Every analysis of variance is based on the same strategy: Define a total variation, partition it into component parts attributable to different sources within the data, form ratios of these components to compare them, and calculate the probabilities that these ratios occur by chance.

The first step is to form a total sum of squares by squaring the difference of each subject's VO2 score from the grand mean, and then adding all these squares. This sum is a measure of the variability of the data from the grand mean. Relatively simple algebraic maneuvers[19] justify the partition of the total sum of squares into two sums. One, the within-group sum of squares, is obtained by squaring the difference of each subject's score from its class or group (column) means, and adding these squares across all the columns. The other, the between-group sum of squares, is formed by subtracting the grand mean from each group mean, squaring the differences, and summing over all the columns. We may write $SS_T = SS_W + SS_B$.

The next step is to convert these sum-squares into variances by dividing each by the appropriate number of degrees of freedom. For the total sum of squares, recall the degrees of freedom, df_T, is N–1, where N is the total number of subjects. The appropriate degrees of freedom, df_B, for the between-groups-sum is $k - 1$, where k is the number of groups (columns). The degrees-of-freedom df_W for the within-group sum can be calculated conveniently from the equation $df_T = df_W + df_B$. When we divide the three sums of squares by the appropriate df's, we have variances or mean squares MS_T (total), MS_W (within-groups), and MS_B (between-groups). Note $MS_T \neq MS_W + MS_B$.

Next, we form the test statistic F as the ratio MS_B/MS_W. The F *distribution* is in fact a family of distributions, each member of which is continuous, unimodal, and positively skewed,[20] and takes on all possible nonnegative values. The particular F-distribution, and its associated probabilities, are entirely determined by two parameters, the two degrees-of-freedom (numerator and denominator). Critical values of F at the .05 and .01 level of significance are tabled and can be used to test the null hypothesis. Computer print-outs give you the probability of your computed value of F.

Thus in testing the null hypothesis $H_o: \mu_1 = \mu_2 = \mu_3 = \mu_4$ against the alternative hypothesis that the subpopulation (group) means are not all equal, we have evaluated the ratio MS_B/MS_W and found the probability that, if H_o is true, this value can occur by chance. If indeed H_o is true, the between-groups and the within-groups contributions to the total variation would not differ significantly, since they both reflect the same variability of subjects' scores. In contrast, if H_o is false and the column means are not equal, then the between-column contribution to total variance should significantly outweigh the within-column contribution, because the former would reflect variability between column means as well as overall score variability.

ASSUMPTIONS UNDERLYING ANALYSIS OF VARIANCE

The use of analysis of variance to make inferences about the equality of subpopulation means requires that several assumptions be made:

1. The dependent variable is normally distributed in each subpopulation (column).
2. The variance of the dependent variable is the same in each subpopulation (column); this is called *homoskedasticity* or *homogeneity of variance*.

3. All observations of the dependent variable are independent; random samples are selected from each of the subpopulations.
4. All the least squares assumptions enumerated previously (p. 285) apply.

These assumptions provide the theoretical basis for one-way analysis of variance. Hence, several tests can be carried out to ensure that the conditions are met. Normality of the sampled subpopulations can be verified through pilot investigations and a chi-square analysis, or through analysis in previous studies of the same groups. Homogeneity of variance is tested by a variety of procedures, including Cochran's[21] C, the Bartlett-Box[22] F, or the Hartley[23] F_{max} tests. Assumptions 3 and 4 require an examination of the data for systematic patterns; such procedures as runs and sign tests can be applied (cf. Chapter 11, section on univariate descriptive measures). The analysis of covariance, to be discussed later in this chapter, represents another approach to the elimination of systematic but unwanted variation.

Many authors observe that it is sometimes necessary to use an analysis of variance procedure even though the assumptions are not satisfied, and assert that, in general, "one can be reasonably confident in applying [it] if none of the assumptions are very badly violated."[24] The procedure is said to be *robust*, if inferences based on it are valid in the face of moderate departures from the basic assumptions. Unfortunately, it is difficult to evaluate the severity of a violation or the special circumstances in which the departure can be overlooked. If the assumptions are relaxed or ignored, serious misinterpretations of the data may result. In general, assumption 3 is essential; the others permit some flexibility if subsamples are large and of approximately the same size. Unless you have expert advice, you would be wise to apply the analysis of variance procedure only when you have verified the assumptions.

If your data do not fit the assumptions it is better to use a multivariate nonparametric statistic such as chi-square, or the Kruskal–Wallis (see Chapter 14).

An analysis of variance is illustrated with a printout from SPSS program ONEWAY. (Figure 12.5) The data are taken from the study described in Chapter 11 (note 3).

We suspect that the VO2 measures (Var 4) may differ according to marital status (Var 78). The program computes means and standard deviations for each of the four groups determined by Var 78, as well as total means and standard deviations for 199 cases. It also calculates between-groups and within-groups df's, sums of squares, mean squares, and F ratio; here $F = 7.508$ with probability 0.0001. Since this is highly significant, we conclude we may indeed reject the null hypothesis that the means of the four groups are equal.

Three multiple comparison procedures are carried out and displayed in Figure 12.5: LSD, Student-Neuman-Keuls, and Scheffe.[25] Each one identifies the widowed group (Label 4) as the subset whose mean on Var 4 differs from the mean of the subset of the other three groups. (See this Chapter, p. 302). Note that the preliminary homogeneity of variance tests indicate a probability in excess of .2 that the groups are drawn from subpopulations with the same variance.

n-WAY ANALYSIS OF VARIANCE AND FACTORIAL DESIGN

In order to extend the procedure described in the preceding section to more complex situations, we first observe that the basic objective of analysis of variance is to study the relationship between a dependent metric (interval- or ratio-level) variable, and one or more independent classifying nonmetric (nominal or discrete ordinal) variables. Many authors call the independent variables *factors*, and the values the factors can assume *levels*. A *random* factor is one whose levels can be regarded as a sample from some universe of levels; a *fixed* factor is one whose levels are the only ones of interest. For instance, sex, age, and marital status are usually considered as fixed, subjects and observers as random, but treatments and locations can be either fixed or random according to the particular study. The distinction is important because when two or more factors are involved, different F-ratios are tested for significance for different configurations of random and fixed factors. Each possible combination of factor levels is called a *cell*: The analysis of designs in which each cell contains one data point is different from those in which the cells contain more than one, and modifications must be introduced if the number of items in all the cells is not the same, or if some cells are empty.

The inclusion of additional independent variables gives rise to increased complication, but the underlying strategy remains the same. The variation of the overall sample is partitioned into components reflecting the contributions of variation within the cells: variation arising from differences between levels of each of the factors (main effects), and variation arising from various combination (interaction and residual) effects of the factors. If interaction effects are significant, it is advisable to test further for so-called simple effects (see SPSS, Hull & Nie, 1981, pp. 30–31). Components are compared using suitable F-ratios.[26] The formulation of an appropriate null hypothesis is correspondingly more complicated, as is the interpretation of the statistical conclusions. It is important to be aware that an early SPSS ANOVA routine computed all F-ratios as for fixed effects model while the update MANOVA has options for other models as well as for variety of designs, for example, nested and repeated measures. BMDP also has a program

VARIABLE VAR4 V02
BY VARIABLE VAR78 MARITAL STATUS

ANALYSIS OF VARIANCE

SOURCE	D.F.	SUM OF SQUARES	MEAN SQUARES	F RATIO	F PROB.
BETWEEN GROUPS	3	1760.7316	586.9104	7.508	0.0001
WITHIN GROUPS	195	15243.9817	78.1743		
TOTAL	198	17004.7109			

GROUP	COUNT	MEAN	STANDARD DEVIATION	STANDARD ERROR	MINIMUM	MAXIMUM	95 PCT CONF INT FOR MEAN		
GRP01	124	37.7581	8.3795	0.7525	13.0000	61.0000	36.2685	TO	39.2476
GRP02	30	37.5000	10.6666	1.9474	13.0000	58.0000	33.5170	TO	41.4830
GRP03	34	38.9706	8.3864	1.4383	24.0000	55.0000	36.0444	TO	41.8967
GRP04	11	25.0909	9.9343	2.9953	7.0000	45.0000	18.4169	TO	31.7648
TOTAL	199	37.2261	9.2673	0.6569	7.0000	61.0000	35.9306	TO	38.5216
FIXED EFFECTS MODEL			8.8416	0.6268			35.9900	TO	38.4622
RANDOM EFFECTS MODEL				2.5492			29.1134	TO	45.3388

RANDOM EFFECTS MODEL - ESTIMATE OF BETWEEN COMPONENT VARIANCE   13.7752

TESTS FOR HOMOGENEITY OF VARIANCES

COCHRANS C = MAX. VARIANCE/SUM(VARIANCES) = 0.3223, P = 0.219 (APPROX.)
BARTLETT-BOX F =   1.139, P = 0.332
MAXIMUM VARIANCE / MINIMUM VARIANCE =   1.620

VARIABLE VAR4 V02
BY VARIABLE VAR78 MARITAL STATUS
MULTIPLE RANGE TEST
LSD PROCEDURE
RANGES FOR THE 0.010 LEVEL -
 3.68 3.68 3.68
THE RANGES ABOVE ARE TABLE RANGES. THE VALUE ACTUALLY COMPARED WITH MEAN(J)-MEAN(I) IS..
 6.2520 * RANGE * SQRT(1/N(I) + 1/N(J))
(*) DENOTES PAIRS OF GROUPS SIGNIFICANTLY DIFFERENT AT THE 0.010 LEVEL

```
          G G G G
          R R R R
          P P P P
          0 0 0 0
          4 2 1 3
```

```
MEAN      GROUP
25.0909   GRP04
37.5000   GRP02    *
37.7581   GRP01    *
38.9706   GRP03    *

- - - - - - - - - - - O N E W A Y - - - - - - - - - -

       VARIABLE  VAR4       VO2
    BY VARIABLE  VAR7B      MARITAL STATUS
MULTIPLE RANGE TEST
STUDENT-NEWMAN-KEULS PROCEDURE
RANGES FOR THE 0.050 LEVEL -
     2.81  3.35  3.67

THE RANGES ABOVE ARE TABLE RANGES.  THE VALUE ACTUALLY COMPARED WITH MEAN(J)-MEAN(I) IS..
    6.2520 * RANGE * SQRT(1/N(I) + 1/N(J))
HOMOGENEOUS SUBSETS    (SUBSETS OF GROUPS, WHOSE HIGHEST AND LOWEST MEANS DO NOT DIFFER BY MORE THAN THE SHORTEST
                        SIGNIFICANT RANGE FOR A SUBSET OF THAT SIZE)

SUBSET 1

GROUP    GRP04
MEAN     25.0909
SUBSET 2

GROUP    GRP02    GRP01    GRP03
MEAN     37.5000  37.7581  38.9706

- - - - - - - - - - - O N E W A Y - - - - - - - - - -

       VARIABLE  VAR4       VO2
    BY VARIABLE  VAR7B      MARITAL STATUS
MULTIPLE RANGE TEST
SCHEFFE PROCEDURE
RANGES FOR THE 0.050 LEVEL -
     3.99  3.99  3.99

THE RANGES ABOVE ARE TABLE RANGES.  THE VALUE ACTUALLY COMPARED WITH MEAN(J)-MEAN(I) IS..
    6.2520 * RANGE * SQRT(1/N(I) + 1/N(J))
(*) DENOTES PAIRS OF GROUPS SIGNIFICANTLY DIFFERENT AT THE 0.050 LEVEL

                  G G G G
                  R R R R
                  P P P P
                  O O O O
                  4 2 1 3

MEAN      GROUP
25.0909   GRP04
37.5000   GRP02    *
37.7581   GRP01    *
38.9706   GRP03    *
```

FIGURE 12.5 An analysis of variance: printout from SPSS program ONEWAY.

for mixed model analysis. Serious errors can arise through the use of an inappropriate model; however, corrections can be easily carried out by hand.

To fix our ideas, suppose that in the example of the preceding section, we classified the subjects by sex as well as marital status. Thus marital status, Var 78, Factor A, has 4 levels, while sex, Var 77, Factor B, has 2 levels. It is possible that the factors interact, so that widowed male subjects have lower VO2 scores than other widowed subjects or other male subjects, and so forth. Such so-called interaction effects can be evaluated and, if significant, suggest that our original linear (additive) model is inadequate: a multiplicative component should be introduced. The printout of SPSS program ANOVA appears as Figure 12.6.

The question posed in the example (see Chapter 11, note 3) used for a one-way analysis is now augmented: If the factor of sex (Var 77) is now taken into account, is the effect of marital status still significant?

The program prints row, column and cell means and number of cases, for the two factors Var 77 and Var 78; thus, the mean value of Var 4 for 10 widowed females is 24.00; for all 54 females, 30.80; and for all 199 cases, 37.23.

The program now computes sums of squares, df's, mean squares, F-ratios, and probabilities for sources of variation: main effects, interaction effects, and residuals. We see that the effect of sex is highly signficant and the effect of marital status is also significant ($p = .038$), but that interaction effects are not ($p = 0.429$). You will observe that the sum of the independent main effect sum of squares for variables 77 and 78 is less the total main effect sum of squares; the discrepancy reflects the "joint additive effect of these two variables."[27]

The multiple classification analysis, which uses a regression viewpoint, gives the deviations of the group means (but not the cell means) from the grand mean, and computes the value of eta: .32 for the pair of variables Var 4 and Var 78, and .42 for the pair Var 4 and Var 77. It also computes beta-weights for the standardized regression equation: $z = .20z_{78} + .36z_{77}$, as well as multiple $R = .464$ and $R^2 = .215$. This analysis suggests that even while the difference in group means is significant, the linear relationship between the three variables is only moderate in strength.

Factorial design is a particularly useful experimental plan if the effects of a number of interacting treatments must be analyzed. In general terms a factorial design can be described as an $l_1 \times l_2 \times \ldots \times l_n$ experiment where n is the number of factors (variables, treatments) and l_i is the number of levels of the ith treatment (see terminology used in Chapter 11 for tables). Such a design presents two important advantages: (1) it makes possible an analysis of the interaction between two or more experimental variables, and (2) even if no interaction occurs, the design is more economical, in time and

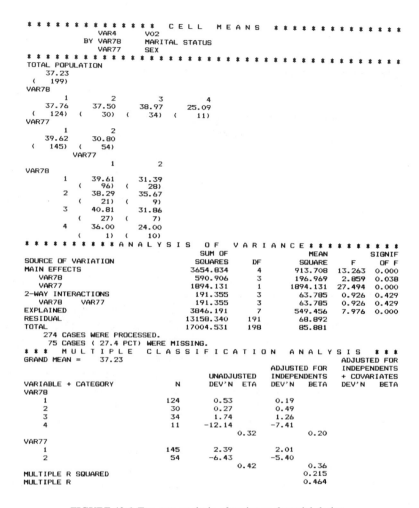

```
* * * * * * * * * * * * *   C E L L   M E A N S   * * * * * * * * * * * * * *
              VAR4      VO2
          BY VAR78    MARITAL STATUS
             VAR77    SEX
* * * * * * * * * * * * * * * * * * * * * * * * * * * * * * * * * * * * * * * *
TOTAL POPULATION
     37.23
  (   199)
VAR78
        1             2           3           4
      37.76         37.50       38.97       25.09
  (   124)   (     30)   (     34)   (     11)
VAR77
        1             2
      39.62         30.80
  (   145)   (     54)
            VAR77
              1             2
VAR78
        1             39.61       31.39
          (     96)   (     28)
        2             38.29       35.67
          (     21)   (      9)
        3             40.81       31.86
          (     27)   (      7)
        4             36.00       24.00
          (      1)   (     10)
* * * * * * * * * A N A L Y S I S   O F   V A R I A N C E * * * * * * * * * *
                              SUM OF                   MEAN          SIGNIF
SOURCE OF VARIATION          SQUARES     DF           SQUARE     F     OF F
MAIN EFFECTS                3654.834      4          913.708  13.263  0.000
  VAR78                      590.906      3          196.969   2.859  0.038
  VAR77                     1894.131      1         1894.131  27.494  0.000
2-WAY INTERACTIONS           191.355      3           63.785   0.926  0.429
  VAR78    VAR77             191.355      3           63.785   0.926  0.429
EXPLAINED                   3846.191      7          549.456   7.976  0.000
RESIDUAL                   13158.340    191           68.892
TOTAL                      17004.531    198           85.881
     274 CASES WERE PROCESSED.
      75 CASES ( 27.4 PCT) WERE MISSING.
* * *   M U L T I P L E   C L A S S I F I C A T I O N   A N A L Y S I S   * * *
GRAND MEAN =     37.23
                                                 ADJUSTED FOR   ADJUSTED FOR
                                                               INDEPENDENTS
                                    UNADJUSTED   INDEPENDENTS   + COVARIATES
VARIABLE + CATEGORY         N       DEV'N  ETA   DEV'N  BETA    DEV'N  BETA
VAR78
        1                  124       0.53         0.19
        2                   30       0.27         0.49
        3                   34       1.74         1.26
        4                   11     -12.14        -7.41
                                           0.32          0.20
VAR77
        1                  145       2.39         2.01
        2                   54      -6.43        -5.40
                                           0.42          0.36
MULTIPLE R SQUARED                                             0.215
MULTIPLE R                                                     0.464
```

FIGURE 12.6 Two-way analysis of variance: factorial design.

number of separate observations, than any sequence of one-treatment-at-a-time studies. Factorial designs can also be utilized in survey studies yielding data cross-tabulated on several classification variables.

Evidently, n-way analysis of variance is a natural for n-factor designs of the type just described, where the dependent variable is metric and the independent variables are nonmetric. It is possible to introduce a factor whose two levels are "experimental" and "control" so as to permit analysis of treatment effects. Moreover, if each cell contains sufficiently many data points, they may be separated into two groups, "original" and "replication", thus creating the appearance of a parallel replication. It is important to randomize the selection procedures for experimental and control groups, and for original and replication groups, so as to lessen possible bias.

A special case of the foregoing is found in so-called *randomized block* design, frequently used when the researcher wishes to control the effects of some independent blocking variable, such as income level. First, stratify the population with respect to this variable, then draw subjects from the various strata to ensure that the distribution of the trait in each subsample (treatment group) grossly matches the distribution of the trait in the population. The analysis for randomized blocks design is precisely the same as for factorial designs. Matched-pairs and repeated measurements designs are also suitable for analysis of variance procedures.[28]

OTHER TYPES OF DESIGN

Certain important designs that appear to preserve the factorial format, and that achieve greater efficiency in sampling or data collection, do not lend themselves to analysis of variance unless the statistical procedure is suitably modified. The simplest example is that of a factorial design in which certain cells are empty or combined, so-called *confounded* designs; hence, certain effects cannot be analyzed. The *nested* or *hierarchical* design is illustrated by a study in which 10 teachers use instructional method *A* and 10 other teachers use instructional method *B*, in classes to which students are randomly assigned. Basically, this is an incomplete two-way factorial. Here, no analysis of interaction effects is possible, and it is incorrect to proceed as if the design were factorial.[29]

Latin (and *Greco-Latin*) *square designs* are another form of incomplete factorial in which empty cells are located systematically. Here again interaction effects cannot be detected without refinements[30] in the analysis of variance procedure.

ANALYSIS OF COVARIANCE (ANCOVA)

Imagine a study in which you identify, in advance, one or more variables, called *covariates*, which you believe to be correlated with the dependent (criterion) variable; in other respects, the study lends itself to an analysis of variance with one or more factors. A simple example would be an investigation of birth weights of full-term infants, where the factors are sex of infant (two levels) and smoking behavior of mother (three levels), and the covariates are birth weights of mother and father respectively. Note that the covariates and the dependent variable are metric (interval or ratio), and the independent variables—factors—are nonmetric (nominal or discrete ordinal). You wish to sort out the effects of the factors, and any possible interaction effects, while suppressing or controlling the effect of the covariates. In other words, you seek to analyze the effects of infant sex and maternal smoking in the portion of the variability in birth weight not accounted for by parental birth weights. We can also refer to "partialling out" the effects of parental birth weights.

The method of choice for data analysis in this and comparable studies is the analysis of covariance. This technique is based on a linear model, of which the simplest case is:

$$Y = b_0 + b_1 X_1 + b_2 X_2 + \epsilon$$

$$\text{dependent} \qquad \text{factor} \qquad \text{covariate} \qquad \text{"error"}$$
$$\text{variable}$$

which yields the equations:

$$Y_j = b_o + b_1 X_{1j} + b_2 X_{2j} + \epsilon_j$$

where $1 \leq j \leq n$, n = number of subjects. Analysis of covariance can be regarded either as an extension of analysis of variance or as an extension of multiple regression analysis. It is adaptable to a wide variety of designs, whether experimental, quasi-experimental, or purely descriptive.[31]

The "classical" problem, in which the researcher is interested in suppressing the effect of one or more quantitative variables, so that the relationships between the dependent variable and one or more factors can be analyzed, involves calculating sums of squares adjusted for the (correlation) effects of the covariates, partitioning the adjusted sums, dividing by degrees of freedom, and comparing the appropriate F-ratios with a table of critical values. This evidently represents a modification of the procedure used in analysis of variance. The closely related problem of removing the effect(s) of one or more categorical or qualitative variables, so that the relationships between the dependent varible and one or more quantitative variables can be investigated, makes use of the flexibility of regression analysis with dummy coding.

It is possible to exploit the multiple regression viewpoint still further and to examine the contribution of each of the independent variables, whether qualitative or quantitative, after adjusting for the effects of all the others. The use of an analysis of covariance procedure assumes a direct causal relationship between the covariates and the dependent variable. The decision to use a coded nominal variable as a covariate rather than a factor may be tricky. Judicious interpretation is essential, since careless inferences can easily be correct answers to the wrong questions. This procedure does not completely replace use of proper controls or comparison groups.

A generalized regression perspective encompasses the different approaches and is generally utilized by computer programs.[32] It is most instructive to look in detail at the computer output (Figure 12.7) of subroutine ANOVA based on data from the study we have been using.

Into the analysis of variance of Var 4 (aerobic measure) with the two factors Var 78 (marital status), and Var 77 (sex), we now introduce the covariate Var 76 (age), because we conjecture that the difference we noticed earlier between the widowed groups and the others reflects the greater age of the widowed.

The first steps are as in the preceding example, but the total sum of squares is decomposed differently, including a contribution of the covariates. We now see, however, that the main effect of Var 78 is no longer significant ($p = .534$), while the main effect of sex remains significant ($p = .000$). This is very striking and makes our conjecture more plausible.

The multiple classification analysis shows a multiple $R^2 = .391$ for a multiple correlation of .626, which underlines the importance of Var 76 as a predictive variable in addition to Vars 77 and 78. The column "unadjusted dev'n" reflects the deviations from the Var 4 mean predictable for each Var 77 or Var 78 group on the assumption the relation between Var 4 and Var 76 is linear. The column "adjusted for independents + covariates" gives the adjustments to the Var 4 mean needed to eliminate the effects of the factors. "Beta" is the standard regression weight; partial correlation ratios ("partial eta") are also given.

MULTIPLE COMPARISON PROCEDURES[33]

If an analysis of variance procedure simultaneously comparing several population means yields a statistically significant F-test, it is then customary to ask: Which specific means are significantly different? For instance, in our comparison of VO2 measures for each of our categories of adults, if we found that the null H_o: $\mu_1 = \mu_2 = \mu_3 = \mu_4$ must be rejected, we may now wish to know whether, on average, single adults differ from married, married from formerly married, divorced from widowed, or whatever. These comparisons can be decided upon in advance (a priori) of data collection, or after (a posteriori) analysis of the data.

The "natural" approach, that of performing all possible t-tests in order to make pairwise comparisons, has a serious drawback: The more null hypotheses (comparisons) there are to be tested, the more likely we are to falsely reject one of them. The bias against the H_o's is exaggerated in exploratory studies where comparisons of only the most discrepant means are made.

Several multiple comparison procedures are available which avoid this difficulty, and which are suitable for a posteriori comparisons. These include:

- Fisher's LSD (Least Significant Difference): reduces the significance level as a way to avoid the problem just described; easy to compute.

```
* * * * * * * * * * * * * *   C E L L   M E A N S   * * * * * * * * * * * * * *
                 VAR4         VO2
           BY VAR78          MARITAL STATUS
              VAR77          SEX
* * * * * * * * * * * * * * * * * * * * * * * * * * * * * * * * * * * * * * * *
TOTAL POPULATION
     37.23
   (   199)
VAR78
      1              2            3            4
    37.76          37.50        38.97        25.09
  (   124)   (      30)   (      34)   (      11)
VAR77
      1              2
    39.62          30.80
  (   145)   (      54)
           VAR77
                 1            2
VAR78
      1        39.61        31.39
            (    96)   (      28)
      2        38.29        35.67
            (    21)   (       9)
      3        40.81        31.86
            (    27)   (       7)
      4        36.00        24.00
            (     1)   (      10)
* * * * * * * * * A N A L Y S I S   O F   V A R I A N C E * * * * * * * * * * *
                 VAR4         VO2
           BY VAR78          MARITAL STATUS
              VAR77          SEX
            WITH VAR76       AGE
* * * * * * * * * * * * * * * * * * * * * * * * * * * * * * * * * * * * * * * *
```

	SUM OF SQUARES	DF	MEAN SQUARE	F	SIGNIF OF F
SOURCE OF VARIATION					
COVARIATES	4070.698	1	4070.698	75.017	-0.000
VAR76	4070.698	1	4070.698	75.017	-0.000
MAIN EFFECTS	2585.895	4	646.474	11.914	0.000
VAR78	119.264	3	39.755	0.733	0.534
VAR77	1926.563	1	1926.563	35.504	0.000
2-WAY INTERACTIONS	37.785	3	12.595	0.232	0.874
VAR78 VAR77	37.785	3	12.595	0.232	0.874
EXPLAINED	6694.379	8	836.797	15.421	0.000
RESIDUAL	10310.152	190	54.264		
TOTAL	17004.531	198	85.881		

```
COVARIATE    RAW REGRESSION COEFFICIENT
VAR76         -0.397
      274 CASES WERE PROCESSED.
       75 CASES ( 27.4 PCT) WERE MISSING.
* * *   M U L T I P L E   C L A S S I F I C A T I O N   A N A L Y S I S   * * *
GRAND MEAN =     37.23
```

		UNADJUSTED DEV'N	ETA	ADJUSTED FOR INDEPENDENTS DEV'N	BETA	ADJUSTED FOR INDEPENDENTS + COVARIATES DEV'N	BETA
VARIABLE + CATEGORY	N						
VAR78							
1	124	0.53				0.45	
2	30	0.27				-1.34	
3	34	1.74				0.22	
4	11	-12.14				-2.09	
			0.32				0.09
VAR77							
1	145	2.39				2.03	
2	54	-6.43				-5.45	
			0.42				0.36

```
MULTIPLE R SQUARED                                                    0.391
MULTIPLE R                                                            0.626
```

FIGURE 12.7 Analysis of covariance.

- Tukey's HSD (Honestly Significant Difference): suitable for any and all simple pairwise comparisons of means provided samples are of equal size; based on the studentized range statistic, for which values are tabled.
- Student–Newman–Keuls (SNK) method.
- Scheffe's method: can be used when samples from different populations are not of equal size and/or when comparisons other than pairwise comparison of means are desired. The Scheffe test, which is based on the F-distribution, imposes a fairly stringent criterion, and it may be difficult to interpret the outcome of "no significance." Moreover, although this method can be used for n-way ANOVA and for analysis of covariance designs as well, it is of the greatest importance that the appropriate choice be made of degrees of freedom, and in the latter case, that adjusted means be used.

These and other multiple comparison procedures are available as options for the SPSS program ONEWAY (see Figure 12.5), and can also be carried out by other programs. They can be applied as part of an analysis of covariance as well, but it is important to verify that the appropriate adjustments for the covariate are incorporated. Moreover, multiple comparison tests are a waste of time unless the cells or subgroups tested are sufficiently large to allow interpretation as representative samples of the population stratum.

In this chapter, we have described the simplest examples of causal relationships involving three variables, and the most commonly used multivariate applications of the general linear model: multiple regression and analysis of variance with covariates. We have also suggested a few of the extensions of these basic procedures, such as multiple and partial correlation, and path analysis, and have indicated some of the special design considerations pertinent to the use of these procedures.

In the next chapter, we will describe additional multivariate techniques that exploit the general linear model.

Notes

[1] On appropriate statistical occasions, data involving only two variables will be treated as multivariate. For example, the function $Y = f(X_1, X_1^2)$, where Y is determined by X_1 and the square of X_1, is such a case.

[2] Classification of techniques based entirely on data characteristics can be found in Stock and Dodenhoff (1982), Uhl (1972), and Andrews et al. (1975). These all incorporate decision trees.

[3] Excellent guides to table construction are Davis (1963, 1971) which also include references. Zeisel (1968) is superb for presentation and interpretation. Rosenberg (1968) is useful for discussion of the way tables suggest analysis. Hirschi and Selvin (1973) present a number of provocative observations on their defects.

[4]See Monkhouse and Wilkinson (1963).

[5]Chernoff's faces offer interesting possibilities (see Wang [1978] and Flury and Riedwyl [1981]), as do dendrograms for analysis of clustering (see Aldendorfer and Blashfield [1984], Lorr [1983], Mezzich and Solomon [1980], Gordon [1981], and Bailey [1974].)

[6]Davis (1963).

[7]See any standard text, for example, Hays (1973), Ferguson (1981), Edwards (1976, 1979). (Notation is not entirely standard, so be careful!)

[8]Achen (1982) points out (pp. 59–61) that social science is interested in prediction errors, for example, residuals, not variance, so other measures than R^2 should be used to measure goodness-of-fit.

[9]For formulas, explanation and discussion, see Edwards (1979, Chapter 3), Kleinbaum and Kupper (1978, Chapter 11), Jacobson (1976, passim under specific measure), and *SPSS Manual*, (Nie et al., 1975, pp. 330–333). Blalock (1979) has an excellent presentation of multiple and partial correlation, with emphasis on causal interpretations.

[10]Roman letters are used here for the parameters to indicate we are dealing with a sample; Greek letters would indicate we are estimating universe (population) parameters. Beware: notation can be very inconsistent from one reference manual to another.

[11]*Multicollinearity* means the determinant of the intercorrelation matrix is too near zero, so variables are "almost" dependent. For a discussion of multicollinearity and its effects in a statistical argument see Asher (1976), Edwards (1979), Lewis-Beck (1980), and *SPSS Manual* (Nie et al. 1975, pp. 340–341).

[12]See Achen (1982, passim); especially useful are pp. 7–30, 35–41, 51–58.

[13]See Lewis-Beck (1980, p. 30).

[14]For details, see Kleinbaum and Kupper (1978, Chapter 13); Lewis-Beck (1980, pp. 66–71); Edwards (1979, Chapter 7); and *SPSS Manual* (Nie et al. 1975, pp. 373–383 and passim). Closely related is the Multiple Classification Analysis procedure; see Andrews et al. (1973) which also includes a comparison of this technique and analysis of variance, or Cohen and Cohen (1983, Chapter 5).

[15]For formulas, see Kleinbaum and Kupper (1978) or Edwards (1979).

[16]References: Hartwig and Dearing (1979); Tukey (1977 [variable transformations]); Hays (1973, pp. 675–684, 700–702); Kleinbaum and Kupper (1978, Chapter 9 [Polynomial Regression]); and *SPSS Manual* (Nie et al., 1975, Chapter 21 [transformations of variables, polynomial regression]).

[17]See, for instance, Stevens' (1972) analysis of social scaling.

[18]Asher (1983) has an excellent recent bibliography, including references to discussions of ordinal and nominal data. Blalock (1961) is more discursive and gives more background. These are both extremely readable and clear. See also *SPSS Manual* (Nie et al. 1975, pp. 383–397); Birnbaum (1981); Boudin (1968); and the data analysis chapter in Bell et al. (1981). Garson (1971) has a very nice chapter on causal modelling and path analysis. Berry (1984) is a good supplement to Asher.

[19]See any mid-level statistics text. We are avoiding formulas in order to eliminate the need to introduce notation.

[20]Most texts—for example, Hays (1973), Roscoe (1975)—illustrate as well as describe these distributions.

[21]See Roscoe (1975, pp. 390–391) or Snedecor and Cochran (1967, p. 290).

[22]See Bradley (1968); Winer (1971); Scheffe (1959); Roscoe (1975, pp. 288–289), Snedecor and Cochran (1975, pp. 296–298).

[23]See Roscoe (1975, pp. 289–290); this can be used only when all columns are of the same length.

[24]See Kleinbaum and Kupper (1978, p. 248) for a succinct summary of this position and necessary safeguards.

[25]The update version also carries out Tukey and Tukey B tests. See Hull and Nie (1981, pp. 397ff).

[26]For an exposition of the technicalities see Kleinbaum and Kupper (1978), Roscoe (1975), Edwards (1979), Ferguson (1981), Winer (1971), Scheffe (1959), and others.

[27]See *SPSS Manual* (Nie et al., 1975, p. 408).

[28]See Roscoe (1975) (several references) for an introductory discussion; also Kleinbaum and Kupper (1978), Winer (1971), and Hull and Nie (1981) for computer options.

[29]Ross and Smith (1968, p. 381); see also Winer (1971) and Spector (1981) for a simple discussion, and Roscoe (1975, passim).

[30]Ross and Smith (1968, pp. 382ff.), Winer (1971), Myers (1979).

[31]A good discussion of alternate problem perspectives is found in Wildt and Ahtola (1977); other excellent references are Edwards (1979, Chapter 12), Kleinbaum and Kupper (1978, Chapter 14); Ferguson (1981); Roscoe (1975, Chapter 41); Cohen and Cohen (1983, passim).

[32]Modifications for special designs and random versus fixed effects models are necessary. See Wildt and Ahtola (1977), Winer (1971), or Scheffe (1959) or Cohen and Cohen (1983); also *SPSS Manual* (Nie et al. 1975; Hull and Nie 1981); and Norusis (1985, Chapter 7).

[33]See Kleinbaum and Kupper (1978, pp. 264–277); *SPSS Manual* (Nie et al., 1975, pp. 426–428); Roscoe (1975, Chapter 28, and pp. 385–388); Winer (1971) (for making decisions); and Scheffe (1959). Keep in mind that there is substantial controversy among statisticians as to the validity and usefulness of a posteriori multiple comparison techniques. It is difficult for the beginner to decide on their relative merits.

Additional Reading

A footnote with references appears in the Notes for each main multivariate technique discussed in this chapter. The references listed here are more general. It would be misleading to label any of them elementary, but we feel they are accessible to the persistent reader.

Causality

See Chapter 1 note 19.

Multivariate Tables

Zeisel (1968): first rate.
Rosenberg (1968)
Davis (1963, 1971)   useful to help conceptualize data layouts.
Wang (1978)
Barnett (1981): emphasis on interpretation.

Exploratory Data Analysis

Hartwig and Dearing (1979)
Tukey (1977)
Mosteller and Tukey (1977): emphasis on regression.
McNeil (1977)
Gordon (1981): multivariate.

General Multivariate Methods

Cohen and Cohen (1983): encyclopedic, many special cases; readable; generalized regression viewpoint.

Scheffe (1959): analysis of variance and multiple comparisons; technical.

Myers (1979): design and modifications in analysis of variance.

Winer (1971): design and modifications in analysis of variance.

Edwards (1979): regression viewpoint in ANOVA, good general discussion.

Bennett and Bowers (1976); straightforward; linear models with emphasis on factor analysis.

Cooley and Lohnes (1962): discriminant analysis and canonical correlation.

Chatfield and Collins (1980): compact, very British; linear models; good section on cluster analysis and scaling.

Shepard et al. (1972): multidimensional scaling, theory and applications.

Anderson (1958): analysis of variance and covariance.

Kleinbaum and Kupper (1978): accessible, lots of examples.

Kachigan (1982): extraordinarily accessible and intuitive; strongly recommended.

Hays (1973): accessible, sensible; but introduction to regression and analysis of variance does not include many of the advanced topics.

Harris (1975): Chapter 1 has a clear heuristic comparison of techniques.

Roscoe (1975): compact, clear; no special cases, tries to be simple.

Overall and Klett (1973): applications viewpoint.

Hair et al. (1979): many examples, heuristic exposition.

Sage Series: a good general "manual" though some units are better; good bibliographies. We particularly recommend Achen (1982) for thought-provoking comments on assumptions and interpretation.

Blalock (1960): clear exposition.

Ferguson (1981): a decent basic text oriented towards psychology and education. The most recent edition has much improved presentation of multivariate procedures.

Bailey (1974)
Bryson and Phillips (1974) } clustering procedures described and compared;
Lorr (1983)   good bibliography; generally readable.
Aldendorfer and Blashfield (1984)

Thompson (1984): good overview of canonical correlation analysis.

Norusis (1985): good chapters on cluster analysis, discriminant analysis, and log-linear procedures.

13

Probabilistic Methods: Multivariate Statistics II

Clustering and Classification Techniques

Introduction

In this chapter, we are concerned primarily with the clustering and classification techniques based on the general linear model. Many of the procedures needed to carry out the classification strategies are highly technical and require extensive practice before they can be comfortably interpreted; therefore, we emphasize geometrical formulations that may help support the analytic descriptions.

Although probability estimates accompany many steps in factor, discriminant, and canonical correlation analysis, these procedures are above all useful for descriptive purposes rather than inferentially for extrapolation from a sample or for comparison of samples. New classification techniques, especially ones that may be used with ordinal or nominal data, are currently being developed in profusion: We will mention them only in passing.

Factor Analysis

Factor analysis is a multivariate "technique" whose purpose is to replace a collection of intercorrelated variables by another set of variables, called *factors*,[1] which will be (1) fewer in number, (2) relatively independent, (3) conceptually meaningful, that is, plausible in theoretical terms. When a factor analysis is successfully carried out in a particular study, the proportion of combined variability accounted for by the factors is approximately the same as that accounted for by the original variables. Factor analysis can be used to find or identify these factors, or to confirm a conjecture as to their number or existence. It is important to keep in mind that factor analysis is, in fact, a large cluster of related strategies for simplifying data, not a single statistical procedure.

These methods were developed initially in the first decade of this century in order to clarify the identification of variables needed to account for individual differences in intelligence and aptitude. The enormous growth in the use of psychological tests, particularly in the past 60 years, spurred research interest in both the mathematical theory and the broadened areas of application. Factor analysis of vast accumulations of social survey data, as in political opinion studies, has been manageable because of the wide availability of computer programs with great flexibility in the choice of alternative approaches. Two "softer" examples may be seen in McNamara and Bahr's (1981) investigation of factors in marital role satisfaction, and James and Kleinbaum's (1976) study of social and economic variables related to hypertension-related mortality rates. The latter is explicated at some length in Kleinbaum and Kupper (1978), Chapter 21.

Any factor analysis starts with a collection of variables and their measures. The "correlation" between each pair of measures can be expressed using any coefficient of association whose values are bounded by -1 and $+1$, such as Pearson's r, Spearman's *rho*, or others listed in Chapter 11.[2]

We adopt the somewhat circular[3] point of view that variables correlate to the extent they measure common attributes, and that data in a large number of intercorrelated variables can be explained in terms of a small number of underlying or inferred variables. Schematically, this can be illustrated in a very simple case by a Venn diagram (Figure 13.1). Suppose that scores on four tests are to be used to predict performance in a specified task and the respective variances are accounted for, as shown by the proportion of overlap in the corresponding circles. The four test scores can be reduced to two so-called factors, one consisting of Scores 1 and 2 suitably combined, the other of Scores 3 and 4, and the explained proportion of the variance of the task score is the same as before. Note that in this example the new factors are independent.

In order to proceed,[4] we will first introduce some vocabulary. Assume the original variables are $X_1, X_2, \ldots, X_n$; a *factor* is a linear combination $F_i = W_{11}X_1 + W_{12}X_2 + \ldots + W_{in}X_n$, $2.i = 1, \ldots, k$. The W's are called *factor weights* and must be estimated from the data. The "correlations" between F's and X's are called *factor loadings*; although they yield much of the same information as factor weights they are not the same thing. "Correlations" between F's are called *factor cosines*, reflecting the standard geometrical interpretation of this technique. To be useful, k should not exceed n. When the value of a factor is calculated for a sampling unit, the resulting number is a *factor score*. The totality of common variance of any two or more factors is called the *factor space*.

Factor analysis rests on the same assumptions of linearity and independence of measurement errors as do the other multivariate techniques we have already described. The mathematical technicalities are formidable; they assume a

FIGURE 13.1 Schematic diagram of a factor space: Scores on four tests $(X_1–X_4)$ used to predict performance on a given task can be reduced to two factors, represented respectively by the overlapping areas of X_1 and X_2, and of X_3 and X_4.

substantial mastery of matrix algebra. It is however possible to acquire an intuitive overview, so we are relegating even a brief description of the formalism to an endnote.[5] We are taking for granted that all calculations are carried out by computer, as in such programs as SPSS, BMDP, or SAS.

The following applies to many if not most factor analysis procedures, but remember there are many modifications and special situations, so that we strongly suggest consulting an expert even if your problem appears quite straightforward.

The first step is the preparation of the correlation matrix. Typically, each variable is correlated with every other variable, and the resulting numbers are set forth in a matrix, that is, a rectangular array (R-type). An alternative, to which we will refer later, uses correlations or measures of association between sampling units to form the matrix (Q-type).

The second step is the extraction of a new set of variables, the so-called initial factors. Either of two approaches can be taken:

1. The first factor is that linear combination of the given variables which accounts for the greatest possible proportion of the variance in the dependent variable. The second factor is the linear combination of the given variables accounting for the greatest possible proportion of the remaining variance in the dependent variable, subject to the further condition that it is uncorrelated with the first factor. Subsequent factors are defined similarly until all the variance is exhausted, but most variance is accounted for by the first few. This approach is called *principal-component analysis* and the new variables *defined factors*.

2. On the basis of empirical evidence or theoretical inference, the existence of several factors is conjectured. Each given variable is written as a sum of a *unique* part and a *common* part, the latter assumed to be a linear combination of the hypothetical factors. The hypothetical *inferred* factors are assumed to be uncorrelated. In order to carry out this approach, called *classical* or *common-factor analysis*, it is necessary to estimate the proportion of the variance of each given variable not accounted for by common factors and not contributing to the intercorrelations of these variables. This is called *unique variance*; its complement is *communality*.

The decision as to which approach to take depends on the purpose of the study and the information available. In practice, common-factor analysis requires a modification of the correlation matrix that incorporates the communalities into the matrix.

The third step is the rotation of the initial factors into *terminal* factors. The set of factors obtained at the second step is not unique but can be transformed mathematically into other statistically equivalent sets of factors, some of which will be more readily interpretable in the context of the original problem. The goal of this step is to achieve a conceptually meaningful set of factors. The major decision is whether to use an *orthogonal* rotation method, yielding *uncorrelated* factors which will be "mathematically simpler to handle," or an *oblique* rotational method, yielding correlated factors which may be "empirically more realistic. . . . [T]he choice should be made on the basis of the particular needs of a given research problem."[6] A variety of strategies for carrying out the rotation is available, many of which have been developed as computer algorithms: varimax, equimax, quartimax and oblimin, quartimin, covarimin. It is essential to find out which ones are employed as options by the particular computer program you select. Naming the terminal factors can be difficult: They do not identify themselves. This aspect involves many subjective considerations; criteria for appropriateness of a name include the magnitude of the factor loadings, as well as theoretical issues. It is easy to fall victim to the illusion that, once named, the factors have "material" existence. (Aldendorfer and Blashfield [1984] observe that other clustering methods offer less danger of reification.)

A final step (R-type) is the computation of the factor scores for each sampling unit so that analysis of these new variables can go forward.

A brief examination of the defects in the factor analysis method is in order. First, not every table of correlations lends itself to factor analysis, either because of the nature of the variables or because of the mathematical character of the table entries. Indiscriminate, turn-the-handle application can lead to erroneous or meaningless conclusions. Second, the decision as to which variables to include, and how to interpret the factors, reflects many metastatistical considerations. Third, the method itself requires decisions at each step, and these generally lead to quite different sets of factors. It may be impossible to evaluate in advance which is the best alternative, so it is necessary to run through the analysis more than once. Fourth, it is necessary to have enough data. Use an R-type factor analysis procedure only if the number of variables is large (over 10) and the number of sampling units (cases) is 10 times the number of variables. For a Q-type analysis, the number of variables should be large (more than ten times the number of proposed clusters), and there should be a high degree of variability between the cases.

Nevertheless, factor analysis can reduce a large number of variables to a small set of meaningful patterns, and as a result it can make a significant contribution to your understanding of a syndrome or a constellation of social variables. A very large number of scales widely used to measure so-called psychological variables (e.g. attitudes) are based on factor analytic reductions of sets of initial variables. More information can potentially be obtained from a thoughtful factor analysis than through alternative multivariate techniques such as regression analysis; factor analysis can also be useful where multicollinearity (high intercorrelations between so-called independent variables) is present.

To illustrate the use of SPSS program FACTOR ANALYSIS, we selected 13 physiological variables, plus age, from those used in the study described in Chapter 11 (note 3), and sought to reduce them to a smaller set which "explains" the same space. The print-out (Figure 13.2) first exhibits the variable list with labels: means, standard deviations, and the correlation matrix for the 62 cases used in the analysis.

The program then computes 14 principal factors, their respective eigenvalues and the percentage of variance each accounts for. Note the first three factors account for 53.5% and the first five for nearly 70%. The computer was instructed to stop forming factors as soon as the percent of variance explained by the factor falls below 7%.

The factor matrix, that is, the factor weights before rotation, is next printed for the first five factors. We can write $F_1 = (-0.74816)$ Var 4 + (-0.66274) Var 7 + (0.16429) Var 8 + ... + (0.73904) Var 76. The communalities (overlap) for the variables are also printed.

We selected rotation of the principal factors using the varimax procedure. The rotated factor matrix is printed in Figure 13.2, showing the factor weights for the rotated factors. The linear functions are expressed as above.

The *transformation matrix* is in effect a correlation matrix of factors. Note however that it is not symmetrical, nor are the main diagonal entries 1's, because the communalities are calculated on a smaller set of factors than the set to which the varimax rotation is applied.

The section of the printout headed Factor Score Coefficients tells us how to evaluate Factor 1, etc. on Case X: Value = $(.0988)(Var\ 4)_x$ + $(-0.05491)(Var\ 7)_x$ + ... + $(-0.32369)(Var\ 76)_x$ and so forth. (This printout also included diagrams showing the location of the selected variables around each pair of factors, but we have deleted most of this section.) It is the task of the researcher to decide whether to use all 14 variables which account for 100% of the factor space, or to use the five factors which leave 30% of the factor space "unexplained." It is also up to the researcher to assign suitable and meaningful labels to the factors.

VARIABLE	MEAN	STANDARD DEV	CASES	LABELS...
VAR4	38.9516	8.3655	62	VO2
VAR7	173.4193	18.6666	62	MAX HEART RATE
VAR8	189.3064	24.4195	62	MAX BLOOD PRESSURE
VAR9	0.5790	0.9587	62	ST DEP
VAR12	67.4677	6.6400	62	HEIGHT
VAR13	175.1129	31.9226	62	WEIGHT
VAR14	138.0806	20.0117	62	RESTING BLOOD PRESSURE
VAR16	75.6452	10.1434	62	RESTING HEART RATE
VAR17	252.0806	43.5329	62	CHOLESTEROL
VAR18	165.8226	77.3726	62	TRIGLYC
VAR19	90.9516	28.1846	62	GLUCOSE
VAR20	10.4644	2.8836	62	PFC
VAR21	3.3452	1.2324	62	FEV
VAR76	52.1774	9.4808	62	AGE

CORRELATION COEFFICIENTS..

	VAR4	VAR7	VAR8	VAR9	VAR12	VAR13	VAR14	VAR16	VAR17	VAR18	VAR19	VAR20	VAR21	VAR76
VAR4	1.00000	0.49984	-0.15601	-0.30695	0.02963	-0.04921	-0.31020	-0.08347	-0.44384	-0.19179	-0.18322	0.56350	0.24445	-0.32275
VAR7	0.49984	1.00000	-0.16853	-0.31582	-0.07911	0.17307	0.00324	0.35050	-0.41754	-0.23612	0.31031	-0.15128	-0.03055	-0.44783
VAR8	-0.15601	-0.16853	1.00000	0.02934	0.18726	0.39855	0.35050	0.10700	0.51747	0.16509	-0.01981	-0.29063	-0.15128	0.15271
VAR9	-0.30695	-0.31582	0.02934	1.00000	0.02934	-0.06404	-0.05579	-0.21437	0.15151	0.20343	-0.01612	-0.20343	0.04799	0.41381
VAR12	0.02963	-0.07911	0.18726	0.02934	1.00000	0.06621	0.21096	-0.16919	0.12712	0.20610	0.12758	0.08804	0.08031	0.14813
VAR13	-0.04921	0.17307	0.39855	-0.06404	0.06621	1.00000	0.33233	0.25372	-0.20078	0.04815	0.34761	0.25279	0.02787	-0.34521
VAR14	-0.31020	0.00324	0.35050	-0.05579	0.21096	0.33233	1.00000	0.02410	-0.08079	-0.08598	0.34710	-0.25969	-0.37437	0.13377
VAR16	-0.08347	0.35050	0.10700	-0.21437	-0.16919	0.25372	0.02410	1.00000	-0.08079	-0.03379	0.29439	0.08375	0.03435	-0.04979
VAR17	-0.44384	-0.41754	0.51747	0.15151	0.12712	-0.20078	-0.08079	-0.08079	1.00000	0.16859	-0.38455	-0.17643	0.39617	0.39617
VAR18	-0.19179	-0.23612	0.16509	0.20343	0.20610	0.04815	-0.08598	-0.03379	0.16859	1.00000	0.36222	0.11226	0.11226	0.21219
VAR19	-0.18322	0.31031	-0.01981	-0.01612	0.12758	0.34761	0.34710	0.29439	-0.38455	0.36222	1.00000	-0.10635	0.02012	-0.31301
VAR20	0.56350	-0.15128	-0.29063	-0.20343	0.08804	0.25279	-0.25969	0.08375	-0.17643	0.11226	-0.10635	1.00000	0.36381	-0.31301
VAR21	0.24445	-0.03055	-0.15128	0.04799	0.08031	0.02787	-0.37437	0.03435	0.39617	0.11226	0.02012	0.36381	1.00000	-0.31301
VAR76	-0.32275	-0.44783	0.15271	0.41381	0.14813	-0.34521	0.13377	-0.04979	0.39617	0.21219	-0.31301	-0.31301	-0.31301	1.00000

DETERMINANT OF CORRELATION MATRIX = 0.00631180(0.63180365D-02)

VARIABLE	EST COMMUNALITY
VAR4	1.000000
VAR7	1.000000
VAR8	1.000000
VAR9	1.000000
VAR12	1.000000
VAR13	1.000000
VAR14	1.000000
VAR16	1.000000
VAR17	1.000000
VAR18	1.000000
VAR19	1.000000
VAR20	1.000000
VAR21	1.000000
VAR76	1.000000

FACTOR	EIGENVALUE	PCT OF VAR	CUM PCT
1	3.33858	23.8	23.8
2	2.39779	17.1	41.0
3	1.74896	12.5	53.5
4	1.20678	8.6	62.1
5	1.02612	7.3	69.4
6	0.84579	6.0	75.5
7	0.73944	5.3	80.7
8	0.68049	4.9	85.6
9	0.54206	3.9	89.5
10	0.46191	3.3	92.8
11	0.33282	2.4	95.1
12	0.29156	2.1	97.2
13	0.24209	1.7	99.0
14	0.14557	1.0	100.0

FIGURE 13.2 SPSS program FACTOR ANALYSIS.

```
FACTOR MATRIX USING PRINCIPAL FACTOR, NO ITERATIONS
                FACTOR  1    FACTOR  2    FACTOR  3    FACTOR  4    FACTOR  5

VAR4            -0.74816     -0.16677      0.03283      0.12340      0.19218
VAR7            -0.66274      0.33194     -0.18956     -0.05209      0.30775
VAR8             0.16429      0.71405     -0.14812      0.43350     -0.00388
VAR9             0.46723     -0.22427      0.15398      0.48940     -0.25893
VAR12            0.03505      0.14641      0.53711      0.54816      0.41695
VAR13           -0.18564      0.70991      0.33623      0.10728     -0.36239
VAR14            0.30419      0.71796     -0.31233     -0.08743     -0.25053
VAR16           -0.14721      0.50987      0.20520     -0.32012      0.47592
VAR17            0.67986     -0.19073      0.13819     -0.37940      0.10661
VAR18            0.42090     -0.04605      0.64746     -0.14615      0.05648
VAR19            0.29671      0.50431      0.49600     -0.31089     -0.04277
VAR20           -0.72916     -0.03257      0.31839      0.08299     -0.11359
VAR21           -0.37312     -0.30839      0.57943     -0.04550     -0.27388
VAR76            0.73904     -0.09930     -0.06108      0.26159      0.35879
VARIABLE        COMMUNALITY

VAR4             0.64080
VAR7             0.68275
VAR8             0.74674
VAR9             0.59887
VAR12            0.78548
VAR13            0.79431
VAR14            0.77596
VAR16            0.65272
VAR17            0.67299
VAR18            0.62303
VAR19            0.68687
VAR20            0.65390
VAR21            0.64714
VAR76            0.75694
        VARIMAX ROTATED FACTOR MATRIX
                FACTOR  1    FACTOR  2    FACTOR  3    FACTOR  4    FACTOR  5

VAR4             0.49148     -0.26079     -0.46213      0.29655      0.17241
VAR7             0.21290      0.11065     -0.45604      0.64351      0.05569
VAR8            -0.27441      0.74814     -0.17660      0.01830      0.28320
VAR9            -0.12824      0.04580      0.11837     -0.70905      0.25212
VAR12            0.06981      0.07729      0.10912      0.00161      0.87334
VAR13            0.39561      0.77380      0.13935      0.10293      0.09496
VAR14           -0.35467      0.75003      0.05173      0.08547     -0.27865
VAR16           -0.02917      0.17891      0.22575      0.73019      0.18901
VAR17           -0.43552     -0.24000      0.62907     -0.11521     -0.12927
VAR18            0.03107     -0.07373      0.73478     -0.10805      0.25503
VAR19            0.02679      0.41116      0.68405      0.21305      0.06156
VAR20            0.74808     -0.03478     -0.21443      0.17470      0.12870
VAR21            0.72982     -0.22059      0.20862     -0.13415      0.06573
VAR76           -0.70949     -0.10824      0.20812     -0.27354      0.35172

TRANSFORMATION MATRIX
                FACTOR  1    FACTOR  2    FACTOR  3    FACTOR  4    FACTOR  5

FACTOR  1       -0.72053      0.08459      0.54123     -0.42450      0.02339
FACTOR  2       -0.10040      0.88869      0.06394      0.43390      0.08823
FACTOR  3        0.54293     -0.02195      0.68219     -0.02923      0.48837
FACTOR  4       -0.01282      0.21890     -0.48515     -0.51621      0.67087
FACTOR  5       -0.41930     -0.39328     -0.04721      0.60348      0.55053
FACTOR SCORE COEFFICIENTS
                FACTOR  1    FACTOR  2    FACTOR  3    FACTOR  4    FACTOR  5

VAR4             0.09881     -0.13245     -0.17137      0.12464      0.16949
VAR7            -0.05491     -0.01878     -0.16574      0.35077      0.09079
VAR8            -0.11435      0.35078     -0.18619     -0.07691      0.22497
VAR9             0.05696      0.11479     -0.05501     -0.46418      0.17116
VAR12           -0.02315     -0.01197     -0.02046      0.02380      0.68403
VAR13            0.26165      0.41253      0.09353     -0.11256     -0.01608
VAR14           -0.08937      0.35788     -0.00669     -0.01348     -0.24167
VAR16           -0.11695     -0.05780      0.17656      0.52437      0.15240
VAR17           -0.13537     -0.16487      0.30665      0.10172     -0.11738
VAR18            0.09055     -0.06268      0.37570      0.02306      0.13110
VAR19            0.08960      0.14820      0.38196      0.15307     -0.03663
VAR20            0.30310      0.02404     -0.02303     -0.02080      0.06779
VAR21            0.38570     -0.03431      0.18818     -0.15965     -0.02440
VAR76           -0.32369     -0.10737     -0.02833     -0.01181      0.32238
```

FIGURE 13.2 (*continued*).

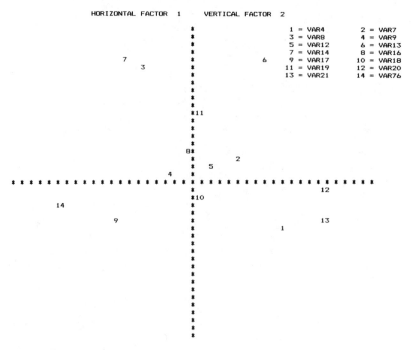

FIGURE 13.2 *(continued)*

Earlier, we mentioned *Q-type factor analysis*: The outcome is a clustering of individuals in such a way that within each cluster the pattern of measures on the given variables is approximately the same. For instance, imagine 25 symptoms observed in 1000 individuals. A factor (cluster) which includes one quarter of the population suggests a common causative agent, so we might seek a unique genetic strain. The "distance" of one case from another can be calculated by applying the usual metric distance formula to the respective factor scores. Q-type analysis is closely related in its goal to discriminant analysis, which we take up in the next section.

Special clustering techniques for special purposes have been developed in great variety. Under the general heading of *cluster analysis* are included multidimensional scaling (see Chapter 7, especially note 31) and others described in Bailey (1974), Bryson and Phillips (1974), Mezzich and Solomon (1980), Chatfield and Collins (1980), Hand (1981), Gordon (1981), and Aldendorfer and Blashfield (1984). All have as their goal reducing the dimension of the data space. Computer routines such as FASTCLUS, available in SAS, are essential if you need to carry out clustering procedures efficiently. Cluster analyses are primarily exploratory (structure-seeking), directed toward the development of a taxonomy to be incorporated in further confirmatory studies.

Discriminant Analysis

Discriminant analysis is a technique designed to serve either, or both, of two purposes: (1) If all the data can be classified a priori into two or more groups,[7] discriminant analysis makes it possible to study the multivariate differences between the groups, identify which variables are the most powerful discriminators (i.e. which contribute the most to placing an observation in its groups), and describe how "close together" or "far apart" the groups lie. (2) If further, as yet unclassified, data are available, discriminant analysis makes it possible to predict their group membership in a systematic way.

Let us first consider an example of two groups. The population of the study we have referred to several times can be classified into two groups according to whether they answer yes or no to the question: "Do you have chest pain?" We may be concerned with the extent to which certain physical status variables discriminate between these groups. Group membership can thus be construed as the dependent variable, while the discriminating variables[8] will be those which, suitably weighted, will yield a linear *discriminating function* whose mean value on group one will be as different as possible from its mean value on group two. It will also be possible to generate two linear *classification functions*, in the same discriminating variables, whose values will allow us to predict to which of the groups an unclassified case will belong, and estimate the error probabilistically. We will also want to know which among the discriminating variables are most important in determining, say, membership in group one, and which among them play virtually no part in discriminating between groups.

A more complicated example is drawn from the domain of medical diagnosis. Imagine that each of five diseases is associated with three or more "symptoms" on a list of ten; the problem of differential diagnosis can be described as that of properly assigning a case exhibiting several symptoms to the appropriate disease category. Assume also that each "symptom" can be measured on an interval scale, for example, temperature, sedimentation rate, etc., and that in a study of a sample of cases, the diagnosis (group assignment) has been made by some means (e.g. observed rash, biopsy) independent of the listed symptoms. Then discriminant analysis of these cases may yield classification functions which will, with high probability, permit assignment of additional cases to the proper disease category on the basis of listed symptoms (discriminating variables). An example from the recent literature is Francken and Van Raiij's (1981) analysis of variables affecting satisfaction with leisure time activities. Once the dependent variable is dichotomized or polyotomized, a discriminant analysis seems a very natural way to proceed.

The basic conceptual strategy involves selecting a set of *discriminating variables* which are associated with group membership, and determining linear combinations of these variables whose means on the different groups are as far apart as possible. These so-called *discriminating functions* can be manipulated to yield the sort of information described above. The mathematical machinery is that of regression analysis and uses matrix theory, the calculus, and probability theory for tests of significance.

Since the details are extremely complicated and require considerable technical sophistication, we will present an overview of the assumptions and the outcomes. Our notation will follow the SPSS manual, or Klecka (1979). For the interested and informed reader, our references[9] provide a further list of mathematical sources.

ASSUMPTIONS AND PROCEDURES

The use of discriminant analysis begins with a population in which two or more groups can be distinguished, such that every case or observation can be assigned to exactly one group. (There may also be unclassifiable cases, but these play no part in the analysis.) Each subject or case has values on one or more discriminating variables. In addition, conditions must be met concerning certain distributions and certain matrices which will be used in the derivation of formulas.

If g = number of groups, p = number of discriminating variables: X_1, $X_2, \ldots, X_p; n_j$ = number of cases in the j th group ($1 \leq j \leq g$); n = total number of cases, we can state our assumptions formally:

1. $g \geq 2$: at least two groups
2. $n_j \geq 2$: at least two cases per group
3. $0 < p < n-2$: any number of discriminating variables, but must be less than the number of cases minus 2.
4. Discriminating variables $X_1, X_2, \ldots X_p$ must be continuous interval or ratio level (as in the case of factor analysis, some authors relax this restriction on level).
5. Discriminating variables are independent: no one is a linear combination of the others, nor are any pair or subset highly intercorrelated. The reason for this should be clear: discrimination based on two correlated or linearly dependent variables will be confused if their effects overlap.
6. Each group is drawn from a population whose distribution on the discriminating variables is multivariate normal.

7. The covariance (intercorrelation) matrices for each group must be approximately equal.

It is important to understand to what extent these assumptions can be violated. Assumptions 6 and 7, which are needed for tests of significance and for computation of the coefficients in the discriminating functions, are fairly robust, but if there are many borderline cases, the accuracy of classification predictions can be impaired. Because of the strong negative effect of the following situations on both accuracy of prediction and interpretation, it is unwise to attempt to apply discriminant analysis[10]

- when there are many unclassifiable cases or much missing data
- when discriminating variables are highly intercorrelated
- when a variable has zero variance on one group or across several groups
- when group sizes n_j are grossly different
- when the data points include several that are far from the others (outliers)

Suppose that we are interested primarily in describing and analyzing the differences between the groups, in terms of the discriminating variables. We start by seeking a *canonical discriminant function* of the form $f = u_o + u_1 X_1 + ... + u_p X_p$ where the u's are numbers; if the mth case in the jth group has value X_{ij_m} on the ith discriminant variable X_i, the function has value

$$f_{j_m} = u_o + u_1 X_{1j_m} + u_2 X_{2j_m} + ... + u_p X_{pj_m}.$$

The *unstandardized coefficients* u for the first such function are determined so that if the mean value of f_j is computed for each j, the group means are as different as possible. The coefficients in the second such function are also derived so that the same maximal-difference-between-means condition is satisfied and also so that the values on the second function are not correlated with values in the first (orthognality). A third function can be defined similarly: Coefficients maximize group-mean differences, values are uncorrelated with those of previous functions, and so forth. The largest possible number of canonical discriminant functions which can be derived in this way is $g - 1$ or p, whichever is fewer. We will denote by q the maximum number of discriminant functions.

Several observations are in order:

1. One or more of the discriminant functions may be statistically insignificant, that is, the information they contribute is not needed in the analysis of which group a case belongs to.
2. There are several procedures for evaluating importance of a later function: a measure of relative percentage of the eigenvalue associated with the function, canonical correlation (see below), and a test of

significance called Wilks' lambda (λ), which tells us the discriminating power of the functions already derived. These are all available in SPSS. It may be appropriate and convenient simply to ignore discriminating functions which are not statistically significant.

3. The details of computing the u's are beyond the scope of this book. Very generally, it requires the formation of three matrices: $T = (n - 1)$ $\times$ total covariance matrix; $W = (n - g) \times$ within groups covariance matrix, and $B = T - W$.[11] The conditions imposed on the discriminant functions can then be translated into equations involving the entries in B and W, which can then be solved. Each solution corresponds to one canonical discriminant function.

4. Since the units in which $X_1, \ldots, X_p$ are measured may be quite disparate, it is extremely difficult to interpret the relative contributions of the discriminating variables by inspecting the coefficients u in the respective discriminant functions. Further tidying up is helpful (see next section).

5. It should also be evident that in some cases the importance of some discriminating variables far exceeds that of others, and this can be exploited to shorten computations and decrease the number of discriminant functions. We take this up briefly below.

INTERPRETING DISCRIMINANT FUNCTIONS

It may be useful to consider a geometrical or spatial interpretation of the discriminant functions. The p discriminating variables define a p-dimensional space in which every data point (case) can be located. Each group, however, is more-or-less concentrated in some portion of the space, and the portion belonging to any group can be summarized by its centroid (mean on each variable). By studying the relative positions of these centroids, we can understand how the data points are grouped. It turns out that q, the number of dimensions needed to describe the "space" of groups, is at most one less than the number of groups. The discriminant functions describe the transformation of the original p-space into the new q-space. A useful way to think about these functions is as "dummy variables" which define the groups.

We can also compute the value of each discriminant function for each data point and compare these discriminant scores with the group centroids. When the number of cases and dimensions is small, this may permit visualization of a sort of territorial map of the data.

Replacement of the canonical discriminant functions by new functions in which each discriminant variable is standardized (z-form) makes possible the interpretation of the *standardized coefficients* as the absolute contribution of each discriminant variable in determining the discriminant score of a data point. These can easily be computed from the unstandardized coefficients u. Further insight into the space of discriminant functions can be achieved by inspecting the *structure coefficients*, which are correlations between single discriminating variables and discriminant functions.

CLASSIFICATION OF CASES[12]

So far we have devoted our attention to the first purpose of discriminant analysis as described on page 317. Classification is a separate—but mathematically related—enterprise whose goal is the assignment of cases to groups. Using either the discriminating variables or the canonical discriminant functions, we can make predictions as to which group a case most likely belongs; we can estimate both the probability of membership and the probability of error. Classification procedures typically involve the comparison of a case to each group centroid and the use of some criterion for evaluating distance.

The simpler approach is adapted from the original suggestion of R. A. Fisher.[13] For each k, $1 \leq k \leq g$, we find a linear classification function of the form where the X's are the discriminating variables and the b's are numerical coefficients derived in terms of the inverse of the matrix W and the means of the X's in the respective groups. (It is not possible to interpret these b's.) The score for the kth group is h_k, a numerical label interpreted as the value of a nominal variable. The group scores can be transformed into probabilities.[14] In order to classify a single case, the group scores $h_1, \ldots, h_g$ are computed for that case, and the case is placed in the group with the highest score (largest h).

(An alternative approach derives the classification functions directly from the canonical discriminant functions. This has the advantage of permitting exploitation of significance tests and of the fact that g may be much less than p. There are, however, drawbacks, and the two approaches may yield different results.)

Unclassified cases can be classified using these functions, and the probabilities of "correct" classification of already grouped data can be tabulated, to give a measure of the effectiveness of the classification functions. From this point of view, discriminant anaysis can be regarded as a natural validation for diagnostic or taxonomic procedures.

CALCULATING PROCEDURES

Discriminant functions can be calculated by either of two procedures. In the direct method, all the discriminating variables are entered concurrently. In the stepwise procedure, variables are entered on the basis of their discriminating power. Five measures of discriminating power are available: (1) Mahalonobis, (2) Maximin, (3) Minimum Residual Distance, (4) Wilks' λ, and (5) Rao's V. The first three criteria yield similar results for groups of equal size. Both Wilks' λ and Rao's V can be converted into chi-square distributions, the values tested for significance and easily interpreted, so they are commonly preferred.

If a discriminating variable contributes significantly to the explanation of a group, as measured by Wilks or Rao, it will be included in the discriminant function, otherwise not. Thus, the discriminant functions will be more parsimonious than if all variables were used in each function, but will differ only insignificantly in effectiveness as predictors of assignment.

The canonical correlation coefficient can be employed to give information on the usefulness of the discriminant function. First, each discriminant function can be compared with the set of $(g - 1)$ dummy variables representing the g groups; the coefficient will have a value between 0 (no relationship) and 1 (perfect relatedness) and can be computed from the function's eigenvalue. The larger the correlation, the better the discriminating variables work to separate the groups.

To illustrate the foregoing we examine a portion of the printout of a set of calculations carried out using the SPSS program DISCRIMINANT ANALYSIS. (We have deleted the covariance matrices which are not directly interpretable, as well as the centroids and unstandardized coefficients.) Using the data from the study described earlier in Chapter 11 (note 3), we seek support for the conjecture that the physiological variables maximum and resting heart rate, cholesterol, maximum blood pressure, systolic depression and fever discriminate between the groups labelled 1 = yes, 2 = no, determined by Var 46 chest pain. Seventy-five cases were available for the analysis (see Figure 13.3).

We first see group and total means and standard deviations for each of the six proposed discriminating variables. "Eyeballing" suggests that Vars 7 and 8 and, possibly, Var 9 may be useful as discriminators. Wilks' lambda is computed for each variable: These numbers can be interpreted as correlations of the variables with the first discriminant function. We see that only the value for Var 7 is significant ($p = .0023$); that for Var 8 ($p = .0741$) may be useful. The other variables are poor discriminators.

The program then prints the instructions it is following in making decisions. There are two classification functions, whose coefficients are listed next. To use this information, select a case, and for it, compute .5809004 Var 7 + .2070816 Var 8 + ... + 3.338217 Var 21 − 110.6833 and compare with .6253420 Var 7 + .2167571 Var 8 + ... + 3.105552 Var 21 − 118.2401. If the first number is the larger, the case should be assigned to group 1, if the second, to group 2.

ON GROUPS DEFINED BY VAR46   CHEST PAIN

```
     274 (UNWEIGHTED) CASES WERE PROCESSED.
     199 OF THESE WERE EXCLUDED FROM THE ANALYSIS.
       2 HAD MISSING OR OUT-OF-RANGE GROUP CODES.
     178 HAD AT LEAST ONE MISSING DISCRIMINATING VARIABLE.
      19 HAD BOTH.
      75 (UNWEIGHTED) CASES WILL BE USED IN THE ANALYSIS.
```

NUMBER OF CASES BY GROUP

VAR46	NUMBER OF CASES UNWEIGHTED	NUMBER OF CASES WEIGHTED	LABEL
1	29	29.0	
2	46	46.0	
TOTAL	75	75.0	

GROUP MEANS

VAR46	VAR7	VAR8	VAR9	VAR16	VAR17	VAR21
1	164.72414	179.13793	0.73448	74.82759	258.34483	3.49655
2	178.10870	190.65217	0.52391	76.15217	248.19565	3.22609
TOTAL	172.93333	186.20000	0.60533	75.64000	252.12000	3.33067

GROUP STANDARD DEVIATIONS

VAR46	VAR7	VAR8	VAR9	VAR16	VAR17	VAR21
1	22.41475	27.20389	0.76591	10.93836	51.39224	1.52888
2	14.37935	26.53988	1.04247	10.40078	43.25306	0.88930
TOTAL	18.94468	27.20691	0.94524	10.55826	46.49498	1.17600

POOLED WITHIN-GROUPS CORRELATION MATRIX

	VAR7	VAR8	VAR9	VAR16	VAR17	VAR21
VAR7	1.00000					
VAR8	0.17416	1.00000				
VAR9	-0.29057	0.15139	1.00000			
VAR16	0.37519	0.01022	-0.15776	1.00000		
VAR17	-0.34225	-0.03479	0.17474	0.01518	1.00000	
VAR21	0.12686	-0.14886	0.06985	0.06870	-0.18002	1.00000

CORRELATIONS WHICH CANNOT BE COMPUTED ARE PRINTED AS 99.0.

WILKS' LAMBDA (U-STATISTIC) AND UNIVARIATE F-RATIO
WITH 1 AND   73 DEGREES OF FREEDOM

VARIABLE	WILKS' LAMBDA	F	SIGNIFICANCE
VAR7	0.88002	9.952	0.0023
VAR8	0.95695	3.284	0.0741
VAR9	0.98807	0.8813	0.3510
VAR16	0.99622	0.2772	0.6001
VAR17	0.98855	0.8457	0.3608
VAR21	0.98729	0.9401	0.3355

FIGURE 13.3 SPSS program DISCRIMINANT ANALYSIS.

```
ON GROUPS DEFINED BY VAR46        CHEST PAIN
ANALYSIS NUMBER        1
DIRECT METHOD:   ALL VARIABLES PASSING THE TOLERANCE TEST ARE ENTERED.
       MINIMUM TOLERANCE LEVEL................. 0.00100
CANONICAL DISCRIMINANT FUNCTIONS
       MAXIMUM NUMBER OF FUNCTIONS..............           1
       MINIMUM CUMULATIVE PERCENT OF VARIANCE... 100.00
       MAXIMUM SIGNIFICANCE OF WILKS' LAMBDA....   1.0000
PRIOR PROBABILITY FOR EACH GROUP IS 0.50000

CLASSIFICATION FUNCTION COEFFICIENTS
(FISHER'S LINEAR DISCRIMINANT FUNCTIONS)
VAR46  =           1                2
VAR7         0.5809004        0.6253420
VAR8         0.2070816        0.2167571
VAR9         1.526166         1.482075
VAR16        0.2739232        0.2584382
VAR17        0.2086576        0.2091652
VAR21        3.338217         3.105552
(CONSTANT)  -110.6833        -118.2401

                    CANONICAL DISCRIMINANT FUNCTIONS

                  PERCENT OF   CUMULATIVE              CANONICAL :  AFTER
FUNCTION  EIGENVALUE  VARIANCE    PERCENT              CORRELATION : FUNCTION  WILKS' LAMBDA  CHI-SQUARED  D.F.  SIGNIFICANCE

                                                                  :     0       0.8450095      11.789      6    0.0669
1*        0.18342    100.00     100.00               0.3936883   :
* MARKS THE   1 CANONICAL DISCRIMINANT FUNCTION(S) TO BE USED IN THE REMAINING ANALYSIS.

STANDARDIZED CANONICAL DISCRIMINANT FUNCTION COEFFICIENTS
             FUNC 1
VAR7         0.91652
VAR8         0.29883
VAR9        -0.04807
VAR16       -0.18937
VAR17        0.02723
VAR21       -0.31548
POOLED WITHIN-GROUPS CORRELATIONS BETWEEN CANONICAL DISCRIMINANT FUNCTIONS AND DISCRIMINATING VARIABLES
VARIABLES ARE ORDERED BY THE FUNCTION WITH LARGEST CORRELATION AND THE MAGNITUDE OF THAT CORRELATION.
             FUNC 1
VAR7         0.86214
VAR8         0.49525
VAR21       -0.26497
VAR9        -0.25655
VAR17       -0.25133
VAR16        0.14389
UNSTANDARDIZED CANONICAL DISCRIMINANT FUNCTION COEFFICIENTS
             FUNC 1
VAR7         0.5122166D-01
VAR8         0.1115166D-01
VAR9        -0.5081790D-01
VAR16       -0.1784747D-01
VAR17        0.5850590D-03
VAR21       -0.2681605
(CONSTANT)  -8.807980
```

FIGURE 13.3 *(continued).*

324

CANONICAL DISCRIMINANT FUNCTIONS EVALUATED AT GROUP MEANS (GROUP CENTROIDS)

GROUP	FUNC 1
1	-0.53215
2	0.33548

TEST OF EQUALITY OF GROUP COVARIANCE MATRICES USING BOX'S M
THE RANKS AND NATURAL LOGARITHMS OF DETERMINANTS PRINTED ARE THOSE
OF THE GROUP COVARIANCE MATRICES.

GROUP LABEL	RANK	LOG DETERMINANT
1	6	24.892591
2	6	23.199974
POOLED WITHIN-GROUPS COVARIANCE MATRIX	6	24.379269

BOX'S M	APPROXIMATE F	DEGREES OF FREEDOM	SIGNIFICANCE
38.695	1.6669	21, 13090.7	0.0283

SYMBOLS USED IN PLOTS

SYMBOL	GROUP LABEL
1	1
2	2
#	ALL UNGROUPED CASES

```
              ALL-GROUPS STACKED HISTOGRAM
           -- CANONICAL DISCRIMINANT FUNCTION 1 --

   16 +                                                                  +
      .                                                                  .
      .                                                                  .
   12 +                                                                  .
      .                                                                  .
      .                                                                  .
F   8 +                                                                  +
R     .                                                2                 .
E     .                                                2                 .
Q     .                                                22                .
U     .                                                22                .
E     .                                                22  2             .
N   4 +                               2 #              22  22 2          +
C     .                     # 2 2            2         12  12222         .
Y     .                     122 122   112212222        2                .
   -1 .            1 2  121112121211111112  22 22                        .
   -1 .   1  1 2  2111                                                   .
  OUT +...+....+....+....+....+....+....+....+....+....+....+....+....OUT
      -3   -2   -1    0    1    2    3
```

GROUP CENTROIDS

CLASSIFICATION RESULTS -

ACTUAL GROUP	NO. OF CASES	PREDICTED GROUP MEMBERSHIP	
		1	2
GROUP 1	29	16 55.2%	13 44.8%
GROUP 2	46	11 23.9%	35 76.1%
UNGROUPED CASES	2	2 100.0%	0 0.0%

PERCENT OF "GROUPED" CASES CORRECTLY CLASSIFIED: 68.00%

FIGURE 13.3 (continued).

325

Since there are two groups, one canonical discriminant function can be computed. The canonical correlation of the "dummy" group membership variable with the discriminant function scores is .3936883, which tells us the function is a relatively poor predictor of group membership. Standardized coefficients of this function are given: Thus if z_7 is standardized Var 7, etc., the linear form $0.91652z_7 + 0.29883z_8 + \ldots + (-0.31548)z_{21}$ will separate Groups 1 and 2 as well as possible with these variables. Unstandardized (raw score) coefficients are also printed, but we have deleted these.

Finally, the correlation between the discriminant functions f_1 and each of the discriminating variables is given. Notice that the correlation between f_1 and Var 7 is .86214, by far the largest of those computed, and that between f_1 and Var 8 is .49525, while all the others reflect a weak association.

We conclude from this analysis that this set of discriminating variables is a relatively poor set of predictors to use in assigning individuals to yes–no groups on the chest pain variable, or for predicting probable future reports of chest pain.

It is disconcerting to note that often variables that are excellent discriminators between groups do not emerge in an analysis of variance with large differences of means. The discriminant analysis and ANOVA procedures exhibit different aspects of the variables' interrelationships.

A LAST WORD ON DISCRIMINANT ANALYSIS

It should be clear from all the preceding that discriminant analysis is analogous to the multiple regression procedure where (1) the dependent variable may be nominal and (2) the equation is recalculated for each value of the dependent variable. The technique can be used to classify cases into groups known in advance and to "explain" the relationship of the classification to the set of discriminating variables. If the group identification or the number of groups is unknown, then factor analysis or some other cluster procedure would be more appropriate.

Finally, the procedure known as canonical correlation analysis (see next section) can be carried out, to investigate how well the set of classification functions "explains" the group labels.

Canonical Correlation Analysis[15]

Canonical correlation analysis (also called conjoint analysis) is a multivariate technique—more accurately, a set of techniques—that represents yet another and perhaps the most general exploitation of the linear model. Bivariate or multiple correlation and regression analysis and discriminant function analysis can all be regarded as special cases of canonical correlation analysis; so also, in many ways, can factor analysis. This procedure offers an approach to the question: Given a set of variables $X_1, X_2 \ldots, X_p$ and a set of variables $Y_1, Y_2, \ldots Y_q$ representing observations on the same N sampling units, what is the pattern of associations between the two sets, and how strong are these associations? Note that the X's and Y's may be labelled independent and dependent, respectively, but this is certainly not essential. The analysis is symmetrical. It seems to us, in view of the accessibility of computers, that "cancorr" analysis might profitably be used for exploration, seeking the subsets X and Y that will maximize the correlations described below.

The basic strategy is conceptually simple. If $\sum_{i=1}^{p} a_i X_i$ and $\sum_{j=1}^{q} b_j Y_j$ are any linear combinations of X's and Y's respectively, these two forms can be thought of as new formal variables which take on values for the N units of observation, so it is possible to compute the (bivariate) Pearson product-moment correlation[16] r between the two combinations. By suitably adjusting the values of the a's and b's, we can make the value of r a maximum, so that a maximum amount of the association between the X's and Y's is "explained."

A few examples will illustrate the sort of problems suitable for canonical correlation analysis:

1. A study of which educational and environmental attributes of individuals have the greatest impact on the pattern of their expenditures under specified headings, for example housing, transportation, entertainment.[17]

2. A study of "the degree to which the distribution of expenditures within nations across various socially desirable activities could be accounted for by the basic socio-economic and political characteristics of the nations".[18]

3. A study of how such variables as family educational and income level, travel time, and number of hours worked, as well as standardized and high-school test scores, "explain" the overall pattern of performance in the college major and in specified required courses.

4. A study of the relationships between amounts of specified nutrients (including polyunsaturated or saturated fats) in a regulated diet, the weight and age of the subject, and blood pressure and levels of blood cholesterols and certain other elements.

It is not easy to find examples of research reports using canonical correlation analysis although some are cited in the listed references: This state of affairs probably reflects a lack of familiarity on the part of most investigators.[19] One of the relatively few examples is Ohnmacht and Olson (1968), which deals with reading readiness measures and visual perception test scores.

Use of the canonical correlation technique rests on a number of assumptions. These include:

1. The data are all interval-level.
2. The data are normally distributed on each variable (this assumption is necessary in order to apply tests of statistical significance).
3. The relationship among variables or sets of variables is linear.
4. The population correlation and covariance matrices are positive definite (all principal diagonal minors are greater than zero).

We now look at the procedure in somewhat greater detail. For each of the N sampling units (individuals, communities, or whatever) a measurement is made on each of the p variables X_i ($l \le i \le p$) and on each of the q variables Y_j ($\le j \le q$).

The first step is to determine

$$x_1 = a_{11}X_1 + a_{12}X_2 + \ldots + a_{1p}X_p$$

and

$$y_1 = b_{11}Y_1 + b_{12}Y_2 + \ldots + b_{1q}Y_q$$

as those linear combinations which meet the conditions:

1. $r_{x_1y_1}$ is the maximum correlation achievable for all possible selections of a's and b's (Thus each pair of candidates for x and y is evaluated at each data point, and the correlation determined. The winner is the pair producing the largest r).
2. $\overline{x}_1 = \overline{y}_1 = 0$ (The means of each of x_1 and y_1 across all data points is zero).

Once found, x_1 and y_1 are called the first pair of *canonical variates* and $r_{x_1y_1}$ the (first) *canonical correlation*. When x_1 and y_1 are evaluated at a particular data point, the result is a pair of canonical variate scores.

Now, for the second step, repeat the first: Seek

$$x_2 = a_{21}X_1 + \ldots + a_{2p}X_p$$

and

$$y_2 = b_{21}Y_1 + \ldots + b_{2q}Y_q,$$

linear combinations such that $r_{x_2y_2}$ is a maximum across all choices of a's and b's across all data points, $\overline{x}_2 = \overline{y}_2 = 0$, and, in addition, $r_{x_1x_2} = r_{y_1y_2} = r_{x_1y_2} = r_{x_2y_1} = 0$, that is, x_2 and y_2 are uncorrelated with x_1 and y_1 and with each other; x_2 and y_2 are called the second pair of canonical variates and $r_{x_2y_2}$ the second canonical correlation.

Continue in this way to form linear combinations

$$x_h = \sum_{i=1}^{p} a_{h_i} X_i$$

and

$$y_h = \sum_{j=1}^{q} b_{h_j} Y_j$$

subject to:

1. $\overline{x}_h = \overline{y}_h = 0$ (means of the canonical variate across the data points are zero),
2. $r_{x_h y_k} = r_{x_h x_k} = r_{y_h y_k} = 0$ for $h \neq k$ (x's and y's formed at different steps are orthogonal [uncorrelated]), and
3. $r_{x_h y_h}$ is the maximum for all possible a's and b's which meet the preceding constraints. (It will always fall between -1 and $+1$.)

The number of such pairs of canonical variates cannot exceed the lesser of p and q.

The outcome of all these calculations can be interpreted, with some caution. If the X and Y variables are standardized, the coefficients a and b indicate the contribution of each variable to the respective canonical variate scores. The square of $r_{x_1 y_1}$ can be regarded as a coefficient of determination, indicating the proportion of variance in y_1, accounted for by variance in x_1, and likewise for the squares of the other canonical correlations. The terminology eigenvalue rather than coefficient of determination is used, because of the underlying matrix-theoretical arguments. The eigenvalues decrease as the process proceeds: $r_{x_1 y_1}^2 > r_{x_2 y_2}^2 > \ldots$.

Needless to say, the calculations required for this analysis are feasible only if a suitable computer program is available. Typically, output will include the coefficients a and b for each canonical variate, each canonical correlation coefficient, and each eigenvalue. The canonical variate scores are optional. Some programs omit another very useful set of calculations: the correlations of the original variables with each canonical variate. The two resulting so-called canonical structure matrices, one for the X's and x's, one for the Y's and y's, are used to define *redundancy*,[20] a concept whose purpose is to allow us to reject variates because they contribute little more to the "explanation" of the relationships between X's and Y's.

Wilks' lambda (λ) should be calculated for each pair of canonical variates, that is for each canonical correlation. This statistic is used to test the null hypothesis that no residual linear association between the X's and Y's remains after the canonical variates are extracted. Lambda is transformed into a chi-square value; a table should be used to compare the actual value with the critical value for the degrees of freedom and the specified level of significance; if a computer program is used, the value and significance level will appear on the printout. If the null hypothesis is rejected, the next variate is calculated; otherwise, the process stops.

There are a number of special problems and extensions of the canonical correlation model. Among these are: verifying linear dependence (multicollinearity) among the variables, which may cause difficulties in inverting the intercorrelation matrix; developing tests of significance; interpreting "variance of the two sets X and Y"; and determining the smallest number of pairs of canonical variates. Three or more sets of variables may be given, so partial canonical correlations may be desirable. (If you are interested in such additional topics, consult Cooley and Lohnes or other references.)

To illustrate the canonical correlation technique and its interpretation, we inspect the printout of the SPSS program CAN CORR. It is based on a relatively simple example in which we select certain of the physiological variables used in the study described earlier, and look at both the pretest and the posttest measurements. Our goal is some insight into "how much of the post-space is accounted for by the pre-space" (see Figure 13.4).

The first item is the list of variables to be used, together with respective means and standard deviations for the 27 complete cases in which the analysis is based. (On consulting the list of variables in Chapter 11 [note 3], you will observe that certain variables have pre- or post-test values only: certain variables were deleted because a preliminary set of calculations revealed that since, for example, pre-height and post-height correlations are essentially perfect, retention of both variables would reduce the rank of the correlation matrix needed to carry out the procedure.) The correlation matrix for these thirteen variables, seven pre-(X's), six post-(Y's), is also printed. It may suggest which pre- and post-variables are doing the work in accounting for any relationship between the pre-space and post-space.

The program next computes six pairs of canonical variates. Thus the first pair of canonical variates has correlation .94721, explaining 89.72% of variance, (correlation squared = eigenvalue, which is a coefficient of determination). Wilks' lambda (λ) tests the hypothesis that no residual linear association between X's and Y's remains; the value .00484 is translated into the chi-square value of 101.29276 with $df = 42$ which is highly significant. The second pair have correlation .89823 and eigenvalue .80681; Wilks' lambda (λ), .04707, has significance at better than .01. For the third pair of canonical variates, the correlation is .82613 but Wilks' lambda (λ) has significance .140

which is "below" .05. Although subsequent pairs of variates are computed by the program, together with their correlations and significance levels, the programmer's instructions were to print out coefficients only for pairs of variates whose significance was .05 or better.

Thus we see the first pair of variates Can Var 1 can be written

$$(-0.77870)\text{Var}4 + (-0.24604)\text{Var } 7 + ... + (-0.21998)\text{Var } 14 \text{ and}$$
$$(-0.70880)\text{Var}173 + (-0.31746)\text{Var}176 + ... + (-0.12209)\text{Var } 186;$$

if the two sets of values for all 27 cases are computed, the correlation .94721 should appear. Similarly for the second pair of variates Can Var 2,

$$(-1.60428)\text{Var } 4 + ... + (-0.39209) \text{ Var } 14 \text{ and}$$
$$(-1.60107)\text{Var } 176 + ... + (-0.02600) \text{ Var } 186.$$

As we have indicated in the text, certain other information that might be useful is not computed by this program.

Our conclusion based on this analysis is that there appears to be a strong relationship between these pre- and post-variables. The researcher, thus, can decide whether to use these two pairs of canonical variables rather than the 7 prevariables and 6 postvariables. A suitable set of labels must also be devised so that the canonical variates will have meanings appropriate to the study, and this may be a challenging task, as in the case of labelling of factors.

Multivariate Linear Methods: Some Comparisons

In Chapter 12 and the preceding sections of this chapter, we have discussed a number of techniques which are related in two senses: through the mathematical assumptions and methods brought to bear on their solution, and through the problems to which they may be applied. Without trying to be exhaustive, we will mention a few of their similarities and differences. Some of these have already been pointed out.

All the techniques rest on the assumed existence of a matrix of pairwise intercorrelations between an assortment of variables, one or more of which may be labelled dependent and two or more independent. The goal of each technique is the transformation of this matrix into a simpler form, usually one with zeroes off the main diagonal, or with specified submatrices of simpler form. (The Sage monographs cited in the Additional Reading list take this view consistently.) This transformation serves two purposes: (1) When it has been accomplished, the outcome can be interpreted as the replacement of the given variables by a smaller number of variables which fill up the same space of data points. We can see this strategy in the cases of factor analysis,

VARIABLE	MEAN	STANDARD DEV	CASES
VAR4	34.8148	9.9268	27
VAR7	155.8889	27.3444	27
VAR8	171.1111	25.8358	27
VAR9	1.1593	1.1946	27
VAR12	68.6296	2.7617	27
VAR13	167.8148	22.9950	27
VAR14	126.0741	16.1196	27
VAR173	39.6667	9.5636	27
VAR176	163.9259	22.8152	27
VAR177	180.3704	27.0841	27
VAR183	133.3333	15.4322	27
VAR185	71.2963	10.7088	27
VAR186	238.8519	49.7089	27

CORRELATION COEFFICIENTS
A VALUE OF 99.00000 IS PRINTED
IF A COEFFICIENT CANNOT BE COMPUTED.

	VAR4	VAR7	VAR8	VAR9	VAR12	VAR13	VAR14	VAR173	VAR176	VAR177	VAR183	VAR185	VAR186
VAR4	1.00000	0.82429	0.36135	-0.58154	0.05352	0.15452	0.09431	0.87644	0.74529	0.18137	-0.07666	0.27334	0.06619
VAR7	0.82429	1.00000	0.46599	-0.61193	-0.03622	0.28091	0.23143	0.70449	0.87603	0.30490	0.01003	0.37143	0.01046
VAR8	0.36135	0.46599	1.00000	-0.19412	-0.28079	0.09423	0.47190	0.21232	0.39908	0.76099	-0.35693	0.24482	-0.03533
VAR9	-0.58154	-0.61193	-0.19412	1.00000	-0.21926	-0.37341	-0.19517	-0.51462	-0.61523	-0.03615	0.04520	-0.21188	0.12153
VAR12	0.05352	-0.03622	-0.28079	-0.21926	1.00000	0.61543	-0.28102	0.25145	0.21014	-0.22126	-0.11612	0.04417	0.01219
VAR13	0.15452	0.28091	0.09423	-0.37341	0.61543	1.00000	-0.08214	0.25348	0.47825	0.06273	-0.01553	0.37868	0.14130
VAR14	0.09431	0.23143	0.47190	-0.19517	-0.28102	-0.08214	1.00000	0.12990	0.16588	0.51266	0.40405	0.18213	-0.17605
VAR173	0.87644	0.70449	0.21232	-0.51462	0.25145	0.25348	0.12990	1.00000	0.79487	0.10265	-0.19232	0.17338	-0.04509
VAR176	0.74529	0.87603	0.39908	-0.61523	0.21014	0.47825	0.16588	0.79487	1.00000	0.31549	-0.15046	0.41773	-0.02131
VAR177	0.18137	0.30490	0.76099	-0.03615	-0.22126	0.06273	0.51266	0.10265	0.31549	1.00000	0.40293	0.29639	0.09152
VAR183	-0.07666	0.01003	-0.35693	0.04520	-0.11612	-0.01553	0.40405	-0.19232	-0.15046	0.40293	1.00000	-0.00714	-0.13681
VAR185	0.27334	0.37143	0.24482	-0.21188	0.04417	0.37868	0.18213	0.17338	0.41773	0.29639	-0.00714	1.00000	0.14076
VAR186	0.06619	0.01046	-0.03533	0.12153	0.01219	0.14130	-0.17605	-0.04509	-0.02131	0.09152	-0.13681	0.14076	1.00000

NUMBER	EIGENVALUE	CANONICAL CORRELATION	WILK S LAMBDA	CHI-SQUARE	D.F.	SIGNIFICANCE
1	0.89720	0.94721	0.00484	101.29276	42	0.000
2	0.80681	0.89823	0.04707	58.06818	30	0.002
3	0.68249	0.82613	0.24363	26.83029	20	0.140
4	0.16235	0.40293	0.76731	5.03249	12	0.957
5	0.08213	0.28659	0.91603	1.66648	6	0.948
6	0.00201	0.04480	0.99799	0.03816	2	0.981

COEFFICIENTS FOR CANONICAL VARIABLES OF THE FIRST SET

	CANVAR 1	CANVAR 2
VAR4	-0.77870	-1.60428
VAR7	-0.24604	1.44162
VAR8	0.07776	0.16459
VAR9	-0.14558	-0.39364
VAR12	-0.16110	-0.02467
VAR13	-0.21076	0.09580
VAR14	-0.21998	-0.39209

COEFFICIENTS FOR CANONICAL VARIABLES OF THE SECOND SET

	CANVAR 1	CANVAR 2
VAR173	-0.70880	-1.60107
VAR176	-0.31746	1.86983
VAR177	0.04359	-0.34012
VAR183	-0.20724	0.12927
VAR185	-0.14430	-0.19278
VAR186	-0.12209	-0.02600

FIGURE 13.4 SPSS program CAN CORR (canonical correlation).

333

discriminant analysis, and canonical correlation analysis. (2) The simplification of a matrix permits the solution of a system of linear equations, determined perhaps by a minimum or maximum condition derived by using elementary calculus. We see this strategy in regression analysis, where we seek the "best" hyper-plane (line) as determined by a least-squares criterion.

A secondary mathematical theme is the decomposition of the variation around some location, whether it be a mean or a "line", into portions attributable to specified sources within the data. Then the respective portions are compared to assess the relative importance of these sources of variation. The form of the argument differs according to whether the independent variables are nominal or interval, but the overall strategy of regression analysis, analysis of variance, and analysis of covariance is the same. In ANOVA, the differences of data points from the group means is the "error" whereas in classical regression analysis, the differences of data points from the best line is the "error": If the group means fall on a line the two approaches coincide.[21] From both the theoretical and the practical (design) points of view it may be convenient to exploit the equivalence of multiple regression/correlation and anova/ancova.

Factor analysis seeks to reduce the number of variables, replacing the given ones by linear combinations that account for the same variance but which are uncorrelated; another way of thinking about this is to observe that factor analysis *seeks* clusters of variables. Discriminant analysis also seeks to reduce the number of variables, to the minimum needed to assign individuals to already specified categories; thus, this technique can be regarded as an extension of regression analysis to the case in which the dependent variable is nominal.

Canonical correlation analysis also resembles (principal component) factor analysis in that its goal is a set of mutually uncorrelated linear combinations. However, in factor analysis the combinations are selected so as to fill up the space determined by the variables; and in canonical analysis, they fill up the space determined by the relationship between two sets of variables. (In discriminant analysis they fill up the space of the relationship between the discriminating variables and the groups). This filling is formulated more precisely in terms of variance accounted for, or in terms of the dimension of a geometrical space.

Problems of interpretation in all methods arise in large part from the need to disentangle overlapping effects, the result of relatively large intercorrelations among the original variables, or of interaction which involves three or more variables.

In this and the preceding chapter we have described and compared the most familiar multivariate techniques based on the general linear model. We have only scratched the surface: Each procedure has many special modifications and extensions; in addition, each has been applied in a wide variety of research situations in that the outcomes of data analysis require careful interpretation. Some authors, such as Cohen and Cohen (1983) believe that multiple regression/correlation analysis, in which they include factor and discriminant analysis, can be adapted to any level of data. We prefer the more traditional conservative point of view that it should be restricted to data that meet the conditions listed in Chapter 12 (section on assumptions). In the next chapter, we describe briefly some of the methods which can be used when these conditions cannot be satisfied.

Notes

[1]Not to be confused with factors as this terminology is used in analysis of variance.

[2]Kim and Mueller (1979b, pp. 73ff.). state very strongly that factor analysis should be restricted to interval variables, use of ordinal variables leads to difficulties in interpretation, and use of dichotomous variables is entirely unjustified. Many other authors such as Kleinbaum and Kupper (1978), adopt a much looser standard, and base the analysis on any measure of association which permit interpretation as proportion of variation.

[3]See footnote *SPSS Manual* (Nie et al. 1975, pp. 471), quoting Rozeboom.

[4]Our discussion follows that of Kleinbaum and Kupper (1978, Chapter 21), and Kim (*SPSS Manual*, Nie et al., 1975, Chapter 24). We have also drawn on Kim and Mueller, (1979a,b). See also Kerlinger (1973, Chapter 37), which is presented very intuitively. Kachigan (1982) also emphasizes heuristic rather than detail. Harmon (1960) is still good. Bennett and Bowers (1976) address a variety of techniques, for example, multidimensional scaling, from a factor analysis viewpoint.

[5]This description applies to R-type principal-component factor analysis, and presupposes an acquaintance with matrix algebra. The machine starts off by calculating a matrix R of intercorrelations.

The correlation r_{12} between two variables, represented as vectors V_1 and V_2, can be interpreted geometrically as $r_{12} = V_1 V_2 \cos \angle (1,2)$ where $\angle (1,2)$ is the angle between the vectors, and V_1, V_2 are their respective lengths. This is illustrated in Figure 13.5.

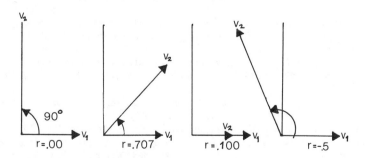

FIGURE 13.5 The correlation between two variables can be represented geometrically as the angle between vectors.

From the mathematics of matrix algebra we know that if R has some rank k, then R has k nonzero eigenvalues (characteristic roots) $\lambda_1, \lambda_2, \ldots, \lambda_k$. Each eigenvalue λ_i will have associated with it a uniquely determined eigenvector V_i, which satisfies the matrix equation $RV_i = \lambda_i V_i$; the eigenvectors $V_1, \ldots, V_k$ are orthogonal. Moreover, the product of the eigenvalues is equal to the determinant of R, and, most important, the largest eigenvalue represents the amount of variance explained by V_1, the second largest the amount explained by V_2, etc. Thus the eigenvalue λ_i can be interpreted as k times the square of the correlation between the ith factor F_i and the dependent variable. Finding the eigenvectors for R constitutes principal-component analysis. The vectors $V_1, V_2, \ldots, V_k$ are regarded as new axes for the factor space.

The third step in factor analysis is usually the rotation of the eigenvectors (axes) or factors into new positions so that for each new factor the factor loadings for most of the original variables are near zero and for the remaining few variables are relatively large. Intuitively this means that the new rotated factors "separate" the data; ideally, such an outcome makes possible meaningful interpretation of the rotated factors. The rotation is accomplished by a linear transformation of the rows of the factor matrix; the choice of linear transformation, that is, of rotation procedure, will depend upon which additional assumptions or constraints are introduced. Most important among these is the decision to preserve orthogonality of the rotated factors, as against permitting a relaxation of this condition (oblique rotation). The latter may be desirable to achieve a low correlation between rotated factors. A variety of computer procedures is available for rotation: Consult your manual.

The preceding suggests that undertaking a factor analysis in the absence of a fair amount of mathematical sophistication would be extremely hazardous to both the validity and the value of the outcome. All authors emphasize the need to buy or otherwise acquire the necessary expertise before proceeding. Our goal has been to acquaint you with the overall purpose of this technique and to give you an overview of the strategy.

[6]SPSS Manual, (Nie et al., pp. 472–473).

[7]It is very important to keep in mind that this procedure requires that the groups be specified in advance, without a reference to the independent variables. This is in contrast to cluster analysis which "finds" the groups a posteriori. See, for instance, Lorr (1983), or Norusis (1985, Chapter 5).

[8]Note that although the discriminating variables can be referred to as independent and the group label variable as dependent there is no implication of causality.

[9]Kleinbaum and Kupper (1978, Chapter 22). This discusses $g = 2$ only and the formulation differs, but is very clear; Klecka (1979) is a good first reference for formulas. A very clear heuristic can be found in Kachigan (1982). Cohen and Cohen (1983) have an interesting viewpoint. Huberty (1984) reviews issues in use and interpretation. Norusis (1985, Chapter 3) gives a well-worked example.

[10]See Klecka (1979, pp. 60–63). Discriminant analysis is also inappropriate if the independent variables are continuous ordinal: Yogev and Jamshy (1983) use a discriminant analysis on Likert-scaled response data.

[11]If we had standard-form variables we would work with correlation matrices.

[12]See SPSS Manual (Nie et al. 1975, p. 445); Klecka (1979, Chapter 4); Norusis (1985, Chapter 3).

[13]R. A. Fisher "The Use of Multiple Measurements in Taxonomic Problems," Annals of Eugenics, Vol. 7: pp. 179–188 (1936), cited in Klecka (1979).

[14]See Klecka (1979, pp. 43–47); also Kleinbaum and Kupper (1978, pp. 426–429).

[15]References: Cooley and Lohnes (1962); Levine (1976); Van der Geer (1971); Anderson (1958); SPSS Manual (Nie et al. 1975, Chapter 25); Muller (1982); and Kachigan (1982). Thompson (1984) is up-to-date and very readable.

[16]Levine (1976, pp. 12–13) observes that substitution of nonparametric measures seems reasonable, but does not permit interpretation in terms of variance.

[17]Suggested in Levine (1976, p. 6).

[18]Levine (1976, pp. 27ff.).

[19]Hirschi and Selvin (1973, p. 170) mention some potential problems in interpreting the outcome of a canonical analysis. Thompson (1984) reviews recent literature on applications and lists types of problems well suited to cancorr analysis (pp. 7–10).

[20]See Cooley and Lohnes (1962).

[21]See Iverson and Nörpoth (1976, p. 81), and Edwards (1979); also Cohen and Cohen (1983, Chapters 1 and 10).

Additional Reading

As for Chapter 12, each main multivariate technique described in this chapter has a corresponding endnote with references.

For general references, also consult Chapter 12 Additional Reading list, under the heading General Multivariate Methods.

14

Probabilistic Methods: Multivariate Statistics III

Techniques Free of Linear Assumptions

Introduction

In this chapter, we are concerned mainly with nonparametric multivariate techniques. Time series analysis, which appears to follow the pattern of other least squares procedures, in fact presents special problems. We consider this topic first.

Time Series: Special Issues in Bivariate and Multivariate Analyses

In many studies, the solution to the research problem requires that measurements of one or more variables be made at regular or irregular time intervals. In the simplest case, the data consists of n pairs (t_i, X_{t_i}) $1 \leq i \leq n$, with $t_1 < t_2 < \ldots < t_n$, and the differences are all equal $0 < t_2 - t_1 = t_3 - t_2 = \ldots = t_n - t_{n-1}$. (This case is illustrated in the section on graphs in Chapter 11.) The goal of data analysis is usually two-fold: to formulate a functional relationship $X_t = f(t)$, which (1) fits the data well enough to satisfy some criterion, and which (2) can be used to predict values X_t for additional $t > t_n$ well enough to satisfy some (possibly different) criterion.

Examples abound: a fever chart reflecting the characteristic course of certain diseases; charts recording fluctuations in birth, marriage, divorce, death rates; records of traffic volume every hour for a month; and charts of sales, stock market activity, Dow–Jones averages, unemployment, volume of exports. Demographers attempting to project population shifts have long exploited time series methods originally developed by economists for the analysis of long-term trend and periodic (cyclic and seasonal) fluctuations in economic indicators. Increasingly, social scientists interested in such questions as changes in voting patterns or religious affiliation, or other attitudinal shifts over time are making use of these techniques.

Perhaps the earliest account of time series analysis is found in the Biblical story of Joseph. Looking at Egyptian wheat production over a period of several centuries, he observed a cyclical pattern: 7 lean years of poor crops alternating with 7 fat years of good crops. More modern descriptions of the basic procedures, such as moving averages, to identify and analyze characteristics of time series can be found in any elementary statistics text directed primarily towards economics or business applications.[1] The analyst seeks a "best" functional equation fitting a line, polynomial of higher degree, or function in some other class. Curve fitting is often done using a least-squares procedure, but unfortunately forecasts tend to be quite inaccurate. This reflects the basic unsuitability of the approach.

If we have two time series

$$\{(t_i, X_{t_i})\}$$

and

$$\{(t_i, Y_{t_i})\},\ 1 \leq i \leq n;\ t_i < t_{i+1},$$

we seek to describe the relationship between the X_{t_i} and the Y_{t_i}, the former being regarded here as the independent variable and the latter as dependent. An example might be TV watching and reading scores for the graduating class of a high school, observed over a period of years; another might be proportion of a specified age group unemployed and number of crimes in some category, recorded over a period of years at monthly intervals. The first impulse may be to follow the procedure for fitting a regression line

$$Y_t^c = a + bX_t,$$

based on the functional relation

$$Y_t = a + bX_t + \epsilon_t.$$

Recall that in order to use this linear model, and to apply the least-squares machinery, it is necessary to make three assumptions concerning the error terms:

1. The error term has mean zero.
2. The error term has constant variance independent of over all observations.
3. The error terms corresponding to different points in time are not correlated.

In many cases, the third assumption is violated: We say the error terms are *autocorrelated* or *serially correlated*. This can be illustrated as in Figure 14.1. Since the data points alternately lie above and below the best line, we infer

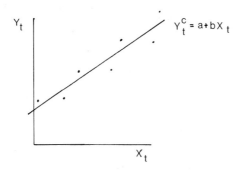

FIGURE 14.1 Autocorrelation in time-dependent bivariate data.

that successive error terms are negatively correlated. Consequently, while it is possible to carry through the regression procedure mechanically, conclusions as to significance are weakened or invalidated. The same objections apply to the predictive use of the obtained equation.

In effect, what is needed is a strategy that will decompose a random variable X_t into parts which reflect the observed periodicities and break the variance σ_t^2 of X_t into components which will achieve their respective maxima at predictable values of t. Thus it will be possible to avoid some of the difficulties described above, and to increase the accuracy of predictions, particularly at turning points of the graph. A relatively new time series forecasting technique designed to carry out this strategy is called *spectral analysis*.[2] It makes use of the sophisticated machinery of harmonic analysis, as well as the mathematical theory of statistics; the technicalities are far beyond the level of this book.

The fluctuations in the series X_t are assumed to reflect the superimposition of a large number of elementary cycles with different frequencies (hence, "spectrum"); each such cycle corresponds to a trigonometric term of the form $R \cos(\omega t + \theta)$. For different values of ω these terms are uncorrelated, so their variances sum to the variance σ_t^2 of X_t. From knowledge of the σ's and R's it is possible to infer the (average) relative contribution of these terms to σ_t^2.

The appropriate terms are found by (1) fitting a "best" trigonometric polynomial to the given time series, by a modified least-squares procedure; (2) smoothing this polynomial by introducing so-called lag windows (there are several conventions for doing this); and (3) identifying the resulting spectrum. These steps can also be incorporated into the analysis of bivariate or multivariate relationships. Computationally, it is desirable to take advantage of the Fast Fourier Transform (FFT) algorithm. Both SAS and P-STAT have computer programs for this technique.

If your study requires precise decomposition of time series and examination of periodicities, you may wish to take advantage of spectral analysis.[3] Its strength lies in its potential for providing better forecasts and its avoidance of the inaccuracies that arise from autocorrelation. However, the methods are untested in that relatively few studies exist to examine interpretations. You may have no choice if you cannot assume statistical independence among independent variables and your dependent variables exhibit periodicities.

Nonparametric[4] Multivariate Methods

INTRODUCTION

In Chapter 11 we described the principal features of a number of procedures used to measure and evaluate location (central tendency), dispersion, differences, and association, for univariate and bivariate data. The information was arranged systematically according to the level(s) of the data as well as the intended goal of the analysis.

So far in Chapters 12 and 13, we have described several multivariate techniques based on the general linear model. While some of these have been extended to nominal (especially dichotomous) variables through the use of dummy coding, and to continuous ordinal variables, such procedures may be controversial and the interpretation of results so obtained, questionable. In any event, there are many circumstances in which the use of these powerful and elegant parametric methods is inappropriate or impossible.

Listing and classifying the alternatives available for the analysis of association between three or more variables or of differences between three or more samples, is difficult for several reasons:

- Variables of one or more of the following types may be present: dichotomous, nominal with more than two values; discrete ordinal, continuous ordinal, ordinal-metric; discrete interval or ratio; continuous interval known not to be normal or not known to be normal, for example, when samples are very small or population very skewed.
- Some techniques on the market are useful for small samples, but because no computer programs are generally available they are unworkable for large samples unless you can develop the programs yourself.
- A great many techniques are available. Some do part but not all the job of the parametric analogue. Some are essentially equivalent to others— differently named—which are better known; some extremely specialized were developed to solve particular problems and involve unusual assumptions. Most ordinal statistics have special forms for ties.

- The nomenclature is maddening: almost all the nonparametric tests are eponymous.
- There are very few comprehensive reference books that include not only the rationale but also the computational algorithm with examples. Understanding the underlying strategy requires a familiarity with combinatorial mathematics and also with the convergence arguments that permit approximation by standard distributions.

We will describe a few of the most widely-used techniques: Our discussion is in no way exhaustive. We believe these will serve your purpose in most cases and will yield interpretable results. Almost all have computer programs available. Before you undertake any procedure, you would be wise to consult with an expert who is experienced in nonparametric analysis and also to examine the reference material on the method(s) you think may be appropriate. Such effort will be well rewarded; at the very least, you will avoid embarassment and error.

NONPARAMETRIC ANALYSIS OF
VARIANCE (KRUSKAL–WALLIS AND FRIEDMAN TESTS)

Several familiar study designs, intended to isolate treatment effects and thus permit comparisons, lead to data of the following form:

Group 1	Group 2	...	Group k
X_{11}	X_{21}	...	X_{k1}
X_{12}	X_{22}	...	X_{k2}
.	.		.
.	.		.
.	.		.
X_{1,n_1}	X_{2,n_2}	...	X_{k,n_k}

n_i is the number of elements in the ith group, so X_{ij} denotes the jth observation (data point) in the ith group, $1 \leq i \leq k$, $1 \leq j \leq n_i$. The dependent variable X is assumed to be continuous and the measurement scale at least ordinal: This means the values of X are rankable. Call

$$N = \sum_{i=1}^{k} n_i,$$

the total number of data points.

In order to proceed, we consider other possible constraints. Assume that the observations are independent both within and among samples (groups), that the samples are selected at random, and that the populations are identical except for a possible difference in the median for at least one population. Note that the n_i's do not have to be equal. The hypothesis to be tested is that the k populations have the same median.

For example, in studying prestige of medical specialists, a researcher may ask pediatricians (1), OB-GYNS (2), psychiatrists (3), neurologists (4), and radiologists (5) the question: If an internist is rated 100, how do you rate a general surgeon?

If the data were interval-level and normally distributed, we could use a simple one-way analysis of variance. In this situation, we use the *Kruskal–Wallis test* which is a fairly straightforward generalization of the Mann–Whitney 2-sample test.

If there is indeed no difference between the groups you would not expect a concentration of high (or low) ranking values in any group(s); hence, the sum of ranks should be about the same for all groups. This is the rationale for the test. The basic procedure is simple. First, all groups are pooled and the values of X_{i_j} are ranked,[5] smallest $= 1$, largest $= N$, within the pool. Denote the rank of X_{i_j} as $R(X_{i_j})$. Next, compute $R_i = \sum\limits_{j=1}^{n_i} R(X_{i_j})$, the sum of ranks for items in the ith group (column). The test statistic is

$$H = \frac{12}{N(N+1)} \sum_{i=1}^{k} \frac{1}{n_i}[R_i - \frac{n_i(N+1)}{2}]^2 .$$

Critical values of H and their corresponding probabilities are tabled for $k \le 3$ and $n_1, n_2, n_3 \le 5$. It turns out that for $k > 3$ and/or at least one $n_i > 5$, H is distributed approximately as χ^2 with $df = k - 1$, and so a table of χ^2 can be used for critical values and probabilities.

To measure the strength of the association between groupings and rankings, once a significant difference has been found, the correlation ratio eta (η) (for ranks) can be used, since the variable X is continuous. Dunn's procedure (see Daniel, 1978, Chapter 6) can be used for multiple comparisons.

A computer program is available to carry out the Kruskal–Wallis test.[6] The printout typically shows number of cases n_i and mean rank $\overline{R}_i = \frac{R_i}{n_i}$ for each group, the value of H (or of χ^2) and significance level. In addition, the value of H corrected for ties and its significance level are provided.

We illustrate the so-called Kruskal–Wallis one-way analysis of variance by ranks, by looking at the printout (Figure 14.2) of the Kruskal–Wallis subroutine in the SPSS program NPAR TESTS applied to the data obtained in the study described in Chapter 11. Our dependent variable is Var 124, total satisfaction, and our independent variable (factor) is Var 78, marital status. For the 58 usable cases, the computer prints the mean rank for each of the four values.

```
FILE    CDIC      (CREATION DATE = 11/15/XX)
VARIABLE          N         MEAN     STD DEV    MINIMUM    MAXIMUM

VAR124            58       35.138     9.271     23.000     89.000
VAR78            210        1.676     0.953      1.000      4.000
- - - - - KRUSKAL-WALLIS 1-WAY ANOVA
    VAR124        TOTAL SATISFACTION
BY VAR78          MARITAL STATUS

       VAR78        1          2         3          4
      NUMBER       37          5        11          5
   MEAN RANKS    31.38      22.30     27.00      28.30
                                             CORRECTED FOR TIES
          CASES   CHI-SQUARE  SIGNIFICANCE  CHI-SQUARE  SIGNIFICANCE
            58       1.633       0.652        1.640       0.650
```

FIGURE 14.2 Kruskal-Wallis one-way analysis of variance by ranks.

It appears the least satisfied category is the single (higher rank means higher satisfaction score) and the most satisfied is the married. Since N is large, the value of the Kruskal-Wallis statistic is approximated by $\chi^2 = 1.633$, with significance 0.652: this means such a value of χ^2 can be expected to arise by chance with probability 65%. The value of χ^2 corrected for ties is also printed. It is perhaps surprising that differences in total satisfaction scores do not seem to be associated with marital status, at least in the sample under study.

In Figure 11.22, illustrating the Mann-Whitney test, we saw that the total satisfaction scores, for this sample, did not reflect significant differences between male and female.

In view of a number of recent writings, such as Bernard's (1972) "His and Her Marriage" analysis, which have suggested that the interaction between gender and marital status may be of major importance, it would be helpful to have at our disposal a technique that permits an evaluation of interaction effects for our data. Unfortunately, the SPSS program does not include such a nonparametric procedure (see pp. 346–347).

Let us return now to an array of data like the one we first considered (p. 343), but with the imposition of different constraints. As before, assume the dependent variable X is continuous. Assume $b = n_1 = n_2 = \ldots = n_k$, so that each row of the array can be interpreted as a sample, or block, of size $k \geq 2$. Assume also that the data in any row are rankable, that is, the level of measurement must be at least ordinal, the blocks are mutually independent, and there is no interaction between blocks and columns (treatments).[7] The hypothesis to be tested is that no treatment tends to yield larger values than any other.

This state of affairs is usually called a randomized complete block design. Typically, the column entries X_{ij} are repeated measures, based on different treatments of instruments, of b individuals selected at random, so each individual is considered a block. As an example, suppose ten medical students are asked the following: If an internist is rated 100, how do you rate: a pediatrician (1), a general surgeon, (2), a psychiatrist (3), an orthopedic surgeon (4), a neurologist (5), an OB-GYN (6), a radiologist (7)? (The list should be presented in random order.) Here we have seven groups (columns) and ten blocks (rows).

		1	2 ... k	Treatments
Blocks	1	X_{11}	$X_{12} ... X_{1k}$	
	2	X_{21}	$X_{22} ... X_{2k}$	
	b	X_{b1}	$X_{b2} ... X_{bk}$	

If the data were interval-level and normally distributed, we would use a two-way ANOVA, mixed model with one item per cell. In this situation, we use the Friedman two-way analysis of variance by ranks; Bradley (1968) points out that this procedure is in fact a one-way analysis because it tests only for column effects.

The first step in using the Friedman test is to rank the scores in each block (row); let $R(X_{ij})$ denote the rank (1 = low, k = high) assigned to X_{ij} in row i. If the column scores are indeed not different from each other, then you would not expect a concentration of high (or low) ranks in any column. This provides the rationale for the test. In effect, the null hypothesis is that each ranking assigned a column is equally likely. Next, compute $R_j = \sum_{i=1}^{b} R(X_{ij})$ $1 \le j \le k$, the sum of ranks for the jth column. The test statistic[8]

$$\chi_r^2 = \frac{12}{bk(k+1)} \sum_{j=1}^{k} [R_j - \frac{b(k+1)}{2}]^2.$$

Tables of χ_r^2 are available for small values of b and k, for example, $k = 2$, $2 \le b \le 15$; $k = 3$, $2 \le b \le 9$; $k = 4$, $2 \le b \le 4$; showing critical values and probabilities. For larger values of b and k, χ_r^2 is approximated by χ^2 with $df = k - 1$. A computer printout will show rank sum for each column, value of χ_r^2 and its significance level, also χ^2, degrees of freedom and significance level.

The Friedman test can be adapted for use as a multiple comparison test.[9]

As described, the Kruskal–Wallis and Friedman tests are one-way analyses. Most texts indicate that no nonparametric tests for main effects and interactions among several variables are available, but Daniel (1978) refers to several suggested procedures. Bradley (1968) illustrates an extension of these procedures to two independent variables (factors) and indicates "several" may be used. However, an additional assumption about the dependent variable X must be made: Both sums and differences of measurements are meaningful. For practical purposes, this means the measurement scale is interval, but no assumptions are made about normality. We do not know of any procedure that permits evaluation of interaction effects in continuous ordinal data.

Both the Kruskal–Wallis and the Friedman tests have asymptotic power efficiency (relative to the parametric F-test) approaching .955, both are easy to compute by hand and easy to interpret. Computer routines are readily available. These procedures should always be considered and are in fact methods of choice for nominal versus ordinal (rankable) data either in conjunction with percentage analysis of cross tabulations or instead of it. Two recent articles in which the data analysis correctly employs these nonparametric procedures are (respectively) Musso and Cranero's (1981) report of an ESP experiment, and Sardy's (1982) "The Economic Impact of Inflation on Urban Areas."

THE COEFFICIENT OF CONCORDANCE

Kendall's coefficient of concordance W may be used in the same sort of situation where Friedman's test is applicable, to measure the agreement in rankings in the b blocks. Of course, if $b = 2$, the Spearman rho (ϱ) or the Kendall tau (τ) will yield the information we want, but they are not usable if $b > 2$.

Just as for the Friedman test, assume we have b sets of k measurements on an ordinal scale (ranks or rankable). Typically, each set corresponds to one object or individual. The null hypothesis is that the b rankings are not associated, that is, the rankings are assigned independently and at random.

W will be 1.0 if the rankings of scores within any block are identical to the rankings in any other. W will be close to zero if there is "perfect disagreement" among rankings, as measured by the variance in column rank sums. Computation is simplified by the following formula:[10] $W = \dfrac{\chi_r^2}{b(k - 1)}$

where χ_r^2 is the Friedman statistic. Critical values of W and their significance level are tabled for small b and k; for larger values, a suitable transformation $b(k - 1)W$ is approximated by χ^2 with $df = k-1$.

COCHRAN'S Q TEST

In some studies using the randomized complete block design, the measurement scale for the dependent variable X may be a dichotomy, so that each X_{ij} ($1 \le i \le b$, $1 \le j \le k$) can be designated a 1 or a 0. As before, we assume that treatments are independent; the null hypothesis to be tested is that each block has the same proportion of 0's and 1's.

While the situation strongly resembles that in which the Friedman test is used, the procedure is an extension of McNemar's test which would apply when $b = 2$. (See Chapter 11.) Cochran's Q can be calculated by a formula[11] whose values are closely approximated by χ^2 with $df = k - 1$. Computer printouts typically provide the contingency table $(2 \times k)$, value of Q, and significance level.

This statistic may be used for instance to decide whether each of 5 test items is equally difficult: Administer the items in random order to each of 10 randomly selected subjects, score 0 if wrong, 1 if correct, and compare the proportions of 0's and 1's for the 5 items.

The labelling of a procedure as nonparametric, because of its applicability to data for which the assumption of normality is impossible or unnecessary, may contradict the labelling of the same procedure as parametric, because its mathematical justification depends on the presence of normally distributed random variables. The family of chi-square distributions provides an example.[12]

The Chi-Square Tests[13]

The need for multivariate categorical analysis has steadily increased in the past several years, partly as a result of increasing use of survey data as a basis for policy decisions in many fields. The wide use of computers for data storage, retrieval, and classification has helped to encourage large-scale studies. Typically, individuals are assigned to classes or categories on each of a number of traits or attributes, and the resulting nominal-variable cross-classifications are examined for evidence of distribution patterns or a variety of possible relationships. In connection with the latter, we may ask whether two (or more) variables are statistically independent, and if not, what is the strength or form of the relationship.

Many techniques have been developed for these purposes.[14] Three types of chi-square procedures are of very broad applicability: a goodness-of-fit test, as test of independence for contingency tables (cross tabulations), and the generalized linear chi-square test. They can be used with all levels of data (interval, ratio, ordinal, or nominal) so they are suitable when only minimal assumptions are made:

1. Each sample is a simple random sample from the population of interest.
2. The samples are independent, if two or more populations are in question.

3. For each characteristic of interest, each subject can be assigned to exactly one class or category, and these classes are mutually exclusive and exhaustive; that is, each variable of interest can be measured on a nominal scale.

The *goodness-of-fit* test can be undertaken when the data consists of N independent values of a random variable X. Suppose the values can be placed into classes; then, the following frequency tabulation can be exhibited:

Class	1	2	3	...	c	
Observed frequency	O_1	O_2	O_3	...	O_c	N = total

O_j denotes the number of items whose X values fall in class j for $j = 1, 2, \ldots, c$. We may ask whether this frequency distribution is statistically different from some known and specified distribution, such as the uniform, normal, binomial, Poisson, multinomial, gamma, etc.

In order to proceed, we must be able to calculate the theoretical or expected frequency for each class. To do this, select the theoretical distribution to which you want to compare your data, and let p_j be the probability that the value of a random variable, so distributed, falls in class j. Define expected frequencies of X by $E_j = p_j N$, $j = 1, 2, \ldots, c$. The test statistic is

$$\chi^2 = \sum_{j=1}^{c} \frac{(O_j - E_j)^2}{E_j}$$

and degrees of freedom $df = $ c–1.

Computer input is the set of observed and expected frequencies; the output is the value of χ^2, the degrees of freedom, and the associated probability or significance level. Using these results, we can decide whether to reject the null hypothesis that there is no statistically significant difference between observed and expected frequencies.

The use of the chi-square for *analysis of contingency tables* involves several very similar procedures based on differing assumptions. We can describe a (two-way) contingency table has having r rows (groups) and c columns (classes). Groups and classes can be thought of as values of two nominal variables, or each group can be thought of as a sample from a different population. The ith row ($l \le i \le r$) and jth column ($l \le j \le c$) intersect in the ijth cell. If r_i is the number of observations in the ith sample, each observation can be placed into exactly one of the c classes. Let O_{ij} be the number of observations from the ith sample in the jth class, that is, in the ij-cell, then $r_i = O_{i1} + O_{i2} + \ldots + O_{ic}$ for $i = 1, 2, \ldots, r$. The data are arranged in a contingency table:

	Variable A			
Variable B	Class 1	Class 2 ... Class c		Totals
Group 1	O_{11}	O_{12}	O_{1c}	r_1
Group 2	O_{21}	O_{22}	O_{2c}	r_2
.	.	.	.	.
.	.	.	.	.
.	.	.	.	.
Group r	O_{r1}	O_{r2}	O_{rc}	r_r
	c_1	c_2	c_c	N

Notice $N = r_1 + \ldots + r_r = c_1 + \ldots + c_c$ where

$$c_j = \sum_{i=j}^{r} O_{ij} \, j = 1, 2, \ldots, c.$$

As before, in order to proceed we must define an expected frequency for each cell, so we let $E_{ij} = \dfrac{r_i c_j}{N}$. E_{ij} is the expected frequency of the ij-cell, Row i, Column j. The null hypothesis to be tested is that the proportions (probabilities) of the observations falling into different cells in any column are the same as the proportions for any other column. The test statistic is defined by

$$\chi^2 = \sum_{i=1}^{r} \sum_{j=1}^{c} \frac{(O_{ij} - E_{ij})^2}{E_{ij}}$$

with $df = (r-1)(c-1)$.

Machine programs require as input r, c, cell frequencies O_{ij} and a statement that you are doing a contingency problem. Output includes E_{ij}'s, value of χ^2, degrees of freedom, and significance level of χ^2.

Certain special cases deserve attention.[15]

- From a 2×2 table, a *correction for continuity (Yates)*[16] is applied to the statistic because χ^2 is continuous, but the distribution of the statistic is discrete.
- If the row totals are held constant (e.g. if each row is an independent sample) but column totals can vary, the same calculations are carried out but the test will determine if the rows are independent of the columns. (Vice versa if column totals are fixed, and row totals vary.) In these circumstances, χ^2 is called a test of independence.
- If both row and column totals, in a 2×2 table, are fixed, the number of possible tables is limited, and the so-called *Fisher's exact test*[17] can be used.

- If the values of the variable are recorded simply as falling above or below a column median or a row median, the chi-square test is called the *median test*. This is extended easily to a multiple median test.[18]
- If the data are classified according to a sign change, + or − , the analysis can be accomplished using the sign test of McNemar's test.

Measures of association for $n \times m$ contingency tables, and their interpretation, are presented at some length in Liebetrau (1983), in Reynolds (1977b), in Jacobson (1976), and quite chattily in Davis (1971). The best known measures are Cramer's V, the contingency coefficient C, Guttman's lambda's, the Goodman–Kruskal gamma, the odds ratio, and Yule's Q.

When categorical data require a three-or-more-way classification, the procedures we have described earlier are inadequate. The use of chi-square statistics to analyze data sets two variables at a time does not do justice to the multivariate nature of the situation. Inspection of what are, in effect, measures of partial association based on the Goodman–Kruskal gamma, Yules's Q, or various other statistics,[19] can yield valuable insight into relationships between effects; however, general methods for analysis of multidimensional tables are clearly needed.

ANOVA or dummy-variable regression are not applicable because all the variables are nominal level. Several modified chi-square techniques usually referred to as log-linear models[20] have been developed in recent years. One of these, the Grizzle–Starmer–Koch[21] (GSK) model, is fairly typical; the following will give you an intuitive idea of how it works.

Assume we have an n-way contingency table; the classification variables are regarded as independent (factors). The terminology—main effects, cells, and so forth—is taken from ANOVA. The dependent variable is the number of observations (frequency) per cell: This frequency can be translated into a probability. In order to use the GSK, or similar, procedure, the first step is to hypothesize a distribution and a set of interrelationships (model) that might account for the observed data. From this model, probabilities and their expected frequencies can be computed for each cell. The next step is to compare the expected frequencies with the observed frequencies using a criterion which for large samples closely approximates the chi-square goodness-of-fit test. If the discrepancies are small, the model is retained. Finally, the parameters of the model can be estimated. For a variety of reasons, mainly reflecting the fact that contingent probabilities are multiplicative, it may be easier to formulate models using the logarithms of all frequencies rather than the frequencies themselves. This tactic converts multiplicative relationships into additive (linear) ones. It also allows a null hypothesis of independence, or no effect, of say, the ith variable, to be stated as a linear relationship. A term or terms can be introduced into the model which may be identified as *interaction*.

In order to carry out a multivariate categorical analysis, a suitable computer progaram is virtually essential. For example, in a straightforward approach, input includes the cell frequencies and the expected cell frequencies: The latter depend on the choice of model which in turn depends on the investigator's experience with both the research area and the log-linear procedure.

The GSK approach incoporates the assertion that *absence of row effects* means that certain linear combinations of the logarithms of cell frequencies are zero, and likewise for column effects and interaction effects involving two or more variables. The GSK program carries out tests of these assertions and the resulting output resembles an ANOVA table. Main effects for each variable, interaction effects, and residual (goodness of fit) effects are listed, with each *df*, χ^2 and significance level printed. The algorithms used in the program are highly technical and we make no attempt to describe them. Most packages contain programs for log-linear χ^2 analysis.

Recent examples of studies exploiting log-linear analysis include Veroff (1981) already described in Chapter 2, and Duncan and Duncan (1978); it seems to us that the Erbe (1962) study would lend itself to this procedure as well.

It is frequently stated that results, especially interaction effects, are difficult to interpret. The same criticism can be leveled against conventional ANOVA, especially when the number of factors is large, but familiarity with the procedure greatly enhances ease and comfort in using information based on elaborate computations.

Partialling Procedures[22]

A fruitful strategy for the exploration of multivariate relationships is the use of first- and higher-order partial measures of association. We have described part and partial correlation in Chapter 12 (pp. 282–283) in connection with the control of sources of variance. When the data are ordinal, or nominal amenable to ordering, partial rho's, tau's or gamma's can point to intervening or antecedent variables. Careful inspection of three- or higher-way cross tabulations, particularly those in which row and column percentages are presented, will permit you to identify possible interactions among nominal variables. Old-fashioned eye-balling should always be your first step.

We cannot emphasize too strongly the importance of imaginativeness and flexibility in interpretation. Reliance on the computer as a device for handling large data sets is understandable but unfortunately often leads to the overuse of formal significance testing and improper application of the multilinear (regression) model to analyze partial and interaction effects.[23] Whether or not you carry out systematic hypothesis testing with the partial measures, you need to exercise judgment and to draw upon your knowledge about pertinent findings in related studies.

Some Last Thoughts on
Multivariate Statistical Techniques

In this chapter and the two preceding, we have described a sample of the available techniques. In very general terms, every multivariate problem can be described as leading to a set of n-tuples. As in the univariate and bivariate cases, data analysis techniques are intended to provide information on patterns of distribution and/or association. Some see the ultimate goal of analysis as the isolation of measured effects so that causal inferences may be made, but this straitjackets the examination of data and prematurely terminates many potentially useful approaches.

The research literature of every field contains many examples of creative modifications and imaginative applications of standard techniques. In addition, reference manuals such as Cohen and Cohen, Winer, Bradley, Daniel and others include many procedures we have not even mentioned and special cases of those we have presented. As we have stated so often, a first-rate experienced statistical consultant can be enormously helpful in assisting you with a revision of your problem formulation to take advantage of existing analytic methods or, if worse comes to worst, in devising a tailor-made technique. Not uncommonly, a moderate effort directed toward sharpening or rephrasing your research question will greatly alleviate your statistical difficulties.

Finally, there is no excuse for failing to plan data analysis *before* undertaking data collection. Much grief can be avoided if time, money, and effort are not spent accumulating data that can't be analyzed, for the effects you seek, by any known method. Some questions can't be answered: Don't base your study on them.

Notes

[1]Lapin (1982), Clelland et al. (1973), Freund (1971), Yamane (1967b), etc. More advanced references: Ostrow (1977); Box and Jenkins (1971); Hull and Nie (1981); see also Cook and Campbell (1979, pp 301–335).

[2]The terminology is derived from physics where radiation (e.g., light) from some source is broken down, by a prism or grating, into its components of various wavelengths or frequencies. The pattern of frequencies is called the *spectrum*.

[3]Unless your mathematical preparation is very strong, you would do best to seek the aid of a consultant, preferably one trained in economics.

[4]We are using "nonparametric" and "distribution-free" interchangeably although they are technically different.

[5]A procedure is available to correct for tied ranks. Consult, for example, Daniel (1978), Jacobson (1976), or Siegel (1956).

[6]See, for example, SPSS subprogram NPAR TESTS (Hull and Nie, 1981).

[7]The terminology is awkward. We shall refer to column scores.

[8]This formula appears in Bradley (1968); a somewhat different but equivalent formula is used in Daniel (1978) and Siegel (1956). Modifications can be introduced to correct for tied ranks.

[9]See Daniel (1978, Chapter 7) for related tests and many references.

[10]For other formulas, including discussion of correction for ties, see Daniel (1978), Jacobson (1976), and Siegel (1956). All these references offer extended comments on interpretation.

[11]See Siegel (1956), or Daniel (1978).

[12]Most elementary texts refer to this issue; for brief discussions, see Daniel (1978, Chapter 5); Roscoe (1975, Chapter 28).

[13]Both Steger (1971) and Haber et al. (1970) contain a selection of articles on pitfalls in the use of the chi-square.

[14]See Reynolds (1977a,b) and their references; also Davis (1971); Kleinbaum and Kupper (1978, Chapter 23); and Daniel (1978, Chapter 5), which considers several important issues. A modification of the contingency chi-square is illustrated in Lyon et al. (1978). Agresti (1984) presents a variety of techniques, including extensions and modifications of the chi-square.

[15]See discussion of special problems and additional issues: Daniel (1978, pp. 184–188); Steger (1971).

[16]See any standard text.

[17]See, for example, Daniel (1978, pp. 110ff.) or Roscoe (1975, Chapter 34).

[18]See Siegel (1956).

[19]See Reynolds (1977b, pp. 52–56); Davis (1971, Chapters 4–7). Fleiss (1981) may also be useful.

[20]See Fienberg (1977); Reynolds (1977b, pp. 57–79; very clear); Duncan and Duncan (1978: App. A) expounds several simple examples. Knoke and Burke (1980) is extremely readable and emphasizes interpretation. Agresti (1984) discusses log-linear models for ordinal data. Norusis (1985, Chapters 8 and 9) displays several worked log-linear procedures.

[21]Discussed extensively in Kleinbaum and Kupper (1978, Chapter 23). It is important to keep in mind that this is only one among many. Other models use odds rather than probabilities; some distinguish between dependent and independent variables in the analysis.

[22]See Kendall (1962) for rank-order statistics, and Davis (1971) or Zeisel (1968) for cross-tabulations. Jacobson (1976) discusses partial measures for each measure of association. Blalock (1979, Chapter 19) is an excellent general discussion of multiple and partial correlation and their interpretation, with special reference to causal models. Pages 462–468 concern multiple and partial correlational techniques for ordinal and nominal data.

[23]Classical regression and analysis of variance models interpret interaction as multiplicative: this is an assumption like any other.

Additional Reading

As in Chapter 12, each main multivariate technique described in this chapter has a corresponding footnote with references.

For general references, also consult list under the heading General Multivariate Methods on page 307.

In addition, you may find useful the following:

Nonparametric Statistical Techniques

Agresti (1984): comprehensive presentation of techniques for ordinal categorical data, difficult to read without a strong background. Excellent bibliography.

Bradley (1968): discursive, emphasis on distribution-free interval-level tests, but has a good general discussion of Friedman and Kruskal–Wallis tests; superb bibliography.

Conover (1980): practical general reference, useful material on multisample comparisons.

Daniel (1978): up-to-date, comprehensive, with good bibliographies for each topic and many worked examples.

Davis (1971): very explicit, emphasis on Yule's Q and its extensions.

Fienberg (1977): linear models for categorical data.

Hildebrand, Laing, and Rosenthal (1977): good bibliography.

Jacobson (1976): especially good on partial measures of association; many worked examples, well-organized.

Kendall (1962): rank-ordered methods.

Liebetrau (1983): comparison of competing techniques.

Reynolds (1977a,b): analysis of cross-classifications, comparisons of competing measures.

Siegel (1956): old reliable, easy to read.

15

Deterministic Problem Analysis Techniques

Introduction

In this chapter we describe a few among an assortment of deterministic techniques for problem analysis which have been rapidly increasing in number and range of application in the past 40 years.

We have already described what is meant by a mathematical model (Chapter 10), and have indicated the distinction between deterministic and probabilistic models. Among the former, we may further loosely distinguish descriptive (structural) and predictive (functional) models. Following are some examples of deterministic models:

- The problem of describing the relationship between a stimulus and the sensation in the responder was attacked by Fechner (among others), who formulated a law expressed mathematically in the form:

$$\text{sensation} = K \cdot \log(\text{stimulus}).$$

Once the constant K is determined a scale can be constructed, based on this model, to measure sensation. As the stimulus is changed, the sensation changes predictably. This point of view has been extended to social class scales.[1] Here, K is a parameter for the model, associated with the particular class of phenomena under study, for example, light of specified wavelength, sound of specified frequency.

- The problem of identifying the effect of childhood resources on adult attainment has led to a variety of models. One, which exploits the scaling model mentioned above, involves income as a function of six variables and seven parameters; it permits an inspection of the effect of parental social class, number of siblings, membership in the majority [sic], etc., on adult income.[2]

- The problem of expressing the relationship between total household income and the proportion spent on necessities as opposed to other goods and services, leads to a conjecture or model of the form:

$$\text{proportion spent on necessities} = \frac{k}{\text{income}}$$

357

This says the one is inversely proportional to the other; the one falls directly as the other rises. The constant k is a parameter for the model, and is associated with such uncontrollable factors as household size, weather in the region, local food cost patterns, and so forth. As the household income changes, the model predicts what proportion is spent on necessities.

- The problems of describing kinship systems, communications nets, and organizational hierarchies have been systematically attacked using graph theoretic techniques. These lead to a set of formal description of relationships and permitted paths within the network.[3]

Much research in the social and behavioral sciences is directed toward the formulation of theory and its translation into a mathematical model.[4] Such a model may, but need not, involve a formula; it may make use of a mathematical structure such as a finite group or a connected graph. Predictive deterministic models are always warmly received, and if such a one is available for your research problem you should take advantage of it.

We do not address the question of model construction, which in any case properly belongs under the heading of hypothesis formulation. The kinds of models in use in your field will suggest appropriate possibilities.[5] In the rest of this chapter, we discuss the mathematical and related procedures used for analysis of deterministic models.

Elementary Mathematical Techniques

Sometimes the model at hand requires us to use only the tools of high school algebra and plane geometry in order to reach a solution:

- In applying the model: Total Profits (P) = Total Revenue (R) − Total Costs (C), we see readily that there are two ways to increase P: Either increase R while C is constant or decreasing, or decrease C while R is constant or increasing. If R and C both increase or both decrease, the change in P cannot be predicted without more information.
- If three distribution or service locations D_1, D_2, D_3 are already established, and you wish to locate a manufacturing plant or diagnostic laboratory so as to equalize shipping or travel costs, elementary geometry tells you that the plant should be placed as near as possible to the so-called circum-center of the triangle with vertices D_1, D_2, D_3. (This model also assumes that small portions of the surface of the earth can be approximated by a plane.) Moreover, you will also learn from geometry that if more than three distribution or service points are built, the equalization goal cannot in general be achieved.

Calculus Based Techniques[6]

The examples presented above require only the most elementary mathematical techniques. Many models either require or permit the use of the calculus for their analysis.

- Learning can be described using Hull's learning function.[7]

$$y = M(1 - e^{-ax}),$$

where
$$\begin{cases} x \text{ is the number of trials;} \\ y \text{ is the response rate, a measure of learning; and} \\ M \text{ and } a \text{ are positive parameters.} \end{cases}$$

To understand the "shape" of this function, we write $\dfrac{dy}{dx} = e^{-ax}$ and see at once that y levels off as x increases, with the horizontal $y = M$ as an asymptote (Figure 15.1).

- Suppose we have determined empirically that a suitable predictive model for the amount of time needed by a single clerical worker to alphabetize and catalogue forms is given by:

$$T = a + bx \log \frac{x}{100} \text{ where } \begin{cases} x = \text{number of forms} \\ a,b = \text{parameters} \end{cases}$$

If we want to know the optimum number of forms to assign each worker in a batch, to keep the time per batch to a minimum, we turn again to differentiation and its applications.

The elementary calculus, based on the powerful properties of the concept of limit, offers three principal classes of techniques: differentiation, integration, and summation of infinite series. When the model involves functions that satisfy the assumptions underlying these techniques, such as

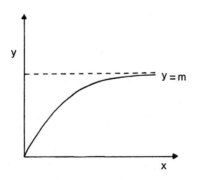

FIGURE 15.1 Function, with horizontal asymptote.

continuity (smoothness), many questions are answerable and many interpretations meaningful. Suppose the model requires only two variables whose relationship can be expressed by the equation $y = f(x)$, with which is associated a plane curve. Differentiation of f, where possible, allows us to evaluate the limiting value of quotients $\dfrac{f(x + \Delta x) - f(x)}{\Delta x}$, interpretable as instantaneous slope $\dfrac{dy}{dx}$ of the curve. Integration of f, when possible, allows us to evaluate the limiting value, denoted $\displaystyle\int_{a}^{b} f(x)dx$, of certain sums $\displaystyle\sum_{i} f(x_i)\Delta x_i$, and is interpretable as area under the curve between specified cut-off x-values. It may also be possible, under suitable assumptions, to approximate the value of $f(x)$ as closely as we may wish by a sequence of sums of the form $\displaystyle\sum_{i=1}^{m} c_i x^i$, by selecting a suitably large m, and to estimate the approximation error. If the model contains three or more variables, the foregoing can be generalized, with appropriate modifications in notation.

In addition to the items already mentioned differentiation can tell us:

- The effect of one variable in a multivariable function, if all other variables are held fixed.
- The number of times a curve changes direction, where it increases or decreases and whether it is "accelerating" or "decelerating."
- Where a curve reaches its highest or lowest values.
- Approximately where a function takes on value zero.
- Whether and where a surface has ridges or peaks.

Integration techniques can tell us, for example:

- The skewness and kurtosis (peakedness) of a curve.
- The volume under a surface.
- The function whose rate-of-change function is $y = f(x)$.[8]

These are, of course, only a small subset of the approaches exploiting these techniques.

If the model with which you are working involves one or more nonlinear functions, and possibly one or more constraints on the variables, then the use of the calculus may provide important information. A number of books have been written specifically for self-directed study (see Additional Readings); ideally, the learner should have an instructor or a study-group with a knowledgeable leader. Much research in economics and biology, but relatively little in other social or behavioral sciences, has exploited calculus-based models. Examination of exemplary studies[9] may suggest useful alternatives to the more standard approaches.

Among the problems whose solutions may be obtainable using the calculus are those which seek the largest or smallest value of a function over some range of the variable(s). A very extensive and varied class of research questions can be formulated as optimization problems, that is, the solutions are maximum or minimum values of some function. More informally, the decision-maker seeks the "best" or "optimum." It is difficult to be more precise except in specific cases. We now present several of these.

Mathematical Programming

This title covers an assortment of techniques designed to optimize decisions. Basically, there are five types: (1) linear programming; (2) integer programming; (3) parametric programming; (4) dynamic programming; and (5) nonlinear programming. Despite their labels, they have nothing in common with computer programming. They all deal with the problem of allocating limited resources among competing activities in the best possible way. For each, there exists an algorithm (prescribed mathematical procedure) that will lead to the solution, providing the assumptions are satisfied and a solution exists at all. Except for the last on the list, all depend on the machinery of linear (matrix) algebra. The main computational strategy, the simplex method, was developed by Dantzig in 1947, and almost at once encouraged a rapid increase in number and breadth of applications. Most of these have been directed toward economic research, but in recent years many have appeared in other social sciences, especially management science. Every application involves three steps: (1) the formulation of the problem as a set of one or more functions, called the *objective function(s)*, to be maximized or minimized, together with a set of *constraints* which may be equations or inequalities; (2) the development of the solution, which is a maximum or minimum value, together with the point(s) in n-dimensional space at which it is achieved; (3) the interpretation of the solution.

LINEAR PROGRAMMING

The general linear programming model can be used when issues such as the following concern you:

- Investment portfolio selection—to maximize return and minimize risk.
- Media selection—to obtain greatest exposure at least cost.

- Marketing strategy—to allocate limited sales force and advertising funds for maximal sales volume.
- Production scheduling—to minimize cost but meet demand for product.
- Transportation routing—to minimize cost but meet demand for product.
- Manpower planning—to achieve optimal deployment of personnel in various job functions.
- Staff assignment—to utilize specialized skills most efficiently.
- Blend specifications—to achieve proportions in a mixture that will meet product specifications at least cost.
- Election campaign strategy planning—to maximize votes when time allocations to districts must be limited.

Certain conditions must be met besides those mentioned earlier. Principally, all the functions that appear in the formulation, including the constraint functions (which define the boundaries of the region in which we can operate), must be linear. We also assume that all the variables are continuous. Thus, in a problem of cost minimization, no quadratic or cubic cost functions are admissible.

The general linear programming model can be expressed[10] as follows:

Maximize

$$z = c_1 x_1 + c_2 x_2 + \ldots + c_n x_n$$

subject to

$$x_j \geq 0, \ (j = 1, \ldots, n)$$

and

$$\sum_{j=1}^{n} a_{ij} x_j \leq b_i \ (i = 1, \ldots, m).$$

There are n variables and m constraints, which must be converted into equations by the addition of a so-called *slack variable* to the left-hand side of each inequality. The model thus becomes

Maximize

$$z = \sum_{j=1}^{n} c_j x_j + \sum_{i=1}^{m} 0 \cdot s_i$$

subject to

$$x_j \geq 0, \ (1 \leq j \leq n), \ s_i \geq 0, \ (1 \leq i \leq m)$$

and

$$\sum_{j=1}^{n} a_{ij} x_j + s_i = b_i, \ (1 \leq i \leq m).$$

The slack variables $s_1, \ldots, s_m$ change the inequalities into equations but do not alter the objective function. They have no effect on the optimum solution.

A point $(\tilde{x}_1, \ldots, \tilde{x}_n)$ is called *feasible* if its coordinates satisfy the original system of inequalities; the set of all feasible points is a convex region in n-dimensional space whose boundaries are the equations $\sum\limits_{j=1}^{n} a_{ij}x_j = b_i$ ($1 \le i \le m$) and $x_j = 0$ ($1 \le j \le n$) and whose corners can be obtained by solving the boundary equations n at a time. It can be shown that any solution of the program must occur at a corner of the feasible region. The *simplex method* incorporates into a relatively simple algorithm a search procedure in which, starting at one specified corner (initial trivial solution) and carrying out prescribed permitted linear transformations of the $(m + n)$ -dimensional space of variables $x_1, \ldots, x_n, s_1, \ldots, s_m$, it is possible to "move around the boundary" until an optimal corner is reached.[11] The simplex algorithm[12] exploits the notation of matrix theory by replacing the given system of equations with a tableau or matrix of coefficients; the criterion of optimality is also stated as the condition that certain tableau entries be nonnegative.

Computer programs for solving linear programs are widely available, for example, in IASML. Output is one or more set(s) of values $\tilde{x}_1, \ldots, \tilde{x}_n$ which maximize the objective function and also satisfy the constraints. The maximal value should also be given. The slack variables drop out of the solution.

The linear programming model as described above requires the maximization of an objective function subject to certain constraints. Minimization problems (with appropriate constraints) can be dealt with very efficiently thanks to the Duality Theorem. This associates to every minimum program a maximum dual program and vice versa, ensures the existence of a solution of the former if and only if one exists for the latter, and exhibits a neat connection between the two solutions. Interpretation of the dual solution can in many cases be very instructive: For example, the problem of maximizing profit has the dual problem of minimizing costs. At the algorithmic level, reading the solution differs for the dual but the steps leading to the solution are the same. The computer printout for a maximum problem includes the solution for the minimum dual.

Several difficulties may arise in the course of applying the simplex method, including:

1. The initial trivial solution may not work.
2. The number of steps (iterations) needed to arrive at an optimal solution may be very large.
3. No optimal solution may exist.
4. Several optimal solutions may exist.

The simplex algorithm can be modified to deal with some of these. If you encounter any of them, you will need to seek assistance from someone experienced with optimization techniques.

INTEGER PROGRAMMING

Some linear programs arise in such a way that the solution set must consist of integers. For example, if the underlying "real" problem seeks the optimal allocation of individuals to tasks, an outcome which suggests that 37.3 workers should carry out Process A, etc., will not be too helpful. Similarly, a problem in which the variables have only the values 1 = choose and 0 = reject and the goal is to select items from an assortment so as to maximize some gain, will of necessity have integer solutions.

It may well occur that in such cases, the optimal noninteger solution is very far from the optimal integer solution, so using the general linear programming approach will yield misleading results. Fortunately, there exist several special algorithms[13] that make use of the concepts underlying the simplex method and which output integers. Many have been programmed for use with computing equipment.

PARAMETRIC PROGRAMMING (SENSITIVITY ANALYSIS)

The general linear programming model requires, for any specific example, three sets of parameters $\{a_{i_j}\}$, $\{b_i\}$, $\{c_j\}$ whose values arise from the "real" problem to which the model is applied. Small changes in one or more of these parameters will, in general, effect changes in the optimal solution. The investigation of the relationships among these changes is called *sensitivity analysis*; the technique for carrying it out is called *parametric programming*.[14] The outcome is some insight into the amount of elbow room in the given problem.

Computer programs based on suitable algorithms are available in which a's, b's or c's are permitted to vary continuously over a specified interval or intervals, and it is thus possible to study the resulting variation in the optimal solution of the given system.

As an example, imagine the problem of preparing a least-cost mixture of several foods, each of which supplies a certain amount of specified minerals; the mixture must meet minimum requirements for each mineral. If the cost of each component now changes slightly, the optimal mixture—as well as its cost—may well change also; if the availability of the minerals in the different foods is not invariant, the optimal mixture can also change.

NONLINEAR PROGRAMMING[15]

Relaxing the assumptions of linearity in an optimization problem yields a system of the form:

Maximize

$$f(x_1, \ldots, x_n)$$

subject to

$$x_j \geq 0, \ (1 \leq j \leq n)$$

and

$$g_i(x_1, \ldots, x_n) \leq b_i, \ (1 \leq i \leq m)$$

where, f, g, $\ldots$, g_m are given functions of the variables x_j. This is general to the point of vacuity! In order to ensure existence of a solution, let alone provide an algorithm to achieve it, we need to make further assumptions. Two important special cases have been extensively analyzed, and procedures have been developed for their solution. Quadratic programs, in which the constraints are linear but the objective function contains terms of the form x_j^2 or $x_j x_k$, can be dealt with through an ingenious modification of the simplex method. Convex programs,[16] in which $f(x_1, \ldots x_n)$ is concave (downward curving) and the $g_i(x_1, \ldots, x_n)$ are all convex (upward curving) are also amenable to solution using a rather complicated algorithmic technique. Even using a high-speed digital computer, calculations take a long time.

Nonlinear programming is an active mathematical field in which rapid progress is being made and major breakthroughs can be anticipated in the next few years.

DYNAMIC PROGRAMMING

Dynamic programming is "a mathematical technique for making a sequence of interrelated decisions. It provides a systematic procedure for determining the combination of decisions that maximizes overall effectiveness."[17] It does not prescribe a single standard formulation, but involves an approach to problem-solving in which a complex problem with many variables is broken down into one-variable sub-problems which can be solved sequentially. Considerable ingenuity and insight may be required to make the conversion.

An elementary example would be the following: A product can be shipped via any one of several routes, not all passing through the same points but all including the same number of transfers enroute, from factory to warehouse. Each link involves different shipping costs. How should the route be planned to minimize total cost? A little reflection will suggest that the overall cheapest route may very well include one expensive link, if the other links balance it. As stated, the problem appears to require an enormous amount of calculation to sort the alternatives.[18]

Selecting or building a manageable model for a multistage problem is by far the most important aspect of the approach to a solution. Many algorithms have been developed and computer programs are readily available for dynamic programming procedures.

Network Models[19]

In Chapter 6 we displayed two networks designed to aid planning for, respectively, a survey research project and an experimental project. These are examples of PERT-type systems. The Program Evaluation and Review Technique was the name first given to a procedure applied to the U.S. Navy's Polaris missile program; since 1958 it has been exploited in government and industry, in both research and development. The DuPont Corporation, concerned with controlling time and costs required to bring new products from research stage to production, developed the network analysis technique called Critical Path Method (CPM). These are the two most widely-used approaches to project planning and control.

PERT

In order that a project be amenable to PERT analysis it must meet a relatively simple set of conditions:

1. There must be a well-defined set of jobs, the completion of which marks the end of the project; it must be possible to list all the jobs.
2. The beginning and end of one job must be clearly demarked from those of another to which it may be linked. Continuous-flow processes cannot be analyzed using this technique.
3. The ordered sequences in which the jobs are to be performed, must be specified. For each job, the immediate predecessor(s) must be identified and listed.

A flow plan is prepared as a way of checking that the information in 1 and 3 is properly assembled. On a particular flow plan there may be two or more alternative paths to completion. It is also necessary to obtain, from competent individuals, three estimates of the time required for each job: t_0 = optimistic (best) time estimate, t_p = pessimistic (worst) time estimate, and t_n = most-likely (normal) time estimate. From these an expected value

$$t = \frac{t_0 + 4t_n + t_p}{6}$$

and a variance

$$\sigma_t^2 = \left(\frac{t_p - t_0}{6}\right)^2$$

can be computed for each job. These are obtained from the beta probability distribution.

Two sets of "deadlines" can now be calculated: first, the earliest time at which each job can be started and finished (E.S. and E.F.), if all predecessor jobs have been started at their respective earliest times and completed in their respective times t. (F is the overall project completion time so computed.) Second, by working backwards from the target completion time T through the flow plan, the latest time at which each job can be started and finished (L.S. and L.F.) (if it and all jobs for which it is a predecessor are completed in their respective times t, so that the project completion will not be delayed beyond T). For each job, *slack time* is the difference between E.S. and L.S.; thus, it represents the time the start can be delayed without delaying the whole project beyond T. A *critical path* through the network is one whose total slack time is zero.

To illustrate how the system works, consider this (simplified) fictitious example: Two third grade classes, A and B, are to participate in an assembly program. Each class must be taught and rehearsed to perform a play; each class needs to prepare costumes, which can be done concurrently with rehearsals, and, in addition, class B must learn and rehearse a song. The program is to be presented in 30 days. Figure 15.2 shows the flow plan for the problem; Table 15.1 gives a list of the jobs, job predecessors, and calculated expected time per job.

We now return to Figure 15.2 and label each job with the pair (E.S., L.S.). If a job has more than one immediate predecessor, or is the immediate

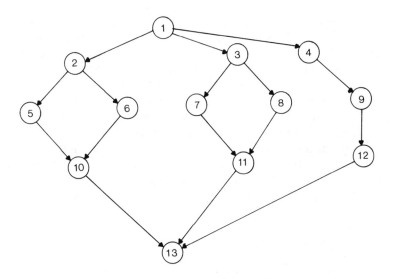

FIGURE 15.2. Flow plan for assembly program.

TABLE 15.1

Jobs for Class Play

Job	Description	Predecessor	Expected time in days
1	Start	—	0
2	Select play for class A	1	5^{20}
3	Select play for class B	1	5
4	Select song for class B	1	2
5	Make costumes for class A	2	10
6	Teach play to A	2	15
7	Make costumes for class B	3	10
8	Teach play to B	3	10
9	Teach song to B	4	5
10	Rehearse play A	5,6	5
11	Rehearse play B	7,8	5
12	Rehearse song B	9	3
13	Present program = Finish	10,11,12	

predecessor of more than one later job, we label it by the latest E.S. (as in the case of Job 10) or the earliest L.S. (as in the case of Job 2). The result is Figure 15.3.

The pair attached to Job 13 tells us that we can complete the task within the scheduled time of 30 days. The pairs attached to Jobs 2 and 3 tell us that to be finished by Day 30, we must select the plays no later than Days 5 and 10 respectively, whereas the song selection (Job 4) can be started as late as Day 20. Note that this network has no critical path.

The total slack time in this network is 5 days: This tells us we can delay starting until Day 5 without necessarily delaying the overall project completion beyond Day 30. Jobs such as Job 12, which has 20 days slack time, offer an opportunity for the scheduler to exercise discretion in setting start times, for jobs can be postponed to the L.S. time without delaying the project, and the persons needed to perform them can be assigned elsewhere in the meantime.

The statistical estimates of the times t also allow calculation of the probability that the project will be completed on time, or in 25 days.

PERT approaches to planning and control can be extremely helpful. A limitation is that this model omits cost and other considerations and is dependent on accurate time estimates. Computer programs are available that output all results from the input of the jobs in sequence and their respective t_o, t_p, and t_n.

CRITICAL PATH METHOD (CPM)

An outgrowth of PERT is CPM, which differs from the original in two important ways. *CPM* is deterministic in that it assumes times can be predicted with (statistical) certainty, so no variability estimates can be made. CPM also

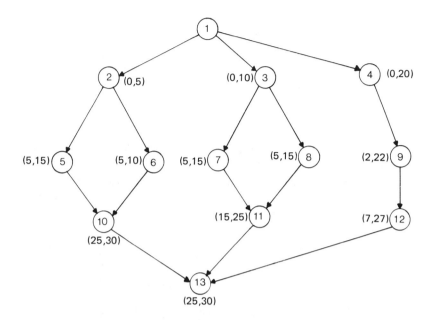

FIGURE 15.3. Network for assembly program.

incorporates a cost versus time trade-off for each job, and thus makes possible the search for a minimal cost solution.[21]

Both CPM and PERT lend themselves to formulation as linear programs (minimization). These generalizations have been called generalized evaluation review techniques: GERT. Network applications can clearly benefit from this useful approach as can any time-sequenced set of tasks.

Decision Theory

Decision-making, in research as in real life, involves the selection of one among two or more mutually exclusive alternatives, in order to achieve a desired outcome. A choice between explanations reflects an evaluation of probabilities in view of the logic of the situation; a choice among causes of action reflects an assessment of probable effectiveness.

A decision is commonly classified[22] according to whether it is made under conditions of:

1. Certainty: each action is known to lead invariably to a specific outcome; typically, decision making under certainty boils down to the solution of a (deterministic) optimization problem. For example, you are offered a dish of dimes and nickels, and must choose coins so that the total

number does not exceed 20 and the number of dimes does not exceed the number of nickels by more than 11. What is the largest value of your selection?

2. Risk: each action leads to one of a set of possible specific outcomes, and each outcome occurs with a probability known to the decision maker. For instance, a fair coin is tossed: If it comes up heads, you win double its value, if tails, you lose its value. How do you bet so as to optimize your gain?

3. Uncertainty: each action leads to a set of possible specific outcomes, but the probabilities of these outcomes are not known to the decision maker. For example, you are presented with a nickel, a dime, and a quarter. Any or all of them may be counterfeit. You may choose one coin and, if it is good, you keep it, but, if it is bad, you forfeit double its value. Which one should you choose?[23]

The literature of this field has focused on decision rules for Condition 3. We will present briefly some of those most frequently mentioned. It is important to keep in mind that the choice of a decision rule involves highly subjective considerations.

The basic formulation is as follows: $A_1, \ldots, A_m$ are actions (strategies) from which a choice must be made; $S_1, \ldots, S_n$ are *states of nature*[24] one of which is true but we do not know which, nor do we know their respective probabilities.[25] To each pair (A_i, S_j) we assign a payoff or utility u_{ij}. The numbers u_{ij} may be positive, negative, or zero; they may arise by theoretical assumptions, or from observation, or they may be purely subjective.[26]

To fix our ideas, consider the Utility Payoff Matrix:

Strategy	State of Nature	
	S_1	S_2
A_1	100	0
A_2	90	50
A_3	45	60

For instance, if you choose Strategy A_1 and the state of nature is S_1, the payoff is 100. Now let us look at a number of possible decision rules:

The maximin criterion: For each strategy A_i, find the worst outcome for that strategy, that is, the least u_{ij}. Now select the greatest among these, in effect, the least worst. This procedure maximizes the minimum gain. In our table, the least worst is $u_{22} = 50$ assigned to A_2 and S_2. Thus our decision is to choose A_2. Sometimes, confusingly, this is called the *minimax criterion* because it can be interpreted as minimizing the maximum loss.

The *maximax criterion* calls for the decision maker to choose the strategy where largest payoff is the greatest (go for broke). In our example, we choose A_1.

The *minimax regret (or risk) criterion*, suggested by Savage (1961), incorporates into the problem the risk, or opportunity loss, of an incorrect decision. To use this rule, locate the largest payoff U_j in each column S_j of the utility payoff matrix; now let $r_{ij} = U_j - u_{ij}$. Using the r_{ij}, form the Regret Payoff Matrix, which in our example is:

	S_1	S_2
A_1	0	60
A_2	10	10
A_3	55	0

Now apply the minimax (least worst) criterion to this matrix: We choose strategy A_2 because it leads to the least regret, 10 as opposed to 55 or 60. Other criteria can also be used with a regret matrix. There are a number of criticisms[27] of this criterion. Perhaps the one most interesting from our point of view is that even though the utilities u_{ij} are comparable (form an ordinal scale) the regrets r_{ij} may not be comparable: In our example, the regret $r_{21} = 10 = 100 - 90$ may not be the same in reality as the regret $r_{22} = 10 = 60 - 50$.

The *pessimism-optimism criterion* or *Hurwicz α criterion* is designed to avoid the excessive conservatism of the minimax criterion by utilizing a weighted combination of the best and the worst outcomes. The decision procedure starts with the selection of a number α between 0 and 1 called the pessimism-optimism α. For each A_i, let $m_i = \min \{u_{ij}\}$, $M_i = \max \{u_{ij}\}$ respectively the least and greatest payoff for that A_i. Now form $\alpha m_i + (1 - \alpha) M_i$ which is called the α-index of A_i. In our example, if $\alpha = 3/4$ and $1 - \alpha = 1/4$, the α-index of A_1 is $(3/4) \cdot 0 + (1/4) \cdot 100 = 25$, of A_2 is $(3/4) \cdot 50 + (1/4) \cdot 90 = 60$, of A_3 is $(3/4) \cdot 45 + (1/4) \cdot 60 = 48\ 3/4$. Since A_2 has the highest index, select strategy A_2. Among several difficulties associated with the use of this criterion is that of determining an α-level in a plausible way; in addition, it does not always resolve a decision in accord with intuitive judgment.

The *expected value criterion* involves a calculation very much like the preceding. It incorporates a set of probabilities p_j = probability of S_j, which may be obtained subjectively or from theory or prior observation. The decision rule is: for each A_i compute a "payoff index" $\sum_j u_{ij} p_j$, then select the strategy whose index is the greatest. If the states of nature are assumed to be equiprobable, in our example we could have $p_1 = p_2 = 1/2$, so the index for A_1 would be $(100) \cdot 1/2 + (0) \cdot (1/2) = 50$ for A_2, $(90) \cdot (1/2) + (50) \cdot (1/2) = 70$, for A_3 $45 \cdot (1/2) + 60 \cdot (1/2) = 52\ 1/2$, so we choose strategy A_2. If, on the other hand, we have reason to believe $p_1 = .9$ and $p_2 = .1$, then the payoff indices for A_1, A_2, A_3 are 90, 86, and 46.5 (respectively) so we would select A_1.

However the probability estimates may be made initially, later experience may suggest a revision of these estimates, which will in turn affect the decision outcome. This can be done effectively by means of a *Bayesian* analysis, a brief overview of which can be found in Luce and Raiffa (1957, p. 312), or Iverson (1984). Simple expositions of Bayes' theorem and examples of its application can be found in most elementary probability texts.[28] Many of these take advantage of decision tree notation and terminology. Mixed criteria such as the combination of a regret rule with a set of a priori probabilities can lead to interesting results. A very simple mixed example is the *maximum likelihood criterion* in which the strategy yielding the largest value of $u_{ij} p_j$ is selected.

It is clear that information has value in the decision-making process if it can help us identify the payoffs in the utility matrix. Frequently, this information is obtained from sample data and thus is probabilistic in character. Sample information is not so valuable as "perfect information" which would reflect the true state of nature. Even though the latter is not available, it is possible to define and calculate an efficiency ratio for the sample information at hand, and thus to determine the relative costs and benefits of collecting additional information.[29]

While decision theory is useful in leading us to an optimal decision, it has a severe limitation: The data needed to complete the utility (payoff) matrix may be unknown, unknowable a priori, or unmeasureable. Assigning utility values u_{ij} to the events or outcomes (A_i, S_j) is extremely difficult; it is basically a subtle measurement problem. Many projects are unable to take advantage of the tools of decision analysis, because the functions which define the objectives of the decision are not clearly identified or explicitly formulated, so payoffs cannot be calculated.

Finite Markov Chain Processes[30]

We now consider two fictitious examples which, because of their common elements, will lead to the same model.

1. An employer carries out a semiannual rating scheme in order to assess need for retraining programs. Experience data reveal that if the last rating was "superior", the employee's chance of being rated "superior" again is 2/3 and of being rated "good" is 1/3; whereas, if the last rating was "good," ratings of "superior" and "good" are equiprobable. Overall, 60% of all employees are rated "superior." After how many years can a cohort of employees be expected to achieve the overall "superior" proportion? What are the implications of this?

2. A transit company offers its passengers two choices of vehicle on a certain commuter route: small jitneys (minibuses) and standard large buses. Schedules and fares are identical. Over a period of several weeks, a large number of passengers are repeatedly interviewed, and the data reveal that of those who use a jitney for any one trip, 90% use it the next trip and 10% switch; whereas, of those who use the big bus for any one trip, 80% use it again and 20% switch. In the long run, what proportion of all passengers can the company expect to use each sort of vehicle? What are the implications?

Each example presents us with a finite set of alternatives, $a_1, \ldots, a_r$, called *states*. In (1) the states are a_1 = "superior", a_2 = "good"; in (2) the states are a_1 = takes the jitney, a_2 = takes the bus. In addition, in each example we have a set of *transition probabilities*, defined so that p_{ij} is the probability that if the system is in state i at a specified time it will be in state j after the next unit of time. Using the p_{ij} we write a transition matrix P, which for our examples are respectively

$$\text{(1) } P_1 = \begin{bmatrix} \tfrac{2}{3} & \tfrac{1}{3} \\ \tfrac{1}{2} & \tfrac{1}{2} \end{bmatrix} \text{ and (2) } P_2 = \begin{bmatrix} .9 & .1 \\ .2 & .8 \end{bmatrix}$$

It is easy to show that

$$P_1^n \longrightarrow \begin{bmatrix} .6 & .4 \\ .6 & .4 \end{bmatrix}$$

as n increases and that in fact, when $n > 3$, P_1^n is very close to its limit. From this we can conclude that after three rating periods, the employees "average" 60% superior. Similarly, it is easy to show that

$$P_2^n \longrightarrow \begin{bmatrix} \tfrac{2}{3} & \tfrac{1}{3} \\ \tfrac{2}{3} & \tfrac{1}{3} \end{bmatrix},$$

which suggests that in the long run, 2/3 of the passengers will be taking the jitney. The transit company might do well either to offer an inducement to bus passengers or to invest in more jitneys.

These examples exhibit some of the characteristics of finite Markov chain processes. The questions we have raised are only a few among the many which can be approached using this model. To use it and to exploit some of the generalizations, you must have or acquire the necessary mathematics background. Apart from terminology, the basic concepts and procedures are quite simple. If you are interested in questions concerning the evolution of systems over repeated trials, such an effort will be repaid in increased flexibility of analysis.

Inventory Models[31]

An inventory control model may be appropriate whenever the situation under study can be formulated as an excess "supply of goods" stored in anticipation of "future orders": When the supply gets low it must be replenished to avoid delaying the orders. The answers to the following questions determine the "inventory policy":

1. What is the per item cost of storage? (This may vary with inventory size).
2. What are the per item capital costs of "producing" the items? (This may vary with the size of the "production" run.)
3. What is the per item cost of placing the order for replenishing "stock"?
4. When should the inventory be replenished? That is, to how low a level can the supply fall before a reorder must be placed?
5. How many items should be ordered when the inventory is replenished?

Mathematical inventory models exist that permit solution using techniques of the calculus or linear programming. Probability estimates can also be introduced into the model.

Certain research problems lend themselves to formulation using this approach. Nagel and Neef present an example[32] concerning the optimum percentage of defendants to hold in jail prior to trial. Their analysis is lucidly written and extremely instructive. Another, perhaps complementary question, involves jurors: Some cities allow those summoned for jury service to phone the court officer each day at 5:00 pm and find out whether to appear in person the next day. On the basis of the progress of the court calendars, how should be the appearance of jurors be scheduled (how should the inventory level of "goods" be set and how should the "supply" be replenished) so as to minimize both jury fees (the "cost of production") paid and salary lost?

If your study leads to questions of this type, the exploitation of an inventory model may be fruitful. It may take some imagination to see a research problem as one to which this technique can be applied.

Waiting Line (Queueing) Models

Many questions concerned with access to services, or passage through a checkpoint or other bottleneck, can be analyzed using the terminology and techniques of waiting line or queueing theory. Problems occurring in all kinds of social science research suggest a waiting line approach if they involve for instance:

- Traffic flow on highways at tollbooths or construction sites;
- Need for staff to serve children during peak and off-peak periods in a school cafeteria;
- Determining number of doctors to be assigned to a hospital emergency room, based on data collected earlier (patient load, seriousness of ailments, season, etc.);[33]
- Waiting time for interviews and/or processing in a social service agency;
- Delay in placement of young babies in foster care (this may also suggest an inventory model, with a "stock" of foster parents);
- Scheduling of court calendars to minimize waiting time for hearings or trials;
- College registration procedures;
- Business applications, such as processing of loan applications or insurance claims, filling mail orders, scheduling a repair service (with a priority system), etc.

To make use of the queueing model, it is necessary to identify several characteristics of the system:

1. What is the statistical or probabilistic distribution of "customers"' arrival times?
2. How many (finite or infinite) are permitted to queue up?
3. How are "customers" selected for service? The *service discipline* may be first-come-first-served or random or may reflect some priority procedures such as triage.
4. How many *service facilities*, for example, bank cashiers, nurses, etc. are there?
5. How long, on average, does a customer require for the service? What is the probability distribution of service times? It is frequently assumed

that arrival time distribution is Poisson and service time distribution is exponential.

From this information, it will be possible to predict:

1. The probability that the system is empty;
2. The probability that there are n customers in the system;
3. The average number of customers in the system;
4. The average number of customers in the queue;
5. The probability that an arriving customer has to wait for service;
6. The average holding time (= waiting time + service time) per customer.

Other information, such as the likelihood that a customer will "balk," that is, leave the system before being served, can also be incorporated. Based on these data, a decision can be made as to the benefits and costs of increasing or decreasing the number of service facilities.[34]

As in the case of the inventory model, the use of a waiting line approach for a research problem requires making the association between the technique and the question as posed. An open mind is a far more important asset in evaluating a possible model than a high degree of expertise, since the latter can always be acquired in one way or another.

Afterword

The methods described in this chapter have been underutilized in research studies. If a problem can be stated so that a specified objective is to be optimized subject to a set of boundary conditions (constraints), then it would be worthwhile to seek a deterministic solution to the problem. Likewise, if your research question falls into a class of problems in which a certain model is conventionally used, but the values of the parameters for the model are unknown, your data can perhaps be exploited for this purpose; a later study can then be predictive, and its analysis statistical in the usual sense. Consider deterministic alternatives in your research.

On the other hand, if the data are such that several outcomes, rather than a single one, are plausible, then a probabilistic formulation is necessary.

Notes

[1]See Stevens (1972). Plutchik (1974 [ed. 2], Chapter 12) is also pertinent and useful. For a critique, see Coleman (1964).

[2]Coleman and Rainwater (1978, pp. 266-275; also Appendix B).

[3]See, for instance, Kemeny and Snell (1972, Chapter 8); Kemeny, Snell, and Thompson (1966 [ed. 2], pp. 424-433). Also, for other approaches, see Boyd (1969), White (1963), or Knoke and Kuklinski (1982).

[4]See, for instance, Blalock (1969). Notwithstanding: "I never learned mathematics, so I had to think." (Joan Robinson, quoted in *New York Times*, August 10, 1983).

[5]The choice of model depends as much on the characteristics of the maker as on those of the problem, and reflects many intellectual and personality variables. It is also fair to point out that the value of mathematical models in the social sciences is still controversial. See Charlesworth (1963) for some very well expressed and thoughtful opinions. See also Blalock et al. (1975) for an insight into the state-of-the-art in sociology, and Rashevsky (1968) for proposed models for historical analysis. See also Miller (1970, pp. 155-159) for examples.

[6]This section assumes you have at least a hearsay acquaintance with the analytic geometry of the plane. For calculus material, see this chapter's Additional Reading list; this is an overview, not a review.

[7]See Hull (1945).

[8]Kemeny and Snell (1972) present in Chapter 3 a model for an ecological problem which leads to a pair of differential equations.

[9]Easily readable is Coleman, (1968).

[10]There are many variations in notation. We will use the max problem as the basic case.

[11]For a very elementary exposition, see Nadler (1973).

[12]Procedure described in Cooper & Steinberg (1970, 1974).

[13]See Cooper and Steinberg (1970, Chapter 9); Anderson et al. (1978, Chapter 12); Hillier and Lieberman (1974, Chapter 27).

[14]Anderson et al. (1976, Chapter 4) or (1978, Chapter 10).

[15]See Hillier and Lieberman (1974, Chapter 18); note that we are emphasizing the max case, but the corresponding min case is also accessible.

[16]See Cooper and Steinberg (1970, p. 90, 101ff.); Hillier and Lieberman (1974).

[17]Hillier and Lieberman (1974, p. 248).

[18]A number of examples can be found in Hillier and Lieberman (1974, Chapter 6). See also Kemeny and Snell (1972, Chapter 9) for an amusing discussion, and Cooper and Steinberg (1970, pp. 350ff.).

[19]See Anderson et al. (1978, Chapter 14) or (1976, Chapter 8); also Hillier and Lieberman (1974, Chapter 5).

[20]This is calculated, for this job, from fictitious data: $t_o = 1$ day, $t_p = 9$ days, $t_n = 5$ days, $t = \dfrac{1+4.5\times 9}{6} = 5$. The estimated variance is then $(9-1)^2 = 1.78$ and σ_t is 1.33 which means that there is a 99.7% probability this job will be completed in between 2.3 and 7.7 days. Of course, this conclusion requires an assumption of normality.

[21]The PERT/Cost system also allows decisions to take in cost as a factor.

[22]We will follow the point of view of Luce and Raiffa (1957, Sec. 2.1 and Chapter 13). Also very useful as a reference is Anderson et al., (1978, Chapters 4 and 7) or (1976, Chapter 10). An elementary presentation can be found in Lapin (1982).

[23]Luce and Raiffa (1957) add a fourth: "a combination of uncertainty and risk in the light of experimental evidence," and observe that this is the province of statistical inference (p. 13; see also pp. 318ff.).

[24]This term is not defined here but should be clear intuitively; roughly, it means "reality possibilities."

[25]If these were available, the problem could be approached differently. See Luce and Raiffa (1957, p. 277). Also, see Scheff (1963) for discussion in the context of medical diagnosis.

[26]Nicely presented in Nagel with Neef (1976, pp. 55-56); their discussion illustrates the role of subjectivity.

[27]See Luce and Raiffa (1957, pp. 280-282).

[28]The discussions in Anderson et al. (1978, pp. 35-39 and Chapter 5) are very clear and helpful.

[29]See Anderson et al. (1978, Chapter 5) or (1976, Chapter 10).

[30]There is no avoiding the dependence of this section on some familiarity with matrix algebra (see any standard text). References include Anderson et al. (1978, Chapter 11) or (1976, Chapter 16); Adams (1979, Chapter 12), Kemeny and Snell (1972, Appendix C); Hillier and Lieberman (1974, Chapter 12 [more technical]).

[31]See Anderson et al. (1976, Chapter 11) or (1978, Chapter 15); Hillier and Lieberman (1974, Chapter 11 [more technical]).

[32]Nagel with Neef (1976, pp. 38ff.).

[33]This example is discussed at some length in Hillier and Lieberman (1974, p. 380); citation is provided.

[34]See Anderson et al. (1976, Chapter 14) or (1978, Chapter 17); Hillier and Lieberman (1974, Chapters 9 and 10 [more detailed and more technical]). Informative examples, useful formulas.

Additional Reading

Ayres (1964), *Calculus*.
Bellman and Dreyfus (1962), *Applied Dynamic Programming*.
Bers (1969), *Calculus* (2 vol.).
Anderson, Sweeney and Williams (1976), *Introduction to Management Science (IMS)*.
Anderson, Sweeney and Williams (1978), *Essentials of Management Science (EMS)*.
Coleman, J. S., *The Mathematical Study of Change*, Chapter 11 in Blalock and Blalock (1968).
Coleman, J.S., *Introduction to Mathematical Sociology* (1964).
Cooper and Steinberg (1974), *Methods and Applications of Linear Programming*: needs strong mathematics background.
Cooper and Steinberg (1970), *Methods of Optimization*: needs strong mathematics background.
Hillier and Lieberman (1974), *Methods of Operations Research*.
Lapin (1982), *Statistics for Modern Business Decisions*: strong sections on decision theory, Bayesian analysis, subjective probability.
Luce and Raiffa (1957), *Games and Decisions*.
Kemeny and Snell (1972), *Mathematical Models in Social Sciences*.
Kemeny, Snell and Thompson (1966), *Introduction to Finite Mathematics*.
Milne-Thompson (1960), *Calculus of Finite Differences*.
Nagel with Neef (1976), *Operations Research Methods*.
Sawyer, W. W., (1949) *Mathematicians' Delight*; (1961), *What Is Calculus About*.
Speigel, Murray (1963), *Advanced Calculus*.
Williams, J., (1954), *Complete Strategyst*: simple and enjoyable introduction to game theory.

In addition, each topic has a reference list (see endnotes).

16

Endgame

This chapter is concerned primarily with setting forth the outcomes of your study: in particular, the presentation of your results and of your overall report according to the most widely used pattern. We offer a checklist which may be helpful, but some departments use a different dissertation model. Therefore, you should check with your committee chairman, or consult the library's file of completed theses, before starting the writing-up phase of your project. Journals and funding agencies such as HEW have other standards, so we have included short sections on preparing articles and evaluation reports, with several references.

At the end of the chapter, we offer some advice on literary style with an emphasis on readability.

Evaluating the Design of Your Study

The design of your study is the plan of the circumstances or conditions within which your observations will be made, and the evidence so obtained will be recorded and analyzed. It thus includes general methodology (research type), procedures, treatments (i.e. selection or manipulation of the internal or external environments of the subjects), selection of population, instruments for measuring and recording effects, and choice of statistical procedures. To present the design is to present the framework for the tests of relationships among the variables, in effect, to describe a set of instructions or descriptions for replication. The design must be so formulated that as the researcher you can isolate, observe, and make an inference about the effects that in your analysis of the problem you have identified as the objects of your study. No matter how interesting the evidence may be, if it does not permit you to decide that the desired solution has been achieved, the design is inadequate.[1]

Throughout this book we have stressed that a number of pieces must fit together smoothly. Evaluating a design thus involves the consideration of compatibilities, including the following:

- Design and Definitions: Do the individuals or events that you will observe truly embody the constructs you want to relate to each other? That is, have you appropriately operationalized the constructs?
- Design and Hypotheses: Are all the variables accounted for? Have you eliminated or accounted for sources of variance other than those associated with the independent variables? Do the hypotheses deal with all the effects you will systematically observe? Is it clear from the design which are the dependent variables?
- Design and Measurement: Do the procedures you specify yield measures of the kind required by your hypotheses? Will your measurement be sufficiently but not excessively refined? Are all the variables measured? Are all the possible combinations of variables accounted for?
- Design and Computer Use: Does your plan for making observations and recording the evidence take advantage of computer sorting, exhibiting, summarizing and analysis? Have you exploited appropriate computerized procedures, for example, recording of data, timing, etc.? (See Chapter 9, passim.)
- Design and Statistical Procedures: Is there a statistical procedure appropriate to your problem? If there are several, have you a clear idea of why you chose the one you did? Are the data you propose to collect susceptible to a statistical analysis of a type which will permit you to make the necessary inferences? Is your population large enough to allow you to argue probabilistically?
- Design and Purpose of the Study: If you will need to use the conclusions to make or implement decisions in "real life", does your design incorporate all relevant issues? Will your conclusions allow for generalization, that is, is your design sufficiently broad?
- Design and the Traditions of Your Problem Area: If you do not use a design analogous to those in comparable studies, are you prepared to account for your decision? Are you familiar with the strengths and weaknesses of your design as opposed to the traditional ones?

The foregoing is summarized in the following:

> Of course, if we are to have any confidence in the results of our analysis, then the construction of reliable and valid indicators of our key concepts is an absolute necessity as are appropriate data collection and data reduction strategies. . . . [T]he success of one's data analysis depends upon proper execution of all the steps in the research process prior to the analysis stage. In fact [we] would go so far as to argue that if one's causal analysis goes astray, it will more likely be due to carrying out the earlier steps in the research process poorly rather than to any misuse of the techniques which are relatively straightforward and easily learned. Poor theory, unsatisfactory operational definitions, and the like are more likely to frustrate analysis than any mistakes in application of techniques. If one errs in the actual application of techniques, the analysis can in most

instances be redone correctly. But if one has omitted a key variable from the data collection or invalidly measured a key concept, then statistically "correct" analysis may still yield incorrect results.[2]

Far better an approximate answer to the right question, which is often vague, than an exact answer to the wrong question, which can always be made precise.[3]

The Overall Structure of the Report

In its structure, the report parallels the study: There are three main parts:

1. The problem: general problem statement, in question form (see Chapter 2, section on stating the problem-question); subproblems, operationalized; hypotheses, preferably in testable form; variables and their definitions; general and research literature related to the problem (previous studies).
2. The methodology: pilot studies and pretesting, if any; population; sampling procedures; method used to test hypotheses; manipulation of independent variables(s): treatments, data gathering procedures, description of instruments (reliability, validity), and measurement techniques; data analysis procedures.
3. The results: findings, presented accurately and completely; support or nonsupport for hypotheses; conclusions and interpretations of the results; limitations and weaknesses of the study; implications for application, for theory, and/or further study.

We discuss these below, in turn.

Review of Related Literature:
Suggesting the Importance of the Study

The presentation of your review of the literature will stand or fall on how well you organize your ideas. You must arrange the material so that the reader can see the logical flow of major and subsidiary theory and can readily associate each report you cite with (1) the theory for which it provides evidence or counterevidence, and (2) previous studies whose findings it confirms or contradicts. The natural progression of concepts, previous findings, and theoretical implications must be apparent, and converge sharply on the proposed problem-question. If several aspects of theory converge or conflict in your problem be sure to summarize them. You do not want to impose a mysterious do-it-yourself project on the reader.

To achieve this organization is not simple, nor is it impossible. It may be convenient to arrange background material according to the major variables in your study, in which case each empirical report cited must indicate which variables were juxtaposed. Another organizational scheme is based on a list of subproblems; yet still another reflects the principal theoretical constructs. You will find it helpful to read as models several examples of recent dissertations or research reports: Ask your mentors to suggest a few titles. A useful undergraduate trick is to make a trial outline by arranging, on the floor, index cards labelled by major topics—beware of pets, roommates, children, and gusts of wind—and to shift the cards around until the sequence pleases you.

Our best advice is to allow sufficient time to think through this aspect of your study. It may be necessary to revise your presentation of the review of the literature after design and data analysis have been more completely planned.

Ideally, at the end of your background discussion, your reader will regard your problem-question as inevitable. It will appear to be a natural outgrowth of earlier studies and will be entirely justified by appropriate theoretical considerations. The importance of your study will be perfectly clear—above all, to you—in the following respects:

- What is the same? Will your results and procedures permit comparisons? innovation in procedure or anaysis will you offer?
- What is different? What alternative viewpoint is embodied? Is there a different population or instrument involved?
- What is better? How will your arguments and results avoid defects or remedy omissions of earlier studies? Are your techniques more refined? Will your evidence permit a more conclusive test of theory?
- What is the same? Will your results and procedures permit comparisons?

Presentation of Design and Methodology

The goal of the section of your report that presents design and methodology is to make unmistakably clear to other researchers what you have done, and what they will have to do in order to replicate your study. It is necessary to include sufficient detail to permit repetition of the experiment or survey, so that any unusual or special aspects should be carefully described. On the other hand, there is no need to do more than refer to readily available descriptions of standard equipment, procedures, analysis, etc.

In your presentation, you should include:

- population: selection, size of sample, assignment of subjects to treatments, specifications;
- procedures: exact treatments, schedule, time lapses between phases, number and training of observers and of those administering treatment, special controls, data-gathering techniques including coding, equipment specifications;
- design: type; if experimental, classification (e.g., 2 × 2); and justification of your choice;
- measurements: instruments used, source, validity and reliability, justification of choice, description of construction if relevant;
- data analysis: method (describe unusual methods or modifications);
- pilot study: purpose, outcomes.

Even though space limitations may require you to abbreviate the report, it is of the greatest importance that you set forth the methodology in sufficient detail so that the hypotheses can be clearly identified and the research procedure reconstructed and evaluated. It is instructive to apply the criteria given in Chapter 3 to your own report.

What To Make of It

It is important to distinguish between the two aspects of the endgame: *arriving* at conclusions and interpretations, and *reporting* them. Every manual for researchers exhibits the same inability to specify guidelines for how to generate explanations or formulate explanatory concepts, how to perceive patterns, how to establish continuity between what is previously known and what is newly observed. (On the other hand, once you have perceived such patterns or begun to formulate explanations, manuals can be very helpful in suggesting ways to describe them and to display them persuasively to your reader.) "Interpretation [which] is the search for the broader meaning of the research findings"[4] requires courage and imagination, the willingness to take risks. We have no prescription, nor did we have one for developing conjectures or models (theories), as in guessing which are the antecedent and which the mediating variables. "The leap from data to discovery"[5] eludes specification, because at the present time no inductive logical step is very clearly understood, and not, we think, because it is intrinsically mysterious or supernatural. We can, however, pass along to you our experience in guiding other beginning researchers.

As in every other component of your research project, the key step is asking the appropriate question(s). Thus, clearly stated problem-questions and their tentative answers in the form of conjectures, whether or not cast in the form of testable hypotheses, are enormously helpful as a guide in your exploration of the data. Keeping these conjectures in mind—preferably right in front of you while you inspect your data and the outcomes of analysis—will prevent you from getting lost in the complexity of comparisons and relationships or distracted by irrelevant patterns. The "let's take a look" strategies for data manipulation and interpretation reflect the absence of hypotheses. While it is surely true that the most interesting outcomes emerge from exploration (as opposed to confirmation), and from insights obtained in thoughtful contemplation of nonquantified data, nonetheless, multivariate exploratory projects are not in general appropriate for novice researchers, and a first project must be closely guided by conjecture.

Most experienced researchers agree that analysis precedes data collection, in the sense that outcomes should be anticipated in the study design, in the classification of variables, in the identification of categories, and in the coding of responses. These decisions are of particular importance when open-ended interview material is in question, but it should be evident that information gathered by whatever procedure (questionnaire, direct observation, or inspection of documents) is useless in their absence.

Theoretical frameworks and findings in related studies suggest appropriate classification schemes. Likewise, previous and cognate studies should guide your search for explanations, that is, for factors other than those identified and measured.

Exploit your rationale, don't just summarize your findings, or simply describe the decisions suggested by statistical testing. The process that led from the background literature, to hypotheses, to data collection, to analysis, must be reversed: Refer your conclusions, in terms of the original problem-question, back to the literature. Figure 16.1 illustrates schematically the successively more focussed refinements, modifications, and decisions which precede data collection and analysis, followed by the successively broader formulations of the outcomes of the project.

Since this is not an ideal world, the most interesting outcomes are often those which contradict one's expectations or occur in the absence of any expectations: "fringe effects." Exceptions are a rich source of speculation, more instructive than predicted patterns because they force you to consider alternatives. Such findings encourage the researcher to take another look at earlier "outlier" studies and to speculate about possible omitted variables.

Our comments boil down to this: Think about your data, play with possibilities, free associate on the findings. Clip the statements of your hypotheses to your print-outs so you aren't distracted by turning pages, or

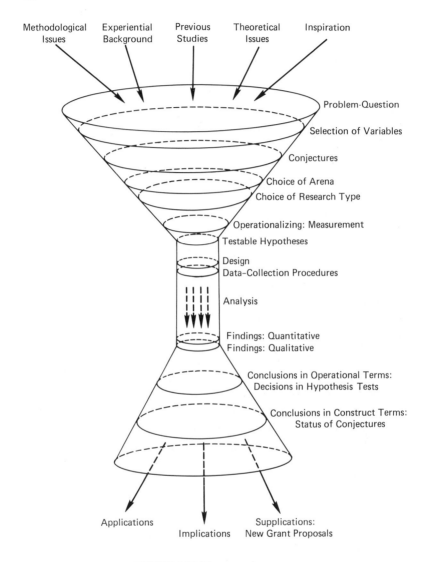

FIGURE 16.1 The research process.

lay the cross tabulations out on the floor, shifting them around physically while you compare effects. Give yourself enough time and do not rush precipitately to cast your conclusions into a standard form. If possible, talk your explanations through with an informed colleague before you begin to write your report.

The Statement of Findings

When you complete the observational phase of your project and the analysis of your data by statistical or other suitable techniques, your remaining tasks are to present your findings and to discuss their implications. Appropriately included in this discussion are:

- verification of hypotheses
- generalizations
- relationship of your findings to those of other studies
- resolution of contradictions
- suggestions for further study or action based on your results
- indication of support—or the reverse—for the theory on which your problem is based.

Some of these items are far removed from the data (evidence obtained from observations).

It is essential that you keep perfectly clear in your mind the distinction between findings and everything else mentioned in the preceding paragraph. The arrangement of your presentation should reflect a strict separation between data (the record of your observations) and their summary and analysis on the one hand, and your interpretations, conclusions, and comments on the other. Articles often combine all these in one section, whereas theses and other long reports usually emphasize the distinction. Each university department (indeed each dissertation committee) and each journal has its own conventional format and its own criteria for deciding which items for deciding are to be regarded as "findings" and which as "conclusions." You will be wise to consult your chairman, editor, or other research supervisor, and follow the prescribed style of organization. Ask for references to suitable models. If no guidelines are offered, adopt a stringent definition of "findings."

WHAT ARE FINDINGS?

Your description of findings is the crux of your report, because it is the base from which you will arrive at an answer to the question originally posed, embodied in your problem statement. By *findings* we mean:

- Data: the record of your observations. These may be numerical, as in the case of measurements (scores) obtained through the use of instruments, or counts of individuals in each of various categories. They may be entirely verbal, as in the case of material obtained through interviews or notes made in the field. They may be pictorial, as in the case of photographs or drawings of specimens or of characteristic dress or posture. In historical studies, newly discovered documents or other source materials are described under findings.

- Summaries of data and the outcome of statistical procedures applied to the data: once again, these may be verbal, but more likely they will involve a greater or lesser amount of numerical analysis carried out by computer. The results may be displayed in the form of graphs. Included here are the statistical measures which you have decided are best for your purpose, and the probabilities associated with their values.
- Descriptions of shortcomings, errors, or omissions in equipment, observations, procedure, assumptions, sampling, or analysis that you noticed in the course of carrying out your study.

Discussion of the foregoing, or conclusions you draw, are not properly "findings" and we believe they do not belong in this section of your report. It is preferable to follow the section on findings with one devoted to conclusions, implications, discussion, and summary.

PRESENTATION OF FINDINGS

It is difficult to give general rules concerning presentation because of the great variety of studies in the social and behavioral sciences. Your best strategy is to read several well-regarded reports of studies related to yours, and note how the findings are presented. However, it is possible to set forth some general criteria that you should make an effort to satisfy.

The presentation may be one or more of the following:

- Visual: Illustrations can have a high value in published research. Photographs of subjects, sketches or photos of artifacts or of the environment, and diagrams of all kinds, as well as graphics such as histograms (see Chapter 11, section on graphs) are among the possibilities you should seriously consider. Graphs should be properly chosen for the kind of data, clearly drawn, and informatively labelled and titled. Photographs or sketches should be easy to make out, clearly titled, and of suitable size.
- Tabular: Tables should be so arranged that the reader cannot fail to notice the aspect of the data you wish to exhibit. When appropriate, percentage figures or cumulative totals or marginal totals should be shown. The outcomes of computation, as opposed to subtotals, etc., should be displayed together with any appropriate probability values or predicted error terms. When there are many variables or numerous tests of association, be sure that each table or other display is clearly labelled and titled. If you have any doubt that your intended reader can understand the tabular material, you can give a brief statement of what the table

shows, but be sure you have really made it easier to understand, not just expanded the section by reformulating the substance of a table or graph in words. You may save effort, and avoid errors, by using computer print-outs, reproduced as an appendix, instead of recapitulating the data analysis in typed form.

- Verbal: Descriptions, particularly of procedures and background information, are often best presented in verbal form. Case study methodologies may require extended verbal presentations. Consider lists and similar abbreviated formats when appropriate, rather than complete sentences or standard paragraphs.

Your presentation, in order to be more intelligible to the reader and to serve as the foundation for your discussion and conclusions, must be both clear and orderly. This means:

- You must accurately gauge the probable level of knowledge and sophistication of your reader.[6] It is as improper to recite the obvious as it is to omit essential definitions, assumptions, and references needed to understand your findings. You cannot presume the presence of special expertise, particularly in the areas of statistics and the use of equipment; neither can you refer to previous research or researchers in an offhand way unless you are certain there can be no confusion. If you are in doubt, a brief statement can provide information without condescension.
- Your description of findings must be complete. When you formulated hypotheses and delineated methodology, you indicated that you intended to make certain observations; all of those proposed observations must now be accounted for. Evasiveness in acknowledging obvious omissions or errors serves no scientific purpose. If you neglected to make certain observations or were unable to obtain certain data, you should say so. If your study attempted to replicate findings in an earlier study, but could not do so, you have an obligation to say this: It is not necessarily the case that *your* results are inaccurate. The previous report may be incomplete or otherwise misleading. Data obtained in a pilot study and used to make decisions about how to proceed in the main study, should be identified as such; likewise, demographic or background data should be exhibited and labelled. You will not be able to discuss or draw conclusions from data which are not available to the reader.
- Your description of findings must be unambiguous. Your reader must have no difficulty understanding what you have observed and what statistical summaries you have computed. In your description, you must make clear what constructs were in question, and what were the in-

dicators. Make an attempt to read what you have written with a naive eye; if it is not entirely clear, rewrite it.

- Your description must be logical, in that findings are grouped according to some plausible principle. The reader should not have to turn back and forth searching for the results of related procedures. The time you spend planning the presentation will be well repaid in superior organization. A liberal use of section headings will guide the reader through the structure of your report.
- Your presentation must be objective. There is no place for justification, value judgments, partisan interpretations, or selective emphasis.
- Your description should be concise. Do not repeat yourself; do not run on; do not vacuously embellish. Discursiveness in this section is no virtue, but avoid the cryptic.

COMMON ERRORS IN PRESENTATION OF FINDINGS

By far the most frequent mistake found in reports prepared by experienced researchers, as well as by beginners, is the contamination of the presentation of findings by interpretive discussion. Try to avoid this unless you are directed by your research supervisor to combine conclusions and generalizations with the findings. Even in this case, be sure the distinction is clear to you. This will be most helpful in the event you give an abbreviated oral version of your report, for example, a talk to a professional society or a thesis defense.

Another common error is an excessive preoccupation with the details of computation. Most readers find this distracting and confusing; the others can find what they want to know about unusual algorithms in an appendix or by referring to a standard manual. It is also tiresome to read lengthy translations or verbal restatements of the statistical summaries and tests; there is little purpose to this, but it is almost epidemic in dissertations. (As always, however, follow your departmental rules where they exist.)

Inadequate titling, labelling, or identification of sources provide the maximum in both mystification and frustration for the reader. A fellow researcher can be most helpful in pointing out such lapses.

A hurried preparation of this section of your report will show up in poor organization. You may be impatient at this stage of your project, and your deadline may be approaching, but it is important nonetheless to allow sufficient time for reflection. Although you should keep separate the findings and the conclusions in your report, you will find that if you mentally place the findings with the corresponding conclusions, and arrange them in a coherent order, many of the problems of developing the organization of both sections will have been solved in advance. Brief topic headings make both writing the report and reading it much smoother.

Your Conclusions

The first item of business in this section of your report is an explicit statement of the status of your statistical hypotheses (if any) in view of your findings. The next is the reformulation of your results in terms of the research hypotheses. It is advisable to restate each statistical hypothesis of the study and then indicate whether the null hypothesis is to be rejected, and at what level of significance; this decision is made on the basis of the probability calculated from your data. (If you are not making use of inferential statistics, then you should refer to whatever distributions are pertinent, for example, comparison of two obtained values of the contingency coefficient; do not force your conclusions into inferential form.) Where there are alternative hypotheses, you must state them and indicate which is supported.

You should now restate the research hypotheses and indicate whether your findings support them; if the evidence suggests that a research hypothesis is false, you must acknowledge this explicitly.[7] Your original problem statement was, we hope, sufficiently straightforward so that you can now indicate succinctly what answer you have obtained to the underlying question. All the conclusions must be phrased in a form that other investigators can understand and subsequently verify.

The foregoing constitute your conclusions in the strict sense, and should be displayed immediately following your findings and preceding your critical comments on the study and your discussion of its implications.

RECAPITULATION OF PROBLEM STATEMENT

It is conventional to set forth in the final chapter of a dissertation a recapitulation of the problem, the theoretical background, description of relevant earlier studies, and description of populations, treatments, and special techniques. (In shorter articles it is appropriate simply to restate the problem in the light of the findings; that is, to provide enough information so that the reader can tell what is your answer to the question originally posed.) Try to avoid burdening your readers with excessive detail which blurs a clear view of the research problem and its solution; on the other hand, offer enough to allow them to see what you have achieved. (You can refer to an earlier section or page of your report in order to avoid repetition.) If your problem was extremely complex or had many parts, this section may be quite long. Do not try to present an entirely self-contained discussion: Work on the assumption that the reader is sufficiently motivated to read the whole of your report or to look back into earlier chapters.[8]

Critical Comment: Implications and (General) Discussion

Following your conclusions, which are more or less narrowly justified by your findings, it is appropriate that you discuss the implications of your study. This section of the report can be quite speculative in tone, so long as you do not suggest that you are making an inference in the usual sense. You may want to comment on any or all of these:

- Meaning of conclusions or findings in the light of theory—Do your findings serve to reject, confirm or synthesize already existing theory, or to suggest new theory? How should your rationale be reinterpreted in the light of your data?
- Meaning in the light of previous studies—Are your findings compatible with those of earlier studies or do they extend them? How do they relate to the history of the ideas you have been exploring?
- Meaning for further studies—Do your findings suggest modifications or new directions for study? In effect, you can offer a re-review of the literature.
- Meaning for application—What predictions in real situations become more plausible?
- Meaning for action[9]—To what use can the evidence in your study be put in making decisions about real situations?

The discussion will reflect your overall knowledge of the field, your familiarity with its ramifications, and your good judgment.

Your overall comment should begin with an indication of the general value of the study. This includes not only remarks concerning the importance of the problem area, but your informed opinion of the importance of the results you have obtained, for example, that they extend to a new population or to one acting under new conditions the expectation that a certain phenomenon will occur. If you have confirmed observations reported by other researchers, you should so state. This is the place to suggest the desirability of further study—or perhaps the uselessness of further study—as justified by your results. You have made a major contribution if your research area makes the problem more interesting or potentially more fruitful.

A close reinspection of your rationale (problem background) may lead to the following organization: Unexpected findings suggest the need for alternative explanations and the construction, and thus the empirical testing, of a new or modified theoretical chain. Expected findings, which appear to confirm the research hypotheses, suggest the need for further refinement of alternative explanations and a search for definitive evidence to eliminate the alternatives. In addition, the logical implications of the theory from which the research hypotheses were deduced can now be pursued with greater confidence.

To the extent that your findings permit generalization, you should set forth these inferences as clearly and logically as possible. (This is true whether you have formulated and tested hypotheses, or your study has been exploratory.) You should explicitly propose further investigations to confirm the validity of such inferences.

On the other hand, if you feel no generalizations are possible but that a replication with modifications would yield new and related information, you should suggest them in enough detail to be useful to other researchers. For example, variables not studied, or restricted in their range of values, call for further research. One of the most valuable parts of any research report is such a section on replication (repetition, modification and/or extension), because it contains both warnings of pitfalls and the considered advice of a knowledgeable person (that's you!) on where to go next. Keep in mind that, at the moment, you know more about this particular problem than anyone else.

The usefulness of your conclusions for application, especially in such fields as education and management science, can be explored by a technique comparable to free association. The ability to ask yourself what-if questions and to combine scholarship and imagination in generating answers will serve you better than the more cautious extrapolations of the kind needed for the making of deductive inferences. To put this another way, the divergent (rather than the convergent) thinker has the advantage here. You will also find that discussion with an informed colleague can be invaluable.

The critical comment portion of your report offers you the opportunity to display both scholarship and imagination: Do not fail to exploit it.

Resolution of Contradictions

Insofar as your study extends, though it need not exactly replicate, other earlier studies, it contributes to existing knowledge.

It is necessary to address explicitly any contradictions between your evidence and that obtained in earlier studies, and between different items of the evidence you have assembled. If it is your necessarily speculative conclusion that the former have arisen because of differences in design or in conditions of observation, it is very important to indicate this in detail. If you cannot resolve such contradictions, or if you attribute them to weaknesses (errors of commission or omission) in your study, it is appropriate for you recommend further research. You can be as specific or as general as you wish, but try to be realistic about what is feasible for other investigators in your field.

Internal contradictions may well be the result of weaknesses such as uncontrolled factors: for example, omitted variables, unsuitable choice of population, nonrandom or too-small samples, contaminated subjects or procedures, errors in recording observations or in scoring questionnaires, subtle researcher bias, instruments with inadequate validity or reliability, erroneous or incomplete data analysis, or implicit assumptions about some aspect of the problem. As a scientist, you have the obligation to acknowledge such shortcomings, even though it may be painful for you to do so. Those who follow you will be grateful for any assistance you can give in the form of identification of pitfalls. Do not be afraid to state that you believe your study needs to be repeated with greater safeguards against errors.

Negative Results

It frequently happens that a study yields so-called negative results, that is, evidence which fails to permit any inference concerning the hypotheses, or permits only the inference that the research hypothesis is implausible. If your investigation falls into this category, you may feel very discouraged. You may be apprehensive that it will be rejected as unsuitable for a dissertation or a publishable article. In fact, some committees and editors have an unalterable rule against negative results: No matter how interesting they may be in themselves and no matter how rich their implications, if the data fail to support the original research hypotheses, the study is unacceptable. We hold to the opposite view: Sidman (1960) and others have pointed out that negative results often suggest fruitful new directions for further study. In addition, the publication of reports on unproductive lines of investigation can save much wasted effort by later researchers.[10]

There follow suggestions for possible ways to deal with and exploit negative results.

Your first obligation is to account for such results. If, in good conscience, you can attribute them only to defects in some aspects of your study, then you are certainly in an awkward position. No conclusions can be properly drawn from evidence improperly obtained or from arguments improperly formulated. If, however, no such defects can be identified, you may be justified in suggesting that the theory on which you have based your study is either false or incomplete. Theory is valuable to the extent that it predicts what can be observed; its most common shortcoming is an overly-restricted specification of variables. You should devote careful attention to the assumptions you have incorporated, and the list of variables you have selected to control or manipulate, then state as an implication of your investigation that it is essential either to modify the theory, to introduce further assumptions, or to replicate the study with additional or different variables. Thus, you may be able to use your results as a basis for raising new questions. This strategy not only emphasizes the value of what you have found, but represents your best hope of salvaging your entire project.

We do not wish to mislead you. It is not always possible to rescue a study that yields negative results. In case of an error in initial formulation, in design, or in data-gathering procedures, your only recourse is to start over.

Your Summary

At the end of your report, you should present a brief abstract of the entire study, including principal findings. To help yourself prepare this, consider: If you were an investigator planning a further study in the same or a related area, what would you need to know about this study in order to decide what it is about, what it has achieved, and whether it deserves a detailed reading. Your experience in abstracting your bibliographic references will come in handy.

Follow the format in use at your university or established by the journal to which you expect to submit your article. *Dissertation Abstracts* provides instructions for submission of abstracts which may also be useful even if your report is not a dissertation.

Journal Articles: Special Considerations

The editors of every journal have prepared instructions for contributors and will send them to you on request. As soon as you have decided to which journal(s) you will submit your report, you should read these instructions carefully because you must meet the requirements in order that your article receive prompt and serious consideration. (Once you have developed a reputation for important research, you may enjoy greater latitude.)

Without question, the limitations on length impose a great burden on the writer. Organization of the material and conciseness of expression assume enormous importance. In general, reports are compressed using the following devices:

1. Problem statement is very compact. The original question or source of the problem may be omitted.
2. Explicit statement of hypotheses is often omitted and the reader is expected to infer their precise formulation from the results and conclusions.
3. Definitions, except of novel and unfamiliar terms, may be omitted. Delimitations are rarely stated.

4. Review of the literature is much compressed, with only the most important previous studies described in any detail. The emphasis is on defects or shortcomings, so as to justify the need for the present study.
5. Procedures such as sample selection, training of subjects or observers, use of equipment, etc. are described in abbreviated fashion. Interview schedules and questionnaires are usually omitted.
6. Only the results of statistical analysis are given, with emphasis on the significance level.
7. Findings and conclusions are presented together. Weaknesses of this study and suggestions for further study may be briefly presented.

Items 2, 5, 6 and 7 in this list involve the greatest hazard for the reader. Whatever else you do, in the article, you must make perfectly clear:

- what you were looking for,
- what you expected to find,
- what you did to obtain evidence,
- what you actually did find, and
- what you conclude.

A critical reading of articles in your field will give you guidance in what to avoid, as well as a familiarity with successful shortcuts.

If you have already prepared a full report, you may experience difficulty in writing a shorter version to meet publication requirements. It may be helpful to lay out a new outline, so that you don't allocate too much space to the relatively inessential portions. One aspect of the revision that may be particularly irksome is changing the form of footnotes and bibliographic citations; be sure to allow time for this if you must meet a deadline.

Evaluation Reports: Special Considerations

If your research project is the implementation of a funded program, your report will necessarily emphasize implications for application and further action. Moreover, evaluation reports must be so formulated that they not only satisfy the requirements of the funding agency, but also address the concerns of the group for whose benefit the program was undertaken. Consequently, the problems of correctly identifying your audience and of taking "political" realities into account, are of great importance.

An excellent analysis of these issues and many useful suggestions can be found in *How to Present An Evaluation Report*, (Morris and Fitzgibbon [1978]). Anyone whose study falls into the "action" category would be wise to consult this little book. The authors indicate that the following items need special attention:

- For whose benefit was the program undertaken?
- How was the original need for the program assessed?
- What resources were available and/or developed for the program?
- How were the outcomes measured and what were the results?
- How were process aspects of the program measured?
- How certain is it that the program caused the results?
- What decisions are facilitated now that the results are available?
- What are the costs and benefits of the program?

Your report must also be interesting and stimulate the enthusiasm of the audience, so as to encourage continued involvement with the program.

Pitfalls in Presentation of Conclusions[11]

Weaknesses in the conclusions and discussion section of your report fall into a few categories. Most can be avoided by allocation of adequate time and by the careful exercise of critical attention to what you have written.

Inadequate knowledge of your field calls for an intensive effort at this stage; otherwise, your discussion will be superficial. Our advice in Chapter 3 that you continue to read background material may pay off, as will your energy and persistence during earlier years of your training. Take advantage of any opportunity to "pilot your conclusions," that is, to describe your results to other researchers in the same area; their reactions may suggest directions for you to pursue. In particular, try out your alternative explanations and make an effort to respond to informed suggestions.

Poor organization usually arises from failure to address the original problem, insufficient reflection, and/or hurried assembling of material. Occasionally, the researcher really does not understand his own findings; in such a circumstance, a well-presented discussion of implications is nearly impossible to achieve. You may find it helpful to subject yourself to an explicitly verbalized interrogation: "What does this mean?" "What is the connection?" etc. Try to control your impatience now the end is in sight.

The intrusion of value judgments, personal bias, "wild" inferences (such as those involving causality) unjustified by the hypotheses or the available evidence, or a "gee whiz" attitude towards the findings, will seriously damage your discussion. So, too, will confusion of significance and importance of the findings.

The best guide is to be found in the library, in the form of much-admired dissertations or well-written reports by competent researchers. Use these as models as far as possible. Be sure to set aside time to edit and revise; you will inevitably have further thoughts.

All tasks of report preparation are enormously facilitated through use of a word-processor (text editor). We strongly urge you to take advantage of the capabilities of this sort of equipment. Do not begrudge the effort required to learn the appropriate skills.

The Research Report:[12] Recapitulation

Reduced to its essentials, the report must tell the reader:

- what problem was investigated,
- what methods were used to obtain evidence concerning the problem,
- what evidence was actually obtained, and
- what conclusions were inferred from this evidence.

The ultimate test of an acceptable report is: Can another investigator replicate the research by following the methodology and analysis described in the report?

Developing a Readable Style

"Since writing is communication, clarity can only be a virtue."[13] The obfuscatory language and tortured syntax of many technical reports have long been a deserving target for parody. It is not easy to write well. For many, writing even a short passage requiring connected sentences is extremely aversive. The two most frequently tendered pieces of advice are:

1. Organize your ideas into a manageable sequence *before* you set words on paper.
2. Excise, revise and edit *after* you have something written down.

Good writing depends ultimately upon a thorough understanding of the topic and a clear identification of the relative importance of its parts. This means that if your knowledge of your subject is inadequate, you will inevitably muddle the exposition. You must decide what you want to say before you start writing: "Before beginning to compose something, gauge the nature of the enterprise and work from a suitable design."[14] An outline, which need not be arranged in the traditional indented form but which must include all the principal items in their logically appropriate places, is an obvious first step. Successively "fatter" outlines then incorporate key phrases and, perhaps, lead or summary sentences. You should find the first draft much easier to prepare on the basis of such an outline, but it never writes itself.

Avoid repetitious elaboration (or elaborate repetitions) of the same point. On the other hand, don't be cryptic. Ask yourself: Would I follow this line of argument if I did not already accept the conclusions? Could I visualize this procedure from the description? Reorganize if necessary: The results are well worth the hard work. Use topic headings liberally but do not expect them to disguise a lack of organization. Write your summaries and introductions last,[15] and be ready to rewrite them several times. Do not expect your first draft to be more than that. You must devote your effort to expressing your ideas in written words; if you try to revise as you go, you will just distract yourself.

Next, read what you have written. "When you say something, make sure you have said it. The chances of your having said it are only fair."[16] You cannot afford to fall in love with your first draft—be prepared to revise and edit ruthlessly, sentences first, then paragraphs and sections in context. Begin your revision by deleting everything which is unnecessary for clarity. Your goals are simplicity, economy and precision. "The writer must strive for the right blend of detail and brevity."[17] A certain amount of drudgery, such as footnotes, presentation of statistical material, citations, etc. is inescapable, but finding and following suitable models will lighten your burden.

Editorial skills can be learned. Like others, they will develop with practice. Four useful strategies for improving your writing are:

1. Keep your potential audience sharply in focus. Imagine a particular person who will read your report.
2. Let the draft sit for a few days or, better, a few weeks. "It is remarkable what a little time will do for (your) objectivity and critical capacity."[18] You will be able to see more readily where you need to revise.
3. Read the manuscript out loud. Your ear picks up awkwardnesses and confusions which your eye slides over. "Style is the sound [a writer's] words make on paper."[19]
4. Have someone else read and criticize your material.[20] This may be uncomfortable but worthwhile. You are not obliged to make the suggested changes, but at least give all comments serious and careful consideration.

An awareness of your own style generally requires attentiveness to style in what you read. Try to distinguish between well-written reports and the others, which make life difficult for their readers: emulate the former. Avoid jargon, hackneyed expressions, and dissertationese; also florid and unusual vocabulary, vogue words, vague circumlocutions, literary affectations ("fine writing"), runaway figures of speech, and clever turns of phrase.[21] Watch out for pronouns without antecedents, awkward gerunds, dangling modifiers. Use parallel constructions for comparisons. If you need a word whose definition or usage is unfamiliar, look it up. Use active rather than passive constructions: They are shorter and more forceful. Don't over-qualify, but state your position firmly, without apparent hesitancy. Keep your sentence structure simple unless you are a practiced and unself-conscious writer. You will observe we have said nothing about elegance, grace, vivid imagery, varied vocabulary, etc. "Style takes its final shape more from attitudes of mind than from principles of composition."[22]

Afterword

At this stage, assemble the parts of your report and *read it through*. DON'T SKIM!

1. If modifications have been introduced at any point, have all consistent changes been made?
2. Does the problem statement at the outset agree with the problem statement as discussed in the conclusions? Is the title informative, suggestive of the problem area, and brief?
3. Do the hypotheses, research and statistical, appear in the same form throughout?
4. Is your background review section focused on main issues, so the reader understands your selection of variables? Does your discussion refer your findings to the problem background? Are your sources clearly identified and any special help generously acknowledged?
5. Is the design/methodology section sufficiently clear as to population, instruments and procedures, so that an investigator who wishes to repeat your study exactly will know what to do?
6. Do your findings, as presented, provide the information you indicated was needed to support your hypotheses?
7. Are your findings and conclusions unmistakeable?
8. Is the entire report equally free of repetitions and mysterious omissions?
9. Does it "stick together" and "flow"? That is, is the underlying organization sound and apparent to the reader?
10. Is your use of terminology consistent throughout?

*   *   *   *   *

By now you will no doubt have begun planning your next research project.

Appendix: Dissertation Checklist

A. Preliminary materials
   1. Title page
   2. Approval sheet
   3. Preface and acknowledgements
   4. Table of contents
   5. Table of tables
   6. Table of charts and illustrations
   7. Description of treatment of references and footnotes
B. Body of the proposal (incorporating the review of the literature)
   1. Statement of the problem
   2. Importance of the problem
   3. Summary of relevant theory
   4. Analysis of related studies[23]
   5. Statement of hypotheses, operationalized
   6. Statement of anticipated inferences
   7. Assumptions of this study
   8. Limitations and delimitations of this study
   9. Definition of terms used
C. Methodology
   1. General description of design
   2. Population and sampling procedures
   3. Treatment or data-gathering procedures
   4. Instruments and measurement
   5. Proposed data analysis
   6. Pilot studies
D. Evidence (Findings)
   1. Text
   2. Tables
   3. Charts
   4. Summary of data analysis
E. Conclusions, discussion, summary, implications
   1. Restatement of problem and procedures
   2. Conclusions in terms of hypotheses[24]
   3. Identification of weaknesses in the study
   4. Discussion and implications
   5. Suggestions for replication and further study
F. Reference materials
   1. Bibliography

2. Appendices

3. Index (if report is very long)

You will also be expected to prepare an abstract of specified length and a set of locations for bibliographic reference. Consult suitable models, or instructions such as those prepared by *Dissertation Abstracts* or the various journals.

Notes

[1]"If you don't know where you are going, you will end up somewhere else" (Lawrence Peter).

[2]Asher (1976, pp. 9-10).

[3]Tukey (1963).

[4]Sellitz et al. (1976, p. 459).

[5]We owe this phrase to an (anonymous) reviewer.

[6]Some general and thought-provoking suggestions about identifying the audience can be found in Morris and Fitzgibbon (1978, pp. 28-30). They point out the importance of the orientation and expectations of the audience, as well as its level of knowledge.

[7]See later section Negative Results.

[8]This advice may be a counsel of perfection. Morris and Fitzgibbon (1981, p. 33 passim) suggest that in an evaluation report you should imagine your reader will be called away in the middle and never return!

[9]"The great end of life is not knowledge but action" (T. H. Huxley).

[10]See discussion in Chapter 2 (pp. 45*ff*, and footnote 19, Chapter 2.) We seriously propose that a journal be established, devoted solely to the announcement of negative results: nonsignificant differences, nonsupport of widely accepted conjectures, inconclusive tests, and weak associations.

[11]Backstrom and Hursh-Cesar (1981) have excellent lists of errors to be avoided in interpretation and presentation.

[12]As previously indicated, this section and the next are directed to those who want to prepare a full report such as a dissertation. Consult your committee for modifications. Many universities publish a dissertation manual as a guide. A good once-over can be found in Kerlinger (1973, Appendix A, pp. 694-698); see also Plutchik (1974, Appendix I, pp. 305-308) and Selltiz et al. (1959, 1976).

[13]Strunk and White (1962, p. 65).

[14]Strunk and White (1962, p. 57). This is advice of very general application!

[15]"The last thing that we find in making a book is to know what we must put first" (Blaise Pascal).

[16]Strunk and White (1962, p. 66).

[17]Kerlinger (1973, p. 694).

[18]Kerlinger (1973, p. 699).

[19]Strunk and White (1962, p. 53).

[20]"No passion in the world is equal to the passion to alter someone else's draft" (H. G. Wells).

[21]"Read over your compositions and, when you meet a passage which you think is particularly fine, strike it out" (Samuel Johnson).

[22]Strunk and White (1962, p. 70).

[23]Items 3 and 4 may be presented as a separate chapter. This is standard for dissertations but journal articles usually combine them with the problem statement.

[24]Items 2 and 3 are frequently placed with findings in dissertations.

Additional Reading

Many comprehensive texts on research methods contain a chapter on report preparation. You may find it helpful to consult:

Kerlinger (1973): Appendix A.
Pound (1977): thesis handbook.
Selltiz et al. (1976): Chapter 15.
Hy (1977): Chapter 4.

Morris and Fitzgibbon (1981): directed to those who must prepare evaluation reports on funded projects.

Backstrom & Hursh-Cesar (1978): practical tips on writing reports on survey studies (pp. 386–399).

Ehrenberg (1982): emphasis on clarity in description of findings. Chapters 18–20 should be read before you try to formulate conclusions. Sensible and helpful.

References on style: Many journals and publishers have brief style sheets that cover details of usage as well as preparation of manuscripts.

There is a large body of reference material whose goal is to help the writer. Everyone has particular favorites for different purposes. Here are some of ours:

Definitions, Historical Meanings, Etymology, Spelling

Oxford English Dictionary: many quotations showing shifts in meaning; word origins.

Webster's New International Dictionary (ed. 2): concise definitions; preferred usage. Ed. 3 shows usage without indicating correctness.

Roget's Thesaurus: synonyms, antonyms, and near misses; can be confusing if you aren't sensitive to fine distinctions.

General Advice On Style

Zinsser (1980): contains many practical suggestions for editing and organizing nonfiction material; has examples.

Strunk and White (1962): lots of rules, opinionated, but peerless for nearly 50 years; their standard of excellence is breathtaking; take this book to the desert island with you.

Gowers (1977): directed to civil servants who produce garble; emphasis on clarity and clean understated British prose; many funny "horrid" examples.

Precision in Word Usage, Rules for Sentence Construction, Use of Connectors and Prepositions

Fowler (1965): the classic, very English, overmeticulous but exact, thorough, and with a high standard of clarity.

Partridge (1963): more relaxed, less complete.

Bernstein (1979): very relaxed, American, journalistic but knows how to be precise in usage; often witty, full of examples.

Overall Organization, General Advice on How to Write

Baker (1966 and 1969): starts from scratch; main concern is expository and persuasive prose.

Perrin (1965): basic composition.

Flesch (1946, 1949): serious but unpretentious; perhaps too discursive.

Zinsser (1980): how to write a draft and manage revisions.

Shaughnessy (1979): if you have serious writing problems, this book may be useful even though its intended audience does not include you.

References

Abelson, R. P. and Tukey, J. S. Efficient Conversion of Non-Metric Information into Metric Information. Proceedings of the Social Statistics Section of the American Statistical Association, Washington, 1959, 226-230. In *The Quantitative Analysis of Social Problems*, Tufte, E. R., pp. 407-417. Reading, MA: Addison-Wesley Publishing Co., 1970.

Achen, C. H. *Interpreting and Using Regression*. Sage University Paper Series on Quantitative Applications in the Social Sciences 07-029. Beverly Hills, CA: Sage Publications, Inc., 1982.

Ackerman, R. *Non-Deductive Inference*. London: Routledge & Kegan Paul, 1966.

Agresti, A. *The Analysis of Ordinal Categorical Data*. New York: John Wiley & Sons, 1984.

Aldendorfer, M. S. and Blashfield, R. K. *Cluster Analysis*. Sage University Paper Series on Quantitative Applications in the Social Sciences 07-044. Beverly Hills, CA: Sage Publications, Inc., 1984.

Allen, E. M. Why Are Research Grant Applications Disapproved? *Science* (1960), Vol. 32, pp. 1532-1534.

Anastasi, A. *Psychological Testing*. (ed. 4). New York: Macmillan, 1976.

Anderson, B. F. *The Psychology Experiment*. (ed. 1). Belmont, CA: Wadsworth Publishing Co., Inc., 1966.

Anderson, D. R., Sweeney, D. J., and Williams, T. A. *An Introduction to Management Science*. St. Paul, MN: West Publishing Co., 1976.

Anderson, D. R., Sweeney, D. J., and Williams, T. A. *Essentials of Management Science*. St. Paul, MN: West Publishing Co., 1978.

Anderson, N. H. Scales and Statistics: Parametric and Nonparametric. *Psychological Bulletin* (1961), Vol. 58, pp. 305-316. Reprinted in *Readings in Statistics for the Behavioral Scientist*, J. A. Steger (Ed.). New York: Holt Rinehart Winston, Inc., 1971.

Anderson, T. W. *An Introduction to Multivariate Statistical Analysis*. New York: Wiley, 1958.

Andrews, F. M., Klem, L., Davidson, T. N., O'Malley, M. O., and Rodgers, W. L. *A Guide for Selecting Statistical Techniques for Analyzing Social Science Data* (ed. 2). Research Monograph. Ann Arbor, MI: University of Michigan, Institute for Social Research, 1981.

Andrews, F. M., Morgan, J. N., Sonquist, J. A., and Klem, L. *Multiple Classification Analysis* (ed. 2), Ann Arbor, MI: Institute for Social Research, University of Michigan, 1973.

Armitage, P. *Sequential Medical Trials*. Oxford: Blackwell, 1960.

Arthurs, A. M. *Probability Theory*. Volume in Library of Mathematics. New York: Dover Publications, Inc., 1965.

Asher, H. B. *Causal Modeling* (rev.). Sage University Paper Series in Quantitative Applications in the Social Sciences 07-003. Beverly Hills, CA: Sage Publications, Inc., 1976, 1983.

Ayres, F., Jr. *Calculus* (ed. 2). New York: Schaum Publishing Co., 1964.

Babbie, E. R. *Survey Research Methods*. Belmont, CA.: Wadsworth Publishing Co., 1973, 1979.

Bachrach, A. J., Erwin, W. J., and Mohr, J. P. The Control of Eating Behavior in an Anorexic by Operant Conditioning Techniques. In *Case Studies in Behavior Modification*, pp. 153-163, Ullman, L. P. and Krasner, L., (eds.), New York: Holt Rinehart Winston, Inc., 1965.

Backstrom, C. H. and Hursh-Cesar, G. *Survey Research* (ed. 2). New York: John Wiley & Sons, 1981.

Bailey, K. D. Cluster Analysis. Chap. 2 in *Sociological Methodology 1975*. D. R. Heise, ed. San Francisco, CA: Jossey-Bass Inc., 1974.

Bailey, K. D. *Methods of Social Research.* (ed. 2). New York: The Free Press, 1982.

Bakan, D. The Test of Significance in Psychological Research. In *On Method: Toward a Reconstruction of Psychological Investigation,* pp. 1–29. San Francisco, CA.: Jossey-Bass, 1967.

Baker, S. *The Complete Stylist.* New York: Thomas. Y. Crowell, Co., 1966.

Baker, S. *The Practical Stylist.* (ed. 2). New York: Thomas Y. Crowell, Co., 1969.

Barber, T. X. *Pitfalls in Human Research.* New York: Pergamon, 1976.

Barber, T. X. and Silver, M. J. Fact, Fiction, and The Experimenter Bias Effect. *Psychological Bulletin,* Monograph Supplement, Dec. 1968, Vol. 70, No. 6, part 2.

Barnett, V. (ed.). *Interpreting Multivariate Data.* New York: John Wiley & Sons, 1981.

Barcikowski, R. S. *Computer Packages and Research Design.* Washington, D.C.: University Press of America, 1982. P.O. Box 19101, Washington, D.C. 20036.

Barnow, B. S. The Effects of Head Start and SES on Cognitive Development of Disadvantaged Children. Unpublished doctoral dissertation, University of Wisconsin, 1973.

Bart, P. and Frankel, L. *The Student Sociologist's Handbook.* Glenview, Ill.: Scott-Foresman & Co., 1981.

Bell, C. and Encel, S. (eds.) *Inside The Whale: Ten Personal Accounts of Social Research.* Oxford: Pergamon Press, 1978.

Bell, A. P., Weinberg, M. S., Hammersmith, S. K. *Sexual Preference: Its Development in Men and Women.* Indianapolis, IN: University of Indiana Press, 1981.

Bellman, R. and Dreyfus, S. *Applied Dynamic Programming.* Princeton, NJ: Princeton University Press, 1962.

Bennett, S. and Bowers, D. *An Introduction to Multivariate Techniques for Social and Behavioral Sciences.* New York and London: Macmillan, 1976.

Bennett, C. A. and Lumsdaine, A. A. (eds.) *Evaluation and Experiment: Critical Issues In Assessing Social Programs.* New York: Academic Press, 1975.

Berelson, B. and Steiner, G. *Human Behavior.* New York: Harcourt Brace & World, 1967.

Bernard, J. *Academic Women.* Cleveland, OH: World Publishing Co., 1966.

Bernard, J. *The Future of Marriage.* New York: World Publishing Co., 1972.

Bernstein, T. M. *The Careful Writer: A Modern Guide to English Usage.* New York: Atheneum, 1979.

Berry, W. D. *Nonrecursive Causal Models.* Sage University Paper Series on Quantitative Applications in the Social Sciences 07–037. Beverly Hills, CA: Sage Publications, Inc., 1984.

Bers, L. *Calculus* (2 vols.). New York: Holt Rinehart Winston, Inc., 1969.

Beveridge, W. I. B. *The Art of Scientific Investigation.* New York: W. W. Norton Inc., 1950.

Billingsley, A. *Black Families In White America.* Englewood Cliffs, NJ: Prentice-Hall, Inc., 1968 (paper).

Binder, A. Further Considerations on Testing the Null Hypothesis and the Strategy & Tactics of Investigating Theoretical Models. *Psychological Review 70* (1963) pp. 107–115.

Birdwhistell, R. *Introduction to Kinesics.* Louisville, KY: University of Louisville Press, 1952.

Birnbaum, I. *An Introduction to Causal Analysis in Sociology.* New York: Macmillan, 1981.

Birnbaum, J. A. Life Patterns and Self-Esteem in Gifted Family-Oriented and Career-Committed Women. Chapter 24 (pp. 396–419) in *Women and Achievement.* Mednick, M. T. S. et al. (eds.) New York: Hemisphere Publishing Co. (Wiley), 1975.

Blalock, H. M. Jr. *An Introduction to Social Research.* Englewood Cliffs, NJ: Prentice-Hall, 1970.

Blalock, H. M. Jr. *Causal Inference in Nonexperimental Research.* Chapel Hill, NC: University of North Carolina Press, 1961.

Blalock, H. M., Jr. *Conceptualization and Measurement in the Social Sciences.* Beverly Hills, CA: Sage Publications, Inc., 1982.

Blalock, H. M., Jr. *Social Statistics.* New York: McGraw-Hill, (ed. 1, 1960; ed. 2, 1972; ed. 2, rev., 1979).

Blalock, H. M. Jr. The Measurement Problem: A Gap Between the Languages of Theory and Research. (Chap. 1) in Blalock H. M. and Blalock A. B. (eds.), *Methodology in Social Research.* New York: McGraw-Hill, 1968a.

Blalock, H. M. Jr. Theory Building and Causal Inferences, pp. 155–198, in Blalock & Blalock (eds.), *Methodology in Social Research.* New York: McGraw-Hill, 1968b.

Blalock, H. M. Jr. *Theory Construction.* Englewood Cliffs, NJ: Prentice-Hall, 1969.

Blalock, H. M. and Blalock, A. B. (eds.), *Methodology in Social Research.* New York: McGraw-Hill, 1968.

Blalock, H. M. Jr., et al. (eds.). *Quantitative Sociology: International Perspectives on Mathematical & Statistical Modelling.* New York: Academic Press, Inc., 1975.

Bliss, E. C. *Getting Things Done: The ABC's of Time Management.* New York: Chas. Scribner's Sons, 1976.

Bloom, B. *Taxonomy of Educational Objectives: The Cognitive Domain.* New York: David McKay, 1956.

Bolles, R. C. The Difference between Statistical Hypotheses and Scientific Hypotheses.: *Psychology Reports,* 1962, Vol. 11, pp. 639–645.

Borg, W. R. and Gall, M. D. *Educational Research.* New York: David McKay Co., Inc., 1971 (ed. 2), 1979 (ed. 3).

Bott, E. Urban Families: Conjugal Roles and Social Networks. *Human Relations,* 1955, Vol. 8, pp. 345–383.

Bottomley, B. Words, Deeds and Postgraduate Research. In *Inside the Whale,* Bell C. & Encel S. (eds.). Oxford: Pergamon Press, 1978.

Bouchard, C., Boulay, M., Thibault, M. C., Carrier, R., and Dulac, S. Training of Submaximal Working Capacity: Frequency, Intensity, Duration and Their Interactions. *Journal of Sports Medicine & Physical Fitness,* March 1980, Vol. 20, No. 1.

Boudon, R. A New Look at Correlation Analysis, Chapter 6 in Blalock, H. M. and Blalock, A. B. (eds.), *Methodology in Social Research.* New York: McGraw-Hill, 1968.

Box, G. E. P. and Jenkins, G. M. *Time Series Analysis.* San Francisco, CA: Holden-Day, 1971.

Boyd, J. P. The Algebra of Group Kinship. *Journal of Mathematical Psychology* 6 (1969), pp. 139–167; Chapter 18 in Leinhart, S. (ed.) *Social Networks.* New York: Academic Press, 1977.

Bradley, J. V. *Distribution-Free Statistical Tests.* Englewood Cliffs, NJ: Prentice-Hall, 1968.

Bradley, J. V. Pernicious Publication Practices. *Bulletin of the Psychonomic Society,* 1981a, Vol. 18, pp. 31–34.

Bradley, J. V. Editorial Overkill. *Bulletin of the Psychonomic Society,* 1981b, Vol. 18, pp. 271–274.

Braithwaite, R. B. *Scientific Explanation.* New York London: Cambridge University Press, 1953. New York: Harper & Brothers, Harper Torchbooks, 1960.

Brier, A. and Robinson, I. *Computers and the Social Sciences.* New York: Columbia University Press, 1974.

Broad, W. and Wade, N. *Betrayers of the Truth.* New York: Simon and Schuster, 1983.

Brophy, J. E. and Good, T. L. Teacher's Communication of Differential Expectations for Children's Classroom Performance. *Journal of Educational Psychology* (1970), Vol. 61, pp. 365–374.

Broverman, I. K., Broverman, D. M., Clarkson, F. E., Rosenkrantz, P. S. and Vogel, S. R. Sex-Role Stereotypes and Clinical Judgments of Mental Health. *Journal of Consulting and Clinical Psychology,* 1970, Vol. 34, No. 1, pp. 1–7.

Bruhn, J. G. and Wolf, S. *The Rosetta Story: An Anatomy of Health.* Norman, OK: University of Oklahoma Press, 1979.

Bryson, K. R. and Phillips, D. P. Method for Classifying Interval-Scale and Ordinal-Scale Data. Chap. 4 in *Sociological Methodology 1975,* D. R. Heise, ed. San Francisco, CA: Jossey-Bass Inc., 1974.

Buros, O. *(Sixth, Seventh, Eighth) Mental Measurements Yearbook.* Highland Park, NJ: Gryphon Press (1965, 1972, 1978).

Buros, O. *Tests in Print.* Highland Park, NJ: Gryphon Press, 1961.

Campbell, D. T. and Stanley, J. C. *Experimental and Quasi-Experimental Designs for Research.* Chicago: Rand-McNally, 1963.

Campbell, N. R. *An Account of the Principles of Measurements & Calculations.* London: Longman, Green, 1928.

Campbell, N. R. *Foundations of Science: The Philosophy of Theory & Experiment.* New York: Dover Publications, Inc., 1957.

Campbell, N. R. *What Is Science?* London: Methuen & Co., Ltd., 1921. New York: Dover Publications, Inc., 1953.

Cannon, W. B. *The Way of An Investigator.* New York: Harper Publishing Co., 1965 (orig. pub. 1945).

Caplovitz, D. *Making Ends Meet: How Families Cope With Inflation & Recession.* Beverly Hills, CA: Sage Publications, Inc., 1979.

Caplovitz, D. *The Poor Pay More.* New York: The Free Press, 1967.

Caplow, T., Bahr, H. M., Chadwick, B. A., Hill, R., and Williamson, M. H. *Middletown Families.* Minneapolis, MN: University of Minnesota Press, 1982.

Carmines, E. G. and Zeller, R. A. *Reliability and Validity Assessment.* Sage University Paper Series in Quantitative Applications in the Social Sciences 07-017. Beverly Hills, CA: Sage Publications, Inc., 1979.

Carr, E. H. *What Is History?* New York: Knopf, 1961. Middlesex, Eng.: Penguin Books, 1964.

Carr-Hill, R. A. and Stern, N. J. *Crime, The Police, and Criminal Statistics.* New York: Academic Press, 1979.

Caudill, W. and Plath, D. W. Who Sleeps by Whom? Parent-Child Involvement in Urban Japanese Families. *Psychiatry* 29 (1966): pp. 344-366. Reprinted in Levine, R. A., (ed.) *Culture and Personality.* Chicago: Aldine Publishing Co., 1974.

Charlesworth, James C. (ed.) *Mathematics and the Social Sciences: The Utility & Inutility of Mathematics in the Study of Economics, Political Science, & Sociology.* Philadelphia, PA: American Academy of Political & Social Sciences, 1963.

Chatfield, C. and Collins, A. J. *Introduction to Multivariate Analysis.* London: Chapman and Hall, 1980. (New York: Methuen, Inc.)

Chein, I. An Introduction to Sampling. Appendix B in Selltiz, C., Jahoda, M., Deutsch, M., and & Cook, D. *Research Methods in Social Relations* (rev.). New York: Holt Rinehart Winston, Inc., 1959.

Cherniss, C. *Professional Burnout in Human Service Organizations.* New York: Praeger, 1980.

Chun, K, Cobb, S., French, J. R., Jr. *Measures for Psychological Assessment: A Guide to 3000 Original Sources and Their Applications.* Ann Arbor, MI: Institute for Social Research, University of Michigan, 1975.

Clelland, R. C., deCani, J. S., & Brown, F. E. *Basic Statistics with Business Applications* (ed. 2). New York: John Wiley Sons, 1973.

Coale, A. J. and Stephan, F. F. The Case of the Indians and the Teenage Widows. *Journal of the American Statistical Association,* June 1962, Vol. 57, pp. 338-347.

Cochran, W. G. *Sampling Techniques.* New York: John Wiley & Sons, Inc., 1953.

Cochran, W. G., and Cox, G. M. *Experimental Designs.* (ed. 2). New York: Wiley, 1957.

Cohen, J. *Statistical Power Analysis for the Behavioral Sciences.* New York: Academic Press, 1969.

Cohen, J. and Cohen, P. *Applied Multiple Regression/Correlation for the Behavioral Sciences.* (ed. 2). Hillsdale, NJ: Lawrence Erlbaum Associates, Inc., 1983.

Cohen, M. R., and Nagel, E. *An Introduction to Logic and Scientific Method.* New York: Harcourt, Brace, and Company, 1934.

Coleman, J., Katz, E., and Menzel, H. The Diffusion of an Innovation Among Physicians. *Sociometry* (1957) Vol. 20, pp. 253–270. Reprinted in Leinhardt, S., (ed.) *Social Networks*, pp. 107–124. New York: Academic Press, 1977.

Coleman, J. S. *The Adolescent Society.* Glencoe, IL: The Free Press, 1961.

Coleman, J. S. *Introduction to Mathematical Sociology.* New York: The Free Press of Glencoe, 1964.

Coleman, J. S. *The Mathematical Study of Change.* (Chap. 11) In Blalock H. M. & Blalock A. B. (eds.) *Methodology in Social Research.* New York: McGraw-Hill, 1968.

Coleman, R. P., and Rainwater, L. *Social Standing in America.* New York: Basic Books, Inc., 1978.

Conover, W. J. *Practical Nonparametric Statistics.* (ed. 2). New York: John Wiley and Sons, 1980.

Conrad, A. H., and Myers, J. R. *The Economics of Slavery and Other Studies in Econometric History.* Chicago: Aldine Publishing Co., 1964.

Converse, J. M., and Schuman, H. *Conversations at Random: Survey Research as Interviewers See It.* Ann Arbor, MI: Institute for Social Research, University of Michigan, 1974.

Cook, D. L. *Program Evaluation & Review Techniques: Applications in Education.* Washington, D.C.: U.S. Dept. of HEW, Office of Education, O.E. 12024, Cooperative Research Monograph, 1966, No. 17.

Cook, T. D., and Campbell, D. T. *Quasi-Experimentation: Design & Analysis Issues for Field Settings.* Chicago: Rand-McNally College Publishing Co., 1979.

Cooley, W. W., and Lohnes, P. R. *Multivariate Procedures for the Behavioral Sciences.* New York: Wiley, 1962.

Coombs, C. H. Psychological Scaling Without A Unit of Measurement. *Psychological Review* (1950) Vol. 57, pp. 145–158.

Coombs, C. H. *A Theory of Psychological Scaling.* Bulletin of Engineering Research, No. 34. Ann Arbor, MI: University of Michigan Press, 1952a.

Coombs, C. H. Theory & Methods of Social Measurement. In *Research Methods in the Behavioral Sciences.* Festinger, L. & Katz, D. (eds.), New York: Dryden Press, 1952b.

Coombs, C. H. *A Theory of Data.* New York: John Wiley, 1964.

Cooper, L., and Steinberg, D. *Methods and Applications of Linear Programming.* Philadelphia, PA: W. B. Saunders Co., 1974.

Cooper, L., and Steinberg, D. *Methods of Optimization.* Philadelphia, PA: W. B. Saunders, 1970.

Coopersmith, S. *The Antecedents of Self-Esteem.* San Francisco, CA: W. H. Freeman & Co., 1967.

Coser, L. A. *The Functions of Social Conflict.* Glencoe, IL: The Free Press, 1956.

Council on Inter-Racial Books for Children. *Stereotypes, Distortions and Omissions in U.S. History Textbooks.* New York: Racism and Sexism Resource Center for Educators, 1977.

Coutts, L. M., and Montgomery, S. An Investigation of the Arousal Model of Interpersonal Intimacy. *Journal of Experimental Social Psychology* Vol. 16 (1980), pp. 545–561.

Cox, D. R. *Planning of experiments.* New York: John Wiley & Sons, 1958.

Crane, D. Social Structure in a Group of Scientists: A Test of the 'Invisible College' Hypothesis. *American Sociological Review* (1969) Vol. 34, pp. 335–352. In *Social Networks*, Leinhardt, S. (ed.) New York: Academic Press, 1977.

Cronbach, L. Test Validation. In *Educational Measurement,* R. Thorndike, (ed.) Washington, D.C.: American Council on Education (ed. 2), 1971.

Cronbach, L. J., and Meehl, P. E. Construct Validity in Psychological Tests. In Feigl, H. and Scriven, M. (eds.) *The Foundations of Science and the Concepts of Psychology and Psychoanalysis.* (Minnesota Studies in the Philosophy of Science) Minneapolis, MN: University of Minnesota Press, 1956.

Croxton, F. E., and Cowden, D. J. *Applied General Statistics.* New York: Prentice-Hall, 1939; with Klein, S. Englewood Cliffs, NJ: Prentice-Hall, (ed. 3) 1967.

Dalton, M. *Men Who Manage.* New York: John Wiley & Sons, 1959.

Dalton, M. Preconceptions and Methods in *Men Who Manage.* Chap. 3 in Hammond, P. E. *Sociologists at Work.* New York: Basic Books, 1964.

Daniel, W. W. *Applied Nonparametric Statistics.* Boston, MA: Houghton-Mifflin, 1978.

Davidson, P. O., and Costello, C. G. *N = 1: Experimental Studies of Single Cases.* New York: Van Nostrand Reinhold, 1969 (paper).

Davis, J. A. Conventions and Strategies for the Presentation of Percentage Tables. Notes: Sociology 307, Chicago, IL: University of Chicago, Winter 1963.

Davis, J. A. *Elementary Survey Analysis.* Englewood Cliffs, NJ: Prentice-Hall, 1971.

Davis, J. A. Great Books and Small Groups: An Informal History of a National Survey. In Hammond P. E., (ed.) *Sociologists at Work.* Glencoe, IL: The Free Press, 1964.

Davis, J. A. Some Pitfalls of Data Analysis Without a Formal Criterion. Excerpt from Review of R. K. Merton, G. Reader & P. Kendall, The Student Physician. *American Journal of Sociology,* January, 1958, Vol. 63, pp. 445-446. Chapter 8 in Morrison, D. E. and Henkel, R. E., (eds.), *The Hypothesis Test Controversy,* Chicago, IL: Aldine Publishing Co., 1970.

Dawber, T. R., Kannel, W. B., and Lyell, L. P. An Approach to Longitudinal Studies in a Community: the Framingham Study. *Annals of the New York Academy of Sciences* (1963) Vol. 107, pp. 539-556.

Denzin, N. K. *The Research Act.* New York: McGraw-Hill, 1978.

Deutsch, M. R. Regional Research and Resource Center In early Childhood: Final Report. New York: New York University, 1971.

Dichter, E. *Handbook of Consumer Motivation.* New York: McGraw-Hill, 1964.

Dixon, W. J. and Brown, M. G. *BMDP: Biomedical Computer Programs P-Series.* Los Angeles, CA: University of California Press, 1979.

Dohrenwend, B. S. & Dohrenwend B. P., (eds.) *Stressful Life Events: Their Nature and Effects.* New York: John Wiley & Sons, 1974.

Dollar, C. M. and Jensen, R. J. *Historian's Guide to Statistics: Quantitative Analysis and Historical Research.* New York: Holt Rinehart Winston, Inc., 1971.

Dubin, R. Industrial Workers' Worlds: A Study of the Central Life Interests of Industrial Workers. *Social Problems,* 1956, Vol. 3, pp. 131-142.

Duncan, B. and Duncan, O. D. *Sex-Typing and Social Roles.* New York: Academic Press, 1978.

Durkheim, E. *Suicide.* (Translated by J. A. Spaulding & G. Simpson.) New York: The Free Press, 1951.

Dziurzynski, P. S. Development of a Content Analytic Instrument for Advertising Appeals Used in Prime Time Television Commercials. Unpublished MA Thesis, University of Pennsylvania, 1977.

Edwards, A. L. *An Introduction to Linear Regression & Correlation.* San Francisco, CA: W. H. Freeman & Co., 1976.

Edwards, A. L. *Multiple Regression and the Analysis of Variance and Covariance.* San Francisco, CA: W. H. Freeman, 1979.

Edwards, A. L. *Techniques of Attitude Scale Construction.* New York: Appleton-Century, 1957.

Ehrenberg, A. S. C. *A Primer in Data Reduction.* New York: John Wiley & Sons, 1982.

Ellis, B. *Basic Concepts of Measurement.* Cambridge: Cambridge University Press, 1968.

Erbe, W. Gregariousness, Group Membership, and the Flow of Information. *American Journal of Sociology.* (1962) Vol. 67, pp. 502-516.

Farley, J. E. and Hansel, M. The Ecological Context of Urban Crime. *Urban Affairs Quarterly* Vol. 17, No. 1. (September 1981), pp. 37-54.

Feigl, H. and Brodbeck, M. (eds.) *Readings in the Philosophy of Science.* New York: Appleton Century Crofts, 1953.

Ferguson, G. A. *Statistical Analysis in Psychology and Education.* (ed. 5). New York: McGraw-Hill, 1981.

Festinger, L. Assumptions Underlying the Use of Statistical Techniques. Chapter 22 in Jahoda, M., Deutsch M., and Cook, S. W. *Research Methods in Social Relations.* New York: The Dryden Press, 1951.

Festinger, L., and Katz, D. (eds.) *Research Methods in the Behavioral Sciences.* New York: Holt Rinehart & Winston, Inc., 1953.

Fienberg, S. E. *The Analysis of Cross-Classified Categorical Data.* Cambridge, MA: The MIT Press, 1977.

Fischer, D. A. *Historians' Fallacies.* New York: Harper (Torchbook), 1970.

Fisher, R. A. *The Design of Experiments.* Edinburgh: Oliver & Boyd, 1966.

Fisher, R. A. *Statistical Methods for Research Workers.* Edinburgh: Oliver and Boyd, 1970.

Fisher, R. A. *Statistical Methods and Scientific Inference.* New York: Hafner, 1973.

Fitz-Gibbon, C. T. and Morris, L. L. *How to Calculate Statistics.* Beverly Hills, CA: Sage Publications, Inc., 1978.

Fleiss, J. L. *Statistical Methods for Rates and Proportions.* (ed. 2). New York: John Wiley & Sons, 1981.

Flesch, R. *The Art of Plain Talk.* New York: Harper & Bros., 1946.

Flesch, R. *The Art of Readable Writing.* New York: Harper & Bros., 1949.

Fowler, H. W. *A Dictionary of Modern English Usage.* (rev.). Oxford: Oxford University Press, 1965.

Flury, B., and Riedwyl, H. Graphical Representation of Multivariate Data by Means of Asymmetrical Faces. *Journal of the American Statistical Association,* (December 1981) Vol. 76, No. 376, pp. 757–765.

Fowlkes, M. R. *Behind Every Successful Man.* New York: Columbia University Press, 1980.

Francken, D. A., and van Raaij, W. F. Satisfaction With Leisure Time Activities. *Journal of Leisure Research,* (1981) Vol. 13, No. 4.

Franzwa, H. Female Roles in Women's Magazine Fiction 1940–1970. In *Woman: Dependent or Independent Variable.* Unger, R. K. and Denmark, F. L. (eds.). New York: Psychological Dimensions, Inc., 1975.

Frazier, E. F. *Black Bourgeoisie.* New York: The Free Press, 1957.

Freedman, D., Pisani, R., and Purves, R. *Statistics.* New York: W. W. Norton & Co., 1978.

Freund, J. E. *Mathematical Statistics.* (ed. 2). Englewood Cliffs, NJ: Prentice-Hall, 1971.

Frieze, I. H. Women's Expectations for and Causal Attributions of Success and Failure. In *Women and Achievement.* Mednick, M. T. S. et al. (eds.) pp. 158–171. New York: Wiley, 1975.

Gale, W. A. and Pregibon, D. Artificial Intelligence Research in Statistics. *The AI Magazine* (Winter 1985): pp. 72–75.

Garson, G. D. *Handbook of Political Science Methods.* Boston, MA: Holbrook Press, 1971.

Gensch, D. Different Approaches to Advertising Media Selection. *Operations Research Quarterly* (1970) Vol. 21, No. 2, pp. 193–219.

Gilbreth, F. B. and Gilbreth, L. M. *Fatigue Study.* London: George Routledge & Sons, 1919.

Glantz, S. A. *Primer of Biostatistics.* New York: McGraw-Hill, 1981.

Glenn, N. D. *Cohort Analysis.* Sage University Paper Series in Quantitative Applications in the Social Sciences 07-005. Beverly Hills, CA: Sage Publications Inc., 1977.

Glock, C. Y. (ed.) *Survey Research in the Social Sciences.* New York: Russell Sage Foundation, 1967.

Glueck, S., and Glueck, E. *Physique and Delinquency.* New York: Harper and Bros., 1956.

Goffman, C. *Presentation of Self in Everyday Life.* Garden City, New York: Doubleday (Anchor), 1959.

Gold, D. Statistical Tests and Substantive Significance. Chapter 20 in Morrison, D. E. and Henkel, R. E. (eds.) *The Significance Test Controversy.* Chicago: Aldine Publishing Co., 1970.

Goldstein, H. *The Design and Analysis of Longitudinal Studies.* New York: Academic Press, 1981.

Goode, W. J. *Women in Divorce (After Divorce)*. New York: Free Press, 1956.

Gorden, R. L. *Interviewing: Strategy, techniques and tactics*. (rev. ed.). Homewood, IL: The Dorsey Press, 1975.

Gordon, A. D. *Classification: Methods for the Exploratory Analysis of Multivariate Data*. London: Chapman and Hall, 1981.

Gordon, M. M. *Social Class in American Sociology*. Durham, NC: Duke University Press, 1958.

Gorer, G. *Exploring British Character*. New York: Criterion, 1955.

Gottlieb, D. and Hodgkins, B. College Student Subcultures: Their Structure & Characteristics in Relation to Student Attitude Change. *School Review* (Fall 1963) Vol. 71, pp. 266–289.

Gottschalk, L. *Understanding History: A Primer of Historical Method*. New York: A. A. Knopf, 1969.

Gottschalk, L., Kluckhohn, C., and Angell, R. *The Use of Personal Documents in History, Anthropology, and Sociology*. New York: Social Science Research Council, 1947.

Gould, P. and White, R. *Mental Maps*. New York: Penguin Books, Inc., 1974.

Gould, R. *Transitions*. New York: Simon and Schuster, 1978.

Gould, S. J. *The Mismeasure of Man*. New York: W. W. Norton & Co., 1981.

Gowers, E. *The Complete Plain Words*. London: HMSO, 1973; New York: Pelican Books (ed. 2), 1977.

Grant, D. A. Testing the Null Hypothesis and the Strategy and Tactics of Investigating Theoretical Models. *Psychological Review* (1962) Vol. 69, pp. 54–61.

Gray, B. H. *Human Subjects in Medical Experimentation: A Sociological Study of the Conduct and Regulation of Clinical Research*. New York: John Wiley & Sons, 1975.

Greer, S. *The Logic of Social Inquiry*. Chicago: Aldine Publishing Co., 1969.

Groves, R. M., and Kahn, R. L. *Surveys by Telephone*. New York: Academic Press, 1979.

Guilford, J. P. *Psychometric Methods*. (ed. 2) New York: McGraw-Hill, 1954.

Guilford, J. P. and Fruchter, B. *Fundamental Statistics in Psychology & Education*. New York: McGraw-Hill, (ed. 5), 1973; (ed. 6), 1977.

Haber, A., Runyon, R. P., and Badia, P. (eds.) *Readings in Statistics*. Reading, MA: Addison-Wesley Publishing Co., Inc., 1970.

Hair, J. F., Jr., Anderson, R. E., Tatham, R. L., and Grablowsky, B. J. *Multivariate Data Analysis*. Tulsa, OK: PPC Books, 1979.

Hall, E. T. Proxemics: The Study of Man's Spatial Relations. In I. Goldstein (ed.) *Man's Image in Medicine & Anthropology*. New York: International University Press, 1963.

Hammond, Phillip E. (ed.) *Sociologists at Work: The Craft of Social Research*. New York: Basic Books, Inc., 1964, (New York: Anchor Books, 1967).

Hand, D. J. *Discrimination and Classification*. New York: John Wiley & Sons, 1981.

Handy, R. and Kurtz, P. A Current Appraisal of the Behavioral Sciences. *The American Behavioral Scientist*. Special Supplement to Vol. 7, No. 1–7. Great Barrington, MA: Behavioral Research Council, 1964.

Harman, H. H. *Modern Factor Analysis*. Chicago: University of Chicago Press, 1960.

Harris, R. J. *A Primer of Multivariate Statistics*. New York: Academic Press, Inc., 1975.

Hartwig, F. with Dearing, B. A. *Exploratory Data Analysis*. Sage University Paper Series on Quantitative Applications in the Social Sciences 07–016. Beverly Hills, CA: Sage Publications, Inc., 1979.

Haynes, S. G., and Feinleib, M. Women, Work and Coronary Heart Disease: Prospective Findings from the Framingham Heart Study. *American Journal of Public Health*, 1980, Vol. 70, pp. 133–141.

Haynes, S. G., Feinleib, M., Kannel, W. B. et al. The Relationship of Psychosocial Factors to Coronary Heart Disease in the Framingham Study. I: Methods & Risk Factors. *American Journal of Epidemiology*. (1978a) Vol. 107, pp. 362–383. II: Prevalence of Coronary Heart

Disease. *American Journal of Epidemiology* (1978b). Vol. 107, pp. 384–402. III: Incidence of CHD. *American Journal of Epidemiology* III (1980).

Hays, W. L. *Statistics for the Social Sciences.* (ed. 2). New York: Holt, Rinehart Winston, Inc., 1973.

Heise, D. R. (ed.) *Microcomputers and Social Research.* Beverly Hills, CA: Sage Publications, Inc., 1981.

Helson, R. The Creative Woman Mathematician. In *Women and the Mathematical Mystique.* Fox, L. H., Brody, L., and Tobin, D. (eds.) pp. 23–54. Baltimore, MD: The Johns Hopkins University Press, 1980.

Hemphill, J. K. and Coons, A. E. Development of the Leader Behavior Description Questionnaire. In *Leader Behavior: Its Description and Measurement.* Stogdill, R. M. and Coons, E. A. (eds.) Columbus, OH: Bureau of Business Research, Monograph 1957, No. 88, pp. 6–38.

Henkel, R. E. *Tests of Significance.* Sage University Paper Series on Quantitative Applications in the Social Sciences 07-004. Beverly Hills, CA: Sage Publications, Inc., 1976.

Hersen, M. and Barlow, D. H. *Single Case Experimental Designs.* Elmsford, NY: Pergamon Press, 1976.

Hildebrand, D. K., Laing, J. D., and Rosenthal, H. *Analysis of Ordinal Data.* Sage University Paper Series on Quantitative Applications in the Social Sciences 07-008. Beverly Hills, CA: Sage Publications, Inc., 1977.

Hillier, F. S. and Lieberman, G. J. *Introduction to Operations Research.* (ed. 2). San Francisco, CA: Holden Day, 1974.

Hilton, E. T. and Lumsdaine, A. A. Chapter 5 in *Evaluation and Experiment: Some Critical Issues in Assessing Social Programs.* Bennett, C. A. & Lumsdaine, A. A. (eds.), New York: Academic Press, 1975.

Hirschi, T. and Selvin, H. *Principles of Survey Analysis.* New York: The Free Press, 1973.

Hockett, H. C. *The Critical Method in Historical Research & Writing.* New York: Macmillan, 1955.

Hoel, P. *Introduction to Mathematical Statistics.* (ed. 4). New York: John Wiley & Sons, 1971.

Homans, G. C. *The Nature of Social Science.* New York: Harcourt Brace & Co. (paper), 1967.

Horner, M. S. *Sex Differences in Achievement Motivation & Performance in Competitive and Non-Competitive Situations.* Unpublished doctoral dissertation. Ann Arbor, MI: University of Michigan, 1968.

Huberty, C. J. Issues in the Use and Interpretation of Discriminant Analysis. *Psychological Bulletin,* 1984, Vol. 93, No. 1, pp. 156–171.

Hull, C. L. *Principles of Behavior.* New York: Appleton-Century-Crofts, 1945.

Hull, C. H. and Nie, N. H. *SPSS Update 7-9.* New York: McGraw-Hill, 1981.

Hy, R. J. *Using the Computer in the Social Sciences: A Non-Technical Approach.* New York: Elsevier North-Holland, Inc., 1977.

Hyman, H. *Survey Design and Analysis.* New York: The Free Press, 1955.

Hyman, R. *The Nature of Psychological Inquiry.* Englewood Cliffs, NJ: Prentice-Hall, 1964.

Innes, J. M. Selective Exposure as a Function of Dogmatism and Incentive. *The Journal of Social Psychology,* (1978) Vol. 106, pp. 261–265.

Isaac, S. with Michael, W. B. *Handbook in Research and Evaluation.* San Diego, CA: Edits Publishers, 1971.

Isen, A. and Levin, P. Effect of Feeling Good on Helping: Cookies and Kindness. *Journal of Social Psychology,* 1972, Vol. 21, pp. 384–388.

Iverson, G. R. *Bayesian Inference.* Sage Univeristy Paper Series on Quantitative Applications in the Social Sciences 07-043. Beverly Hills, CA: Sage Publications, Inc., 1984.

Iverson, G. R. and Norpoth, H. *Analysis of Variance.* Sage University Paper Series in Quantitative Applications in the Social Sciences 07-001. Beverly Hills, CA: Sage Publications, Inc., 1976.

Jacob, H. *Using Published Data: Errors and Remedies.* Sage University Paper Series on Quantitative Applications in the Social Sciences 07-042. Beverly Hills, CA: Sage Publications, Inc., 1984.

Jacobs, G. (ed.) *The Participant Observer.* New York: George Braziller, 1970.

Jacobson, G. C. The Effects of Campaign Spending in Congressional Elections. *American Political Science Review,* 1978, Vol. 72(2), pp. 469–491.

Jacobson, P. E., Jr. *Introduction to Statistical Measures for the Social & Behavioral Sciences.* New York: Holt Rinehart Winston, Inc., 1976.

Jaeger, R. M. *Statistics: A Spectator Sport.* Beverly Hills, CA: Sage Publications, Inc., 1983.

Jahoda, M., Deutsch, M. & Cook, S. W. *Research Methods in Social Relations* (2 vols.). New York: The Dryden Press, Inc. 1951.

James, S. A., and Kleinbaum, D. G. Socioecologic Stress and Hypertension-Related Mortality Rates in North Carolina. *American Journal of Public Health,* 1976, Vol. 66(4), pp. 354–358.

Jencks, C. *Inequality: A Reassessment of the Effect of Family and Schooling in America.* New York: Harper & Row, 1972.

Jennings, H. H. *Sociometry in Group Relations; A Manual for Teachers.* (ed. 2). Washington D.C.: American Council on Education, 1959.

Jones, M. C. A Laboratory Study of Fear: The Case of Peter. *The Pedagogical Seminary and Journal of Genetic Psychology,* 1924, Vol. 31, pp. 308–315.

Kachigan, S. K. *Multivariate Statistical Analysis.* New York: Radius Press, 1982.

Kahn, R. L. and Cannell, C. F. *The Dynamics of Interviewing.* New York: John Wiley & Sons, 1957.

Kalton, G. *Introduction to Survey Sampling.* Sage University Paper Series in Quantitative Applications in the Social Sciences 07–035. Beverly Hills, CA: Sage Publications, Inc., 1983.

Kanter, R. M. *Men and Women of the Corporation.* New York: Basic Books, 1977.

Kaplan, A. *The Conduct of Inquiry.* San Francisco, CA: Chandler Publishing Co., 1964.

Karachi, L. and Toby, J. The Uncommitted Adolescent: Candidate for Gang Socialization. *Sociological Inquiry,* 1962, Vol. 32(2).

Katz, D. The Practice and Potential of Survey Methods in Psychological Research. In *Survey Research in the Social Sciences.* Glock, C. Y. (ed.) New York: Russell Sage Foundation, 1967.

Katzer, J., Cook, K. H., and Crouch, W. W. *Evaluating Information: A Guide for Users of Social Science Research.* Reading, MA: Addison-Wesley, 1978.

Kazdin, A. E. *Single-Case Research Design: Methods for Clinical and Applied Settings.* Oxford: Oxford University Press, 1982.

Kemeny, J. G. and Snell, J. L. *Mathematical Models in the Social Sciences.* Cambridge, MA: The MIT Press, 1972.

Kemeny, J. G., Snell, J. L., and Thompson, G. *Introduction to Finite Mathematics.* (ed. 2). Englewood Cliffs, NJ: Prentice-Hall, 1966.

Kendall, M. G. *Rank Correlation Methods.* (ed. 3). London: Charles Griffin, 1962.

Kerlinger, F. N. *Foundations of Behavioral Research.* (ed. 2). New York: Holt Rinehart Winston, Inc. 1973.

Keynes, J. M. *A Treatise on Probability.* London: Macmillan & Co., 1921. New York: Harper & Row, 1962.

Kim, J. O. and Mueller, C. W. *Introduction to Factor Analysis.* Sage University Paper Series on Quantitative Analysis in the Social Sciences 07–013. Beverly Hills, CA: Sage Publications, Inc., 1979a.

Kim, J. O. and Mueller, C. W. *Factor Analysis: Statistical Methods and Practical Issues.* Sage University Paper Series on Quantitative Analysis in the Social Sciences 07–014. Beverly Hills, CA: Sage Publications, Inc., 1979b.

King, R. S. and Julstrom, B. *Applied Statistics Using the Computer.* Palo Alto, CA: Mayfield Publishing Co., 1982.

Kinsey, A. C., Pomeroy, W. B. and Martin, C. E. *Sexual Behavior in the Human Male.* Philadelphia, PA: W. B. Saunders, 1948.

Kinsey, A. C., Pomeroy, W. G. and Martin, C. E. *Sexual Behavior in the Human Female.* Philadelphia, PA: W. B. Saunders, 1953.

Kish, L. Selection of the Sample. In *Research Methods in the Behavioral Sciences.* Festinger L. and Katz, D. (eds.) New York: Holt Rinehart Winston, Inc., 1953, 1966.

Kish, L. Some Statistical Problems in Research Design. *American Sociological Review,* June 1959, Vol. 24, pp. 328–338.

Klecka, W. R. *Discriminant Analysis.* Sage University Paper Series on Quantitative Analysis in the Social Sciences 07-019: Beverly Hills, CA: Sage Publications, Inc., 1979.

Kleinbaum, D. G. and Kupper, L. L. *Applied Regression Analysis and Other Multivariate Methods.* Belmont, CA: Wadsworth Publishing Co., 1978.

Knoke, D. and Burke, P. J. *Log-Linear Models.* Sage University Paper Series on Quantitative Applications in the Social Sciences 07-020. Beverly Hills, CA: Sage Publications, Inc., 1980.

Knoke, D. and Kuklinski, J. H. *Network Analysis.* Sage University Paper Series on Quantitative Applications in the Social Sciences 07-028. Beverly Hills, CA: Sage Publications, Inc., 1982.

Kornhauser, A. and Sheatsley, P. B. Questionnaire Construction and Interview Procedure. Appendix C in *Research Methods in Social Relations.* (rev.). Selltiz, C., Jahoda, M., Deutsch, M. and Cook, S. New York: Holt Rinehart Winston, Inc., 1951.

Krippendorff, K. *Content Analysis: An Introduction to its Methodology.* Beverly Hills, CA: Sage Publications, Inc., 1980.

Kruskal, J. B. and Wish, M. *Multidimensional Scaling.* Sage University Paper Series on Quantitative Applications in the Social Sciences 07-011. Beverly Hills, CA: Sage Publications, Inc., 1978.

Kuhn, T. S. *The Structure of Scientific Revolutions.* International Encyclopedia of Unified Science, Vol. 2(2). Chicago, IL: University of Chicago Press, 1962, 1970.

Kurtz, N. R. *Introduction to Social Statistics.* New York: McGraw-Hill, 1983.

Labovitz, S. Criteria for Selecting a Significance Level: A Note on the Sacredness of .05. Chap. 19 in Morrison, D. E. and Henkel, R. E. (eds.). *The Significance Test Controversy.* Chicago: Aldine Publishing Co., 1970.

Lakein, A. *How to Get Control of Your Time and Your Life.* New York: McKay, 1973.

Langbein, L. I. and Lichtman, A. J. *Ecological Inference.* Sage University Paper Series on Quantitative Applications in the Social Sciences 07-010. Beverly Hills, CA: Sage Publications, Inc., 1978.

Lapin, L. L. *Statistics: Meaning and Method.* (ed. 2). New York: Harcourt Brace Jovanovich, 1980.

Lapin, L. L. *Statistics for Modern Business Decisions.* (ed. 3). New York: Harcourt Brace Jovanovich, 1982.

Lastrucci, C. O. *The Scientific Approach: Basic Principles of the Scientific Method.* Cambridge, MA: Schenckman Publishing Co., 1967.

Latane, B., and Darby, J. M. Bystander Apathy. *American Scientist* (1969) Vol. 57, pp. 244–268.

Lazarsfeld, P. F., and Rosenberg, M. *The Language of Social Research.* New York: The Free Press, 1955.

Lazerwitz, B. Sampling Theory and Procedures. Chapter 8 in *Methodology in Social Research.* Blalock, H. M., Jr. and Blalock, A. B. (eds.) New York: McGraw-Hill, 1968.

Leinhardt, S. (ed.) *Social Networks: A Developing Paradigm.* New York: Academic Press, 1977.

Leontieff, W. W. *Input-Output Economics.* New York: Oxford University Press, 1966.

Levine, G. *Introductory Statistics for Psychology: The Logic and the Methods.* New York: Academic Press, 1981.

Levine, M. *Canonical Analysis and Factor Comparison.* Sage University Paper Series on Quantitative Applications in the Social Sciences 07-006. Beverly Hills, CA: Sage Publications, Inc., 1976.

Levinson, D. J. cum al. *The Seasons of a Man's Life.* New York: Alfred A. Knopf, 1978.

Lewis, O. *The Children of Sanchez.* New York: Random House, 1961.

Lewis-Beck, M. S. *Applied Regression: An Introduction.* Sage Paper Series on Quantitative Applications in the Social Sciences 07-022. Beverly Hills, CA: Sage Publications, Inc., 1980.

Liebetrau, A. M. *Measures of Association.* Sage University Paper Series on Quantitative Applications in the Social Sciences 07-032. Beverly Hills, CA: Sage Publications, Inc., 1983.

Light, R. J. and Pillemer, D. B. *Summing Up: The Science of Reviewing Research.* Cambridge, MA: Harvard University Press, 1984.

Lindner, W. *Statistics for Students in the Behavioral Sciences.* Menlo Park, CA: Benjamin Cummings Publishing Co., 1979.

Lipset, S. M., Trow, M., and Coleman, J. S. *Union Democracy.* Glencoe, IL: The Free Press, 1956.

Lodahl, T. M. and Kejner, M. The Definition and Measurement of Job Involvement. *Journal of Applied Psychology* (1965) Vol. 49, No. 1, pp. 24-33.

Lodge, M. *Magnitude Scaling: Quantitative Measurement of Opinion.* Sage University Paper Series on Quantitative Applications in the Social Sciences 07-025. Beverly Hills, CA: Sage Publications, Inc., 1981.

Lorr, M. *Cluster Analysis for Social Scientists.* San Francisco: Jossey-Bass Publishers, 1983.

Lortie, D. *Schoolteacher: A Sociological Study.* Chicago, IL: University of Chicago Press, 1975.

Luce, R. D. and Raiffa, H. *Games and Decisions.* New York: John Wiley & Sons, Inc. 1957.

Lutz, G. M. *Understanding Social Statistics.* New York: MacMillian, 1983.

Lynd, R. S. and Lynd H. M. *Middletown.* New York: Harcourt Brace, 1929.

Lynd, R. S. and Lynd, H. M. *Middletown Revisited.* New York: Harcourt Brace, 1937.

Lyon, J. L., Wetzler, H. P., Gardner, J. W., Klauber, M. R., and Williams, R. R. Cardiovascular Mortality in Mormons and Non-Mormons in Utah, 1969-1971. *American Journal of Epidemiology,* (1978) Vol. 108, No. 5, pp. 357-366.

MacCorquedale, K., and Meehl, P. E. On a Distinction Between Hypothetical Constructs and Intervening Variables. *Psychological Review,* (1948), Vol. 55, pp. 95-107.

Madge, J. *The Tools of Social Science.* London: Longmans, Green, 1953. Garden City, New York: Anchor (Doubleday), 1967.

Madge, J. Free Speech on Sexual Behavior. Chap. 10 in *The Origins of Scientific Sociology.* New York: The Free Press of Glencoe, 1970.

Madge, C., and Harrison, T. (eds.) *First Years Work by Mass-Observation.* London: n.p. 1938. *Manual of Style.* Chicago: University of Chicago Press (ed. 12), 1969.

Markus, G. B. *Analyzing Panel Data.* Sage University Paper Series on Quantitative Applications in the Social Sciences 07-018. Beverly Hills, CA: Sage Publications, Inc., 1979.

Mayhew, H. *London Labour and the London Poor.* London: n.p.:1851. Available abridged under title *Mayhew's London.* Quennell, P. (ed.). London: Spring Books, no date.

McIver, J. P., and Carmines, E. G. *Unidimensional Scaling.* Sage University Paper Series on Quantitative Applications in the Social Sciences 07-024. Beverly Hills, CA: Sage Publications, Inc., 1981.

McMillan, J. H. The Effect of Effort and Feedback on the Formation of Student Attitudes. *American Educational Research Journal.* Summer 1977, Vol. 14, No. 3, pp. 317-330.

McNamara, M. L. and Bahr, H. M. The Dimensionality of Marital Role Satisfaction. *Journal of Marriage and the Family.* February 1980, Vol. 42, No. 1.

McNeil, D. R. *Interactive Data Analysis.* New York: John Wiley & Sons, 1977.

McNemar, Q. At Random: Sense and Nonsense. *American Psychologist,* 1960, Vol. 15, pp. 295-300.

McWilliams, P. A. *The Personal Computer Book.* (ed. 2). Los Angeles, CA: Prelude Press, 1983.

McWilliams, P. A. *The Word Processing Book: A Short Course in Computer Literacy.* Los Angeles, CA: Prelude Press (Ballantine Books), 1982.

Mead, M. *Coming of Age in Samoa.* New York: W. Morrow & Co., 1928, 1961.

Mead, M. *Growing Up in New Guinea.* New York: W. Morrow & Co., 1930, 1975 (rev.).

Mechanic, D. *Medical Sociology.* New York: The Free Press, 1968.

Mechanic, D. *Students Under Stress: A Study in the Social Psychology of Adaptation.* New York: The Free Press, 1962. Madison, WI: University of Wisconsin Press, 1978.

Medawar, P. B. *Advice to a Young Scientist.* New York: Harper & Row, 1979.

Medawar, P. *Induction and Intuition in Scientific Thought.* Philadelphia, PA: American Philosophical Society, 1970, 1969.

Meehl, P. E. *Clinical vs. Statistical Prediction.* Minneapolis, MN: University of Minnesota Press, 1954.

Merton, R. K. *Social Theory and Social Structure.* New York: The Free Press. 1968 (rev.).

Merton, R. K., Fiske, M., and Kendall, P. L. *The Focused Interview: A Manual of Problems and Procedures.* Glencoe, IL: The Free Press, 1956.

Mezzich, J. E., and Solomon, H. *Taxonomy and Behavioral Science.* New York: Academic Press, 1980.

Michelli, D. W., Stein, R. A., Glantz, M., Sardy, H., and Cohen, A. *A Comparison of Exercise Training Intensities on Lipoprotein Cholesterol Functions.* Abstracts of the American College of Sports Medicine, Summer 1981.

Milgram, S. *Obedience to Authority.* New York: Harper and Row, 1974.

Miller, A. G. *The Social Psychology of Psychological Research.* New York: The Free Press, 1972.

Miller, D. C. *Handbook of Research Design & Social Measurement* (ed. 2). New York: David McKay Company, Inc., 1970.

Milne-Thompson, L. M. *Calculus of Finite Differences.* New York: Macmillan & Co., 1960.

Mithaug, D. and Burgess, R. The Effects of Different Reinforcement Contingencies in the Development of Social Cooperation. *Journal of Experimental Child Psychology,* 1968, Vol. 5, pp. 441–454.

MLA Handbook. New York: Modern Language Association, 1977.

Monkhouse, F. J., and Wilkinson, H. R. *Maps and Diagrams: Their Compilation and Construction* (ed. 2). London, Methuen & Co., Ltd., 1963; also University Paperbacks (paper), 1963.

Mood, A. M. and Graybill, F. A. *Introduction to the Theory of Statistics.* (ed. 2) New York: McGraw-Hill, 1963.

Moore, D. S. *Statistics: Concepts & Controversies.* San Francisco, CA: W. H. Freeman & Co., 1979.

Moore, R. W. *Introduction to the Use of Computer Packages for Statistical Analysis.* Englewood Cliffs, NJ: Prentice-Hall, 1978.

Morris, L. L., and Fitz-Gibbon, C. T. *How to Present an Evaluation Report.* Beverly Hills, CA: Sage Publications, Inc., 1978.

Morrison, D. E., and Henkel, R. E. (eds.) *The Significance Test Controversy.* Chicago, IL: The Aldine Publishing Company, 1970.

Moses, L. E., Emerson, J. D. and Hosseini, H. Analyzing Data from Ordered Categories. *New England Journal of Medicine,* Vol. 311, No. 7 (August 16, 1984):442–447.

Mosteller, F., and Tukey, J. W. *Data Analysis and Regression.* Reading, MA: Addison-Wesley, 1977.

Moyer, I. L. Demeanor, Sex and Race in Police Processing. *Journal of Criminal Justice,* (1981) Vol. 9, No. 3.

Muller, K. E. Understanding Canonical Correlation through the General Linear Model and Principal Components. *The American Statistician,* November 1982, Vol. 36, No. 4, pp. 342–354.

Musso, J. R., and Cranero, M. U Effects in an ESP Experiment With Concealed Drawings. *The Journal of Parapsychology,* June 1981, Vol. 5, No. 2.

Myers, J. L. *Fundamentals of Experimental Design.* (ed. 3). Boston, MA: Allyn & Bacon, 1979.

Nadler, M. A Geometric Interpretation of the Simplex Method of Linear Programming. *Mathematics Teacher,* March 1973, pp. 257–264.

Nagel, E. *The Structure of Science: Problems in the Logic of Scientific Explanation.* New York: Harcourt, Brace & World, Inc., 1961.

Nagel, S. S. with Neef, M. *Operations Research Methods.* Sage University Paper Series on Quantitative Applications in the Social Sciences 07-002. Beverly Hills, CA: Sage Publications, Inc., 1976.

Namboodiri, N. K. (ed.) *Survey Sampling and Measurement.* New York: Academic Press, 1978.

Neter, J., Wasserman, W., and Whitmore, G. A. *Applied Statistics.* Boston, MA: Allyn & Bacon, 1978.

Nie, N., Hull, C. H., Jenkins, J. G., Steinbrenner, K., and Bent, D. H. *Statistical Package for the Social Sciences (SPSS).* (ed. 2). New York: McGraw-Hill, 1975.

Norusis, M. J. *SPSS-X Advanced Statistics Guide.* New York: McGraw-Hill, 1985.

Nunnally, J. *Psychometric Theory.* (ed. 2). New York: McGraw-Hill, 1973.

Nye, F., and Hoffman, L. W. *The Employed Mother in America.* Chicago, IL: Rand McNally, 1963.

Oakley, A. Interviewing Women: A Contradiction in Terms, pp. 30–61 in *Doing Feminist Research,* H. Roberts, ed. London: Routledge & Kegan Paul, 1981.

Oakley, A. *Becoming a Mother.* Oxford: Martin Robinson, 1979.

Ohnmacht, F. W., and Olson, A. V. Canonical Analysis of Reading Readiness Measures and the Frostig Developmental Test of Visual Perception. *Educational and Psychological Measurement,* (Summer 1968) Vol. 28, No. 2.

Oppenheim, A. N. *Questionnaire Design and Attitude Measurement.* New York: Basic Books, 1966.

Ostrow, C. W., Jr. *Time Series Analysis: Regression Techniques.* Sage University Paper Series on Quantitative Applications in the Social Sciences 07–009. Beverly Hills, CA: Sage Publications, Inc., 1977.

Overall, J. E., and Klett, C. *Applied Multivariate Analysis.* New York: McGraw-Hill, 1973.

Parsons, J. E. Social Forces Shape Math Attitudes and Performance. In *Association for Women in Mathematics Newsletter,* (May–June 1982) Vol. 12, No. 3.

Partridge, E. *Usage and Abusage.* Baltimore, MD: Penguin Books, 1963.

Payne, S. L. *The Art of Asking Questions.* Princeton, NJ: Princeton University Press, 1951.

Perrin, P. G. *Writer's Guide and Index to English.* (ed. 4). Chicago, IL: Scott Foresman & Co., 1965.

Peters, D. P., and Ceci, S. J. A Manuscript Masquerade. *The Sciences.* September 1980, Vol. 20, No. 7, pp. 16–19.

Pfeiffer, P. E. *Concepts of Probability Theory.* (ed. 2). New York: Dover Publishers, 1978.

Phillips, B. *Social Research: Strategy & Tactics.* New York: Macmillan, 1966.

Phillips, D. C. Toward an Evaluation of the Experiment in Educational Contexts. *Educational Researcher,* AERA June/July 1981, pp. 13–20.

Phillips, J. L. *Statistical Thinking: A Structural Approach.* (ed. 2). San Francisco, CA: W. H. Freeman, 1982.

Piaget, J., and Inhelder, B. *The Psychology of the Child.* New York: Basic Books, Inc., 1969.

Plutchik, R. *Foundations of Experimental Research.* (ed. 2). New York: Harper and Row, 1974.

Poll, S. *The Hasidic Community of Williamsburg.* New York: Free Press of Glencoe, 1962.

Polya, G. *How to Solve It.* Princeton, NJ: Princeton University Press, 1945.

Polya, G. *Mathematics and Plausible Reasoning.* Vol. 1 *Induction and Analogy in Mathematics.* Vol. 2 *Patterns of Plausible Inference.* Princeton, NJ: Princeton University Press, 1954.

Popper, K. *Conjectures and Refutations.* New York: Basic Books, 1962.

Popper, K. *The Logic of Scientific Discovery.* New York: Basic Books, 1959.

Pound, G. *A Handbook for Writing Graduate Theses.* Dubuque, IA: Kendall/Hunt Publishing Co., 1977.

Proctor, C. H., and Loomis, C. P. The Analysis of Sociometric Data. Chap. 17 in Jahoda, Deutsch, Cook *Research Methods in Social Relations.* New York: The Dryden Press, 1951.

Rapaport, A. *Operational Philosophy.* New York: Harper & Bros., 1953.

Rashevsky, N. *Looking at History through Mathematics.* Cambridge, MA: MIT Press, 1968.

Resta, P. E., and Baker, R. L. *Formulating the Research Problem.* Inglewood, CA: Southwest Regional Laboratory for Educational Research & Development, 1967.

Reynolds, H. T. *Analysis of Cross-Classifications.* New York: Macmillan, 1977a.

Reynolds, H. T. *Analysis of Nominal Data.* Sage University Paper Series on Quantitative Applications in the Social Sciences 07–007. Beverly Hills, CA: Sage Publications, Inc., 1977b.

Riecken, H. W., and Boruch, R. F. (eds.) *Social Experimentation.* New York: Academic Press, 1974.

Rist, R. C. On the Means of Knowing: Qualitative Research in Education. *New York University Education Quarterly,* Summer 1979, p. 17–21.

Rist, R. C. On the Relations Among Educational Research Paradigms: From Disdain to Detente. *Anthropology and Education Quarterly* (1977) Vol. 8, No. 2, pp. 44–45.

Robinson, J., and Shaver, P. *Measures of Social Psychological Attitudes.* Ann Arbor, MI: Institute for Social Research, 1969.

Roethlisberger, F. J. and Dickson, W. J. *Management and the Worker.* Cambridge, MA: Harvard University Press, 1939.

Rohrer, J. H., and Edmonson, M. S. (eds.) *The Eighth Generation Grows Up.* New York: Harper & Row, Inc. (Torchbooks), 1960.

Rokeach, M. *The Open and Closed Mind.* New York: Basic Books, 1960.

Rokeach, M. *Beliefs, Attitudes and Values.* San Francisco, CA: Jossey-Bass, 1968.

Roscoe, J. T. *Fundamental Research Statistics for the Behavioral Sciences.* New York: Holt Rinehart Winston, Inc., 1975.

Rose, G. *Deciphering Sociological Research.* Beverly Hills, CA: Sage Publications, Inc., 1983.

Rosenberg, M. *The Logic of Survey Analysis.* New York: Basic Books, Inc., 1968.

Rosenthal, R., and Jacobson, L. *Pygmalion in the Classroom: Teacher Expectation and Pupils' Intellectual Development.* New York: Holt Rinehart Winston, Inc., 1968.

Ross, J., and Smith, P. Orthodox Experimental Design. Chapter 9 in Blalock, H. M. and Blalock, A. B. (eds.). *Methodology in Social Research.* New York: McGraw-Hill, 1968.

Rossi, P. H., Berk, R. A., and Lenihan, K. J. *Money, Work and Crime.* New York: Academic Press, 1980.

Rossi, P. H., and Williams, W. (eds.). *Evaluating Social Programs.* New York: Seminar Press, 1972.

Rozeboom, W. W. The Fallacy of the Null-Hypothesis Significance Test. *Psychological Bulletin,* 1960, Vol. 57, pp. 416–428.

Rozeboom, W. W. *Foundations of the Theory of Prediction.* Homewood, IL: The Dorsey Press, 1966.

Rubinstein, J. *City Police.* New York: Farrar Straus, 1973.

SAS Institute, Inc. *SAS Programmers Guide: SAS Users Guide.* P.O. Box 10066, Raleigh, NC 27605.

Sardy, H. The Economic Impact of Inflation on Urban Areas. In *Inflation Through the Ages: Social, Psychological and Historical Aspects.* Schumuckler, N. and Marcus, E. (eds.). Brooklyn, New York: Brooklyn College Press, 1982.

Savage, L. J. *The Foundations of Statistics.* New York: Wiley, 1954.

Savage, L. J. The Theory of Statistical Decision. *Journal of the American Statistical Association,* 1951, Vol. 46, pp. 55–67.

Sawyer, W. W. *Mathematicians Delight.* Baltimore, MD: Penguin Books, 1949.

Sawyer, W. W. *What Is Calculus About?* New Mathematical Library (Yale University & SMSG). New York: Random House, Inc., 1961.

Schachter, S., and Singer, J. Cognitive, Social, and Physiological Determinants of Physiological State. *Psychological Review,* 1962, Vol. 69, pp. 379–399.

Schaffner, P. E. A self-paced CAI package for selecting statistical methods. *Behavior Research Methods and Instrumentation,* 1983, Vol. 15, No. 2, pp. 130–134.

Scheff, T. J. Decision Rules and Types of Error, and Their Consequences in Medical Diagnosis. *Behavioral Science,* 1983, Vol. 8, pp. 97–107.

Scheffe, H. *The Analysis of Variance.* New York: John Wiley & Sons, 1959.

Schiffman, S. S., Reynolds, M. L., and Young, F. W. *Introduction to Multidimensional Scaling.* New York: Academic Press, 1981.

Schmid, C. F. and Schmid, S. E. *Handbook of Graphic Presentation.* (ed. 2). New York: John Wiley & Sons, 1979.

Schrodt, C. A. *Microcomputer Methods for Social Scientists.* Sage University Paper Series on Quantitative Applications in the Social Sciences 07–040. Beverly Hills, CA: Sage Publications, Inc., 1984.

Schuman, H., and Presser, S. Public Opinion and Public Ignorance: The Fine Line Between Attitudes and Nonattitudes. *American Journal of Sociology,* 1980, Vol. 85, No. 5, pp. 1214–1225.

Schuman, H., and Presser, S. *Questions and Answers in Attitude Surveys.* New York: Academic Press, 1981.

Scott, D. *How To Put More Time In Your Life.* New York: Rawson Wade Publishers, Inc., 1980.

Sedelow, S. Y. *Stylistic Analysis.* Santa Monica, CA: SDC, 1967.

Selltiz, C., Jahoda, M., Deutsch, M., and Cook, S. W. *Research Methods in Social Relations* (rev). New York: Holt Rinehart Winston, Inc., 1959.

Selltiz, C., Wrightsman, L. S., and Cook, S. W. *Research Methods in Social Relations.* (ed. 3). New York: Holt Rinehart Winston, Inc., 1976.

Shaughnessy, M. P. *Errors and Expectations: A Guide for the Teacher of Basic Writing.* New York: Oxford University Press, 1977; (paper) 1979.

Shaw, M., and Wright, J. *Scales for the Measurement of Attitudes.* New York: McGraw-Hill, 1967.

Sheatsley, P. B. The Art of Interviewing & A Guide to Interviewer Selection and Training. Chapter 13 in *Research Methods in Social Relations.* Jahoda, M., Deutsch, M., and Cook, S. W. New York: The Dryden Press, 1951.

Sheldon, W. H. (with Stevens, S. S. and Tucker, W.B.) *The Varieties of Human Physique .* New York: Harper & Bros., 1940.

Sheldon, W. H. *The Varieties of Temperament.* New York: Harper & Bros., 1942.

Shepard, R. N., Ramney, A. K., and Nerlove, S. B. (eds.) *Multidimensional Scaling: Theory & Applications in the Behavioral Sciences.* New York: Seminar Press (Harcourt Brace Jovanovich), 1972.

Sherif, M., and Sherif, C. W. *An Outline of Social Psychology,* New York: Harper & Row, 1948; rev. 1956.

Shulman, L. S. Disciplines of Inquiry in Education. *Educational Researcher,* June/July 1981, pp. 5–12.

Sidman, M. *Tactics of Scientific Research.* New York: Basic Books, 1960.

Sidner, C. L. On Being a Woman Student at MIT or How to Miss the Stumbling Blocks in Graduate Education. *Association for Women in Mathematics Newsletter,* January/February 1982, Vol. 12, No. 1, pp. 13–17.

Siegel, S. *Non-parametric Statistics for the Behavioral Sciences.* New York: McGraw-Hill, 1956.

Simon, H. A. *Models of Discovery: and Other Topics in the Methods of Science.* Boston, MA: D. Reidel Publishing Co., 1977.

Simon, H. A. *Models of Man: Social and Rational; Mathematical Essays on Rational Human Behavior In A Social Setting.* New York: Wiley, 1957.

Simon, J. L. *Basic Research Methods in Social Science: The Art of Empirical Investigation.* (ed. 2). New York: Random House, 1978.

Singer, S. F. *Is There an Optimal Level of Population?* New York: McGraw-Hill, 1972.

Singleton, R., and Smith, E. R. Does Grade Inflation Decrease Reliability of Grades? *Journal of Educational Measurement,* Spring 1978, Vol. 15, pp. 37–41.

Skinner, B. F. The Operational Analysis of Psychological Terms. From *Psychological Review* (1945) 52. In *Readings in the Philosophy of Science,* Feigl H., and Brodbeck, M. (eds.) New York: Appleton Century Crofts, 1953.

Sklare, M. *America's Jews.* New York: Random House, 1971.

Skyrms, B. *Choice and Chance: An Introduction to Inductive Logic.* Belmont, CA: Dickenson Publishing Co., Inc., 1966.

Slonim, M. J. *Sampling.* New York: Simon & Schuster (Fireside), 1960. Original title: *Sampling in a Nutshell.*

Smart, R. The Importance of Negative Results in Psychological Research. *Canadian Psychologist,* 1964, Vol. 50, pp. 225–232.

Smith, G. *Statistical Reasoning.* Reading, MA: Allyn and Bacon, 1985.

Smith, G. R. A Critique of Proposals Submitted to the Cooperative Research Program. In Culbertson, J. A., and Hencley, S. P., *Educational Research: New Perspectives,* pp. 277–287. Danville, IL: Interstate Printers & Publishers, 1963.

Snedecor, G. W. and Cochran, W. G. *Statistical Methods.* (ed. 6). Ames, IA: Iowa State University Press, 1967.

Social Science Research Council. *Theory and Practice in Historical Study: A Report of the Committee on Historiography.* New York: Social Science Research Council, 1946.

Sommer, *Expertland.* Garden City, NY: Doubleday & Co., Inc., 1963.

SPSS: see Nie et al. (1975) or Hull et al. (1981).

Spear, M. E. *Charting Statistics.* New York: McGraw-Hill, 1952.

Spector, P. E. *Research Designs.* Sage University Paper Series on Quantitative Applications in the Social Sciences 07–023. Beverly Hills, CA: Sage Publications, Inc., 1981.

Spiegel, M. R. *Advanced Calculus.* New York: Schaum Publishing Co., 1963.

Spiegel, M. R. *Theory and Problems of Statistics.* New York: Schaum's Outline Series (McGraw-Hill), 1961.

Spielman, S. The Logic of Tests of Significance. *Philosophy of Science,* September 1974, Vol. 41, No. 3, pp. 211–226.

Srole, L., et al. *Mental Health in the Metropolis: The Midtown Manhattan Study.* (rev.). New York: Harper and Row, 1977.

Stanley, J. C. Special Fast-Mathematics Classes Taught by College Professors to Fourth- through Twelfth-Graders. In *Intellectual Talent: Research and Development.* D. P. Keating, (ed.) pp. 132–159. Baltimore, MD: Johns Hopkins University Press, 1976.

Steger, J. (ed.). *Readings in Statistics for the Behavioral Scientist.* New York: Holt Rinehart Winston, Inc., 1971.

Stephan, F. F., and McCarthy, P. J. *Sampling Opinions: An Analysis of Survey Procedure.* New York: John Wiley & Sons, Inc., 1958, 1963.

Sternberg, D. *How to Complete and Survive a Doctoral Dissertation.* New York: St. Martin's Press, 1981.

Sternleib, G. S., Burchell, R. W., and Sagalyn, L. B. *The Affluent Suburb: Princeton.* New Brunswick, NJ: Transaction Books (E. P. Dutton & Co., distributor), 1971.

Stevens, S. S. Mathematics, Measurement, and Psychophysics. In *Handbook of Experimental Psychology,* S. S. Stevens (ed.). New York: John Wiley & Sons, Inc., 1951.

Stevens, S. S. On the Theory of Scales of Measurement. *Science,* (June 1946), Vol. 103, pp. 677–680.

Stevens, S. S. *Psychophysics and Social Scaling.* Morristown, NJ: General Learning Press, 1972.

Stewart, C. J., and Cash, W. B. *Interviewing: Principles and Practices.* Dubuque, IA: William C. Brown Co., 1974.

Stinchcombe, A. L. *Constructing Social Theories.* New York: Harcourt Brace & World, 1968.

Stinchcombe, A. L. Should Sociologists Forget Their Mothers and Fathers. *The American Sociologist,* February 1982, Vol. 17, pp. 2–11.

Stock, W. A., and Dodenhoff, J. T. Characteristics of Research Variables and Choice of Statistical Analyses. *Phi Delta Kappa CEDR Quarterly,* 1982 Spring, Vol. 15, No. 1, pp. 9–13. Bloomington, IN: Center for Evaluation, Development and Research, 1982.

Stogdill, R. M., Goode, O. S. and Day, D. R. New Leader Behavior Description Subscales. *Journal of Psychology,* (1962), Vol. 54, pp. 259–269.

Stouffer, S. A. Some Observations on Study Design. In *Handbook of Research Design & Social Measurement.* Miller, D. C. (ed.) New York: David McKay Co., Inc., ed. 2, 1970.

Stouffer, S. A., Guttman, L., Suchman, E. A., Lazarsfeld, P. F. et al. *Measurement and Prediction.* Vol. 4 in Studies in Social Psychology in World War II. Princeton, NJ: Princeton University Press, 1950.

Stout, C., Morrow, J., Brandt, E. N., Wolf, S. Study of an Italian-American Community in Pennsylvania. *Journal of the American Medical Association,* 1964, Vol. 188, p. 845.

Strunk, W., Jr., and White, E. B. *The Elements of Style.* New York: Macmillan Co., 1962. (paper)

Sudman, S. *Applied Sampling.* New York: Academic Press, 1976.

Sullivan, J. L., and Feldman, S. *Multiple Indicators.* Sage University Paper Series on Quantitative Applications in the Social Sciences 07-015. Beverly Hills, CA: Sage Publications, Inc., 1979.

Survey Research Center *Interviewer's Manual.* Ann Arbor, MI: Institute for Social Research, University of Michigan, 1973 (rev.).

Swingle, P. G. *Social Psychology in Natural Settings.* Chicago, IL: Aldine Publishing Co., 1973.

Taylor, F. W. *Shop Management.* New York: Harper & Bros., 1911.

Terman, L. *Genetic Studies of Genius.* Stanford, CA: Stanford University Press, 1975.

Thompson, B. *Canonical Correlation Analysis: Uses and Interpretation.* Sage University Paper Series on Quantitative Applications in the Social Sciences 07-047. Beverly Hills, CA: Sage Publications, Inc., 1984.

Thorndike, R. L. (ed.) *Educational Measurement.* (ed. 2) Washington, D.C.: American Council on Education, 1971.

Thorndike, R. L. Review of "Pygmalion in the Classroom" by R. Rosenthal and L. Jacobson. *American Education Research Journal* 1968 (5) 711.

Thorndike, R. L. and Hagen, E. *Measurement and Evaluation in Psychology and Education.* New York: John Wiley & Sons, 1961, 1969.

Thornton, A., and Freedman, D. Changes in the Sex Role Attitudes of Women, 1962–1977: Evidence From A Panel Study. *American Sociological Review,* October, 1979, Vol. 44, pp. 831–842.

Townsend, J. T. and Ashby, F. G. Measurement Scales and Statistics: The Misconception Misconceived. *Psychological Bulletin,* 1984, Vol. 96, No. 2, pp. 394–401.

Trachtman, J. N., Giambalvo, V. and Dippner, R. S. On the Assumptions Concerning the Assumptions of a t-Test. *Journal of General Psychology,* 1978, Vol. 99, pp. 107–116.

Travers, J., and Milgram S. An Experimental Study of the Small World Problem. *Sociometry,* 1969, Vol. 32, pp. 425–443.

Trinkaus, E. The Shanidar 3 Neandertal. *American Journal of Physical Anthropology,* January 1982, Vol. 57, No. 1.

Tufte, E. R. *The Visual Display of Quantitative Information.* Cheshire, CN: Graphics Press, 1983.

Tukey, J. W. *Exploratory Data Analysis.* Reading, MA: Addison–Wesley, 1977.

Tukey, J. W. The Future of Data Analysis. *Annals of Mathematical Statistics,* 1963, Vol. 33, pp. 13–19.

Tukey, J. W., and Wilk, M. B. Data Analysis and Statistics: Techniques and Approaches. Proceedings of the Symposium on Information Processing in Sight Sensory Systems, Nov. 1-3, 1965. California Institute of Technology. In *The Quantitative Analysis of Social Problems,* Tufte, E. R. (ed.), pp. 370–390. Reading, MA: Addison–Wesley Publishing Co., Inc., 1970.

Turabian, K. *A Manual for Writers of Term Papers, Theses and Dissertations.* (ed. 2). Chicago, IL: University of Chicago Press, 1969.

Uhl, N. P. *The Statistical Interface System:* Vol. 1, Design Selection Guide. Durham, NC: National Laboratory for Higher Education, 1972.

Ullman, L. P., and Krasner, L. (eds.) *Case Studies in Behavior Modification.* New York: Holt Rinehart & Winston, Inc., 1965.

Underwood, B. J. *Psychological Research.* New York: Appleton-Century-Crofts, 1957.

Uspensky, J. V. *Introduction to Mathematical Probability.* New York: McGraw-Hill, 1937.

Vaillant, G. E. Natural History of Male Psychologic Health. *New England Journal of Medicine,* 1979, Vol. 301, No. 23, pp. 1249–1254.

Van Dalen and Meyer. *Understanding Educational Research.* (rev.). New York: McGraw-Hill, 1966.

Van de Geer, J. P. *Introduction to Multivariate Analysis for the Social Sciences.* San Francisco, CA: Freeman, 1971.

Verba, S., and Nie, N. H. *Participation in America: Practical Democracy and Social Equality.* Appendix G: Methodological Notes in Our Use of Parametric Statistics. New York: Harper & Row, 1972.

Veroff, J., Kulka, R. A., and Douvan, E. *Mental Health in America.* New York: Basic Books, Inc., 1981.

Vickery, D. M., and Fries, J. F. *Take Care of Yourself: A Consumer's Guide to Medical Care.* Reading, MA: Addison-Wesley Publishing Co., 1976.

Wakeford, J. *The Cloistered Elite: A Sociological Analysis of the English Public Boarding School.* New York: Fred. A. Praeger, Inc., 1969.

Walker, H. M., and Lev, J. *Statistical Inference.* (ed. 3). New York: Holt Rinehart Winston, Inc., 1969.

Wallace, S. E. *Skid Row as a Way of Life.* Totowa, NJ: The Bedminster Press, 1965.

Wang, P. C. C. (ed.) *Graphical Representation of Multivariate Data.* New York: Academic Press, 1978.

Warner, S. B., Jr. *Streetcar Suburbs.* Cambridge, MA: Harvard University Press, 1962.

Warner, W. L., Meeker, M., and Eells, K. *Social Class in America.* New York: Science Research Associates, 1949.

Webb, G. J., Campbell, D. T., Schwartz, R. D.; Sechrest, L. *Unobtrusive Measures: Nonreactive Research in the Social Sciences.* Chicago, IL: Rand-McNally & Co., 1966.

Weber, M. *Protestant Ethic and the Spirit of Capitalism.* (Trans. T. Parsons) London: George Allen and Unwin, 1930.

Weidenborner, S., and Caruso, D. *Writing Research Papers: A Guide to the Process.* New York: St. Martin's Press, 1982.

Weisberg, H. I. Statistical Adjustments and Uncontrolled Studies. *Psychological Bulletin.* (1979) Vol. 86, pp. 1149–1163.

Welkowitz, J., Ewen, R. B., and Cohen, J. *Introductory Statistics for the Behavioral Sciences.* New York: Academic Press, 1982.

White, Harrison C. Models of Kinship Systems with Prescribed Marriage. In *An Anatomy of Kinship: Mathematical Models for Structures of Cumulated Roles.* Englewood Cliffs, NJ: Prentice-Hall, 1963.

Whitehead, A. N. *Science and the Modern World.* New York: Macmillan Co., 1967.

White, R. W. *Lives in Progress.* New York: Dryden Press, 1952.

Whittemore, A. S. Small Size for Logistic Regression With Small Response Probability. *Journal of the American Statistical Association,* March 1981, Vol. 76, No. 373.

Wiggins, J. A. Hypothesis Validity & Experimental Laboratory Methods. Chap. 10 in Blalock, H. M. and Blalock, A. B. (eds.) *Methodology in Social Research.* New York: McGraw-Hill, 1968.

Wildt, A. R., and Ahtola, O. T. *Analysis of Covariance.* Sage University Paper Series on Quantitative Applications in the Social Sciences 07–012. Beverly Hills, CA: Sage Publications, 1977.

Willemson, E. W. *Understanding Statistical Reasoning.* San Francisco, CA: W. H. Freeman & Co., 1974.

Williams, J. D. *The Compleat Strategyst.* New York: McGraw–Hill Book Co., Inc. 1954 (The RAND Series).

Williams, W. *A Sampler on Sampling.* New York: John Wiley & Sons, 1978.

Wilson, E. B., Jr. *An Introduction to Scientific Research.* New York: McGraw–Hill Book Co., Inc., 1952.

Winer, B. J. *Statistical Principles in Experimental Design.* (ed. 2). New York: McGraw Hill, 1971, (ed. 2).

Winston, S. *Getting Organized.* New York: W. W. Norton, 1978.

Woodham-Smith, C. *The Great Hunger: Ireland 1845–1849.* New York: Harper and Row, 1962.

Woolbridge, S. *Software Selection.* Philadelphia, PA: Auerbach Publishers, 1973.

Yamane, T. *Elementary Sampling Theory.* Englewood Cliffs, NJ: Prentice-Hall Inc., 1967a.

Yamane, T. *Statistics* (ed. 2). New York: Harper & Row, 1967b.

Yankelovich, D. *New Rules.* New York: Random House, 1981.

Yogev, A., and Jamshy, H. Children of Ethnic Intermarriage in Israeli Schools: Are They Marginal? *Journal of Marriage and the Family,* November 1983, pp. 965–974.

Zborowski, M. Cultural Components in Responses to Pain. *Journal of Social Issues,* 1952, Vol. 8, pp. 16–30.

Zeisel, H. *Say It With Figures.* (ed. 5). New York: Harper & Row, 1968.

Zeisel, H. The Significance of Insignificant Differences, *Public Opinion Quarterly,* 1955, Vol. 19, p. 319. Chapter 5 in *The Significance Test Controversy.* Morrison, D. E. and Henkel, R. E. (eds.). Chicago: Aldine Publishing Co., 1970.

Zeller, R. A., and Carmines, E. G. *Measurement in the Social Sciences.* Cambridge: Cambridge University Press, 1980.

Zetterberg, H. L. On the Decisions in Verificational Studies. In *Handbook of Research Design & Social Measurement.* D. C. Miller (ed.) New York: David McKay Co., Inc., 1970, (ed. 2).

Zinsser, W. *On Writing Well.* (ed. 2). New York: Harper & Row, 1980.

Zweigenhaft, R. L. Signature Size: A Key To Status Awareness. *Journal of Social Psychology,* 1970, Vol. 81, pp. 49–54.

Index

425